PET PROJECTS

ANIMALIBUS
OF ANIMALS AND CULTURES

Nigel Rothfels, General Editor

Books in the Animalibus series share a fascination with the status and the role of animals in human life. Crossing the humanities and the social sciences to include work in history, anthropology, social and cultural geography, environmental studies, and literary and art criticism, these books ask what thinking about nonhuman animals can teach us about human cultures, about what it means to be human, and about how that meaning might shift across times and places.

Other titles in the series:

Rachel Poliquin, *The Breathless Zoo: Taxidermy and the Cultures of Longing*

Joan B. Landes, Paula Young Lee, and Paul Youngquist, eds., *Gorgeous Beasts: Animal Bodies in Historical Perspective*

Liv Emma Thorsen, Karen A. Rader, and Adam Dodd, eds., *Animals on Display: The Creaturely in Museums, Zoos, and Natural History*

Ann-Janine Morey, *Picturing Dogs, Seeing Ourselves: Vintage American Photographs*

Mary Sanders Pollock, *Storytelling Apes: Primatology Narratives Past and Future*

Ingrid H. Tague, *Animal Companions: Pets and Social Change in Eighteenth-Century Britain*

Dick Blau and Nigel Rothfels, *Elephant House*

Marcus Baynes-Rock, *Among the Bone Eaters: Encounters with Hyenas in Harar*

Monica Mattfeld, *Becoming Centaur: Eighteenth-Century Masculinity and English Horsemanship*

Heather Swan, *Where Honeybees Thrive: Stories from the Field*

Karen Raber and Monica Mattfeld, eds., *Performing Animals: History, Agency, Theater*

J. Keri Cronin, *Art for Animals: Visual Culture and Animal Advocacy, 1870–1914*

Elizabeth Marshall Thomas, *The Hidden Life of Life: A Walk Through the Reaches of Time*

Pet Projects

Animal Fiction and Taxidermy in the Nineteenth-Century Archive

ELIZABETH YOUNG

The Pennsylvania State University Press
University Park, Pennsylvania

Library of Congress Cataloging-in-Publication Data

Names: Young, Elizabeth, 1964– author.
Title: Pet projects : animal fiction and taxidermy in the nineteenth-century archive / Elizabeth Young.
Other titles: Animalibus.
Description: University Park, Pennsylvania : The Pennsylvania State University Press, [2019] | Series: Animalibus : of animals and creatures | Includes bibliographical references and index.
Summary: "An analysis of how animals were represented in the nineteenth century in fiction, taxidermy, and other media, threaded together with the author's reflections on animal illness and on the field of animal studies"—Provided by publisher.
Identifiers: LCCN 2019028824 | ISBN 9780271084947 (cloth)
Subjects: LCSH: Saunders, Marshall, 1861–1947—Criticism and interpretation. | Saunders, Marshall, 1861–1947. Beautiful Joe. | Animals in literature—History—19th century. | Dogs in literature—History—19th century.
Classification: LCC PN56.A64 Y68 2019 | DDC 809.93362—dc23
LC record available at https://lccn.loc.gov/2019028824

Printed in the United States of America
Published by The Pennsylvania State University Press,
University Park, PA 16802-1003

The Pennsylvania State University Press is a member of the Association of University Presses.

It is the policy of The Pennsylvania State University Press to use acid-free paper. Publications on uncoated stock satisfy the minimum requirements of American National Standard for Information Sciences—Permanence of Paper for Printed Library Material, ANSI Z39.48-1992.

Contents

Illustrations

Introduction

The place is New England, Massachusetts, Northampton; the time is March 2008, spring break in my academic calendar but closer to wintry, not at all summery. A summary: It is a weekday morning and I am walking my golden retriever, Frankie, to his veterinarian, just a five-minute stroll through my neighborhood, for his annual checkup, during which she finds a lump in his abdomen, and a worried look crossing her kind face; as we return home, he zigzags and collapses, disoriented, and I drive him to the small hospital here in western Massachusetts for animal emergencies, twenty minutes north up the highway, where he is given an abdominal ultrasound and an unfamiliar doctor says, brusquely, "This is cancer, a large tumor is hemorrhaging, you need to go to Tufts"—the big veterinary hospital near Worcester—"*immediately*"; now it is late afternoon, now the dog is whimpering in pain, now I call a friend for help and she comes right away and drives us an hour eastward on the turnpike, from which we turn off into unfamiliar central Massachusetts and are immediately lost on country roads; now it is evening, quite dark, and finally the hospital looms up in front of us, and we bring in Frankie, who is admitted, stabilized, and scheduled for surgery; now we get back into the car for the long drive back. It is the dead of night, and I am somewhere in the middle of my own gothic landscape, holding Frankie's collar in my hand, as if he is already dead. He is seven.

There is more to this canine plot—not yet a funeral plot—and I will narrate it in these pages, though a personal dog story of some shagginess will, I know, interest some readers more than others. But the animal stories underneath, prior, and adjacent to this personal one will be, I hope, of general interest. They map a nineteenth-century cultural landscape—New England, old England, North American—with some surprising views.

For example, in the months that follow this opening scene, I return many times to the animal hospital in central Massachusetts; it is where the Tufts University Cummings School of Veterinary Medicine trains its students. It turns out that the Tufts animal hospital was built on the site of the former Grafton State Hospital, which was established in 1901 as part of the Worcester Lunatic Hospital; the Grafton hospital was known as the "farm colony" for the Worcester one, which means it was where the latter's "chronic insane" lived out their lives in agricultural and domestic pursuits. I learn about Grafton's history from the website of an artist, Anna Schuleit, who has meticulously documented the interlocking histories of Massachusetts mental institutions.[1] Another of these institutions is in the town where I live: the Northampton Lunatic Hospital—later known as the Northampton State Hospital—which was founded in 1856, riding the wave of social reform advocating better treatment for the mentally ill. Soon, however, the institution offered less emphasis on treatment and more on incarceration; by the 1950s, the Northampton State Hospital had thousands of patients and few psychiatrists. This history is typical of the American asylum, as was the deinstitutionalization of Northampton patients in the 1960s part of a national trend; the last patients were released in 1993.[2]

So Tufts's Cummings School of Veterinary Medicine, née Grafton State Hospital, was on the same asylum atlas as the Northampton State Hospital, which is connected to me through several paths. I live in Northampton about a mile from Smith College, whose fields the state hospital abuts. I teach American literature and film at Mount Holyoke College, which is, like Smith, historically a women's college; they are two of the original "Seven Sisters." And Mount Holyoke is sibling to the state hospital by design: the seminary system from which the college emerged bore "a marked resemblance to the structure of asylum life."[3]

The Northampton State Hospital is also in my life in an off-label way. In 2008, when my story about Frankie starts, I see its buildings daily: they are on the verge of redevelopment, but for now, they stand, looming and crumbling, straight out of Gothic Central Casting. In 2000, Anna Schuleit broadcast Bach through the speakers facing out from the empty buildings' windows. This installation was an attempt to render the uncanny audible—in the artist's words, "to make the building sing."[4] Other sounds are heard there now, especially those of dogs, because the grounds of the defunct state hospital have become Northampton's unofficial dog park; they are where I walk Frankie most days, especially after I write. I am finishing a book entitled *Black*

Frankenstein, a study of the transformation of the Frankenstein story in U.S. culture with a focus on its relation to race. Frankie loves this park, which is leash-free, a canine paradise of paths cutting through fields and woods and winding alongside a river, with on-site birds, squirrels, turtles, and the occasional deer and bear. So I walk Frankie, when he is well, at the site of one former state hospital, and now I have brought him, unwell, to another. Both of these sites have been repurposed for dogs—or, to put it another way, all roads in New England seem to lead to a nineteenth-century insane asylum.

The road to the Tufts animal hospital also leads to a famous mental health destination from the past: Worcester was the city Sigmund Freud visited on his only trip to America, in 1909 at the invitation of G. Stanley Hall, psychologist and president of Clark University. In Worcester for a week, Freud delivered five lectures at Clark, to an audience that included William James, who went on a long walk with him—a familiar story: the meeting of great male minds—and found him "a man of fixed ideas," even "a *hallluciné*." The audience also included Emma Goldman, anarchist, feminist, revolutionary—a less familiar story: woman radical in the picture—who was sympathetic to Freud but asked him hard questions.[5] The Clark lectures were an experience about which Freud later happily wrote: "As I stepped onto the platform at Worcester . . . it seemed like the realization of some incredible day-dream: psycho-analysis was no longer a product of delusion, it had become a valuable part of reality."[6] There is a neat symbolic parallel between the asylum patients near Worcester and Freud the visiting *halluciné*—and, conversely, a contrast between the ongoing ailments of the patients and the end of psychoanalysis as a "delusion." The Tufts animal hospital is near enough to Freud's Worcester to be part of the history of psychoanalysis; my nightmare with Frankie has led back to the "incredible day-dream" of Freud.

Down the turnpike past Tufts is Angell Animal Medical Center, a Boston center of animal care named for a nineteenth-century New Englander: George Thorndike Angell (1823–1909), founder in 1868 of the Massachusetts Society for the Prevention of Cruelty to Animals (MSPCA) and editor of its journal, *Our Dumb Animals*, whose slogan on the masthead was "Speaking for those who cannot speak for themselves." The language of speaking for the voiceless is still prominent in today's avalanche of nonfiction books about dogs: a surgeon at Angell, for example, has written *Tell Me Where It Hurts: A Day of Humor, Healing, and Hope in My Life as an Animal Surgeon* while a veterinarian in California has published *Speaking for Spot: Be the Advocate Your Dog Needs to Live a Happy, Healthy, Longer Life*.[7] I have read both of these books, as "pleasure" reading rather than "work" reading, if dealing with canine oncology can be called a pleasure. Really, it cannot. But it is, oddly, a pleasure (for me) to look back at nineteenth-century animals and learn about the people who spoke about and for them.

George Angell, I learn, was a pioneering activist on behalf of animals; through him, Massachusetts became an inspiration to other states, a model for animal welfare societies and animal cruelty legislation. Angell also participated in other reform movements saturating postwar Boston, including the "war on adulteration"—a public health campaign against "poisonous and dangerously adulterated" food and drink. For example, he deplored that "a large portion of our pickles were more or less poisonous" and that "so-called milk . . . did not contain one drop of the genuine article."[8] To vanquish poisoned pickles and fake milk, he advocated for "pure food" laws, a project complementary with his animal advocacy; one campaign improved how nonhuman animals were treated, the other how they were eaten, and both the health of the body politic across species. His campaigns for animals (pro) and adulteration (con) seem a suitable combination for a New England reformer, one Angell in America.

He also exemplified the biggest reform movement in nineteenth-century New England: in the antebellum era, Angell was an ardent abolitionist.[9] The connection between the antislavery and animal welfare movements runs deep. In *Animal Liberation*, the manifesto of the modern animal rights movement, Peter Singer starts with this analogy: "The tyranny of human over nonhuman animals . . . has caused . . . pain and suffering that can only be compared with that which resulted from the centuries of tyranny by white humans over black humans."[10] One wing of the contemporary movement adopts the term "abolition" to express the radicalism of its goals—ending all human ownership and use of animals—and uses the term analogously with human slavery: "The abolition of animal slavery is required by any moral theory that purports to treat animal interests as morally significant . . . just as the abolition of human slavery is required by any theory that purports to treat human interests as morally significant."[11]

But in the nineteenth century, the connection between political movements was more than analogical. For example, the masthead for *Our Dumb Animals* repurposed that of William Lloyd Garrison's abolitionist newspaper *The Liberator*. I find this connection disturbing: it sweeps enslaved people into the orbit of animals so that both may be protected by others. A historian confirms this orbit, describing the focus of nineteenth-century reform as the "enlarged 'household circle' of dependent beings who could not defend themselves in the world: the insane, the worthy poor, the orphan, the aged, the penitent prostitute, the slave—and the animal."[12] And this was the liberal view: helping those perceived incapable of self-defense, not to mention self-representation.

Representation of a literary kind abounds in Boston's nineteenth-century animal welfare movement. Famous writers populate this movement at every turn: Ralph Waldo Emerson, for example, served on the first board of directors of the MSPCA. I am more drawn, however, to the obscure. This is my usual mode: for example, while my book on *Frankenstein* features some established literary figures, like Frederick Douglass and Stephen Crane, it includes many more lesser-known writers, as well as lowbrow films, political cartoons, and ephemera of popular culture. Now too I swerve away from Emerson and toward less canonical names: namely, Marshall Saunders. In 1892, the American Humane Education Society—a partner organization to the MSPCA—sponsored a contest for the best story on "Kind and Cruel Treatment of Domestic Animals and Birds in the Northern States," with a first prize of two hundred dollars. The winner was a Canadian woman writer, Margaret Marshall Saunders (1861–1947); her winning entry, the making of her career, was *Beautiful Joe: An Autobiography* (1894), a novel written in the voice of a dog.

Beautiful Joe was following the lead of Anna Sewell's *Black Beauty* (1877), the novel in the voice of a horse, blurbed by George Angell as "the *Uncle Tom's Cabin* of the horse."[13] This endorsement again bespeaks the connection between abolitionism and animals, not to mention the way the antislavery novel *Uncle Tom's Cabin* (1852) pops up in just about every nineteenth-century account of reform; Harriet Beecher Stowe, it turns out, was a contributor to *Our Dumb Animals*. I am familiar with this pop-up: my first book was on women writers and the American Civil War, and it traced a history in which Stowe—allegedly greeted by Lincoln as "the little woman who made this great war"—loomed large.[14] *Black Beauty* I remember only dimly, but *Beautiful Joe*'s debt to it is made clear in the novel's introduction, written by a then popular author named Hezekiah Butterworth: "The wonderfully successful book, entitled *Black Beauty*, came like a living voice out of the animal kingdom. But it spake for the horse . . . it followed naturally that some one should be inspired to write a book to interpret the life of a dog to the humane feeling of the world. Such a story we have in *Beautiful Joe*."[15]

So *Black Beauty* "spake for the horse," and *Beautiful Joe* continued this project, speaking for Spot in a nineteenth-century voice. *Black Beauty*'s original subtitle was "translated from the equine," and *Beautiful Joe* is presumably

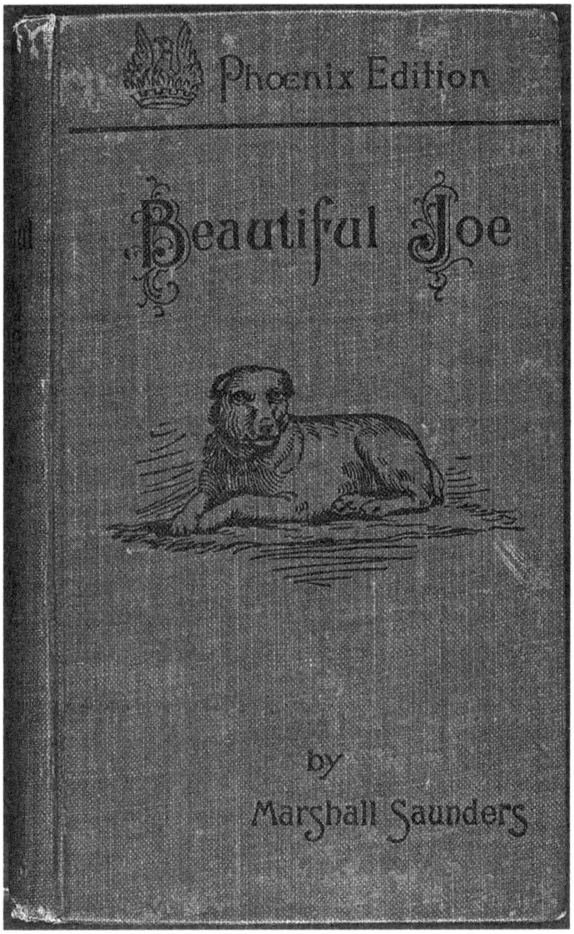

FIG. 1. *Beautiful Joe*, Phoenix Edition cover, 1903. Photo: James Gehrt.

"translated" from the canine. And, it turns out, from the Canadian: Saunders based her novel on a real dog in Ontario, but because the contest stipulated that the winning story be set in the United States, she changed the setting to New England. She also published it under the name Marshall Saunders, defeminizing her name while de-Canadianizing her story. The novel, dedicated to George Angell, was first published by the American Baptist Publication Society. Behind so many reform movements in the nineteenth century is some form of Christianity; behind Saunders herself, it turns out, was her minister-author father, Rev. Edward Saunders. *Beautiful Joe* became a phenomenon, the first Canadian book to sell a million copies, and the first to become a best seller worldwide; it was translated into eighteen languages.[16]

I first read this novel in May 2008, by the sea, where I have come with Frankie shortly after his cancer surgery, during which the surgeon removes most, but not all, of his tumor. Frankie and I go to the tip of Massachusetts: Provincetown, at the end of Cape Cod, originally a Portuguese fishing village, then an artists' colony, now a gay and lesbian resort town—also, not coincidentally, "Eden for dogs."[17] This phrase is from a memoir by a distinguished poet mourning his golden retriever, only one of several books about dogs in Provincetown.[18] It is preseason in P-town, when dogs are welcome on beaches. I have brought with me a variety of pleasure reading, including a copy of *Beautiful Joe*.

The book itself is a thing of beauty. My copy is from the Smith College library, a 1903 edition—a little hardcover object, about six by four inches, bound in dark red cloth with an illustration of a dog on its cover and 359 thin-skinned pages of text.[19] The object is so charming, the cover so cute, that the librarian stops as she is checking it out for me to look it over and says, "Adorable." Later, I will obtain many other editions of *Beautiful Joe*, including three Canadian reprints: one produced by the Beautiful Joe Heritage Society in Meaford, Ontario, whose members I eventually meet; one introduced by Gwendolyn Davies, whose scholarship on Saunders I frequently consult; and one edited by Keridiana Chez, whose version of the novel, with helpful historical documents appended, I use as my reference point here.[20] While these modern reprints are paperbacks, the first copies I see are beautiful hardbacks; I also buy ugly versions printed on-demand through Amazon and read electronic copies downloaded from Google. The versions in which I read *Beautiful Joe* move between old and new book forms, but they all, for me, heighten its intrinsically literary conundrum: What does it mean to narrate, in first person, the voice of a subject who cannot read, write, or speak?

It would be disingenuous to deny that this is a personal question. As I watch my dog in pain, I wish for him to have his own voice; he cannot tell me where it hurts, even though it clearly hurts. The basic criterion for animal rights is the question asked in the eighteenth century by Jeremy Bentham, answered in the twentieth by Peter Singer: "The question is not, can they *reason*? nor, Can they *talk*? but, Can they *suffer*?"[21] Singer answers yes, as do I: Frankie is, unmistakably, suffering. There is little I can do about this; I can take care of him and hope that the cancer does not come back. Meanwhile, I can read and—maybe—write. I am (only) a literary critic, after all.

So I decide to write about *Beautiful Joe*. I have finished my book about the Frankenstein story in America, and it is not such a big leap from monsters to dogs; sometimes there is no leap, and the monster arises, Cujo-like, from within the dog.[22] In fact, I have been collecting some dog-related *Frankenstein* references in a folder along the way, footnotes attached to nothing. Now I have discovered a something, *Beautiful Joe*, to which the footnotes can be leashed. Also, it is a novel by a nineteenth-century American woman writer, and this is an area of my scholarly expertise, although by "American" I customarily have meant "U.S. American." Nineteenth-century Canadian women writers will be new to me—as will the field of animal studies, which has developed rapidly in the last academic generation. It is time to educate myself in this field.

I will analyze *Beautiful Joe* as the work of a woman writer, in relation to other women writers, and I will analyze *Beautiful Joe* as a novel about animals in relation to other nineteenth-century forms of animal representation, such as photography, painting, and especially taxidermy. Also, I will explore some presumably nonanimal topics, including—in alphabetical order—death, mourning, race, slavery, ventriloquism, and women. Other writers at issue in this investigation, many from nineteenth-century America, include Alcott, Baum, Brown, Cable, Chesnutt, Chopin, Douglass, Dunbar, Freeman, Gilman, Hornaday, Jacobs, Phelps, Seton, Stowe, Twain, Wharton, and Wilson. I also interpret writers from other places, at roughly the same moment—Cobbe, Darwin, Sewell, Wells—and from other times, including now: Atwood, Bonaparte, Davis, Derrida, Freud, Gary, Hill, Moore, Munro, and Woolf. Besides dogs and humans, there are other animals under discussion, including birds, cats, cows, horses, monkeys, pigs, rabbits, and sheep. Also, filmmakers: Fuller, Hitchcock, and Reichardt. These alphabetical lists are satisfying to me—menageries of nouns, proper and improper—but perhaps less so to you. So let me describe them another way.

In the following chapters, I read my way through and around *Beautiful Joe* along several scholarly routes, including American studies, animal studies, cultural history, feminist criticism, and psychoanalysis. Most generally, I argue for the importance of two themes, voice and skin, in understanding nineteenth-century animal representation; more particularly, I identify in *Beautiful Joe* and other writing by Saunders the workings of two unusual rhetorical forms, which I term "first-dog voice" and "literary taxidermy." Both of these terms are paradoxes, even oxymorons: first-dog voice is the canine narration of a novel, an impossibility given that nonhuman animals do not use words; "literary taxidermy" combines literature with an activity that requires not human words but animal skins. But both terms describe practices that flourished in the late nineteenth century. This was when the animal-voiced novel grew, along with the animal welfare movement and its vocabulary of speaking for animals, and this was when taxidermy surged as personal souvenir and natural history spectacle—and, concurrently, as a topic in literature.

In addition to their historical concurrence, first-dog voice and literary taxidermy also offer, I will argue, complementary modes for representing animals. Novels depict interiors of selves, especially as expressed in first-person voices, while taxidermy displays exteriors, exhibited as skins. The verbal interiors of first-dog voice overtly contrast with the visual exteriors of taxidermy, although these forms have some structural affinities. In a half dozen works, Saunders develops first-dog voice and literary taxidermy as complementary forms. In her writing and in that of others, these practices have a particular payoff: they offer imaginative avenues for revivifying the dead and remediating loss. They suggest intrinsic connections, in this period, between mourning animals and mounting them in literary form.

What follow, then, are arguments about animals and form, but also claims about animals and politics. I will argue that works by Saunders and other authors illuminate power relationships in a late nineteenth-century world, including species relations between human and nonhuman animals, gender relations between male and female humans, and racial relations between white and nonwhite humans. Her writing also suggests some of the political complexities involved in representing nations through animals. In *Beautiful Joe*, she remounts Canada under the skin of a New England setting, while her other novels point toward the complexities of crossing boundaries of race and culture along with those of species.

Now this summary zigzags; let me try a more linear route. Five chapters and a coda follow. In the first chapter, I explore the literary implications of a novel written in first-dog voice, arguing that this voice is built, in the case of *Beautiful Joe*, on recovery from death and mutilation; that this voice conjoins literary issues of reading, speaking, and writing with the symbolism of canine fidelity; and that it relies on a series of analogies likening dogs to people with disabilities, children, servants, and—especially—women. I argue that first-dog voice in the novel functions as a kind of ventriloquism for the female author, who also surfaces across the novel's characters and in the illustrations that accompany *Beautiful Joe*. I highlight ambivalence as well as enthusiasm in my own first-person voice, using the novel to move among academic fields, particularly animal studies and feminist criticism.

The implications of first-dog voice for the representation of race are the focus of the second chapter, in which I argue that *Beautiful Joe* is inseparable from themes of racial hierarchy and enslavement. A quarter century past emancipation, the novel revivifies earlier genres for representing slavery—the slave narrative, the abolitionist novel, and the animal trickster tale—while turning away from the imperative for emancipation. *Beautiful Joe* reshapes these genres with fidelity to the "master's voice," a phrase named by a famous painting of the era and given material form by new technologies of sound recording. I conclude this chapter with discussion of later works that link race and dogs in more radical ways, focusing on a film, Samuel Fuller's *White Dog* (1982).

In the third chapter, I turn to taxidermy, shifting emphasis from the theme of voice to that of skin. I note the vitality of taxidermy in contemporary art and then analyze taxidermy's relationship to literature, both as a theme represented within literary texts and as a formal structure incorporated by them. Moving from canine to avian taxidermy, I interpret its representation in turn-of-the-century fiction by H. G. Wells, handbooks by William T. Hornaday, and writing in several genres by Marshall Saunders. In contrast to the violently masculine accounts of taxidermy in Wells and Hornaday, Saunders develops a counterimagery of avian taxidermy as a female literary practice in *Beautiful Joe* and in her memoir *My Pets: Real Happenings in My Aviary* (1908). Visits to taxidermy museums in Britain and elsewhere punctuate this chapter, and film flutters at its margins in the forms of *Psycho* and *The Birds*.

The fourth chapter pursues the theme of animal mourning. Revisiting Freud, I use psychoanalysis—another "master's voice"—to suggest the expansive psychic power, generative as well as shattering, of representations of mourning for and by animals. Turning to Saunders, I argue for the organizing role of animal mourning in *Beautiful Joe* and then in the novel's sequel, *Beautiful Joe's Paradise* (1902). A sustained fantasia of animal afterlife and an implicit extension of literary taxidermy, *Beautiful Joe's Paradise* turns melancholic mourning into uncanny revivification. I find a sequel to this sequel in a recent film about women, dogs, and loss: Kelly Reichardt's *Wendy and Lucy* (2008).

In the fifth chapter, I move from psychic to national geographies, turning to the Canadian dimensions of this study. I emphasize shifting versions of Canada—less a fixed locale than a space for taxidermic remounting—in Saunders's biography; in her novels *Rose of Acadia* and *Jimmy Gold-Coast*, which feature Acadian and black Nova Scotian characters; and in *Beautiful Joe*, whose settings both erase and retrace considerations of Canada. I revisit the preoccupation with animals in the world of Canadian literature, analyzing animal imagery in fiction by Margaret Atwood and Lawrence Hill. I visit the Marshall Saunders archive in Nova Scotia, where the themes of national and animal bodies emerge in new ways. Finally, in a coda, I circle back to the original "beautiful Joe" dog, travel to the sites in Ontario where he is memorialized, and reflect on the challenges and opportunities afforded by a "pet project" such as this one.

Some common themes: Race is important throughout as the focus of the chapter on *Beautiful Joe* and slavery, a theme in discussions of literary taxidermy, and the starting point for my analysis of Canadian literature. Women are central to all chapters, as in the analysis of female characters in *Beautiful Joe*; the interpretation of (Margaret) Marshall Saunders; the attention to women writers, artists, and scholars throughout; and the bits of my own story threaded throughout the book. I like to cite women scholars and artists, although in addition, there are also citations of men. All of these citations are variously eccentric and exemplary; I like to wander outside the canon but also to make sure I understand its norms and credit its authors. I submerge many titles in the endnotes, partly to keep the main text relatively uncluttered and partly to entice you to look through the notes, where I hope you will find surprises, even treats. In the body of the text and in its citational extremities, this book is a deliberate pastiche—a stitching together of parts with the seams showing.

Actually, there is already a name for similar activities in the contemporary art scene: "botched taxidermy," wherein artists deliberately mismatch and misassemble animal parts so that things "appear to have *gone wrong* with the animal, as it were, but . . . it still *holds together*." These words are by the art historian and artist Steve Baker, who highlights botched taxidermy as "an attempt *to think a new thing*."[23] I am also attempting, in terms of style and method, "to think a new thing." There are lots of mismatched pieces here, some quite disjunct: for example, discussions of films that fall well outside of the chronological scope of Saunders's era. You do not, of course, have to call this approach "botched taxidermy," which is a term Baker reserves for contemporary art, and anyway, by the time I finish this project, he will have moved beyond, if not actively disavowed, the whole concept.[24] There are other cultural reference points for a project that deliberately amalgamates disparate parts. You could, for example, think of this book as a Frankenstein monster running amok from New England to Nova Scotia.

A few more words about method: The voice for this project is first person and self-reflexive. I craft it to make visible and track the scholarly movements so often effaced in scholarly writing.[25] The voice is real, but its various hues—ambivalence, diffidence, frustration, hesitation, confidence, enthusiasm—are strategically assumed and stylized throughout. The tone sometimes moves toward the comic, like that of an art historian in a book on dogs in art who describes himself as "both smiling and serious."[26] But sometimes I am only serious; some of this material demands it. I try to keep the puns under control—not only because of the question of tone but also because a cultural study of "dog love," to which I am indebted, pretty much told this tail.[27] I do, however, use some of the idioms related to dogs that allow me to dramatize making leaps among ideas. For example, I often employ the imagery of the leash—being dragged along by it, being tangled up in it, and being let off of it, at least by myself.

I leash this stylized "I" to activity that I sometimes describe in the present tense, although that present is now past; you are not reading this in 2008, when it begins. I am using this technique—the "historical present"—partly to narrate Frankie's plot as it unfolded to me then and, more importantly, to narrate a process of intellectual development. Scholarly research takes place in several time zones not only because writing a book often takes a long time but also because it involves encounters with both new works and older ones; the scholar zigzags between the old and the new, which loses its newness by the time it is incorporated into the published work. These encounters and zigzags are usually repressed in academic scholarship: footnotes are either current or not, and the reader finds the work useful or out of date. I want to make that repressed material return, to highlight the time travel involved in scholarly work as well as the relation of that work to the events of everyday life. At times, I will link a specific moment in the Frankie story to that of books appearing at that moment: for example, I have just done this in identifying *Speaking for Spot* and *Tell Me Where It Hurts* as dog books appearing at the moment, 2008, when Frankie first fell ill. At times, though, I will update the "now" of scholarship as close as I can to when this book is published. I do this both to convey my current thinking and to make these pages more useful to you as you read, especially if you are trying to track down my sources or otherwise follow my lead.

The story should give you a shifting sense of place as well as time. I proceed here by an associative scholarly process, forging connections among authors, works, artifacts, and locations. Customarily, these associations too are rendered seamlessly in scholarship. By contrast, the goal of the seam-showing method I use here is to provide an atlas in which place signals intellectual as well as geographic locations, and movement among them is less a direct path than a picaresque wandering. The literal geography of research sites here is centered in New England but includes trips to old England, Nova Scotia, and Ontario. The intellectual geography often involves boundary crossing: animal studies travels to American studies, while taxidermy encounters literary criticism. These journeys are powered by the protocols of scholarly research, but I also highlight more serendipitous movements through space: from the book on the shelf to the one adjacent, from the artifact to the container that holds it, and from the footnote to the memory it dislodges. Through these spatial movements, I assemble an archive, albeit an eccentric one. It includes traditional archival materials, like the papers of Marshall Saunders, and less traditional ones, like a museum collection of taxidermied dogs; it associates texts and terms from the twentieth and twenty-first centuries as well as from the nineteenth.

The figure of speech that proceeds by an association between terms is "metonymy"; it is defined in contrast with "metaphor," the figure for resemblance between terms. I favor metonymy, to lend you a hand—or perhaps a paw, for this common example of metonymy, "lend me a hand," is one of many things that changes when the dog is introduced—though there are metaphors aplenty here too. My favored punctuation mark is the semicolon; I use it as another tool to mark adjacencies and affinities within sentences. My favorite form of movement, like that of the dog racing around the dog park, is the zigzag; the book's archive emerges from a series of zigzags, alternately serendipitous and planned. Metonymy, semicolon, zigzag: these are features of literary style but also of method—here, of style as method.

This project is risky in several ways. There is the risk of scholarly solipsism, of the project sparked by a pet that becomes a "pet project"—a pejorative term, implying narrowness, eccentricity, and a misguided personal dedication to, if not monomania for, a subject. In writing about dogs, there is the risk of the cute, which is not, generally, an adjective of academic inquiry, let alone praise.[28] Nor is "sentimental," a term that seems taboo for those writing about pets, especially women and pets. This taboo is infamous in the writing of two canonical theorists in animal studies, whose praise for "becoming-animal" emphatically excludes "the little cat or dog owned by an elderly woman who honors and cherishes it" in "a sentimental or domestic relation."[29] But even a woman scholar who sympathetically analyzes literary women-dog relationships wants to avoid "the trap of a mawkish, sentimental anthropomorphism."[30] In animal studies, "sentimental" seems an evil that must be warded off; the attitude is—to use one of my favorite two-bit words—apotropaic.

But "sentimental" is a complicated term, not least for scholars of nineteenth-century America. Thanks to feminist critics, we now identify nineteenth-century sentimentalism as a major political tool in the writing of this era, used not only by women—it is time for another pop-up from Harriet Beecher Stowe—but also by men. For example, here is George Angell again, in an article called "Sentiment, Sentimental": "Some of our friends most deeply interested in animal-protection societies are frequently charged with being *sentimental*. We admit it. . . . Thank God for sentiment! When a nation loses it, we shall cease to be a nation."[31] Sentimentality is built into nineteenth-century nationalism and certainly into *Beautiful Joe*, although its sentimentality does not preclude other modes—for example, irony. It may also be built into my own first-person voice; I am not apotropaic about sentiment. But I too balk at mawkishness. I will try to cut the schmaltz with salt.

And, of course, there is the risk of mess: "botched taxidermy" gone to the dogs. Others have successfully essayed pastiche—for example, the feminist theorist whose animal studies book oscillates between theoretical manifestos about companion species and personal accounts of her Australian sheepdog at agility events.[32] This theorist, Donna Haraway, has made a scholarly shift from cyborg to canine manifestos; this change also expresses kinship, her focus staying on creatures "in the same litter."[33] It is not dissimilar to my own scholarly movement, albeit in a more minor key, from monsters to dogs, *Frankenstein* to Frankie. I am not sure if I have the agility, as she does, to pull this kind of thing off, but I will try.

The goals here are several: to recover a particularly interesting author; to use her work as a point of entry into nineteenth-century representations of animals; to reconsider animal studies as a field, along with feminist criticism and American studies; and to illuminate scholarly processes by dramatizing movements within and between fields. The intended trajectory is outward: from *Beautiful Joe* to other novels, memoirs, and materials by Saunders; from literary questions to fields outside literature; and from the particularities of the "I" who speaks here to larger questions of scholarly process. I can't promise that what follows will escape the backyard confines of the pet project. But I want to try. And you know me—just a little—by now; I will take all of these risks anyway.

CHAPTER 1

First-Dog Voice

1.

In March 2008, Frankie survives his surgery, during which an eight-by-eight-centimeter mass is removed from a part of his large intestine called the cecum. The pathology report indicates that it is a "gastrointestinal stromal tumor," a form of cancer abbreviated GIST, an acronym that seems ripe for wordplay about the gist of the matter, though I cannot bring myself to engage in it. Also, the report indicates that some cancer cells have been left behind in his guts—"dirty margins" is the term, in canine oncology as in human, again an evocative phrase for a literary critic, but again a no-go zone for me. For two weeks, Frankie wears, unhappily, a plastic cone to keep him from biting the dozens of metal staples, which stretch from midstomach down to his genitals; he has been eviscerated—the cancer in his guts taken out, mostly—and then reviscerated, stitched together with the stapled seam showing. After the cone comes off, he convalesces quickly, and he seems remarkably happy in his new state, postcolon and postcone—may I say postcolonial, semicolon?

I guess I am happy too: I am punning again. And I am reading and reflecting: What does it mean to write a novel in the first-person voice of a dog? The phrase "first-person voice" does not sound right to me when the literary "I" is not a person. I decide to call this literary technique "first-dog voice."

This voice is not uncommon, especially now—now-ish; remember, the now in which I start this chapter is not the same as the now in which you are reading. Around this moment, circa 2008, two novels in first-dog voice appear: an American best seller narrated by a dog whose human companion is a race-car driver mourning the death of his wife and an English canine-historical novel reconstructing the early 1960s from the perspective of Marilyn Monroe's actual dog.[1] A decade earlier, John Berger's novel *King* (1999) embedded first-dog voice in a narrative of homelessness, while Paul Auster's novel *Timbuktu* (1999), written in third person, similarly entered a canine consciousness to develop a homeless theme.[2] Many of the poems in *Unleashed: Poems by Writers' Dogs* (1995), written with long tongues in canine cheeks, had first-dog lyric speakers.[3] The memoir *Millie's Book: As Dictated to Barbara Bush* (1990) ostensibly offered the autobiography of the presidential English springer spaniel; the memoir *Angus* (2000), written in first-dog voice, conveyed the anguish of author Charles Siebert over the death of his Jack Russell terrier.[4] Also emerging in newer media are first-dog "animalographies," such as "dog blogs" written by individual humans, animal rights groups, and pet-food companies.[5] Around the turn of the twenty-first century, first-dog voice seems to be proliferating across contemporary media and by authors of varying literary pedigrees.

But all of these examples come long after Marshall Saunders's *Beautiful Joe* (1894), and perhaps I should start with what comes before. There was a robust tradition of animal autobiographies in nineteenth-century England, novels written in the voices of animals, including a horse—this is the famous one, Anna Sewell's *Black Beauty* (1877)—and a mouse, donkey, cat, and dog.[6] This last is *The Confessions of a Lost Dog* (1867) by Frances Power Cobbe, a novel told by a Pomeranian about her separation from, and ecstatic reunion with, her mistress.[7] Cobbe's canine "confessions" are, in turn, indebted to Francis Coventry's *The History of Pompey the Little; or, The Life and Adventures of a Lap-Dog* (1751), one of numerous eighteenth-century "it" narratives, which animated property into literary personae; these included works narrated by a bank note, shoe, jacket, flea, corkscrew, and hackney coach.[8] I could go as far back as Lucian, whose depiction of Cerberus has been identified as "the first example in Western literature of a philosophical dialogue involving a talking dog"; the scholar who makes this identification finds the culmination of the talking-dog canon in Franz Kafka's story "Investigations of a Dog" (1922).[9] In analyzing first-dog voice, it is hard to know the best—or at least, the least hackneyed—place to start.

I will come back to many of these examples, but I decide to start in the place where, academically speaking, I feel most at home: late nineteenth-century U.S. culture. A quick survey of dogs in this era: This is when the animal welfare movement took form, evidenced in the American Society for the Prevention of Cruelty to Animals (founded 1866), in George Angell's American Humane Education Society (1889), and in the American Anti-Vivisection Society (1883). This was the moment of dog breeds codified (American Kennel Club, 1884), dog shows launched (Westminster, 1877), veterinary schools founded (University of Pennsylvania, 1884), and more generally, dogs welcomed in great numbers as pets in the parlor and beasts in the boudoir, in America as in Europe.[10]

And dogs in U.S. literature? The best known in this period appear in the ferociously determinist fiction of naturalism, by writers like Jack London, Frank Norris, Stephen Crane, and Theodore Dreiser. Actually, not "writers like": until recently, this was the naturalist canon *tout court*—doggedly male, centered on masculinity. Naturalist novels feature men obsessed with acting like men but behaving like dogs—a good example is Norris's McTeague, a dentist who murders his lover—as well as male dogs themselves. Jack London's animal stories *The Call of the Wild* (1903) and *White Fang* (1906) are wilderness narratives of dogs as men, with an emphasis on themes of bondage and discipline.[11] As dogs came into the feminine parlor at home, they leapt, in novels, into the masculine wild.

This account of canine literary history does not seem complete, though, and not only because the naturalist literary canon is more complicated, its practitioners more diverse than this list, nor even because other writers in this era, as we will see, represent dogs in fiction so differently. This account also seems incomplete because a simile such as "men behaving like dogs" needs to be analyzed, on both the "men" front and the "like dogs" rear. There is a new scholarly field of animal studies that makes the animal simile itself an object of interest, of shifting historical meaning and ideological complexity.

New-ish: I seem to have missed a big wave of scholarship while I was writing on *Frankenstein*. It is hard to date its start: Peter Singer's *Animal Liberation* appeared in 1975, but the academic field of animal studies did not develop comprehensively for a few decades; now "presses, journals, and meetings buzz with Animal Studies."[12] I look around and immediately see books relevant to my interest in dogs in nineteenth-century America. For example, here is *Dog* by Susan McHugh, one in a series of nicely designed single-species animal studies books; I can tell it will be a valuable overview.[13] Here is what looks like an important specialized study of animals in late nineteenth-century American literature by Jennifer Mason.[14] And here in my mailbox is an issue of *PMLA* with a focus on animal studies. This issue confirms that it is past the moment for opening manifestoes, but it includes state-of-the-field summaries and close readings.[15] Everywhere are references to a seminal article by the most famous French theorist of the last century, which has just been published in book form but was translated into English in 2002 and which, clearly, I must read pronto.[16]

I feel some ambivalence about this prospect. I am excited to read these works, but the obligation to get "up to speed" in a new field is also having a dispiriting effect on me. I am being yanked on the leash of academic training, the compulsion to catch up on major theorists, key critics, founding declarations, later revisions, and footnotes for all—being told: sit, down, stay. I want to be responsible to this field, but I also want to wander; I decide, for the moment, to slip the leash. I start with the novel itself.

Beautiful Joe: An Autobiography is a mock-memoir of around three hundred pages, retrospectively narrated by the titular character, "a brown dog of medium size" at the end of a long life that has a horrific beginning (53).[17] The first two chapters describe the dog's youth, in which his master, a cruel milkman named Jenkins, kills his siblings and cuts off Joe's ears and tail. Rescued and nursed back to health by a kind young woman, "Miss Laura," he goes to live with her family, the human Morrises—Laura, her four brothers, and her parents, Rev. and Mrs. Morris—and their many pets, including fox terrier Billy, spaniel Jim, parrot Bella, and cat Malta. After various adventures, Joe accompanies Miss Laura on a visit to family friends on a farm, where they attend a "Band of Mercy" meeting. Back home, Joe meets a visiting circus troupe of performing animals who suffer horribly in a fire. At the end, old and happy, he updates readers on the fates of the book's humans and animals—though I can tell from even a cursory look at new scholarship about animals that this is not the right way to put it; "humans and animals" disavows the animal identity of humans. The appropriate phrase would be "humans and other animals" or "human and nonhuman animals."

Now I have gotten through the plot summary, though I can see from my last sentences that I will not be able to hold off the deluge of new scholarship on animals any longer; I am already getting tangled up in terminology. I realize that my hesitation is not about ingesting the new scholarship but about doing so as I had planned: by reading a dozen foundational works and more specialized studies—in effect, preparing a seminar syllabus for myself—before starting to write. Numerous scholars in the field have, in fact, posted their syllabi to a valuable internet resource about animal studies.[18] But I am too restless to read my way more systematically through syllabi and to postpone working on *Beautiful Joe* until I am done. I decide, instead, to start writing right now and to read as needed.

Already, there is something needed: an explanation of a proper noun in this plot summary. "Band of Mercy" was an organization for children to promote kindness to animals, started in England and then brought to America by

George Angell; at its height in the 1890s, it had nearly half a million members. This name was revived by British Animal Liberation activists in 1972 working in a more militant vein, attacking fox hunts and animal laboratories.[19] The relation between activist movements on behalf of animals—variously "welfare," "rights," "liberation," "abolition": the terminology matters—and animal studies scholarship is complicated, with some scholars going to some lengths to establish distance from activists.[20] I am not concerned with this distance, but then again, I have not put myself to the test. I do not have a dog in this fight, I might say—except that this violent idiom seems as suspect as the absence of activism it here connotes. I write these words from a scholarly location at a double distance, both outside the field of animal studies, at least for now, and outside the world of animal activism, but I understand that there is no "outside" if you are inside. Frankie's illness, for example, may be part of the staggeringly high incidence of cancer among today's golden retrievers, a characteristic that, in turn, seems inseparable from the ruinous health and eugenic elitism with which the history of the purebred dog is intertwined.[21] To animal activists, even my account of my own dog, let alone any analysis of *Beautiful Joe*, might seem—in the most witheringly pejorative sense of the term—academic.

Marshall Saunders herself did not separate her literary ambitions from her political ones: *Beautiful Joe* was written to protest animal cruelty but also to win a prize; a writer's motives—my own, say—are seldom pure. A little biography seems in order. Margaret Saunders was born in 1861 in Nova Scotia and educated briefly in Scotland and France, then returned to live with her family, including her father, a Baptist minister and writer of some renown. She began writing fiction in the late 1880s and became famous with *Beautiful Joe*. After the novel's success, Saunders wrote more, some two dozen books in total; she traveled widely in the United States and Canada and eventually moved to Toronto; she never married or had children; she had many pets; she campaigned against animal cruelty and for women's suffrage, child labor laws, temperance, and other causes; she cofounded an organization for women journalists with her friend Lucy Maud Montgomery, author of *Anne of Green Gables*; she died at age eighty-five in Toronto in 1947. There is no full-length biography of Saunders, but several scholars of Canadian literature have written about her—Gwendolyn Davies, Carole Gerson, and Elizabeth Waterston—and to them I am greatly indebted.[22] There are also brief discussions of *Beautiful Joe* by scholars writing about animals—Tess Cosslett, Janet Davis, Annie Dwyer, Erica Fudge, Marjorie Garber, Roxanne Harde, Susan McHugh, Teresa

Mangum, and Justin Prystash—and by the time I finish this project, there is a longer one, complementing her edition of the novel, by Keridiana Chez.[23]

That scholars of Saunders and *Beautiful Joe* seem mostly to be women is no surprise: the recovery of obscure women writers is usually undertaken by women; I have undertaken this recovery myself. As a feminist critic, I am interested in studying women writers and in pursuing gender questions—pursuing them doggedly, but also waggishly; illustrating the coexistence of these qualities in a feminist scholarly voice is one goal of this project.

Saunders's life story, even in the brief outline I have just given, seems to invite feminist analysis. The absence of a husband and children, for example: in the late nineteenth century, the spinster was a suspect figure, swerving away from gender norms, and the spinster with pets—especially cats, also dogs—even more so.[24] Several scholars term Saunders's adult life in Toronto, surrounded by animals but no other humans, "eccentric."[25] There is a connection, historically, between dog stories and women authors leading lives that were "eccentric" in being lesbian. Frances Cobbe, author of *Confessions of a Lost Dog*, lived openly for decades with a woman partner, Mary Lloyd. Her biography has been revisited for the insights it provides into nineteenth-century lesbian lives, while her *Confessions* has been read as an exploration of "the eroticism of female-centered discipline."[26] The spinster protagonist of Mary Wilkins Freeman's story "A New England Nun" (1891) lives quietly with her canine companion, Cesar, and views her human fiancé as an intrusion: "Louisa looked at the old dog munching his simple fare, and thought of her approaching marriage and trembled."[27] Rejecting the fiancé, the spinster stays single—or rather, she remains coupled with the dog, who functions as "Louisa's double."[28] In a swerve away from human heterosexuality, the story embraces a dog who is a woman's nonhuman partner as well as her nun-hermit double.

Again, though, I feel some hesitation about the project of recovering Saunders's life and works. I do not know if studying her will yield a lesbian or queer biography; more generally, I am not certain how her works will withstand the usual criteria for scholarly recovery. Recovery projects of obscure writers often proceed by celebrating the aesthetic sophistication or political radicalism of the writer; a good example from nineteenth-century American literary history is Charlotte Perkins Gilman's short story "The Yellow Wallpaper" (1892), recovered and celebrated by feminist critics as a brilliant meditation on women, power, madness, and writing.[29] I do not think *Beautiful Joe* merits celebration on aesthetic grounds, and I can already see some severe political limits on the horizon: Saunders's biography reflects a set of norms—white, middle class, Christian—whose biases are likely to be reproduced in her writing. Saunders is no Gilman, although Gilman is no longer the same Gilman, having been raked over the coals politically for her advocacy of eugenics, xenophobia, and racism.[30] The celebration of recovered women writers for their prose often seems to be followed by the condemnation of their politics. I am not interested in assuming these stances for Saunders.

A well-known meditation on nineteenth-century women's writing shifts the terms of discussion: "novels and stories should be studied . . . because they offer powerful examples of the way a culture thinks about itself, articulating and proposing solutions for the problems that shape a particular historical moment"—in short, for the "cultural work" they do.[31] The cultural work model is an oldie but a goodie; I like to return to feminist classics, as you will see. With its best-selling global celebrity, *Beautiful Joe* clearly did important cultural work—for the animal welfare movement, overtly, and perhaps in other ways. My scholarly work is to figure out her cultural work, although that sounds too serious. I will try, also, to have some fun—to keep the waggish in the dogged.

Still, there is one more problem: I feel as though I am following the wrong scent, biographically speaking, for a project in animal studies. Shouldn't I start with the biography of the animal, not the human? Saunders based *Beautiful Joe* on a dog whom she had met while on a visit to Ontario; in the preface, she verifies that "Beautiful Joe was a real dog, and 'Beautiful Joe' was his real name. . . . Nearly all of the incidents of the story are founded on fact."

It would be fitting to start with this "real dog," although difficult. Erica Fudge names the historiographic problem: "Animals are 'inarticulate'; they do not leave documents."[32] There are some exceptions: for example, famous animals with biographical trails.[33] But I am a literary critic, not a historian, and I decide to stick—for now—to the fictional dog. In the novel, Joe seems the very opposite of "inarticulate": he is all voice. Bringing to light an actual case of dog cruelty, Saunders brings to life an impossible literary voice. These two activities, I decide, are closely related: the way Saunders represents animal cruelty is the key to understanding Joe's first-dog voice.

2.

Beautiful Joe contains two scenes of animal cruelty near the start. (Warning: they are terrible.) First is Joe's description of the murder of his siblings by Jenkins, his master:

> He took one pup after another, and right there, before his children and my poor distracted mother, put an end to their lives. Some of them he seized by the legs and knocked against the stalls, till their brains were dashed out, others he killed with a fork. It was very terrible. My mother ran up and down the stable, screaming with pain, and I lay weak and trembling, and expecting every instant that my turn would come next. . . .
>
> . . . Mother picked up all the puppies and brought them to our nest in the straw and licked them, and tried to bring them back to life, but it was of no use. They were quite dead. . . .
>
> My mother never seemed the same after this. She was weak and miserable, and though she was only four years old, she seemed like an old dog. . . . One day she licked me gently, wagged her tail, and died. (59–60)

This material was so graphic that Saunders muted it for later editions of the novel, cutting the second sentence ("Some of them he seized . . . others he killed with a fork.").[34] This omission does not undo the overall horror of the scene; it is hard to believe that *Beautiful Joe* was known as a "children's book"—more on this shortly—when this scene is so grim. Jenkins's violence leads immediately to the death of the puppies and shortly to the death of Joe's mother, here "screaming with pain" from grief. These deaths provide a foundation for the novel to follow, as does the mother's failed effort to "to bring [the puppies] back to life." Her failed effort of revivification will be, at least partially, redeemed.

Before I get to the redemption, here is the second scene of cruelty, in the same chapter. After the death of Joe's mother, Jenkins seems at first "a little sorry," but then he kicks Joe; Joe bites him, and Jenkins becomes enraged:

> He seized me by the back of the neck and carried me out to the yard where a log lay on the ground. "Bill," he called to one of his children, "bring me the hatchet."
>
> He laid my head on the log and pressed one hand on my struggling body. I was now a year old and a full-sized dog. There was a quick, dreadful pain, and he had cut off my ear, not in the way they cut puppies' ears, but close to my head, so close that he cut off some of the skin beyond it. Then he cut off the other ear, and turning me swiftly round, cut off my tail close to my body.

> Then he let me go, and stood looking at me as I rolled on the ground and yelped in agony. (60–61)

In this scene of the body in pain, the dog stretched on the log "yelp[s] in agony." The suffering dog is a sadistic spectacle for both the man who "stood looking at [Joe]" and his son Bill, who is an actual hatchet man for his father. Although Joe notes that this cutting is "not in the way they cut puppies' ears," the scene evokes cropping and docking; later he makes this evocation explicit, describing "my cropped ears and docked tail" (80). These practices were then customary in the world of purebred dogs. For example, it was common to crop the ears of German shepherds and to dock the tails of spaniels. As the animal welfare movement grew, cropping and docking were increasingly criticized. *Beautiful Joe* implicitly extends this critique, making the removal of ears and tail into deliberate acts of violent cruelty.

More important, this scene in *Beautiful Joe* also criticizes the greater extremities of vivisection—the use of live animals in scientific research—which was a major focus of the Anglo-American animal welfare movement. For example, Frances Cobbe's fiction was a sideline to her political career as an antivivisection activist, condemning the men who were "devoted to it as completely and professionally as butchers cutting up carcasses."[35] This analogy appears in Cobbe's memoir, which I encounter appended to a modern edition of H. G. Wells's *The Island of Doctor Moreau* (1894), a novel that offers the most graphically dystopian exploration of vivisection in this era. In Wells's novel, the titular doctor, forced to leave England after "a wretched dog, flayed and otherwise mutilated" escapes from his house, exults on the island in making "animals carven and wrought into new shapes," including a "Dog-Man" who has been surgically crafted from a St. Bernard.[36]

Dog vivisection was the focus of the novel *Trixy* (1904) by Elizabeth Stuart Phelps, a writer who became famous for her novels of human grief after the Civil War—*The Gates Ajar* (1868) and its successors—and was later active in animal welfare campaigns. The novel's male scientist, Dr. Steele, persists in canine vivisection even though "the saddest sight he had ever seen was the expression of the dogs as they were brought to the laboratory from the cellar for sacrifice"; the novel's turning point comes when the titular dog, kidnapped and held in a vivisection laboratory, rescues another dog who has been experimented on there for two years.[37] Canine vivisection also anchors Mark Twain's short story "A Dog's Tale" (1903), written in first-dog voice. Twain's story starts with a comic tone that seems to parody *Beautiful Joe*—"My father was a St.

Bernard, my mother was a cur, but I am a Presbyterian"—but it quickly turns horrific. The narrator witnesses her master and other vivisectionists test ideas about "optics" on her puppy, blinding and killing him: "It put its head against mine, whimpering softly. . . . Then it dropped down . . . and it was still, and did not move any more."[38] The "whimpering" of the vivisected dog was noted in nonfiction as well. Here is a journalist's account in 1893 of "a fine, large dog" in a Philadelphia laboratory, "with one of its ears gone, the brains on that side of its head having been removed. It lay there in its darkened cage, making a continual distressing, moaning sound."[39]

Beautiful Joe dramatizes such radical losses of body and voice, conveying canine mutilation as both a literal injury and a symbolic form of muting. "If I had had any ears, I would have pricked them up at this," Joe notes (122), a potentially comic phrase. But not at all comic is this line about mutilation: "Ever since Jenkins cut my ears off, I had had trouble breathing" (118). There are embedded similes at work here: the loss of ears is like both the muffling of a lung and the stifling of a tongue, precluding the "pricking up" of ears that is the dog's usual expressive response to the world. The amputation of Joe's tail constrains his ability to communicate even more strongly. When a woman is kind to him: "I always wagged my tail, or rather my body, for I had no tail to wag" (80); when he and another dog foil a crime: "[We] wagged our tails, at least Jim did, and I wagged what I could" (127). His missing tail, like his missing ears, both symbolizes and enacts the loss of speech.

These figurative connections are not new. For example, Alfred Elwes in *The Adventures of a Dog* (1857) proposes that "a good portion" of language "finds its way to [the dog's] tail. The motion of that eloquent member is full of meaning."[40] Elwes is another obscure nineteenth-century writer, but a similar idea shows up in works by heavier hitters: for example, Charles Darwin, an avid dog-lover as well as dog-observer.[41] In *The Expression of the Emotions in Man and Animals* (1872), Darwin details how dogs communicate through tail and ears: when the dog is hostile, "the tail is held erect and quite rigid" and "the pricked ears are directed forwards," whereas when the dog is in an "excited condition from joy," the tail "is lowered and wagged from side to side" and the "ears are depressed and drawn backward."[42] In Darwin's world, dog ears and tails connect to each other and to human speech.

In this context, the first-dog literary voice of *Beautiful Joe* seems an act of restoration for a dog who has become mute from mutilation. The voice symbolically reverses the animal cruelty scenes: Joe's mother cannot revive her children, but Joe's author can alter the terms of his mutilation. First-dog voice restores to Joe his ears and tail, allowing him to communicate as his body no longer can.

Within the novel, this communication is explained by way of an unnamed human assistant: "I am an old dog now, and am writing, or rather getting a friend to write, the story of my life" (53). Tess Cosslett shows that nineteenth-century animal autobiographies often include a device that "metafictionally directs our attention to the incongruities of the convention" of animal speech; here, "getting a friend to write" is the metafictive device.[43] The friend is a kind of translator, another convention in the animal autobiography, as in Anna Sewell's *Black Beauty*, "translated from the equine." *Beautiful Joe* was itself translated in traditional ways, as Saunders later summarized: "I have had the honour of leading the old Ontario dog around the world on a chain of translations."[44] This metaphor is already intrinsic to the novel: the interspecies "chain of translations" is present both in the "friend" who writes the story and, more fundamentally, in the form of its first-dog voice that translates doglish to English.

An analogy for the "friend" is lurking here, one introduced in the original introduction to *Beautiful Joe* by Hezekiah Butterworth, who was well known as an author of children's books and of a Zig-zag Journeys travel series, to which I will return. Introducing *Beautiful Joe*, Butterworth applauds Saunders's effort "to understand the languages of the creatures that we have long been accustomed to call 'dumb,' and the sign language of the lower orders of these dependent beings" (47). "Dumb"—denoting mute, connoting stupid—had been intertwined with "deaf" at least since ancient Greece; in nineteenth-century America, as deaf education developed, these terms were institutionally coupled, starting with the Connecticut Asylum for the Education and Instruction of Deaf and Dumb Persons (1817).[45] "Sign language" was then newly standardized in the United States, though also fiercely opposed by oralists, who saw it as "making deaf people foreign, peculiar, and isolated from the nation."[46] Butterworth's descriptions of "dumb" creatures—denotatively, animals; connotatively, people—intersect with the history of deafness.

In Saunders's time, the denotative and connotative often collapsed: animal metaphors were used pejoratively to describe deaf humans. For example, "deaf and dumb" people were described as only capable of "mere animal enjoyment" while sign language was excoriated as "a set of monkey-like grimaces and antics."[47] The movement of the last half century for Deaf culture (capital *D*—Deaf pride, community, and culture: deafness not as disability but as identity) has been a sustained struggle against these painfully dehumanizing metaphors.[48] Butterworth's language exemplifies such earlier dehumanization, implicitly marking deaf people as disabled and placing them, along with animals, within the "lower orders" of "dependent beings."

Within *Beautiful Joe*, though, the themes of animality, deafness, and disability seem to converge in more complicated ways. Joe is not deaf—indeed, he hears very well and is always listening to stories—but he is "dumb" in the sense of nonspeaking; the novel presents the injuries to his ears and tail, as much as his nonhuman species, as the source of his muteness. While the common negative comparison of people with disabilities to animals assumes that animals are able-bodied, Joe is a figure of animal disability. The novel's first-dog voice thus seems a different form of "sign language," one whose effect is not to animalize humans but to humanize animals.

The novel's first-dog voice also seems to reverse the usual model of the dog serving as a tool for the disabled human. The "guide dog" for the blind person, a twentieth-century development, is a concentrated example of this model; Susan McHugh, whose work I am following closely, will soon publish an analysis of fiction about such dogs—a robust literary subgenre often conjoining dogs with blind men.[49] *Beautiful Joe* is the reverse of this model, making the human "friend" writing the story into a guide for the dog. In a nineteenth-century culture that often demoted "deaf and dumb" people and people with disabilities to the status of animals, Marshall Saunders, conversely, seems to move in the other direction. *Beautiful Joe* seems to use first-dog voice to move the dog whose communicative organs have been severed into the realm of the human.

But I am hesitant to make these claims; I made the "seems" show in the last two paragraphs to signal my hesitation. I know that these topics, and the scholarly fields addressing them, are complex. For one thing, Deaf studies and disability studies are not the same fields, with the former often rejecting affiliation with the latter.[50] For another, disability studies and animal studies have often developed in tension with each other, most starkly over the contrasting status of the work of Peter Singer in each field. By the time I finish this chapter, Sunaura Taylor has published an important book on this tension, which includes a critique of the very idea of animals as lacking voice: "Considering animals voiceless betrays an ableist assumption of what counts as having a voice."[51] Much of the vocabulary of animal welfare replicates this assumption, from *Our Dumb Animals* to *Speaking for Spot*; certainly *Beautiful Joe* does so. It leaves an ableist assumption of what counts as "voice" intact—as does my own discussion of Joe's need for voice thus far.

Taylor moves beyond this impasse: analyzing conflicts between the fields of animal studies and disability studies, she affirmatively conjoins them. She advocates for "cripping the animal," wherein "to crip something does not mean to break it but to radically and creatively invest it with disability history, politics, and pride."[52] Marshall Saunders does not "crip" the dog in this modern sense of radical reclamation. But Saunders does seem to allow for a focus on disability as inseparable from an animal's story: "To call an animal a crip is no doubt a human projection, but it is also a way of identifying nonhuman animals as subjects who have been oppressed by ableism."[53] Joe shares this oppression, which is violently marked on his mutilated nonhuman body. More affirmatively, his distance from the domain of the able-bodied seems the source of the novel's distinctive voice.

I am back to the "seems" in my own voice; I will leave them unfinished for now and move to a second analogy. *Beautiful Joe* equates the dog with the child, or more specifically, the first-dog voice of the animal autobiography with the novel for children. The novel's subtitle, "An Autobiography," suggests memoir, but its opening words—"My name is Beautiful Joe, and I am a brown dog of medium size"—makes autobiography impossible; there cannot be a nonfictional, nonhuman animal who says "my name," so this must be fiction.

Specifically, fiction for children. While *Beautiful Joe*, like *Black Beauty*, was read by many adults, it was positioned for a particular audience, as Butterworth outlined in his introduction: "The day-school, the Sunday-school, and all libraries for the young, demand the influence that shall *teach* the reader *how* to live in sympathy with the animal world" (47). Butterworth locks the novel into the didactic space of the Sunday school and the library "for the young." As scholars of childhood have shown, this library has long been devalued: "'children's literature' . . . is still often viewed as something of an oxymoron in the context of Great Books."[54] There are various ways to break out of this zone, to move a work from "kiddie lit" to "Great Book," though this move is easier, in American literature, for books linked with boys rather than girls. Exhibit A: *The Adventures of Huckleberry Finn*.[55]

I do not feel the need to give *Beautiful Joe* a defensive upgrade, to age it out of the category of "the young," but I do want to point out some connections between children and animals in *Beautiful Joe*. Within the novel, children can be the perpetrators of animal cruelty—remember Jenkins's son Bill, carrying the hatchet—but more often, they are positioned as animals' protectors, from beginning to end. Beginning: "I have heard [Miss Laura] say that if all the boys and girls were to rise up and say that there should be no more cruelty to animals, they could put a stop to it" (53). End: "My last words are: 'Boys and girls, be kind to dumb animals, not only because you will lose nothing by it, but because you ought to; for they were placed on the earth by the same Kind Hand that made all living creatures" (270). The appeal to children is revolutionary ("rise up") but also pragmatic ("you will lose nothing by it") and disciplinary ("you ought to"). The discipline runs in two directions: protecting animals, children also discipline themselves. The novel even self-reflexively stages its own scene of pedagogic discipline: the Band of Mercy meeting, where young people raise their hands to recite from *Our Dumb Animals*. After one recitation, the audience clamors for "The dog story—The dog story!" (158). As a pedagogic tool, *Beautiful Joe* will itself become a "dog story" for children to study and repeat.[56]

Children are also one of the novel's major analogies for animals. Nineteenth-century movements for animal and child protection were conjoined, the former emerging before the latter. Both relied on widespread cultural "associations between animals and children as petted members of the family and vital elements in its affective glue."[57] In *Beautiful Joe*, this affective glue imposes sticky responsibilities: Miss Laura's mother says, "A dog . . . is something like a child. If you want it clean and pleasant, you have got to keep it so" (75). The analogy stretches beyond pleasantness. Late in the novel, when circus animals are dying in a fire, "their voices" are "like the voices of children in mortal pain" (253). Not only does the novel address itself to children; it also represents first-dog voice, in its most urgent register, as analogous to that of a child screaming.

But this analogy too is inexact. "A child has a voice to tell its wrong," says Miss Laura, but "a poor, dumb creature must suffer in silence; in bitter, bitter silence" (66). Also, children grow up, and dogs do not. The nineteenth-century pedagogy of kindness to animals helped enforce this contrast between children and animals, with animals "used as objects for children's transition into adult authority and responsibility, from being *like* an animal to being *above* an animal."[58] By contrast, animals could never make this transition. In "Rights of Dumb Animals" (1869), her article in support of the new animal welfare movement, Harriet Beecher Stowe declared, "If there be any oppressed class that ought to have a convention, and pass resolutions asserting their share . . . it is that hapless class who not only can neither speak, read, nor write, but who have no capacity for being taught any of these accomplishments."[59] Stowe's vindication of the rights of animals as an "oppressed class" centered on their inability even to learn, much less to speak or write.

Here is another analogy for the dog, based on an "oppressed class" in the classic sense, from Joe himself: "If men and women are kind in every respect to their dumb servants, they will be astonished to find . . . how faithful and grateful their dumb animals will be to them" (270). "Dumb" migrates here from "deaf and dumb," the vocabulary of disability, to the language of class servitude. The voice of the dog in *Beautiful Joe* is like that of the servant, "faithful and grateful."

Grateful, presumably, because faithful: enter fidelity, the preeminent virtue of the domestic dog. The assumption of dog fidelity was long-standing—faithful Argos waits twenty years to see his master in the *Odyssey*—but its construction changed over time. It ramped up in Victorian Britain: for example, "Greyfriars Bobby," a Skye terrier, became famous for having kept longtime vigil over the grave of his master (a policeman, hence "Bobby") in the Edinburgh cemetery Greyfriars; the dog was enshrined in 1863 in a statue paying tribute to his fidelity.[60] The historical motor for this enshrinement may have been anxiety, with the dream of dog fidelity policing more unruly specters of human disloyalty. A historian of nineteenth-century Paris, for example, argues that interest in canine fidelity surged as a substitute for the fragmentation of modern urban life: "Faithful dogs took the place of faithless people."[61] Back in Boston, Sarah Bolton, in *Our Devoted Friend the Dog* (1902), based a book-long plea against animal cruelty on an extensive catalog of faithful dogs who "have saved people from drowning, houses from burning."[62]

The fidelity of the canine servant even has a proper name, Fido, which was well established in the nineteenth century as the name of Abraham Lincoln's beloved dog.[63] Fido is a servant whose job description is to serve the emotional health of the master. To put it another way, he—the name is male, though the dog can be female; I will come back to this—is a quintessential pet. A historian locating the origin of pets in early modern Europe gives three defining criteria: pets were animals who were allowed inside the house, given individual names, and not eaten.[64] Katherine Grier, a historian of pets in America, notes that the term entered *Webster's Dictionary* in 1828 as "any little animal fondled and indulged"; the word itself signaled human power—"no people, no pets."[65] Other scholars of pets are harsher still: "Domestication means domination."[66]

Beautiful Joe, victim of brutality turned household pet, is happy to be domesticated and dominated by his rescuers. Like a good servant, his tone is deferential: "If it is not wrong for a dog to say it, I should like to add, 'God bless you all'" (270). The dog can offer the blessing of God only by clarifying his submissive place. Darwin, noting that dogs "sometimes throw themselves on the ground with their bellies upwards," concludes that "the feeling of affection of a dog towards his master is combined with a strong sense of submission."[67] Joe's tone is that of the dog who goes belly-up, the servant whose affection is inseparable from his submission.

Keridiana Chez develops a related model of canine servitude in her analysis of the animal literature of this era, characterizing the dog as an "emotional prosthesis" for humans. Chez publishes *Victorian Dogs, Victorian Men* after I first draft this chapter, and our ideas overlap. As she outlines in her introduction, her idea of "emotional prosthesis" emphasizes the complex intimacy between the dog and the human in Anglo-American literature of the period. She gives an extraordinary example from *Scientific American* of 1890: a story of an ailing boy who had a live dog's bone grafted onto his leg, with the dog immobilized for the surgery, its vocal cords cut to "relieve the boy from the annoyance of frequent whinings."[68] Literalizing the bodily intimacy of human and dog, this story also highlights the anxieties generated by their bond. The boy's "annoyance" must be minimized, because "the more important the prosthesis, the more vulnerable its user . . . the more valuable the prosthesis, the greater the need to diminish it as well as the relationship."[69]

With its advocacy of "faithful and grateful" dogs, *Beautiful Joe* indeed represents the dog as an emotional prosthesis—a servant so necessary that his deference must be rendered hyperbolically. However, the novel's first-dog voice also inverts the *Scientific American* story Chez discusses: rather than severing the dog's vocal cords, *Beautiful Joe* restores speech to the mutilated dog through its narrative voice. The first-dog voice of the novel is itself a kind of prosthesis—or, to put it another way, Joe is not only the embodiment of prosthesis but also its user.

This formulation returns me to the terms of disability studies: "Our phrase *narrative prosthesis* is meant to indicate that disability has been used throughout history as a crutch upon which literary narratives lean for their representational power."[70] Their idea—"our" is David Mitchell and Sharon Snyder—seems thematically relevant to *Beautiful Joe*, whose narrative leans on Joe's disability for its power. And it seems formally relevant: the first-dog voice of the novel is a prosthetic voice box built on Joe's disability. I will build on the work of Mitchell and Snyder as well as Chez. Within the novel, Joe serves humans as an emotional prosthesis, while its first-dog voice also functions as a literary prosthesis—a narrative voice box—for him.

To recap: So far I have argued that *Beautiful Joe* uses "first-dog voice" to revivify the mute and mutilated dog; that this first-dog voice is a kind of prosthetic voice box, at once speaking for, translating into words, and writing as fiction the expressions of the dog; and that this voice brings dogs into the orbit, analogically, of people with disabilities, children, and servants. The dog is a figurative Fido, which is another name for the prosthetic "friend" who writes down the story, faithfully translating Joe's thoughts. And this friend is Saunders herself. She is the woman who is faithfully, if fictionally—faithfully because fictionally—giving voice to his voice. Joe is Saunders's fiction, but she is also his Fido.

3.

Now I have come to a fourth analogy: a dog is like a woman. I am back to feminism, though it has been here all along. The antivivisection movement, for example, was closely connected to feminism, Frances Cobbe and Elizabeth Stuart Phelps providing good examples on the British and American sides. Cobbe divided her activist energies between animal welfare and women's suffrage; Phelps wove them into the romance plot of *Trixy*, in which the novel's male scientist, for whom "the subserviency of women had been a matter of course," is rejected by the novel's antivivisection human heroine, who cannot "take a vivisector's hand."[71] The campaigns for animals and women went more violently hand in hand in the Brown Dog Riots of 1907, in which British suffragists fought with medical students over canine vivisection. For these antivivisection feminists, vivisection was a horror akin to contemporary gynecology, with the anger of women at their treatment by male doctors "projected into the figures of animals, captured and tortured at the hands of the vivisectionist."[72]

Later in the twentieth century, a feminist made an influential case that mainstream culture privileges meat and men while butchering animals and women. This critic, Carol Adams, was ahead of the animal studies curve; now she is one of many writing on "Sexism/Speciesism: Interlocking Oppressions."[73] The interlock is visible elsewhere in feminist writing. A feminist legal theorist stipulated a generation ago that "man fucks woman; subject verb object"; more recently, she has analyzed animals with self-echoing precision: "People dominate animals, men dominate women."[74] Some feminist writing is more species-specific, as well as more upbeat: "I consider dog writing to be a branch of feminist theory, or the other way around," writes Donna Haraway in her *Companion Species Manifesto*. Having chosen cyborgs over goddesses in the first wave of women's studies, she now celebrates dogs over cyborgs, as "better guides through the thickets of technobiopolitics."[75]

Before Haraway, there was an even more foundational feminist writer guided by dogs: four years after *A Room of One's Own*, Virginia Woolf wrote *Flush* (1933), a mock-biography of Elizabeth Barrett Browning's cocker spaniel. Woolf liked dogs, as did Browning, Edith Wharton, and the Emilys, Brontë and Dickinson; dogs served all as their "shaggy muses."[76] Relatedly, Woolf also liked women: one of her dogs, Pinka, was a gift from her lover, Vita Sackville-West, and the photographic frontispiece for *Flush* was of Pinka on Woolf's bed. I have already named two women writers in a genealogy of queer-friendly dog stories, Frances Cobbe and Mary Wilkins Freeman; Virginia Woolf is another. For these reasons and others, *Flush* is now catnip, as it were, to scholars in animal studies.[77]

I focus here on one theme in *Flush*: its metaphorical affiliation between male dog and female writer. *Flush* is a novel written in third-person voice but with a modernist interest in getting inside the consciousness of both women and dogs and with a feminist interest in showing similarities between their conditions. Woolf presents the characters of Flush and Elizabeth Barrett, both living in her father's house, as similarly domesticated, and she makes their physical resemblance explicit: "Heavy curls hung down on either side of Miss Barrett's face; large bright eyes shone out; a large mouth smiled. Heavy ears hung down on either side of Flush's face; his eyes, too, were large and bright; his mouth was wide. There was a likeness between them." Yet she turns immediately to the limits of likeness: "Between them lay the widest gulf that can separate one being from another. She spoke. He was dumb. She was woman; he was dog."[78] The sentences "She spoke. He was dumb" mark the gulf between woman and dog, period—literally, with a period. But the last sentence punctuates the point differently. The semicolon that joins "she was woman" and "he was dog" is a sign of proximity as well as difference.

I cannot ascribe the same degree of self-reflexivity to Marshall Saunders's sentences nor equivalent stylistic nuance to my own semicolons; however, *Beautiful Joe* is also an animal story that enacts the joins of "She was woman; he was dog." The most overt link is between Joe and Miss Laura, who is Beautiful Joe's greatest love ("I love her better than any one else in the world" [53]) and his surrogate mother: "'I am not going to let you die, Joe.' And she set her lamp on the ground, and took me in her arms" (70). This lady with the lamp, Joe's nightingale, nourishes him maternally: "She dipped her finger in the milk and held it out to me" (71). The cruelty of Jenkins, a milkman, is replaced by the mother's milk of Miss Laura. A human revivification of Joe's mother, she has even greater sway over him and over others in the world. By the end of the novel, Joe reports, "I do not think that there is any one in all the country around who is as much beloved as she is. . . . Riverdale has got to be a model village in respect of the treatment of all kinds of animals" (269). Riverdale is Joe's utopia, and Miss Laura its beloved female leader.

This fantasy of female leadership has historical contexts. It redresses what Elizabeth Waterston has suggested was Saunders's own experience of gender constraint: "Sent to finishing school when her brothers went to college, saddled with family responsibility for aging parents, [and] impoverished by publishing practices that exploited and underpaid women writers."[79] Susan McHugh maps *Beautiful Joe*'s Laura onto larger developments of social change, an "emerging world of women's suffrage, organized labour, and the social regulation of industry."[80]

Keridiana Chez makes a different map: for her, women in *Beautiful Joe* "function as victims, sensitive barometers of moral outrage, and producers of pleasant affect." Chez views *Beautiful Joe* as a novel oriented toward its male characters, aiming to teach Victorian boys about appropriate masculinity; such pedagogy in the novel means both encouraging boys to be kind and masculinizing characters like Laura's bookish brother.[81]

I like her arguments about boys in *Beautiful Joe*, but they do not preclude mine about women in *Beautiful Joe*. I think the novel both schools boys in masculinity and fantasizes more power for girls. There is even a politically radical female leader name-checked within the novel itself: a friend tells Miss Laura of Louise Michel, who "is an anarchist, and she used to wear a uniform, and shoulder a rifle, and help to build barricades. She was arrested and sent as a convict to one of the French penal colonies. She has a most wonderful love for animals in her heart" (229–30). Michel—French anarchist, Communard, revolutionary—seems an outlier in the world of *Beautiful Joe*: its well-regulated world shuns lawbreaking, let alone anarchy and revolution.

Saunders's vision of Laura as a leader reminds me, instead, of a different woman writer: Louisa May Alcott. In *Little Women*, continuing in *Little Men*, Alcott establishes a model institution—Plumfield—over which a woman presides, producing better boys. For her, female power and better boyhood go hand in hand, and the fictional world affords Alcott more freedom than the actual social world, in which women did not even vote, much less lead. In both *Little Women* and *Beautiful Joe*, the spinster-leader weds by novel's end; *Little Women*'s Jo March marries Professor Bhaer before she establishes Plumfield, and Miss Laura too marries, in her case Harry, an old family friend—she is "Miss Laura no longer, but Mrs. Gray" (266). As Mrs. Bhaer retains at least some of the force of the unmarried Jo March, so too does Mrs. Gray absorb the power of Miss Laura. And the parallel between Alcott and Saunders holds in another way: like Alcott, Saunders has written a nineteenth-century New England novel about the march of a beautiful Jo.[82]

That is a pun, but there is a point: it is not just that Joe inspires female leadership but that Joe is himself like a woman. Joe is, to be sure, a male dog, but he seems neutered. I do not mean that only anatomically, although Joe does not father any puppies, or even symbolically in the sense that a mutilated tail might imply castration (remember Darwin: the dog's tail may be "held erect and quite rigid"). It is more that Joe's character seems, approvingly, feminized. Teresa Mangum makes this argument: Joe operates as an "ungendered heroine," carrying forth feminine virtues of "modesty, affection, submission, and loyalty."[83]

I am not sure about this last trait: the loyalty of a Fido to his master seems a strengthening of bonds between men, within and across species. Sarah Amato shows how dogs in Victorian Britain were viewed as pets for men and models of masculinity; they "were believed to exemplify a chivalric heroism, guilelessness, and loyalty, traits which had long been associated with an idealized masculinity."[84] Famous stories of dog fidelity usually combine male pets with male masters, from Argos to Greyfriars Bobby. But not always: in *Beautiful Joe*, feminized dogs are loyal to women.

The best comparison here may be to that most famous of nineteenth-century novels, Harriet Beecher Stowe's *Uncle Tom's Cabin* (1852). In Stowe's novel, Uncle Tom is infused with traditionally feminine virtues; in the influential formulation of another feminist critic, he is one of the novel's heroines.[85] Joe, the fictional dog, is not the same as Tom, the fictional black man—the racial connotations of *Beautiful Joe* will be the subject of the next chapter—but both Joe and Tom are feminized heroes. In *Beautiful Joe* as in *Uncle Tom's Cabin*, a nineteenth-century woman writer feminizes a male character as both a sign of his virtue and a source of female authority.

Here she is: Marshall Saunders, the woman writer on display, in the photographic frontispiece of the 1903 edition of the novel. She is formally dressed, her face posed at a stiff angle, her eyes looking indistinctly out beyond the frame; a dog sits on her lap. The photograph embraces the woman-animal analogy, aligning woman with dog: they look in the same direction, necks similarly in shadow, white arm and pale fur touching. The animal is both similar and adjacent to the woman, metaphor and metonymy for her. Even the textiles surrounding her—ruffled dress, wrinkled skirt, and what looks like a fluffy blanket—seem fur-like.

FIG. 2.
Beautiful Joe, frontispiece, 1893 [1894]. Photo: James Gehrt.

But the signature below the photograph, "Marshall Saunders," also makes of the author a first-person voice, with her own name—sort of. Saunders published from 1889 onward as "Marshall Saunders," initially without author photographs that would reveal her gender.[86] As male pseudonyms go, "Marshall" packs a wallop compared to, say, George for Eliot or Sand; it is a verb as well as a name, marshaling authority. However, the pseudonym does not operate here as a form of concealment. In this 1903 edition, almost a decade after the novel's publication, the gender of the author was public. The photograph confirms the author as female, while the pseudonym captions the photograph in the terms—or at least in the name—of masculinity.

And in the words of masculine authority: notice the caption adjacent to the author's name, "Open thy mouth for the dumb." This is the voice of God—or at least, the Bible, specifically Proverbs 31:8. The voice of the dog leads back to God, with Saunders lending the proverbial hand through her writer's pen. And her lap: the dog is on her lap, usually a position of subservience to the woman, if not also of woman to man. But Saunders does not seem anyone's lapdog. Here the woman marshals authority, not despite but because of her photographic alignment with an animal.

This observation seems at odds with most of the scholarship I have now read on nineteenth-century animal photography, which focuses on images of wildlife and posits an inverted relation between animals and photographs. As the number of actual wild animals waned, the number of animals shot by cameras waxed. This line of argument parallels an influential analysis of the rise of the zoo by John Berger, who wrote that "everywhere animals disappear. In zoos they constitute the living monument to their own disappearance."[87] These arguments about how photographs and zoos replaced wildlife are persuasive, but they seem incomplete; they ignore the domestic—often the feminized—side of things: the pet in the parlor.

A countergenealogy of canine photographs, less studied, tells this story. Posed solo or with people, in studio and exterior settings, leashed and unleashed, dogs flourished in private family photographs. A pioneering study of these photographs by Ann-Janine Morey suggests that "in American photography, the dog becomes part of the patriotic iconography embracing all the meanings of home—family, fidelity, comfort, protection, nurturance, and love—as well as symbolizing some of the less palatable meanings of home and family—domination, subservience, violence."[88] Fidelity seems particularly important in these photographs not only as a virtue enshrined in the dog but also as a material necessity in the making of the image: early photographic technologies, with their long exposure times, required the dog to sit obediently for a long time.[89] There is also a metaphoric connection to fidelity in the medium of the photograph, which faithfully—indexically—represented an object actually there. In the dog photograph, the animal ostensibly most faithful to humans met the artistic medium ostensibly most faithful to its subject.

Here, the photograph shows the dog sitting faithfully with the writer, and the writer herself looking faithful to respectability and femininity—although the latter was initially disguised; the pseudonym "Marshall" was an initial infidelity to a female name. As for seriousness, she is unsmiling, her face stiff, but the dog on her lap looks lively. In photographs of dogs with stiff-looking humans, sometimes "the dog filled in that missing smile."[90] Perhaps the dog is smiling for Saunders; certainly, Saunders is speaking for the dog. "Open thy mouth for the dumb": the mouth is that of Saunders, inaugurating the first-dog voice to come.

The caption reminds me again of Woolf's Miss Barrett and Flush: "She spoke. He was dumb. She was woman; he was dog." The Saunders photograph confirms that semicolon of affinity. But the frontispiece also scrambles these terms. Not only is the affinity, for Saunders, between speaking woman and dumb dog; it is also between speaking dog and dumb woman.

4.

There is another figure waiting to be introduced: the speaking dummy. The topic of ventriloquism comes up often in animal studies as metaphor. For example, Margo DeMello, introducing a useful anthology on literary representations of speaking animals, describes this topic as "human-animal ventriloquism."[91] But ventriloquism is a material practice as well as a metaphoric frame—a practice whose history is relevant to *Beautiful Joe*.

First, a short historical zigzag: for centuries, ventriloquism was a widespread cultural phenomenon, "dangerously spiced with the demonic or supernatural," before it narrowed into a niche theatrical entertainment "fringed with a sense of the tawdry and the ridiculous."[92] These terms are provided by Steven Connor in a cultural history that emphasizes how late the narrowing came. Only in the twentieth century did ventriloquism take the form it still, largely, retains: a single practitioner, a nonhuman dummy, a comic routine, and a vaudeville stage. Before, it had a broader meaning and a greater cultural importance, wherein the ventriloquist seemed to possess "not just certain skills of suggestion and dissimulation, but . . . the power of voice itself, focused and magnified."[93]

There are many fictional explorations of this theme—for example, Charles Brockden Brown's novel *Wieland, or The Transformation: An American Tale* (1798). In *Wieland*, what seems to be a narrative of the supernatural, with mysterious voices emanating from odd places, is revealed late in the novel to be one of ventriloquism when a character confesses, "A power which I possess . . . enables me to mimic exactly the voice of another, and to modify the sound so that it shall appear to come from what quarter, and be uttered at what distance I please."[94] This is ventriloquism in what was called its "distant voice" mode, here presented as free-floating omnipotence, more religious in authority than vaudevillian.[95] I have read *Wieland*—it is part of the American literary canon—but I only paid attention to ventriloquism as the novel's supernatural substitute, its thrill-killer. Read for itself, ventriloquism anchors the novel, turning other characters—and, by extension, the novel's readers—into dupes.

That is the other reputation that the ventriloquist develops by the twentieth century: as a con man. In L. Frank Baum's novel *The Wizard of Oz* (1900), the Wizard, unmasked as "the great humbug," reveals to Dorothy, "When I grew up I became a ventriloquist," progressing from there to balloonist.[96] One possible model here is P. T. Barnum, who called himself a "humbug" and was known as the "marvellous, wonderful wizard"; another context is the nineteenth-century circus, which often included both ventriloquists and balloonists.[97] Baum's *The Wizard of Oz* combines these elements. In the Wizard's origin story—omitted from the film—ventriloquism is the hot-air foundation for both wizardry and humbuggery.

It is not only that ventriloquism is important as a plot to fiction, from *Wieland* to *Wizard*, but that all fiction seems a form of ventriloquism. In fiction written in first-person voice, the literary "I" is a condensed ventriloquist's dummy; in fiction written in first-animal voice, that dummy is a nonhuman—a practice common in the longer history of ventriloquism. Animals were often used in distant voice ventriloquism, as when the Wizard of Oz explains to Dorothy, "'I can imitate any kind of bird or beast.' Here he mewed so like a kitten that Toto pricked up his ears and looked everywhere to see where she was."[98] Animals assume two roles in this scene: a cat is the conjured but absent dummy, and the dog his credulous mark. In the twentieth century, when ventriloquism narrowed, animal dummies were fewer: the best known was Lamb Chop, voiced by television performer Shari Lewis. Also, Nina Conti, a contemporary English actor-ventriloquist, features a dummy named Monkey in her act; I will return to her.[99]

Lewis and Conti are women ventriloquists, exceptions to the rule; ventriloquists have traditionally been men, and ventriloquism itself was seen to require masculinity. As one nineteenth-century commentator put it, "In those cases in which the ventriloquial effects have been produced by the female organs of speech, there has always been a marked deficiency of power."[100] As ventriloquism narrowed, the ventriloquist's dummy was almost always male, usually a "cheeky boy" who acted as alter ego of the male ventriloquist.[101] A father-son variant: the character of Charlie McCarthy was so closely identified with his ventriloquist, Edgar Bergen, that Bergen's human daughter, Candice, was known as "Charlie's sister." Candice Bergen's own memoir, *Knock Wood*, offers a tart coming-of-age story in which the metaphorical dummy-girl, conflated with the stereotype of the icy blonde, speaks for herself.[102] In a more scholarly vein, a recent study argues for feminist uses of the idea of ventriloquism in Victorian and neo-Victorian fiction. For women writers, ventriloquism offered "the possibility of the 'passionate puppet'; an ostensible dummy that can 'talk back' to the master discourses by which she is manipulated."[103]

Now to return to *Beautiful Joe*: I have positioned the first-dog voice of Saunders's novel as a form of literary prosthesis, enabling the nonhuman to speak; that voice also seems an enactment of ventriloquism. "Open thy voice for the dumb," the Biblical catchphrase for Saunders's authorial voice, seems an exhortation to a ventriloquist—here, unusually, a woman—to throw her voice and have it issue, magically and powerfully, from an animal mouth elsewhere. In the 1890s moment of *Beautiful Joe*, a woman writing a novel in first-dog voice seems less an analog of what the ventriloquist was becoming—a stage performer speaking through a dummy—than an incarnation of what the ventriloquist had been: an omnipotent source for voices that seemed to come from everywhere and nowhere.

I have already quoted one version of this figure contemporary with *Beautiful Joe*: the Wizard of Oz, who can "imitate any kind of bird or beast" well enough to fool Toto. Saunders is the ventriloquist as nonhumbug wizard, both writer and woman. In her use of first-dog voice, she invents a world of animal sound and then keeps going: Joe not only speaks but gets to tell the novel's story in toto.

5.

Even in my zigzag way, I am making some progress in the dog park of animal studies; by now, I have read the celebrated essay by the famous French philosopher—written at the end of his life, an old dog coming up with a new trick—and his voice too seems relevant to that of *Beautiful Joe*. I know that Marshall Saunders and Jacques Derrida are an unlikely couple, even unlikelier than Saunders and Woolf, and I feel confident that this is the only time that they have ever been mentioned in the same sentence. Nonetheless, they seem, in some small way, to be barking up the same tree.[104]

Derrida's essay is about recognizing the usual vectors of power between human and animal—the human looks at, defines, and controls the animal—and reversing them; he wants to open a way to seeing the human as constituted through an animal's gaze. The most famous moment in this essay comes when Derrida sees his cat gazing at him naked in the bathroom: "Can we say that the animal has been looking at us? . . . I often ask myself, just to see, *who I*

FIG. 3.
Beautiful Joe, illustration of Joe, with the caption "My name is Beautiful Joe," 1893 [1894]. Photo: James Gehrt.

am . . . (following) at the moment when, caught naked, in silence, by the gaze of an animal, for example, the eyes of a cat, I have trouble, yes, a bad time overcoming my embarrassment."[105] This is an instance of identification, the theorist "ashamed of being as naked as a beast," but also a recognition of difference: the animal's gaze is "the point of view of the absolute other."[106] From this gaze, a reversal follows: "The animal looks at us, and we are naked before it. Thinking perhaps begins there."[107]

I begin there in Derrida because *Beautiful Joe* also—I understand the stretch in that "also"—reverses the usual vectors of looking. Back to Hezekiah Butterworth's introduction to the novel: "Through [the story] we enter the animal world, and are made to see as animals see" (47). Or at least, as Saunders sees Joe seeing, as when he is given a new collar "with my name on it—*Beautiful Joe*!" and "Mrs. Morris held me up to a glass to look at myself. I felt so happy. Up to this time I felt a little ashamed of my cropped ears and docked tail, but now that I had a fine new collar I could hold up my head with any dog" (80). In this mirror scene, the dog's shame is reversed by the sight of his new collar, the finery of his servitude; his gaze, like his voice, deepens his domestication but also reverses the mutilations of his body.

So too does he gaze repeatedly upon Miss Laura: "I thought then, that I never had seen such a beautiful girl" (63), and later, "She looked more beautiful than I had ever seen her before" (230). Saunders also depicts Joe reading, after a fashion: "I have seen my mistress laughing and crying over a little book that she says is a story of a horse's life, and sometimes she puts the book down close to my nose to let me see the pictures" (53). This is a reference to *Black Beauty*, which Joe is absorbing by looking at its illustrations. His gaze is his form of "reading," an optical complement to the first-dog voice with which he "speaks."

Beautiful Joe is itself a picture book: in the original edition of the novel are five illustrations. The first faces the beginning of chapter 1: a portrait of Joe, medium sized, reclining, carefully posed atop a covered stand, with his foreshortened ears and tail in view. This is the human-made view; the non-human animal is always the object of the image, never its maker. Except that this image is captioned with the first line of the novel, "My name is Beautiful Joe," linking it to the novel's first-dog voice. The portrait becomes another extension of that voice, seemingly claimed by its canine subject as well as its unnamed human maker.

Elsewhere, Joe names his control over a particular kind of image: the photograph. Late in the novel, he describes the visit of a family with a dog to Riverdale: "One day a friend of Miss Laura's came with a little boy and girl, and 'Collie' sat between the two children, and their father took their picture with a 'kodak.' I like him so much that I told him I would get them to put his picture in my book" (266–67). The illustration opposite this passage is a conventionally idealized photographic portrait of a collie with two children. Less conventional, though, is Joe's description. The Kodak camera, launched in 1888, had recently become the standard technology for the home photograph, released from the confines of the studio and available to all. Here, while the father "[takes] their picture with a 'kodak,'" Joe controls the circulation of the image: "I told him I would get them to put his picture in my book." The presence of this photograph affirms his success. In another enactment of photographic fidelity, the publishers of *Beautiful Joe*—"them"—have been faithful to his command to include the image.

Photographic and canine fidelity converge even more fully in the novel in a photographic illustration of the fox terrier named Billy, another canine member of the Morris household. In this image, Billy perches obediently on his hind legs, facing a hand holding a ball up for him. This image is of Saunders's own dog, a fox terrier—presumably the same dog as in the novel's frontispiece. The photographic image neatly captures two kinds of fidelity: the dog's fidelity to the human inside the image and the photograph's fidelity to the real dog outside it.[108]

But there are some complications to this interpretation. The caption underneath the image, a quotation from elsewhere in the chapter, seems at odds with the image: "Billy would take his ball and go off by himself." Billy's story, as sketched across several chapters, is one of a mischievous puppy successfully trained, but the caption emphasizes his autonomy, if not his outright disobedience. This autonomy is echoed, in the photograph, in the self-contained wholeness of the canine body, as contrasted with the human body, which is dismembered—cropped, photographically, into a hand. Billy's full body also contrasts, within the novel, with the mutilated body of Joe. Significantly, Billy's own tail is undocked: "I must say a word about Billy's tail before I close this chapter. It is the custom to cut the ends of fox-terrier's [*sic*] tails, but leave their ears untouched. Billy came to Miss Laura so young that his tail had not been cut off, and she would not have it done" (103). The comment reinforces the temperamental contrast between Joe and Billy with a physical one. In contrast to the subdued deference of the mutilated Joe, Billy is photographically, physically, and psychologically uncropped.

The story of the real Billy, told elsewhere, emphasizes his rebelliousness. In *My Pets: Real Happenings in My Aviary* (1908), Saunders's memoir about her pets and herself—more on this later—she fills in the picture of this family dog:

> Billy would cheerfully pose when he saw a camera, and follow us whenever we went to the photographers in the town. One day when my mother was having her picture taken, Billy placed himself at her feet. The photographer took him up and lifted him to what he considered a more attractive position.
>
> I shall never forget the look of doggish reproach that Billy gave him. . . . It seemed to say "Don't you know, sir, that I am a dog that is used to posing? I know how to show off my good points better than you do."
>
> Strangers sometimes remarked that no member of our family was photographed without this pet dog.

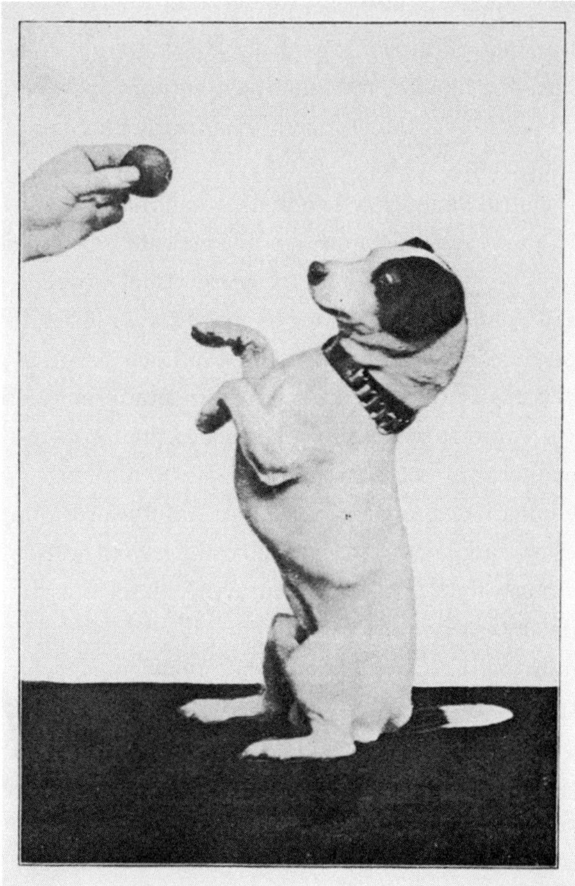

FIG. 4.
Beautiful Joe, illustration of Billy, with the caption "Billy would take his ball and go off by himself," 1893 [1894]. Photo: James Gehrt.

> "We cannot help it," we used to reply, "Billy follows us and gets into the picture. We can't keep him out."[109]

This anecdote again turns on fidelity but alters its terms: the photograph is faithful not to the dog's fidelity but to his assertiveness. Billy seems to be subordinate, placing himself at the foot of the human, but this posture is in service of his assertiveness; acting with "doggish reproach," he knows how to pose. This account reframes the Billy photograph in *Beautiful Joe*, in which the human hand seems to enforce discipline; here, the dog does whatever he wants.

Perhaps it reframes the woman writer too: perhaps Marshall Saunders is less like the submissive Joe than like the defiant Billy; perhaps Billy is both her smile and her voice. In an annotated personal copy of *Beautiful Joe*, Saunders added this handwritten caption to the photo: "My father's hand."[110] This caption is itself intriguing—it denotes a literal hand, but it also connotes the idea of a hand as metonymy for authorship, even leadership. And it raises a question: If the cropped hand in the photograph is that of the father, is Billy equivalent to the daughter? The Billy passage from *My Pets*, written in Marshall Saunders's own first-person voice, aligns the woman and dog again in a tone more defiant than domesticated. Ordinarily, in the human-animal relation, the human exerts control, visual as well as physical; whereas in this story about Billy, the dog shapes his own place in the image. This species reversal in turn reinforces the novel's challenge to gender hierarchies, with animals as well as women complementarily engaged in vocal self-fashioning.

Another recap: I have suggested that *Beautiful Joe*'s illustrations extend connections between the domestication of dogs and women, but they also emphasize, through canine autonomy, the possibility of female disobedience. They complement the ways that the novel's first-dog voice acts as a feminist strategy for a nineteenth-century woman writer to voice her own authority—like a ventriloquist with an animal act—through her use of a dog. It is not only that women provide an additional analogy for dogs in the novel, along with children, servants, and people with disabilities, but that they provide the primary vocal cords with which its first-dog voice box speaks. Speaks, that is, in a particular voice: white, middle class, religious, reform minded rather than revolutionary. This is a common voice in nineteenth-century feminism, important despite its limits—or rather because of its limits. The dummy can only speak with the tools of the ventriloquist.

You could term my method here—showing how *Beautiful Joe* destabilizes, at least modestly, some hierarchies of species and gender—"deconstructive." You could bring this back to Derrida, the most influential voice of deconstruction and now a powerful posthumous voice in animal studies. You could say that I too am ventriloquizing Derrida, both making him speak for me and forming my words through his voice.

Of course, there are many differences: for one thing, Derrida, in his scene of being looked at by an animal, is writing about his cat, and my subject is dogs. Also, the naked part: "The animal looks at us, and we are naked before it." We are? I wonder if Derrida's account of his pet would be less effective if he were less famous or if the naked body in question were female. The latter seems likely: the naked woman would be reduced to the corporeal and, probably, the sexual; embarrassment would not follow after this moment, as it does for Derrida, but would precede and suffuse the scene with the naked lady. There are other feminist critiques of this moment in Derrida, including one by Donna Haraway, who argues that Derrida "failed a simple obligation of companion species; he did not become curious about what the cat might actually be doing, feeling, thinking."[111] And there are metacritiques that decry the privileged role of Derrida in animal studies, questioning whether his primacy has come at the cost of displacing women scholars in the field.[112]

I do not want to compound this displacement, but I do appreciate Derrida's voice and his scene of a human pausing before the gaze of the animal, which is ripe for its own playfully appreciative deconstructions: see, for example, *Lily Does Derrida* (2010–12) by Kathy High, "a dog's video-essay" in which the artist's pet Lily, featured on-screen, seems to analyze Derrida's essay in a human voiceover.[113] I especially like the way Derrida privileges the idea of the "autobiographical animal": "the sort of man or woman who . . . chooses to indulge in or can't resist indulging in autobiographical confidences."[114] The autobiographical animal is Derrida, naked in front of his cat. The nude scene becomes a mirror scene, which in turn becomes a memoir: we might call his essay "beau Jacques, an autobiography." Beau Jacques, beautiful Joe: top dog, underdog.

And, of course, the autobiographical animal, *c'est moi*: a woman writer with a dog, writing on women writers and dogs. In this observation, I know, I am not alone: while I am writing this chapter, for example, Susan McHugh, whose work I continue to follow doggedly, publishes an article on what she terms "feminist/dog-writing": the convergence of autobiographical criticism, feminist theory, and contemporary writing about dogs, by Haraway and others. This essay, which also analyzes the backlash such stories have engendered, has the unimprovable title "Bitch, Bitch, Bitch."[115]

The overlap of this essay with my own concerns could be dispiriting—the leash of keeping up with animal studies pulling tight once again, leaving me with little space to play. But I do not feel cowed or sheepish. For one thing, after drafting this chapter, I find that mine is no longer an entirely novice voice: I heard this article delivered as a talk, I met the author, I made suggestions. I have been teaching some of these books—*Flush*, *Black Beauty*, *The Island of Doctor Moreau*—in a course called "The Nonhuman"; I have been reading journal special issues about animal studies. Actually, these last are starting to forecast the end of the field: "By now its wave seems to have crested, and everyone's watching to see what's been left on the beach."[116] This seems premature, and I find it frustrating that people are starting to say good-bye to animal studies when I have just said hello.

But I am not alarmed: reports of a field's death are often greatly exaggerated. And I am no longer ambivalent. I have decided not to worry about my voice in relation to the field. One should faithfully acknowledge the scholars who have come before—especially, I think, the women, because acknowledgment to them so often drops out. Otherwise, though, one may speak in the voice that comes out—usually third person but sometimes first dog. I am neither Fido nor Joe; I might be closer to Billy, the dog who runs off with the ball but keeps putting himself in the picture. We are autobiographical animals all. Every dog must have her day.

CHAPTER 2

His Master's Voice

1.

A year after Frankie's cancer erupts, I return to Provincetown with him for a weekend and read a best-selling new book on dogs by a cognitive scientist. The author, Alexandra Horowitz, argues that to understand a dog, we must recognize his *umwelt*—initially a biologist's term, now repurposed in animal studies, meaning his "self-world," his subjective understanding of the world. The dog's *umwelt* is dominated by his olfactory skills, his sense of smell being vastly more powerful than that of humans; the dog's point of view is his "point of nose."[1] This concept is immediately applicable: Frankie, whose seaside behavior includes sniffing the salty air and pungent seaweed of Cape Cod, seems to be blissing out in his *umwelt.*

This is often the case. Attuned to tactile as well as olfactory pleasures, Frankie will roll ecstatically in dirt, mud, grass, leaves, sand, and snow; though I know this trait is generic to the golden retriever, it seems to me supremely personalized—dog-ized—in him. In return, his *umwelt* loves him back. For example, when Frankie was young, a neighbor frequently left old tennis balls for him in the waist-high knot of a tree on our local morning walk; now, long after the supply has dried up, Frankie continues to jump up to this knot every time he is on this walk, believing—not unreasonably, given the evidence—that tennis balls grow on trees. He does have his contrary side, with mellow retriever morphing into Frankenstein's monster. For example, almost every day for several years, he would refuse to get into the car for me, even though he was capable of jumping in from a sitting start and even when he was en route to the dog park; instead, he would stop short at the car and throw his weight back on his haunches, civilly disobedient. For anyone else, though—the little girl down the road, the older woman across the street—he would immediately jump in the car. This habit elicited human responses ranging from unsolicited advice to uncontrollable laughter; it was less funny to me, but Frankie himself seemed to be having fun, as he usually does. His cancer—the pain caused by tumor and treatment—is the rare exception to his exceptionally joyful *umwelt*.

Frankie rolls "ecstatically," has "fun," and is "joyful": I understand that these are anthropomorphizing terms, imposing my own *umwelt* on the dog. Anthropomorphism, the ascription of human traits to nonhuman animals, leads to major distortions of animal behavior; there are books in animal studies devoted to this issue.[2] Alexandra Horowitz has read nineteenth-century animal autobiographies, and she dismisses them for their anthropomorphism: "It's a sham: there is no perspective of the dog in them. Instead, it is a dog with the human's voice box transplanted to the dog's snout."[3] Her image of interspecies transplantation gets my attention. I can see what she means. I have looked at the "voice box" of *Beautiful Joe*, and it has led to a series of similes (dogs are like children, servants, people with disabilities, and women) that are inventions of the human. Some of these similes are productive—I argued that the "voice box" of the dog provides a feminist forum for a woman writer—but they are all human projections nonetheless, obscuring the actual animal.

Simile seems itself seems part of the problem: a dog is not like anyone; a dog is a dog. Still, it is hard to avoid simile, metaphor, metonymy, analogy—the whole bag of figurative chew-toys—in writing about dogs. It is not only that there are so many figurative phrases linked to dogs (one website lists them alphabetically: "barking up the wrong tree" leading dozens of entries later toward "working like a dog").[4] It is also that there is no getting away from the traces of figurative language embedded in any kind of writing. In Horowitz's own exhortation that "we try to imagine how [the dog] sees the world," the visual metaphor implicit in her phrase "sees the world" contradicts, or at least complicates, the idea of a smell-centered *umwelt*.[5] Certainly I would be constrained, writing here about dogs, without figurative language, even though—as with the "GIST" and "dirty margins" of Frankie's cancer—I sometimes call a halt to linguistic play. For the writer depicting actual animal behavior, perhaps the goal is not to halt metaphor but to use it more carefully: "The challenge is to anthropomorphize well."[6]

And for the cultural critic, the goal is to make anthropomorphism more visible, to subject it to scrutiny. I like using dog idioms in my own prose because they highlight human assumptions about animals and open them for reflection. I am working hard on such reflection—not, perhaps, "working like a dog," but then Frankie himself does not seem to work like a dog either.

FIG. 5.
Francis Barraud, *His Master's Voice*, 1899. Photo: James Gehrt.

Within a novel like *Beautiful Joe*, the metaphors I have identified are important precisely as metaphors, made by humans for humans; here as elsewhere in animal studies, what is revealed is "not so much the problem of the animal, as the problem of the human."[7] The simile "the dog is like the human" is most interesting when you reverse it—sniff around its back end—and see what the human is like. I would not mistake *Beautiful Joe* as giving any sense of the canine *umwelt*, but neither would I close my nose to the odors it airs of the human. *Beautiful Joe* shows "the human's voice box transplanted to the dog's snout"—exactly so. It is not that Saunders has failed to capture an animal's behavior but rather that she captures a human *umwelt*, circa 1900. What the novel illuminates is not Joe's but his master's voice.

This last is a phrase with its own history, its origin contemporary with *Beautiful Joe*: *His Master's Voice* is an 1899 painting by English artist Francis Barraud in which a dog stands before a wax-cylinder phonograph, apparently listening intently to a sound issuing from it, which the title suggests is the voice of his human master. Barraud sold the painting the next year to a gramophone company, and the image was accordingly altered to show a gramophone, and thereafter used to advertise RCA records. The dog became known as "Nipper" and his image trademarked as *HMV*—"his master's voice." While the use of fine-art paintings in advertisements was not uncommon in this period, Barraud hit the jackpot: the advertisement became "the best known of all dog pictures and arguably the most frequently reproduced painting in the world."[8]

As a picture of a dog, *His Master's Voice* is also a picture of a voice—one that emerges mysteriously from elsewhere to perplex the dog. This voice seems another variant of ventriloquism, then narrowing into its theatrical niche, eclipsed by new technologies of recorded sound. Another scholar notes the combination of new technology with old canine virtue in Barraud's painting: "The high fidelity of the sound finds its perfect match in the high fidelity of the dog."[9] This duality applies more to the painting *His Master's Voice*, which shows a phonograph, than the advertisement, which shows a gramophone: while the gramophone played records produced commercially, only the phonograph could be used to make home recordings, and thus to record the local voice of a dog's "master." As the image moved across media, its connotations of fidelity multiplied. The machine was presented as a faithful worker, as in an 1893 advertisement declaring that "the Phonograph needs no holiday."[10] As an ad, *His Master's Voice* enshrined the loyalty of worker to boss and consumer to corporation, with RCA holding the leash, selling the product. The voice of the corporation was the enduring ghost in the machine.

Ghost in more ways than one: this was originally a painting about death. Francis Barraud maintained that Nipper was mourning the painter's brother: "He never left my brother's heels . . . when my brother died, Nipper attached himself to me."[11] The painting was first called *His Late Master's Voice*, and the dog's table may have been modeled on a coffin. Steven Connor situates the image in a Victorian culture that emphasized modes of communication with the dead—spiritualism, séances, mediums—along with new technologies like the telephone, gramophone, and phonograph. In this reciprocal relationship between technologies of sound and the supernatural—between new media and new mediums—the haunting voice in *His Master's Voice* suggests not only the ghost in the machine but also "the machine in the ghost."[12]

Ghosts dog both *His Master's Voice* and *Beautiful Joe*. There are deaths in both—the dead master of Nipper, the dead mother and siblings of Joe—and attempts at revivification, through voice, in both. And both have masters, although here is a difference: in *His Master's Voice*, the master is presumably male; in *Beautiful Joe*, the master, Miss Laura, is a mistress. These are asymmetrical terms. The male version, as usual, registers more authority: think of the ruling role of "governor" versus the supplementary work of "governess."

But I am focusing on the gender connotations of "master" when what really strikes me now is something else about the word. As a noun, "master" is multiuse: the *Oxford English Dictionary* definition begins, "A person or thing having control or authority."[13] For a scholar of nineteenth-century American literature, a particular kind of person comes to mind: "My master! And who made him my master? . . . What right has he to me? I'm a man as much as he is. I'm a better man than he is" (13).[14] That is George Harris, an enslaved African American, talking with his wife, Eliza, protesting his white human "master" in Harriet Beecher Stowe's *Uncle Tom's Cabin* (1852). For Stowe as for many nineteenth-century writers, "master" means slavemaster.

Even when the word comes up in her novel in another context—as, say, the standard honorific used for a young man—it comes back to slavery. Here is George Harris again, describing an encounter with the master's son: "Young Mas'r Tom stood there, slashing his whip so near the horse that the creature was frightened. . . . [He] ran to his father, and told him that I was fighting him. [The father] came in a rage, and said he'd teach me who was my master; and he tied me to a tree, and cut switches for young master, and told him that he might whip me till he was tired;—and he did do it! . . . Who made this man my master?" (14). The Harris son, "young Mas'r," is an extension of the senior slavemaster—as much his whip as his son. The slave, rather than the horse, is the whip's true target. For a reader of *Uncle Tom's Cabin*—at least, for me—the title *His Master's Voice* evokes the voice of a slavemaster; the ghost in the machine is slavery.

Beautiful Joe, I suggest, should be seen in this light: as a novel that metaphorically links animal "master" with human slavemaster, and dog with human slave, at a turn-of-the-century moment when the representation of slavery was an intervention into the racial violence of the present as well as the past. This is my interpretation, prompted by—among other evidence—the very first paragraph of the novel: "Mr. Morris, the clergyman, in whose family I have lived for the last twelve years, says that he thinks I must be called Beautiful Joe for the same reason that his grandfather, down South, called a very ugly colored slave-lad Cupid, and his mother Venus" (53). I will return to this quotation, but note for now that it links the novel's first-dog voice to the Southern "slave-lad." *Beautiful Joe*, I will argue, revivifies several literary genres that represented antebellum slavery: the slave narrative, the abolitionist novel, and the trickster tale. The result is a literary hybrid whose topic is enslaved humans as well as abused dogs, and whose narrative is, paradoxically, against emancipation as well as slavery. This paradox muddles the novel's political critique of slavery, but it does not, I will suggest, undercut that critique entirely.

I will make this case with evidence from within the novel, but I start with some context from without, some of the many examples of connection between animals and black people in U.S. literature of the nineteenth century, particularly as focused on dogs and especially as shaped by African American writers. Turning to *Beautiful Joe*, I move from its representations of dogs as slaves to its racialized depictions of monkeys and parrots. I then migrate beyond the novel to a more recent work on related themes, Samuel Fuller's film *White Dog* (1982), whose own literary source includes a racially explicit evocation of *His Master's Voice*.

In this chapter, I will modulate my own scholarly voice, retaining the first person but writing less punningly and playfully. To discuss symbolic conjunctions between African Americans and animals, especially as a white critic, is to move onto some of the most painful terrain of U.S. history. I am mindful of how these conjunctions have so often functioned, historically, to deepen racism; I do not want to replicate this racism through ambiguities in my own tone. I will argue throughout for the centrality of racial themes to representations of animals and for the complexity of those themes. Even when depictions of animal enslavement do not lead to human emancipation, I will argue that they may operate to unexpectedly uneven effect—not silencing the white master's voice but distorting its sound.

2.

The "dreaded comparison"—animals and slaves—is often made in the animal rights movement; it is, for example, the title of a book condemning the contemporary exploitation of animals in hunting, trafficking, meat production, and medical research.[15] Peter Singer begins *Animal Liberation* with this comparison and reworks it as a historical connection: "The overlap between leaders of movements against the oppression of blacks and women, and leaders of movements against cruelty to animals, is extensive; so extensive as to provide an unexpected form of confirmation of the parallel between racism, sexism, and speciesism."[16] But this confirmation is not always clear; historically, the parallel has often been a contradiction. Some nineteenth-century supporters of slavery also opposed animal cruelty, insofar as they thought enslaved Africans and animals were all part of one big happy white-ruled family; in one apologia for slavery, "slave children [were] pets in the house."[17] One scholar challenges the parallels even more strongly, exhorting others to "de-couple animal protection from the history of social liberation."[18] An example at the extreme end of the need for this decoupling: the Nazis passed laws protecting animal welfare.[19]

Comparison, overlap, parallel, contradiction, decoupling: all of these relationships connect dog and slave in *Beautiful Joe*, published in 1894. This was forty years past *Uncle Tom's Cabin* and thirty years past emancipation but deep in a period of escalating racism, from the imposition of Jim Crow segregation to the rise of lynching. Animals were central to the most infamous racist imagery of the era: the depiction of black men as rapists of white women. For example, this comparison is made in Thomas Dixon's *The Clansman* (1905)—a novel celebrating the birth of the Ku Klux Klan and the basis for D. W. Griffith's film *Birth of a Nation* (1915)—when an African American man, Gus, recalls his rape of a white girl: "His thick lips were drawn upward in an ugly leer and his sinister bead eyes gleamed like a gorilla's."[20]

The gorilla was only one species invoked in a larger condemnation of the African American man as "beast," a ubiquitous word in this era. As Michael Lundblad shows, "beast" could connote black savagery rather than animality or, as the *Atlantic Monthly* wrote, that "[negroes were] an uncivilized, semi-savage people."[21] This shift to a rhetoric of savagery had its own dire consequences, moving away from the explanatory idea that the criminal was "an animal whose amoral 'heat of passion' could be somewhat excusable."[22] The African American man condemned as beast lost either way: he was perceived as a nonhuman animal like a gorilla or as a semihuman "savage" who lacked even the alibi of animal instinct.

The racist animal symbols of the era included the domesticated dog as well as the wild gorilla. Writers at the turn of the century often used dogs to emphasize the alleged fidelity of former slaves to their masters. In Thomas Nelson Page's short story "Marse Chan" (1887), for example, a former slave, Sam, waxes nostalgic about slavery: "Dem wuz good ole times." At one point, the narrator is surprised to overhear Sam apparently expressing racial protest: "Think 'cuz you's white and I's black, I got to wait on yo' all de time. . . . I ain' gwi' do it!"[23] But it turns out that Sam is talking to his former master's dog, and the tone is affectionate; Sam is happy to serve the dog. Page, a white Southerner, here creates the voice of a black man so naturalized into servitude that he is not only doglike but happily submissive to a dog.

The image of the doglike black man might seem to contrast with that of the gorilla-like beast, but these racist metaphors were complementary: "Blacks [were seen as] docile and amiable when enslaved or severely repressed, but savage, lustful, and capable of murder and mayhem when free and uncontrolled."[24] In postwar depictions of African Americans, the symbolic dog could snap and become beast, just as the "faithful" antebellum slave could become a violent rebel. As Fido could become Cujo, so too could Sambo turn into Nat Turner.[25]

The turn of the century was also a period of extensive antiracist activism, and among its many strategies were reworkings of animal imagery. Paul Laurence Dunbar, then the most well-known African American writer of the era, tackled the metaphoric equation between black men and dogs repeatedly. In his short story "The Lynching of Jube Benson" (1904), a white man narrates his involvement years earlier in the lynching of a black handyman, Jube Benson, mistakenly thought to have raped a white woman, Annie. The narrator, named Melville, first offers an approving canine simile, remembering that Jube "would fetch and carry for [Annie] like a faithful dog." When Melville accuses Jube of rape, he calls him "you hound"; the dog becomes monster, or as Melville says, "I saw his black face glooming there in the half light, and I could only think of him as a monster."[26] These metaphors implode when the actual murderer is exposed as a white man in blackface; both "hound" and "faithful dog" are revealed as false constructions of the white man—literally in the case of the murderer in blackface and symbolically in the mind of the narrator who demonizes him. The story condemns white men for thinking of black men as metaphoric dogs, whether faithful or monstrous, and shows the deadly stakes of these racist metaphors.

A more complicated critique of dog metaphors appears in Dunbar's novel *The Sport of the Gods* (1902). Here too, white men condemn black men as dogs—a black character falsely accused of theft is called "that black hound"—and Dunbar clearly condemns their racism. But in a plot that focuses on the dissolute life of an African American man in New York, black characters also characterize each other as dogs. Joe Hamilton, alcoholic and violent, is condemned by his lover, Hattie:

> There was an expression of a whipped dog on his face.
>
> . . . She sprang up and struck him full in the face with the flat of her hand. . . .

> "Get up!" she cried. . . . "Now, go, you drunken dog, and never put your foot inside this house again."

The canine metaphors of this passage chart Joe's abjection before Hattie; they also revise the animal imagery from earlier in the novel. The innocent black man condemned as metaphoric "hound" by white men has become a ruined figure seen as "drunken dog" by a black woman. Joe kills Hattie, strangling her; afterward he is catatonic, his only interest her "little pet dog. . . . He would sit for hours with the little animal in his lap, caressing it dumbly."[27] Dog metaphors become the basis of a triple critique: of the black man who reduces himself to feminized "pet dog," of the black woman who calls him a "drunken dog," and especially, of a white world that originates these canine metaphors.

At least, this is one interpretation: the tone of this novel is difficult to interpret, as is its disturbing depiction of violence against women. I know how difficult and disturbing this is because I wrote a chapter about Dunbar in my book on American versions of the Frankenstein story; I adapted my own prose from it in the last two paragraphs.[28] But when I was writing about *The Sport of the Gods*, I was thinking about something else: why the chapter in which Joe kills Hattie is called "Frankenstein." I went through dog metaphors on the way to monster ones; I argued that Dunbar uses the Frankenstein story to develop a critique of racist monster-making. Now I see that Frankenstein's monster is himself a talking animal; a book in animal studies devotes a whole section to Shelley's novel.[29] Now I am looking afresh at my own writing, looking at dogs—or at least their metaphors—straight in the eye.

Now that I am looking, I see anew how complicated the relation of African Americans to dogs is in writing at the turn of the century. Colin Dayan, for example, shows the contiguities between legal decisions of the era that reinforced racial segregation and those that cemented the status of dogs as property; for example, the same judge decided *Plessy v. Ferguson* and a Louisiana case that "subjected dogs to the . . . discrimination of a subjagated population." Her comparison is not an equivalence: "I do not suggest that what happens to dogs is an injustice equal to segregation, but that law can be used to make men dogs and dogs trash."[30] Newly codified forms of racism deepened the trash-making connections between black people and dogs at the same moment that new forms of the animal welfare movement sought to elevate the sufferings of animals to the status of humans. Not surprisingly, antiracist activists worked to opposite ends, severing any cross-species affinities in a world in which black people had long been treated as animals. As historian Mia Bay summarizes, "Ex-slaves remembered being fed like pigs, bred like hogs, sold like horses, driven like cattle, worked like dogs, and beaten like mules."[31]

But it was not only that the animal welfare movement had less appeal for people already equated with animals; it was also that the movement was often racist. Here is William James: "Among the many good qualities of our 'Anglo-Saxon' race, its sympathy with the feelings of brute animals deserves an honorable mention."[32] This sympathy of the white "Anglo-Saxon" for the animal reinforced antipathy for nonwhite people. As Lundblad shows, "Humane reform actually became a new and flexible discourse for claiming superiority over various human 'races', reinforcing the logic that only the more 'civilized' group had evolved enough to treat other groups 'humanely.'"[33] At the same time, the rhetoric of this era often encouraged white men to rejuvenate their masculinity in ways that affirmed their proximity to animals, whether through Boy Scout camping or Rooseveltian hunting.[34] In the self-justifying logic of racism, black men were condemned to animality, but when white men responded to their inner-animal call of the wild, they were reinforcing their hold on whiteness.

Some writers protested both the racism of animal metaphors and cruelty to actual animals. For example, Mark Twain: I have already cited his short story, "A Dog's Tale," for its critique of vivisection. Twain's novel *Pudd'nhead Wilson* (1893) is filled with analogies between dogs and slaves, which Twain presents in order to challenge the logic of racism. In the novel, a slave mother switches two identical-looking light-skinned boys, one her own, with the result that her son grows up believing that he is white and that his mother "was merely his chattel . . . his convenience, his dog, his cringing and helpless slave." When Tom learns that he is black, he declares of the man he knows as his uncle, "He is white; and I am his chattel, his property, his goods, and he can sell me, just as he could his dog."[35] Twain's metaphors, like those of racist writers like Page, connect Africans Americans with dogs, but Twain deliberately makes these metaphors misleading; the effect is to unfix rather than cement racial stereotype.

The antiracist novel *Pudd'nhead Wilson* and the antivivisection story "A Dog's Tale" may seem like separate spheres for Twain, but not really. For example, the canine narrator of "A Dog's Tale," recounting her love for her own mother, remembers, "I was sold and taken away, and I never saw her again."[36] A Twain scholar notes that "A Dog's Tale" "might . . . be read as a deft and wrenching parable about the treatment of the self-sacrificing Mammy's own children under slavery, as well as a scathing condemnation of vivisection."[37] It might be read this way; I will do so, to suggest that these twin sides of Twain converge.

Another example, more directly combining antiracism and animal advocacy: the writing of Charles Chesnutt. In *Civilized Creatures*, Jennifer Mason shows how Chesnutt, well known for his antiracist fiction, also participated in the animal welfare movement. For example, he wrote short fiction protesting animal abuse and a positive review of Susanna Louise Patteson's *Pussy Meow* (1901), an animal autobiography intended to serve as the *Black Beauty* of the cat.[38] Throughout Chesnutt's fiction, Mason argues, he brought together the rhetorics of race and animal rights, "strategically (re)associating black men and dogs . . . to attack the animal-based stereotypes that informed both plantation fiction nostalgic for a slave-holding past and defenses of lynching inspired by the desire for an Anglo-Saxon future."[39] In contrast to Paul Laurence Dunbar, whose critique of racist metaphor operated at a remove from the language of animal welfare, Chesnutt embraced this language. Objecting to depictions of "dog-like fidelity" in black characters of the era, he combated such depictions not by divorcing dog and man imagery but by bringing them, rhetorically, closer together.[40]

Chesnutt, Twain, and Dunbar are famous writers from late in the century, decades postemancipation. Lesley Ginsberg and Brigitte Fielder, who have written important essays on animals and race in nineteenth-century literature, find complex forms of affiliation between dogs and African Americans in earlier writing for children. Harriet Beecher Stowe is famous for *Uncle Tom's Cabin*, but not for her children's stories, which included one, "Our Dogs" (1865), about Carlo, a mastiff who "declared himself as . . . the slave and property of our little Prince Charley"—a human boy—and whose growl Stowe parses as meaning "I am your slave for love.[41] Ginsberg argues that the story offers "a wishful, sentimental fantasy of race relations in the postwar period.[42] But Fielder suggests that such stories had antiracist potential, particularly for African American readers.[43] Elsewhere, she specifies this potential as that of "affective kinship" between enslaved people and animals.[44] In a third essay, Fielder anatomizes three kinds of relationships between dogs and African Americans in Stowe's *Uncle Tom's Cabin*: that of analogy, wherein black people and dogs are symbolically aligned; that of ally, wherein black people care for and benefit from dogs; and that of adversary, wherein dogs pursue black people as slave-trackers.[45]

There is abundant evidence for each. Analogy: throughout *Uncle Tom's Cabin*, the slave is frequently compared to a dog, as when Legree says contemptuously of Tom, "He'll beg like a dog" (328). Ally: George Harris remembers a pet, Carlo, who was "all the comfort I've had" (14); another dog, Bruno, a "great Newfoundland," was a "pet and playmate" of George's wife, Eliza (32). Other writers developed this imagery of alliance too: in Harriet Wilson's *Our Nig* (1859), the young protagonist, Frado, has a dog who is her "entire confidant. . . . She told him her griefs as though he were human."[46] This dog is named Fido, like the dog of Abraham Lincoln, but here serving radically, as Karen Kilcup has discussed, as cross-species confidant to an indentured black servant girl in New England.[47] However, the affirmative relationships between Wilson's Frado and Fido, or Stowe's George and Carlo, were the exception; the most common literary relationship depicted between African Americans and dogs was adversarial, with dogs acting as slave-trackers. In *Uncle Tom's Cabin*, this tracking leads to unspeakable horror, as when Cassy warns Emmeline, "You'd be tracked by the dogs, and brought back, and then—then—" (325).

The horror of the slave-tracking hound had a broader hemispheric history: dogs—specifically bloodhounds—were earlier used to track Native Americans, while "Cuba bloodhounds" were employed against black people in the Caribbean. These deployments of dogs as state-sponsored weapons then crystallized in the nineteenth century in the use of the slave-tracking hound of the U.S. South.[48] This hound was often invoked by abolitionists to protest slavery, but it could also reinforce racism. As Marcus Wood notes, the enslaved person attacked by the hound became pinioned as victim, "a figure to be protected and not admired."[49]

An indispensable book theorizing the importance of animals in American culture specifies the abolitionist collapse of slave into hound. In *Animalia Americana*, Colleen Glenney Boggs shows how the image of the slave-tracking dog often eroded species difference: "The encounter with the companion species places [the slave] not only in the position of the animalized human but creates an excess by which he becomes the animalized animal."[50] In the postwar era, the violent dog remained a tool of contemporary antiblack violence, with dogs used as trackers in lynch mobs.[51] The newly dominant racist metaphor of the black man as metaphorical "beast" displaced the ongoing real-life violence inflicted by dogs. It also extended the long-standing conflation of black people and dogs implicit in some abolitionist imagery as well as in proslavery discourse.

Throughout the century, African American writers responded to the image of the dog as slave-tracker, repositioning it in terms of African American humanity. For example, in *The House of Bondage* (1890), her collection of oral histories of slavery, Octavia V. Rogers Albert recounts the story of an escaped woman who was recaptured by dogs: "I picture to my mind a poor woman marching before six men, six horses, and ten blood-hounds with blood oozing from her feet."[52] The bloodhound multiplies here into a complex group antagonist, both metaphor and metonymy for slavery's violence, with the blood of the hounds made manifest in the woman's bleeding feet. Albert's own mental "picture," as both audience and writer, restages the horror of the scene with the power of her own literary imagination.

African American writers also used the image of the slave-hunting hound to reverse the terms of animal metaphor. In Harriet Jacobs's slave memoir *Incidents in the Life of a Slave Girl* (1861), Jacobs condemns both actual "hounds trained to tear human flesh" and the white Northerners who "consent to act the part of bloodhounds, and hunt the poor fugitive back to his den."[53] Boggs shows that Frederick Douglass reworked the slave-tracking hound along several rhetorical routes, from animalizing the slavemaster to reclaiming the intimacy between African Americans and dogs in new ways. For example, when Douglass describes this experience in England: "A dog actually came up to the [lecture] platform, put his paws on the front of it, and gave me a smile of recognition as a man. . . . The Americans would do well to learn wisdom upon this subject from the very dogs of Old England; for these animals, by instinct, know that I am a man."[54] In this scene of cross-species encounter, Douglass uses the dog's "smile of recognition" to elevate black humanity and manhood.

I have been building a case, aided by scholars—particularly Boggs, Dayan, Fielder, Ginsberg, Lundblad, and Mason—for a genealogy of nineteenth-century literature addressing the racist association of African Americans with dogs. I have emphasized the work of African American writers—including Albert, Chesnutt, Douglass, Dunbar, Jacobs, and Wilson—to stress their centrality in revisiting and revising dog imagery. My intervention is meant as an introduction: there are many more nineteenth-century examples of the symbolic overlap between animals and African Americans and of the transformation of this overlap by writers across race. Increasingly, more scholarly discussions of the dog-race overlap in nineteenth-century U.S. culture appear, including a special issue of *American Quarterly* on "Species/Race/Sex" and a book arguing for a nineteenth-century history of "fugitive humanism" that emphasizes moments when racial and animal struggles were conjoined.[55] There are vital new theorizations of race and animal studies, led by scholars of color, including Mel Y. Chen, Che Gossett, Sharon Holland, Zakiyyah

Iman Jackson, and Claire Jean Kim.[56] As this chapter goes to press, I learn of Bénédicte Boisseron's important new book *Afro-Dog: Blackness and the Animal Question*, which elucidates connections between animal studies and black cultural studies in ways that intersect with my interpretations here. Bringing together U.S. American with Caribbean and French diaspora texts, Boisseron advances understanding of conjunctions between blackness and dogs, not least in her insistence on looking at "human-animal encounters through the prism of black and animal defiance."[57]

I will add one more nineteenth-century example to the mix, albeit one that seems far afield: *His Master's Voice*. Like Twain's "A Dog's Tale," the painting seems to be about dogs, not race. In Twain's case, there is ample evidence from elsewhere in his career to make the connection between dogs and race; for the painting, the evidence will have to come from the cultural moment. In the context of racist rhetoric praising black people for their doglike fidelity, we might see this painting as a dramatization of the hierarchies of power—including racial ones—in representations of dogs and masters. *His Master's Voice* offers a depiction of canine fidelity so great that it extends beyond the grave, with the dog posthumously enslaved—commanded, haunted, hounded—by the master's voice.

However, the painting also suggests its own form of resistance to this scenario of hierarchies, of race as well as species. For the wax-cylinder phonograph depicted in the original painting could record as well as play back voices. In so doing, the device offers "a reversible physiology for what we see. For the horn now becomes an ear as well as a mouth; the dog who listens may also seem to be being tempted by the mechanical apparatus to make some answering sound."[58] Nipper could become animate voice as well as listening animal; he could, possibly, bark back.

3.

Now it is time to make the turn back to Marshall Saunders, and it may seem an unlikely one: the writers I have been discussing were overtly attuned to racial politics, as she does not seem to have been; many were radical intellectuals, while she was not; and, of course, she was writing from a different national context—Canada—a locale that I have, so far, sidestepped.

A small step, the beginning of the turn: Saunders published a mini-memoir in 1927, a three-page essay called "The Story of My Life." It includes this anecdote about her childhood in Nova Scotia: "The first six years of my life passed in a dream of bliss, marred only by one unfortunate occurrence. I was held up to view a dead body in a coffin, probably by the irresponsible though kind-hearted Ellen, the coloured woman who assisted my mother in the care of her children."[59] Saunders returns to Ellen elsewhere in her writing, describing her as "our colored maid, who was like a Southern mammy."[60] These descriptions reinforce racial hierarchy: there is no apparent critique of stereotype in her use of the phrase "like a Southern mammy," and in the anecdote of the coffin, Ellen is caricatured as an "irresponsible" servant who creates an "unfortunate occurrence" for the white child. Nonetheless, Ellen serves importantly as what Toni Morrison famously termed an "Africanist presence," signaling "the denotative and connotative blackness that African peoples have come to signify" for white writers.[61] In Saunders's formative memory of an Africanist presence, the white girl's first encounter with death is dependent on the black woman who—literally and thematically—both bears her weight and props her up to see.

An Africanist presence surfaces differently in *Beautiful Joe*, which begins, as I have already noted, with a reference to slavery in the U.S. South. On the first page: "Mr. Morris, the clergyman, in whose family I have lived for the last twelve years, says that he thinks I must be called Beautiful Joe for the same reason that his grandfather, down South, called a very ugly colored slave-lad Cupid, and his mother Venus" (53). Slavery is named from the outset, both displaced to the United States and evoked in the North, grandfathered in through the grandfather, and linked to dogs. And to the question of naming: like the "ugly colored slave lad" called Cupid, the "Beautiful" in Beautiful Joe is an ironic inversion in which Joe is ridiculed and renamed by a white master.[62]

Joe's ugliness is linked, in the next paragraph, to his breeding—or lack thereof: "I know that I am not beautiful, and I know that I am not a thoroughbred. I am only a cur. When my mistress went every year to register me and pay my tax, and the man in the office asked what breed I was, she said part fox-terrier and part bull-terrier; but he always put me down a cur" (53). "Cur" is here both a synonym for a mixed-breed dog and a general term of debasement, a put-down used by the tax assessor. The phrase "only a cur," also Saunders's title for this chapter, was common in nineteenth-century animal welfare; it was, for example, the title of a Band of Mercy song.[63] "Cur" did not necessarily have racial connotations.

Nor, at this moment, did "bull terrier," a breed that was then a favorite family dog in America. It was not until the mid-twentieth century that the bull terrier became, along with some dozen other kinds of dogs, consolidated under the category "pit bull" and demonized in racial ways; I will come back to this demonization.[64] Earlier, fox terriers and bull terriers were both beloved, and "bull-and-terrier dogs" featured positively in several novels.[65] Nipper, the dog of *His Master's Voice*, has been claimed for both terrier breeds; indeed, Laura's description of Joe—"she said part fox-terrier and part bull-terrier"—sounds a bit like Nipper.[66]

So Joe's self-description does not have an overt connection to race, though its placement immediately after the "very ugly colored slave lad" raises the possibility of a covert one. In the history of "nonbreed" dogs, racial connotations often hover: "Terms like mongrel and mutt make breed a kind of measuring stick, according to which most dogs fall short. Paralleling their use as ethnic and racial epithets among humans, these words imply degeneracy, degradation and ultimately social chaos."[67] Writers in the nineteenth-century United States developed this parallel in more positive terms as well. For example—again—Harriet Beecher Stowe writes in another children's story, "Dogs and Cats" (1865), "All dogs which do not belong to some of the great varieties . . . are classed together as curs, and very much undervalued and decried; and yet among these mongrel curs we have seen individuals quite as sagacious, intelligent, and affectionate as the best blood-dogs."[68] Fielder shows that this passage strongly echoes positive descriptions of mixed-race characters in fiction of the period.[69] Saunders revalues Joe along similar lines, making him "sagacious, intelligent, and affectionate." As a "mongrel cur," Joe's relation to the image of the "slave-lad" is one of potential analogy—both affirmative and anxious—as well as direct adjacency on the page.

Whether or not Joe's breeding refers to race, he is unmistakably situated within an orbit of ownership. His ironized reversal from "ugly" to "beautiful" changes his place in this orbit, but it does not release him from it. As a Morris boy recounts, the new name comes from Miss Laura: "If you call him 'Ugly Joe' her ladyship [Miss Laura] will say that you are wounding the dear dog's feelings. 'Beautiful Joe', would be more to her liking" (68). The Morrises are latter-day slavemasters, more benevolent, but still naming him—and, of course, owning him; Miss Laura, "her ladyship," is a symbolic plantation mistress, albeit a "good" one. The novel's animal welfare language is based on a paradox: it opposes a system that would treat animals as cruelly as slaves, but it does not advocate for their emancipation.

It is within this paradoxical space that the novel negotiates its goal of ending animal cruelty. Dramatized in the early account of Jenkins's violence, cruelty reverberates throughout the novel in the imagery of whipping. In slave narratives, the witnessing of whipping is central, as, for example, when Frederick Douglass sees his master with his Aunt Hester: "[He used to] whip upon her naked back till she was literally covered with blood. . . . He would whip her to make her scream, and whip her to make her hush. . . . I remember the first time I ever witnessed this horrible exhibition. . . . I never shall forget it whilst I remember any thing."[70] So too in *Beautiful Joe*; its primal scene is that of Joe witnessing his mother's whipping by Jenkins: "I have seen him use his heavy whip to punish her till her body was covered with blood" (54). This scene is later repeated when Beautiful Joe encounters a horse and driver in the street: "The poor horse kept looking at his master, his eyes almost starting from his head in terror. He knew that the whip was about to descend on his quivering body. And so it did. . . . He whipped his horse, and whipped him, till every lash made my heart ache" (248–49). As in Douglass's memoir, the greatest horror is a scene of subjection not only as enforced by a master but also as witnessed by other slaves.[71]

And *Beautiful Joe* shares with the slave narrative its greatest moment of pathos: the separation of the slave mother from her children. Harriet Jacobs, who is motivated by the desire to prevent such separation—"I was resolved that I would foil my master and save my children, or I would perish in the attempt"—tells the story of "the slave mother [who] sits on her cold cabin floor, watching the children who may all be torn from her the next morning; and often does she wish that she and they might die before the day dawns."[72] *Beautiful Joe* features a similar plot of suicidal maternal grief, when Jenkins kills Joe's siblings: "My mother never seemed the same after this. . . . One day she licked me gently, wagged her tail, and died" (60).

Another example: Like many slave narratives, *Beautiful Joe* includes a scene of learning the alphabet from a white slavemistress. Here is Harriet Jacobs: "As a child, I loved my mistress . . . she taught me to read and spell."[73] Here is Frederick Douglass: "I was utterly astonished at [my mistress's] goodness . . . she very kindly commenced to teach me the A, B, C."[74] And here is an analogous scene of Joe and the alphabet:

> It took Miss Laura a long time to teach us. We never began till a book was laid before us. Then we stared at it, and Miss Laura said, "Begin, Joe and Billy—say A."
>
> For A, we gave a little squeal. B was louder. C was louder still. . . . When we got to Z, we gave the book a push, and had a frolic around the room. (102)

The similarities of these scenes are complicated by material and rhetorical contrasts. Material: Douglass and Jacobs learned the alphabet; Joe, a dog, cannot. Rhetorical: *Beautiful Joe* knows the alphabet of the slave narrative—here, the alphabet of its alphabet—but it pushes away the arc of its plot. This is a slave narrative in which the slave seems happy to stay enslaved.

Something similar happens in Anna Sewell's *Black Beauty*, Saunders's inspiration. Its connections to slavery are hard to miss. It is not only the color of Black Beauty that aligns him with enslaved people, though it is emphasized: "How is your little Darkie?" the owner asks Beauty's mother, and Beauty explains, "I was a dull black, so he called me Darkie" (40).[75] It is also that Sewell's Beauty lives in a condition of total servitude—a horse must never "have any will of his own; but always do his master's will" (44)—and that his narrative is filled with auction-block scenes and cruel masters, as when Beauty's horse-friend Ginger's master, who "punishe[s] [Ginger] cruelly with his whip" (57), More specifically, the violence against Ginger echoes the sexual abuse of enslaved women: "[One man] took my underjaw in his hard hand and wrenched my mouth open, and so by force they got on the halter and the bar into my mouth; then one dragged me along by the halter, another flogging behind, and this was the first experience I had of men's kindness; it was all force" (56). In the ironic chasm between "men's kindness" and "all force" is symbolic rape.[76] Ginger dies, but Sewell gives Black Beauty a happy ending in which he celebrates his two benevolent mistresses: "My ladies have promised that I shall never be sold, and so I have nothing to fear; and here my story ends" (193). "Nothing to fear" comes from being well owned rather than from being free.

In their protagonists' embrace of servitude, Sewell and Saunders are part of a larger literary menagerie. Annie Dwyer, analyzing animal autobiographies, argues for the conservatism of the genre's use of the slave narrative: "Blithely appropriating and repurposing the slave narrative, the animal autobiography in fact creates and upholds new modes of racial figuration, new mechanisms of racial subjection."[77] The "new mechanism" she foregrounds is the "increasingly virulent discourse of black criminality" in turn-of-the-century America, which she finds in the animal autobiography's narratives of animals who "are hopelessly, incorrigibly bad."[78] In the genre's correction of bad behavior, animal autobiographies provide "an education in white innocence and black culpability."[79]

Dwyer draws important attention to the politics of "bad" behavior in the animal autobiography, as well as to the through-line of white innocence and black guilt that structures so much American culture.[80] I am not as convinced as she, though, that *Beautiful Joe* unambiguously fosters forms of racism; I go back to *Uncle Tom's Cabin*, the source for both Saunders and Sewell. For Sewell's abused and resistant Ginger, see Stowe's Cassy, the sexually terrorized slave who outwits Simon Legree; behind Sewell's Black Beauty, see Stowe's Uncle Tom, suffering and sympathetic.[81] The lineage is Uncle Tom, Black Beauty, and Beautiful Joe: all suffering symbolic slaves, male protagonists approvingly feminized by their female authors. And all apparently embracing "good" masters, with "Uncle Tom" later becoming a proper name for the black man condemned as a lackey and sellout.[82] Saunders's Joe—in his worship of his owner and his embrace of enslavement—seems closer to the model of the sellout. In addition to extending the approvingly feminized model of Stowe's Tom, Joe anticipates the more pejorative idea of the emasculated "Uncle Tom" as well.

Within the novel, however, Stowe's own character possesses considerable resistant force, and he never embraces his owner in the way that Black Beauty and Beautiful Joe do: Stowe's Uncle Tom is no "Uncle Tom." And there are other humans in *Uncle Tom's Cabin* connected to the animals of *Beautiful Joe*. At the Band of Mercy meeting in Saunders's novel, a child tells a story about a pony named Topsy: "Well, Topsy *would* run away, and a big, big man came out to papa and said he would train Topsy. So he drove her every day, and beat her, and beat her, till he was tired, but still Topsy would run away. Then papa said he would not have the poor pony whipped so much, and he took her out a piece of bread every day, and he petted her, and now Topsy is very gentle, and never runs away" (166–67). For nineteenth-century readers, the name Topsy was indelibly associated with the unruly black girl of Stowe's novel; Saunders's Topsy evokes Stowe's Topsy, albeit through the equine language of *Black Beauty*. So too does the pedagogy of benevolent rather than violent authority—petting, not beating—evoke Stowe's Topsy. Inspired by little Eva, trained by Aunt Ophelia, Stowe's Topsy turns herself topsy-turvy and eventually rights others, "approved as a missionary to one of the stations in Africa" (377). While Saunders's Topsy cannot become a missionary, she too is gentled.

So Stowe's humans, from Tom to Topsy, offer a basis for Saunders's animals. Both authors work with metaphoric connections between species, though the valence of the metaphor shifts: for Stowe, enslaved people are the focus, or the tenor, of the metaphor, and animals their metaphoric vehicle; for Saunders, by contrast, animals are the focus and slaves the metaphoric vehicle. But that contrast is still too absolute: animals, especially, dogs, are already the tenor as well as vehicle of metaphor within *Uncle Tom's Cabin*.

I go back to Fielder's three-part framework—dog as analogy, ally, and adversary in *Uncle Tom's Cabin*—and pause again at the novel's pets.[83] Carlo, George Harris's dog, is one of several canine Carlos in nineteenth-century literary history: Carlo was the name of Emily Dickinson's own beloved Newfoundland and of St. John Rivers's pointer in Charlotte Brontë's *Jane Eyre*.[84] Stowe's Carlo is mentioned very early in the novel; he is no sooner introduced as George Harris's comfort—"[he] kind o' looked at me as if he understood how I felt" (14)—than he is remembered as a victim of violence. George recalls, "[The master] ordered me to tie a stone to [Carlo's] neck and throw him in the pond," and when George refused, master and son—slavemaster and "young Mas'r"—drowned Carlo and then "pelted the poor drowning creature with stones" (15). Looking ahead, we could see Carlo as a precursor to Beautiful Joe: a sympathetic dog whose horrific victimization introduces the novel. Both have a connection to women too. Carlo is described as a gift to George from his wife, Eliza, and the novel's second pet dog, the Newfoundland called Bruno, is Eliza's "old pet and playmate," who happily "patter[s] along after her" (332). The template Stowe provides for Saunders, then, is one in which male dogs are linked to women, as well as one in which male heroes are affirmatively feminized—an amalgam of canines Bruno and Carlo and human Uncle Tom.

In Saunders's era, though, the best-known dogs of *Uncle Tom's Cabin* were not its friendly pets but its newly represented antagonists. Stage productions of *Uncle Tom's Cabin*, already popular in the 1850s, proliferated after the war on a fantastic scale, and a featured new element was their use of actual dogs: "By the early 1880s, dogs large and small were added to even the most bare bones travelling Tom show, first as harmless bloodhounds and later as fierce English mastiffs, Siberian Bloodhounds, or Great Danes."[85] Dogs were especially indispensable to the scene of Eliza fleeing with her child, Harry, across the icy Ohio River. This was a theatrical invention, since for all the canine references in the novel, its depiction of this scene, as Fielder notes, contains no dogs.[86]

An 1881 theatrical poster for the Jay Rial Company production of *Uncle Tom's Cabin* highlights this innovation, depicting "Eliza pursued by bloodhounds" while crossing the Ohio River with Harry. The poster is centered on two giant, sharp-toothed dogs, mouths open, bodies pushed forward, and paws touching Eliza. The image opposes human and canine as victim and villain, with a gender contrast as well: feminized mother and child flee masculinized hounds. Eliza's feminization is linked visually to her light skin, as in the novel, where the most idealized black characters are mixed race. Here, the image of

FIG. 6.

Jay Rial's Ideal Uncle Tom's Cabin, lithograph by Strobridge Lithographing Co., 1881. Photo: Library of Congress, Washington, D.C.

the imperiled light-skinned woman threatened by rapacious dogs also moves toward the emerging iconography of the white woman under threat of rape from black "beasts."

But while the poster thematically opposes dogs and humans, it also visually aligns them. Eliza and the hounds are pitched at the same angle, the folds of the hounds' skin echo those of her clothes, and her facial coloring seems close to the hue of their fur. This is another version of the equivalence Boggs identifies in antebellum imagery, wherein the slave's "encounter with companion species . . . creates an excess by which he becomes the animalized animal."[87] Here, the dogs visually connote not only the beastly white world that tracks Eliza but also the animalistic blackness whence she came.

In *Beautiful Joe*, conversely, woman and dog save rather than menace each other. Joe is more like the poster's Harry, the enslaved child rescued from evil by a benevolent mother figure. If the later theatrical history of Stowe's novel strengthened its connections between slaves and dogs by making dogs into villains, then Saunders's novel strengthened these connections by emphasizing dogs as victims. Saunders's novel is, in this context, a truer heir to Stowe's than were theatrical productions like Rial's. Her dog story preserves the novel's affective core its appeal to sympathy, approvingly feminized—against the horrors of enslavement across species.

So *Beautiful Joe* borrows from slave narratives—their narrative grammar, their moments of horror and pathos—and from the dog metaphors, characters, and afterlives of *Uncle Tom's Cabin* but with a big difference: unlike the slave narrative and the abolitionist novel, *Beautiful Joe* lacks the goal of freedom. The realization of that goal in *Uncle Tom's Cabin* is, to be sure, constrained. Topsy is turned upright, and other African American characters end up exiled or dead. Still, Stowe exhorts the reader to end slavery, while *Beautiful Joe* ends happily with unfreedom. The novel cannot imagine a happy ending without enslavement.

Or rather, without mastery: this is the governing term. Here is Stowe once again, in her children's story "Dogs and Cats": "A dog without a master is a forlorn creature; no society of other dogs seems to console him; he wanders about disconsolate, till he finds some human being to whom to attach himself."[88] In "Rights of Dumb Animals," Stowe protested animal cruelty but upheld mastery; her goal, pedagogic and political, was for human masters to be "right and generous," understanding their "duty to an animal."[89] *Beautiful Joe* shares in those goals, teaching humans to be better masters by showing animals who celebrate their improved enslavement.

However, there are other animals in *Beautiful Joe* who tell a different story: the monkey and the parrot. I have already noted that primate metaphors were at the center of racist discourse, as in the black character called "gorilla" by Thomas Dixon. There are several monkeys mentioned in *Beautiful Joe*, but they differ from Dixon's. For example, here is a story a boy tells during the Band of Mercy meeting about his English uncle, a former "soldier in India": "One day when he was hunting in the Punjab, he saw a mother monkey carrying a little dead baby monkey. Six months later [he saw the] same monkey still carrying dead baby monkey, all shriveled up. Mother monkey loved her baby monkey, and wouldn't give it up" (159). The context here is imperial England in India; the relation to American slavery is twice removed—from people to monkeys, from America to India—but recognizable nonetheless. Here is a further ratification of the theme of maternal loss central to the slave narrative.

And here is a different monkey story from *Beautiful Joe*, as told by a girl at the Band of Mercy meeting:

> My dranfadder says . . . dat when he was a little boy his fadder brought him a little monkey from de West Indies. De naughty boys in de village used to tease de little monkey, and he runned up a tree one day. Dey was drowing stones at him, and a man dat was paintin' de house druv 'em away. De monkey runned down de trees, and shook hands wid de man.
>
> . . . [My] dranfadder says dat afterward de monkey upset de painter's can of oil, and rolled in it, and den jumped down in my dranfadder's flour barrel. (160)

The child's childish voice marks the anecdote as comic, but the narrative carries serious racial freight: that of the West Indian monkey brought against his will to America and abused. The plot is initially one of reconciliation—the monkey is grateful to the house painter, shaking his hands—but the anecdote takes a more surprising turn. The monkey turns the paint can topsy-turvy, like another version of Stowe's Topsy. Undoing the handshake, the monkey rolls in oil, then flour—like a minstrel in whiteface.

And like a trickster: in the animal trickster tradition, typically, a weak animal like a rabbit outwits a powerful and strong one like a fox through cunning and guile. African in origin, these stories were adapted by African Americans, partly as a protest against slavery; they were transformed by, and transformed, black culture and consciousness.[90] In Saunders's era, the African trickster tale had become famous in a white American version: Joel Chandler Harris's Uncle Remus stories of the 1880s, which enclosed the animal tales of Br'er Rabbit in the frame of the former slave "uncle" narrating them to a white boy. Contemporary readers understood that the victories of Br'er Rabbit over stronger animals like the fox were "motivated by the most transparent aggression and obsequious mocking contempt of the slave for his master, or the black man for his white boss."[91]

Contemporary with Harris's tales, Saunders's monkey rolling in flour seems a Br'er Rabbit story without the Uncle Remus frame. Or perhaps Saunders's monkey is a version of the signifying monkey, a specialized trickster. He has been made famous in literary theory: "The ironic reversal of a received racist image of the black as simianlike, the Signifying Monkey . . . ever embodying the ambiguities of language, is our trope for repetition and revision."[92] Saunders's monkey repeats the gestures of a grateful recipient of charity, shaking the human hand, but then revises his position, flowering into floury reversal. It may be in these trickster subplots that the dog-slave's rebellion is most fully revealed.

I test this argument with a third monkey story in *Beautiful Joe*, this one from an account of a performance by a visiting troupe of circus animals. It is narrated by one of the Morris brothers, as retold by Joe: "A monkey dressed as a lady, in a white satin frock and a bonnet with white veil, came on the stage. She was Miss Green and the dog Bob was going to elope with her. He was all rigged out as Mr. Smith, and had on a light suit of clothes, and a tall hat on the side of his head, high collar, long cuffs, and he carried a cane" (247). This pantomime of the romantic couple, Miss Green and Mr. Smith, turns femininity into a monkey suit and masculinity into a top-hatted dog. The plot is comic, but it has a kick: the monkey "family" of Miss Green "seized the dog and kicked his hat, and broke his cane, and stripped his clothes off, and threw them in a corner, and bound his legs with cords . . . and one of them pulled out a little revolver, pointed it at the dog, pretended to fire, and he dropped down as if he was dead" (247–48). This seems a punishment of the dog for crossing boundaries—clearly between species, perhaps between races.[93] I have already linked the monkey, via the animal trickster, to African Americans. But what if the reverse is at work here, and the monkey is the "whiter" animal? Then the dog in this story seems a symbolically black dandy, punished for venturing beyond his kind.

This kind of interpretation is tricky; I turn for support to a scholar who has made the case for seeing interracial themes in unexpected places—for example, in Garth Williams's *The Rabbits' Wedding* (1958), a children's book pairing light- and dark-skinned rabbits, which was seen as "a dangerous text promoting racial integration." Such interracial interpretation "has to appear plausible *in the text*, and not just in the power generated by public contexts, be they advanced by governments, ideologues, or critics."[94] I am a critic; I want this reading to be plausible in the text; I think that it is, especially because it appears in a novel that openly shows its debts to *Uncle Tom's Cabin*.

The monkey-dog performance in *Beautiful Joe* features an interracial tableau in which the man-dog who violates boundaries is punished, but the dog has the final joke: "After a while, [Miss Green] crept up to the dead dog, pawed him a little, and didn't he jump up as much alive as any of them? . . . I wish he'd give another performance" (248). This performance seems a specifically canine story of trickster reversal: the dog's signature trick, "playing dead," grants him vitality, if not rebellion. The story also converges with images of human interracial boundary crossing: the animal-like black man who crosses boundaries preempts his punishment by staging it himself. The trick of playing dead, presumably taught by the master, is reappropriated by the trickster dog-slave.

So here are three monkey stories, each telling a slightly different tale—progressively more tricksterish—than the central canine plot of the novel. And here is one more trickster: the parrot. Since the early modern period, the parrot has functioned as "one of the signature beasts of the New World"—an emblem of empire—but also as a figure of disturbance in his mimicry of the human.[95] A study of animals in eighteenth-century English literature shows that the literary parrot often resembles a "non-European human."[96] This scholar, Laura Brown, groups the parrot with the dog and monkey, arguing that "the fable of the nonhuman being served as a powerful and common resource for structuring the encounter with cultural difference."[97]

In *Beautiful Joe*, a parrot is brought to the Morrises from the West Indies by a ship's cabin boy. Originally named "Beelzebub," her name has been shortened by the Christian Morrises to "Bella," but she retains her devilish side. She taunts Joe, "Ha, Joe, Beautiful Joe! Where's your tail? Who cut your ears off?" (96). But she is also Joe's double: like "Beautiful" Joe, Bella is an animal whose name suggests beauty and whose speech is unusual. Bella has been trained to talk, but "the boy said he had been careful to buy a young one that could not speak [yet], for he knew the Morris boys would not want one chattering foreign gibberish" (94). Stripped of "foreign gibberish," the bird is still West Indian, from a former anchor of the slave trade; like the dog and the monkey, the West Indian parrot draws *Beautiful Joe* into the orbit of race.

These animals each refract aspects of racial encounter: the dog as slave, the monkey as trickster, and the parrot as foreigner.

The parrot is also a rebel. Bella initially rejects her own confinement: "She hated her cage, and used to put her head close to the bars and plead: 'Let Bella out; Bella will be a good girl. Bella won't run away'" (97). Eventually, the Morrises build a cage handle that she can open herself; she lets herself out and then back in, and she "kept her word and never tried to get away" (97). So her resistance ends in her own embrace of confinement, just as Joe ends up adoring his master; as Dwyer suggests of the genre as a whole, the correction of bad behavior is the goal. Dog and parrot are aligned as self-leashing after all.

Still, Bella does get in a good last word at novel's end: Joe reports that she is living with Mrs. Morris and is "as smart as ever . . . she calls out to me: 'Keep a stiff upper lip, Beautiful Joe. Never say die, Beautiful Joe'" (268). As the novel closes, the bird continues to speak, and her mimicry of human stoicism unsettles metaphors; "keep a stiff upper lip" seems an impossibility for a presumably lipless parrot. Her final imperative to Joe offers him a kind of battle cry. The animals of *Beautiful Joe* stay on the leash, but they also pull on it, from the dog "playing dead" to the parrot who says "never say die."

At the very least, this pull makes the tautness of the leash visible. And this visibility, in the case of racial metaphor, is valuable in itself. Racist equations between black people and animals rely on seeming natural and unremarkable; in the racist simile "a black person is like an animal," the "like" of the simile—its sound of similitude pulling two things into relation—is expected to be silent. But the first-dog voice of *Beautiful Joe* calls attention to the simile. With its unnaturally speaking dog, the novel makes the simile visible—or rather, in the auditory terms of literary "voice," audible. Colleen Boggs, assessing this issue, asks me, "The intention in slavery is to have the claim that slaves are animals function literally, not symbolically. . . . [So is] the ventriloquized first-dog voice precisely a way to . . . fictionalize the literal . . . as a means for opening up the space for critique?"[98] This is an excellent question. In this case, in this novel, I answer: yes.

4.

I have brought *Beautiful Joe* into conversation with slave narratives, abolitionist novels, and animal trickster tales; now I will update this conversation to a more recent era. There are many ways to do so. For example, in the twentieth and twenty-first centuries, the symbolic association of dogs with black people has flourished in ideas about the pit bull, a breed that now sees "a one-on-one lamination . . . onto the African American male."[99] These constructions converged in the case of Michael Vick, the African American athlete convicted for running an illegal dogfighting business and condemned for acts of cruelty to his pit bulls, in a case wherein, as Claire Jean Kim summarizes, "the distinctively tangled relationship between Black masculinity and animality runs like a bright thread throughout the narrative," even as "animal advocates and race advocates adopted a posture of disavowal toward each other's claims."[100] Others have followed this bright thread; I will focus here on some modern versions of the dog depicted as slave-hunting hound—a visual and verbal embodiment of the master's voice.

This imagery reemerges directly in the visual culture of the civil rights movement, particularly in photographs of protestors being restrained in Birmingham by dogs; these famous images by Charles Moore, a white photographer, were initially published in *Life* magazine and then circulated widely. In one photograph, two dogs flank an African American man, one lunging at him from the front, the other tearing off the seat of his pants. In the foreground of the photograph is a second dog, almost facing the viewer; several other dogs circulate in the background. These dogs were the crux of Moore's own political awakening: "The police dogs were what really did it for me. I knew that those high-pressure hoses hurt people . . . but somehow I didn't see them getting hurt that badly. But the sight of snarling dogs, and the possibility of dogs ripping flesh, was revolting to me."[101]

These photographs have their critics: one scholar suggests that Moore's "photographs of policemen loosing attack dogs . . . scripted the 'problem' of race as violence. This narrative let whites who condemned or simply avoided racial violence off the hook."[102] I understand this argument; I have identified another version of it in critiques of the abolitionist imagery of violent slave-tracking hounds. Nonetheless, as animal photographs, the Moore images radically revise contemporary idealizations of the dog as benign household pet. This is the early 1960s, the heyday of TV's Lassie, the white boy's collie. The dog here does not so much replace the helpmeet of Lassie as show the gothic underside of the idealized bond between dog and white boy.

And the underside of this particular breed, the German shepherd—inheritor of the mantle of the slave-tracking bloodhound. The German shepherd was invented in Germany at the turn of the twentieth century and associated there with the police and military. In the United States, its image was recuperated into that of Hollywood star—namely, Rin Tin Tin and, before him,

FIG. 7.

Charles Moore, *Birmingham, Alabama Policemen Use Police Dogs During Civil Rights Demonstrations*, from *Pictures That Made a Difference: The Civil Rights Movement*, May 1963 negative; 1989 print. Gelatin silver print photograph on Kodak Elite fine-art paper, S-surface. Gift of anonymous donor. Mount Holyoke College Art Museum, South Hadley, Massachusetts. Photo: Laura Shea, 2015.2.6. Used by permission of Mount Holyoke College Art Museum and Getty Images.

Strongheart; in the 1920s, they were "analogous to . . . the decade's leading male Hollywood stars, especially the strong, athletic, loner heroes of action films."[103] But the German shepherd continued to be used as a police dog, and in the civil rights era, the breed was reconnected to police violence.

In the Moore photos, the dogs return to their disciplinary origins as collectivized police weapons. In this photograph, the dog in the foreground—mouth closed, facing the camera—could be a domestic pet or a matinee idol if his head were the entire image. But the photograph leashes him systematically to police violence. The dog's leash leads to the white policeman's hand, where it is twinned with his baton; the baton visually bisects the torso of the dog grabbing at the man's pants, and the man, in turn, is twinned with the lunging dog on the other side. Together, the dogs offer an armed extension of the white policeman—in two senses, as both an extension of his arms and an armed weapon.

Meanwhile, the bared teeth of the dog on the left emphasize his mouth as an organ of violence; this organ is presumably also producing sounds, growling or barking, which are then ratified by the vocal commands of the police. The unheard sounds of the image suggest another version of the master's voice. The photograph offers a recognition of the link between canine violence and the sight, if not also the sound, of whiteness.

Andy Warhol chose this photograph, which he described as "the dogs in Birmingham," and gave it the Warholian treatment: silk-screening, repeating, and recoloring Moore into the group of paintings collectively known as *Race Riot* (1963).[104] I will also pursue the legacy of Moore, but in a less pedigreed artwork: a film called *White Dog* (1982) by Samuel Fuller, director of films noir (*Pickup on South Street*), films war (*The Big Red One*), "exploitation" films (*Shock Corridor* and *Naked Kiss*), and other B-movies; he was a low-budget director with, sometimes, a high-art following. Based on a 1970 French novel by Romain Gary, *White Dog* depicts a young Hollywood actress, Julie Sawyer (Kristy McNichol) who accidentally hits a white German shepherd with her car, adopts him, and bonds with him, only to discover that the dog has been trained to attack black people; politically as well as literally, he is a "white dog." To change the dog's behavior, she visits a company that trains animals for Hollywood films. One trainer, a black man named Keys (Paul Winfield), persists in trying to transform the dog, even after he escapes and kills another black person. In the end, the dog goes crazy and attacks another trainer, and Keys kills him.

This is a strange film with a strange history. *White Dog* did not have a regular commercial release; the studio, which had intended "*Jaws* on paws," shelved it after the NAACP protested that its premise was inflammatory.[105] Fuller, who had a history of liberal politics, was apparently devastated and left Hollywood for Paris. The film received a limited release a decade later, and more recently, its critical fortunes rising, it has been rereleased in a high-prestige Criterion DVD, with accompanying admiring essays.[106]

This rerelease is merited: *White Dog* is the only Hollywood film I know that takes as its main topic the use of dogs as tools of racist violence in American history. Despite its pulp status—or because of it: the B-movie genre often provides a sheltering lens for political topics—the film names this history, dramatizing it as a metaphor for racism. It does not refer to the Moore photographs directly, but it carries forth their imagery in a pulpy style whose excesses have their own bite. For example, it features a scene in which the dog, having escaped from the trainer, chases a terrified black man into a church, eviscerates him, and emerges, bloodied, from the scene. The tone is hyperbole: the bloodbath happens underneath a stained-glass window of St. Francis of Assisi being kind to animals—an over-the-top touch. But the attack carries the symbolic weight of a real history of violence. The "white dog" embodies the aggressive force of racist ideology as well as an account of the inculcation of that ideology.[107]

White Dog develops this account with a self-reflexive interest in cinematic image-making. With its Hollywood animal-trainer characters, the film takes as its thematic focus the construction of the dog as loveable cinematic symbol. Also, the camera keeps its actual focus on animals: the dog (dogs—five dogs portrayed the white dog) receives the point-of-view shots ordinarily accorded a human character. These techniques simultaneously humanize him and render humans beastly, as do repeated close-up shots of his eye. Close-ups of an animal's eye in film are often juxtaposed with close-ups of human eyes, so that, as Jonathan Burt notes, "the exchange of the look is, in the absence of the possibility of language, the basis of a social contract."[108] In *White Dog*, that social contract is racism.

The original novel ties this history closely to the racial politics of the 1960s. Romain Gary's *Chien Blanc* (1970) was based on an episode in which his wife, actress Jean Seberg, a participant in civil rights and Black Power groups, unwittingly adopted a "white dog." Gary's novel uses this episode to meditate on the politics of race in 1968 America, including the rise of the Black Panthers, riots in Watts and Detroit, the assassination of Rev. Martin Luther King, and anticolonial struggles. His French narrator is scathing about black activists—"Professional Negroes . . . people who make a living for *themselves*

FIG. 8.
Man and dog in *White Dog*, dir. Samuel Fuller, 1982.

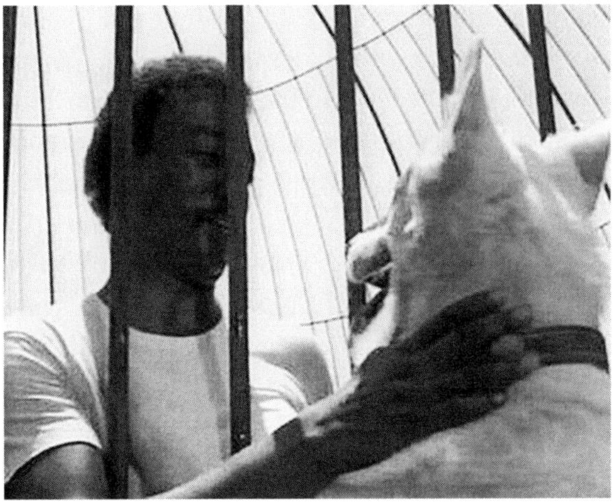

by being black and nothing else, gaming whitey"—but also white liberals and, ultimately, himself (52).[109] The dog becomes a symbol of the narrator: "I am too old a dog now to be able to learn new tricks. So I let go, lash out, ashamed of myself" (74). When he declares that "the White Dog was assuming symbolic proportions in [his] mind," those proportions are his own: "I was identifying myself with that dog in his cage" (135, 136).

Eliminating this first-person narrator, the film also makes several changes to advance the story's antiracist dimensions. In the novel, the trainer, Keys, is a militant activist who goes insane: "He is standing on the stairs almost naked. . . . *And he is laughing*" (273). In the film, by contrast, Keys is heroic, albeit obsessed with the white dog; he seems "like a black Captain Ahab."[110] Keys is also filmed in ways that suggest racial critique, as in scenes of man and dog near the dog's cage. The animal is the one who is caged, but the composition of the shot makes it look as if the black man is behind bars. A critique of the construction of black criminality, these scenes also make whiteness—of fur and skin—look strange.

As it does throughout: the most chilling sequence, to me, comes late in the film, when Julie is visited by an old white man and his two granddaughters. Arriving with a candy sampler in hand, he seems kind, gentle, and soft-spoken until he proudly confirms that he has trained the dog to be racist: racism with a human as well as canine face. The horror of this face is all the greater because the kind-looking man is bearing candy for strangers and has in tow the little girls, presumably also the recipients of his racist tutelage. One girl is played by Fuller's own daughter Samantha: "I made sure Samantha got a line to say on camera with her lovable baby lisp: 'Where is my dog?'"[111] The ostensibly sweet white child in the film is as leashed to the dog as her venomous grandfather, her "lovable baby lisp" a junior version of the master's voice. This is not just my metaphor: the protagonist of Romain Gary's novel is obsessed with white dogs because "he wanted to fill himself with it. The howls, I mean, the rage . . . His Master's Voice . . . you get it? Every morning, he comes here to . . . refresh his memory, I bet. To wind up his hate machinery" (25; ellipses in original). His rage at racism is a rebellion against "His Master's Voice"—"*la Voix de son Maitre*," italicized, in Gary's original.[112] "You get it?" he asks, and I do: here is "His Master's Voice," named directly in *Chien Blanc* as the force that propels the "hate machinery." Here is the connection I have posited between *His Master's Voice* and racial hierarchy, named directly: *voilà*.

I also find an even closer connection between the material surrounding Fuller's *White Dog* and the nineteenth-century animal autobiography. It appears in "The White Dog Talks—to Sam Fuller," a mock-interview written by Fuller and published in the film journal *Framework* in 1982, and now included with the Criterion DVD of the film.[113] This weird but perceptive document consists of purported dialogue between Fuller and "the title actor of the movie":

> **Dog:** Now what's this about?
>
> **Samuel Fuller:** You've heard of *Black Beauty*.
>
> **Dog:** Every animal knows the horse that told his story first-person for children. . . .
>
> **SF:** I thought it would be just as unpredictable to get a dog's critique of the movie we worked on. . . .
>
> **Dog:** Who'd want to hear *my* bark?
>
> **SF:** Who *wouldn't* want to hear it?[114]

Here is *Black Beauty* is in the orbit of *White Dog*, the animal autobiography tradition made explicit, the dog's bark accompanying his bite.

And here is one more important reference the "interview":

> **Dog:** You saw a chance to rip off the KKK skin and expose to what inhuman depths a racist sinks when he created a white dog.
>
> **SF:** Right. In *Frankenstein*, the monster's crimes were great, but the greater crime was Dr. Frankenstein's, for having created the monster.[115]

The first part of this quotation has a biographical precedent: Fuller's work as a journalist in the South during the 1930s, during which he witnessed the phenomenon of the "white dog." Fuller credited his reporting on the Klan as the moment he realized that "[he] could better convey emotions with words *and* images" and thus was launched as a filmmaker.[116] But I am more interested in the *Frankenstein* reference, which is probably to the classic James Whale films of the 1930s, *Frankenstein* (1931) and *Bride of Frankenstein* (1935). Fuller uses *Frankenstein* as a metaphor for understanding the making of racism, to argue that the greatest fault in a narrative of violence lies not with the monster but with the monster-maker. I agree with this argument. I should: in *Black Frankenstein*, I made a fuller version of this argument for understanding the Whale films as racial allegories.[117]

Fuller's comments about *White Dog* lead him to *Black Beauty* and *Frankenstein*, and I would go one more step—to *Beautiful Joe*, with its dog likened from the outset to a "slave-lad": "Who'd want to hear *my* bark?" Beautiful Joe gives one answer: the "my" is not that of a dog, but of the human, the white human writer, imagining both animal and Africanist presences. Saunders's novel, I have suggested, belongs in the orbit of nineteenth-century works that represent American racial hierarchies—an orbit in which the idea of a "master's voice" evokes the owners as slaves as well as animals.

As a narrative of enslavement, *Beautiful Joe* does not offer a critique of racist metaphors, as do the literary works of Twain or Chesnutt—or, later, the visual works of Moore and Fuller. But it does open the door to these and others who adopt more overtly antiracist strategies. Saunders's novel suggests, to me, the value of making visible racist metaphors that would otherwise invisibly naturalize people as dogs—or, to switch to the vocabulary of sound, the value of turning up the volume on metaphors that would otherwise be silent. The canine-voiced novel may not speak back directly to masters, but it shows low fidelity to the soundtrack of racism. In so doing, it offers the potential to distort, remix, or at least to remaster the master's voice.

CHAPTER 3

Literary Taxidermy

1.

After Frankie recovers from his surgery in 2008, I start him on a regimen of daily experimental chemotherapy, which I special-order from a pharmacy in Arizona and administer myself. One medication is a liquid that makes my hands shake every time I use it: the bottle has a skull and crossbones on it, and I must handle it with safety precautions—plastic gloves, hazmat bottle disposal, careful cleanup of everything that, in turn, comes out of Frankie. The medicine has a name, "etopicide," which seems a nonsensical amalgam of other words: email, ectopic, utopia, homicide. Also, it is very expensive; I am worried I will knock the bottle over, wasting money while spreading toxicity. I loathe everything about this drug, but I also laugh every time its package comes in the mail, because it is addressed to "Canine Frankie Young."[1]

This medicine seems to work for quite a while, and mercifully, it does not have the same side effects as human chemo; Frankie stays furry, lively, live. But after two years and nine months, the cancer comes back: an ultrasound reveals that his gastrointestinal stromal tumor—GIST—has recurred, with a tumor on the original site and at least one elsewhere; after much consultation, I decide for him to have surgery again, the news from which is mixed: the tumors visible on the ultrasound were successfully removed, but several others were newly found; these are scattered throughout the intestine in such Latinate locales as the jejunum, the omentum, the ileum, and the duodenum and as far away as the diaphragm; they seem to be newly "seeded," grown from cancer cells randomly flung into new places when the original tumor was removed; they are also "pedunculated"—supported with stalks: I am told to picture broccoli, which I do, and then regret, the imagery of broccoli-tumors too odd even for me—and they are not surgically removable. The surgeon sews Frankie back up with these tumors still inside, making a neat foot-long incision that looks, once the stitches have been removed, like a zipper. Frankie is like a child's stuffed animal—a freshly restuffed animal—with cancer unfortunately mixed in the stuffing.

Or he is like a real stuffed animal: a specimen of taxidermy. Although I should not say "stuffed": taxidermists prefer the term "mounted." I am fascinated by taxidermy. I know this might seem strange, for a feminist critic. Taxidermy is associated with the macho sportsman who turns hunted-down animals into cut-up wall trophies—not to mention with Norman Bates in Hitchcock's *Psycho*, who fills his parlor in the Bates motel with his own taxidermied birds. Norman aside, the norm of taxidermy is the display of dead animals. Often, these animals have been killed by hunters, sometimes by naturalists, occasionally by accident; but always, they are dead, with their corpses gutted, their skins preserved, and their forms mounted on display.

Myself, I like the horrors of Hitchcock's films—I will come back to them—but taxidermy most appeals to me in the space of the natural history museum. There, animals are usually displayed whole, often situated in habitat dioramas, and look, to me, not recently killed but on the verge of coming alive again; I think about their futures, not their pasts. There, I find them strange but wonderful—strange and wonderful, the strangeness pumping the heart of the wonder.

In 2009, I see a wonderful example, in a place known as "Tring," more formally the Natural History Museum at Tring, a town in Hertfordshire, England, which houses a collection of taxidermy animals amassed by the late Walter Rothschild, more formally the 2nd Baron Rothschild (1868–1937). A scion of the banking family, Lord Rothschild eschewed finance for natural history; at seven, he declared his intent to make a museum; at twelve, he hired his first curator; at twenty-four, in 1892, he opened his taxidermy collection to the public; and over time, he amassed the largest individual collection of taxidermy specimens in the world. Even by British standards, he was an eccentric: for example, he traveled in a carriage pulled by zebras. According to his biographer, his niece, "paralysing shyness afflicted him all his adult life and he lived in a shell of silence," but he had "a fanatical attention to detail, coupled with [a] peculiar computer-like mind"—obsessive-compulsive traits that probably made possible the scale and detail of Tring.[2]

All this I learn later, from the biography; what draws me to Tring initially is a story about the reopening of the museum's Gallery 6—the largest gallery of taxidermied dogs in the world.[3] Allow me to describe, briefly, my visit there:

taxidermy is too site-specific to introduce in generalities, and I will get back to Marshall Saunders, Lord Rothschild's contemporary, as soon as I can. I have come to England for a week—Frankie is in remission—and I am staying with friends in Brighton; I decide to make a day trip to Tring. Once a self-contained village, now a town within commuting distance to London, Tring is not usual tourist territory; I get there easily enough by train, but face a small hurdle once I arrive: the station is a good two miles from the museum, allegedly so located because the Rothschilds apparently did not want the hassle of hoi polloi that would come with a train station near their estate. Here, as so often in England, a sense of place begins with a sense of class. Apparently, in the early twentieth century, "the King used to drop in at Tring," a phrase that sounds like the beginning of an A. A. Milne poem but is more the prose of the English aristocracy—Edward VII chilling chez Rothschild.[4]

When I finally make it to the museum—thanks to the kindness of strangers—I am not entirely naive. Going in, I know that taxidermy has a sobering political history. I have read Donna Haraway's influential essay on taxidermy in the Hall of African Mammals at the Museum of Natural History in New York. This essay is a classic of cultural studies and, now, animal studies. In it, Haraway analyzes the taxidermy dioramas in the museum, designed by Carl Akeley, as cultural rather than natural history—or rather, she shows how natural history is itself culturally constructed. For Haraway, Akeley's taxidermy dioramas were shaped by norms of national power, such norms being closely linked at this turn-of-the-century moment to Teddy Roosevelt—friend of Akeley, taxidermist, president, sportsman, conservationist, builder of U.S. empire, and the Teddy of teddy bear. For Akeley as for Roosevelt, the goal was the assertion, at once triumphant and anxious, of white American masculinity. In an era of perceived encroachments upon white male authority—immigration, black emancipation, feminism, "overcivilization"—taxidermy attempted to secure what Haraway terms "Teddy Bear Patriarchy."[5] Tring seems a British version of Rooseveltian empire, Edward picking up from Teddy, with Victoria shaping the British scene before them. Tring's taxidermy was of a piece with Britain's desire to colonize nonhuman as well as human worlds.

Still, inside the museum at Tring, I am captivated: the rooms seem cabinets of curiosities, the glass cases stuffed with stuffed animals in vast quantities and on every conceivable scale, from tiny insects to gigantic hippopotami. Making my way up to the top-floor dog gallery, I am overwhelmed by the strange looks of the animals—how they look at me as well as how they look to me; for example, the polar bear seems to be grinning. The museum guidebook explains, "Giving animals expressions sometimes happened when these skins were mounted."[6] This is an odd sentence: the passive voice behind "sometimes happened" obscures the hand of the human. That hand is doubly important, as absence and as presence. Absence: For all the variety of species here, there are no human specimens. That is, after all, how taxidermy is defined: as a practice using only nonhuman animals; human taxidermy would be something different, propelled directly into horror. But also presence: All the taxidermied animals were made by human hands—"made" as in mounted, then made to smile; "made" often by murder. I understand that the violence intrinsic to this display should make me feel horrified, but I cannot help it. Looking at the bear, I grin too.

Now I am in the top-floor gallery of Tring, where the dogs are positioned in a long shallow case against one wall. Here, it is all about the human-made purebred, with displays of taxidermied hounds, setters, retrievers, bulldogs, collies, terriers, spaniels, and pugs. The collection was assembled by a zoologist at the turn of the twentieth century to show breed diversity, then a recent notion. The majority of dog breeds as we now know them were invented in the Victorian era, in the context of the burgeoning middle-class culture of pet ownership and display. A book on the Tring dogs celebrates the moment: "[These] dogs are in a category all of their own. . . . Collectively they encapsulate the period of greatest importance to dog breeders when the development of breeds reached a peak."[7] More critically, Harriet Ritvo shows the connection to class, arguing that the development of breeds symbolized class instabilities rather than certainties: "The prizewinning pedigreed dogs of the late nineteenth century seemed to symbolize simply the power to manipulate and the power to purchase—they were ultimately destabilizing emblems of status and rank as pure commodities."[8] Susan McHugh provides an imperial frame: "[The] canine breed system . . . emerged as part of the process by which the world's people were for the first time scientifically catalogued according to race, sex and gender. And this taxonomic process was inseparable from the imperialist politics it served."[9] Reflecting the unstable norms of human hierarchies, the Tring dogs magnify imperialism with both taxonomy and taxidermy.

The dogs here were not only purebreds but prize winners. Dogs who were taxidermied in the Victorian era were somehow "exceptional in life. They were champions of their breed, extraordinary athletes, heroes."[10] Sometimes they were community mascots, like Owney (1885–1897), a terrier with the U.S. Post Office, who rode the rails with the mails all over the country; his mounted body is now at the National Postal Museum in Washington.[11] Sometimes, though,

FIG. 9.

Natural History Museum at Tring, Gallery 6. Used by permission of Natural History Museum.

they were pets taxidermied out of private grief—I will come back to this topic—exceptional only to their owners. The Tring dogs, as champions, were more the taxidermic rule, although it was also unusual for any taxidermied dogs to be included in natural history museums. Barry, a taxidermied St. Bernard famous for heroic rescues, was exhibited in the Natural History Museum in Bern, but he was an exception; such museums customarily represented animals at the level of species.[12] Tring, by contrast, has many dogs named as individuals. Also, a few of the Tring dogs are just heads, mounted on the wall; this is stranger still, combining the sportsman's trophy with the natural history museum.[13]

The labels reflect this strangeness. Some give the years of the individual's birth and death ("Afghan hound, 1894–1901"), others dates that signal the biography of the breed, like the bloodhound, "brought to the United Kingdom in 1066." The biggest dog here is Britain itself, from its Norman Conquest puppyhood to its imperial adulthood. Here is a recent addition, a bulldog: "Spike, kennel name Boatswain, 1992–2004." The bulldog has long been a symbol of English power, and Spike presumably carries the nation forward into the postimperial world.[14] However, his names, nick and proper, seem almost oxymoronic. "Boatswain" sounds nautical, historical—*The Tempest* starts with a Boatswain character; Lord Byron's favorite dog, a Newfoundland, was named Boatswain—but "Spike" seems oddly casual, even sweet. This is not to say that this is a kinder, gentler version of canine taxidermy. The eugenic quest for what was deemed "breed purity" has been ruinous to the health of many dogs, and the bulldog is a poster child for such ruin. Enthusiastically promoted in the nineteenth century, bulldogs were bred in ways that produced severe respiratory problems, skin infections, joint malformations, and other health concerns.[15] Whether "Spike" or "Boatswain," the bulldog was a breed in pain.

Here, the pain of the purebred is quieted by death, further silenced by taxidermy, then arranged for display in a long and narrow line. The gallery at Tring looks to me like a Westminster Dog Show of the dead, especially at those moments when the dogs trotting in the ring freeze to hold a pose. This connection could be chilling, since dog shows like Westminster and its British equivalent, Crufts—both begun in the Victorian era, Westminster first—paraded pedigrees for prizes. Except that now I am thinking of the comic film *Best in Show* (dir. Christopher Guest, 2000), an affectionate satire of the Westminster world. Looking at Tring's version of best in show, I am speculating on the comic potential of "Spike" a.k.a. "Boatswain." Again, I understand that this is not the right response, politically: a more appropriate reaction would be disgust. One scholar theorizes disgust as a form of resistance to the violence of taxidermy, a step toward enabling "flayed animals . . . to undo their butchers."[16] I understand the need for disgust, for resistance, for undoing. But still, looking at Spike/Boatswain, I smile.

On my way downstairs, I stop in the "Rothschild Room," where more taxidermy specimens flank an elaborate Rothschild family tree, the taxonomy of nonhuman animal species abutting a human genealogy of aristocratic kinship. This seems an ironic juxtaposition, given the obsession with breeding on display in the dog gallery, but probably the irony is not intentional. Nor does it seem to be intended in the postcard I buy in the gift shop, which features five dogs—a German shepherd, Pekingese, Welsh corgi, Dalmatian, and Afghan hound—against a bright green background. These dogs, each exemplifying some form of national as well as breed identity, look alive and alert—note the poised posture of the Dalmatian, the perked-up ears of the German shepherd—but of course, they are dead. I suppose you might not even notice this if you received the postcard in snail mail, except that the background is strange: too evenly green, too empty, altogether stylized and unreal. Now the dogs themselves look to me too posed, oddly grouped, their gazes mismatched and unfixed; they look like "dogs." Now I am lapsing into ironic scare quotes. Visiting a Victorian museum, I seem, instead, to be approaching the postmodern.

I am not the only one going in either direction: in the twenty-first century, taxidermy is undergoing a new wave of popularity, its biggest since the Victorian era, with as many as a hundred thousand people in the United States alone involved in taxidermy businesses, conferences, and competitions. There are trade books reporting on the contemporary taxidermy scene and providing histories, appreciations, and how-tos; there are taxidermy reality television shows; there are scholarly books providing ethnography and critique.[17] At the hipster end of the new wave are bars, shops, and homes furnished with taxidermy as ironic antiquarian decor, as well as classes at death-friendly venues like the Morbid Anatomy Museum in Brooklyn.[18] It is hard to keep up, and I am happy to find that Rachel Poliquin, a scholar and curator, keeps track of all things taxidermy on a website and that she has written a scholarly book, *The Breathless Zoo*, which indispensably pursues the paradox I have experienced, "the troubled relationship between the aesthetics and ethics of taxidermy: the compelling urge to look and the worry about what made that looking possible."[19]

There has been a particularly vibrant wave of international interest in taxidermy among contemporary visual artists, who use the medium in ways that are political, sophisticated, and—as it were—cutting edge. Some artists reuse existing taxidermy, while others create new specimens; some work with taxidermy in part and some in whole—a part or whole of the animal, a part or whole of their oeuvre.[20] This development is less an organized movement than a shared approach, and genealogies of it vary. But no summary would exclude *Nanoq* (2001–6), a project undertaken by Bryndís Snæbjörnsdóttir and Mark Wilson—Icelandic and English, respectively; known as Snæbjörnsdóttir/Wilson, collectively—to photograph every taxidermied polar bear in the United Kingdom, in situ. The themes *Nanoq* raises include the violent contexts

FIG. 10.

Natural History Museum at Tring, dog postcard. Used by permission of Natural History Museum.

of collecting, the historical relations between the polar bear and empire, and the present and future connections of the polar bear to climate change.[21]

As *Nanoq* suggests, contemporary taxidermy art raises political questions, especially when artists are using newly dead animals. Mark Dion (American) has developed ethical guidelines for animal use; Emily Mayer (English) starts from the principle "I never touch animals that are taken illegally"; and Polly Morgan (English) declares, "Taxidermy today is green, humane and respectful."[22] Perhaps the most overtly political of contemporary taxidermy artists is Angela Singer (English but based in New Zealand; I suspected at the start of this paragraph that a one-word parenthetical for national identity would be insufficient). She is known for her deliberately shocking reuse and alteration of sportsman's trophies. This is how she describes a work entitled *sore (flay)*: "My trophy echoes the just-killed animal, antlers hacked out, blood pouring from its head, hung to be skinned, gutted and bled out. . . . The glass eyes bulge." This last is a deliberate visual address: "I wanted to emphasize the animal looking at the viewer."[23] Here the viewer cannot avoid the visceral violence of taxidermy, as the animal—flayed and bloody—looks back.

I have launched directly into the political concerns of artists working with taxidermy, but I also want to emphasize their aesthetic experiments—one kind of experiment in particular. In 2000, Steve Baker coined the term "botched taxidermy" to describe the work of Singer and other artists: "A botched taxidermy piece might be defined as referring to the human *and* to the animal, without itself being either human or animal. . . . It is an attempt *to think a new thing*." Artists make this attempt with mixed materials, hybrid forms, and deliberate messiness, "with no attempt at perfection but equally with no implication of the thing falling apart"; "botching" is a "provisional, playful, loosely experimental" mode.[24] Baker's own embrace of this idea was provisional: soon he was concerned that "botched taxidermy" had become "a rather clumsy catch-all phrase," and he later declared that "the term has now lost much of its critical purchase."[25] While he found the idea of "botched taxidermy" initially useful to legitimate artistic interest in animals, it now seems to him dated; its terms are "too blunt, too emphatic." In a contemporary art scene where the legitimacy of animal-based art has been proven, "the artist's perplexing responsibility is now to get the animal out of its own way."[26]

I am disconcerted to read this renunciation; I don't want artists to get the animal out of its own way yet. As usual, I seem to have embarked on my own catching-up strategy just as others are moving on: Poliquin has suspended her blog, and the Morbid Anatomy Museum—which I happily visited twice, the second time for an exhibition devoted to taxidermy—has closed.[27] Giovanni Aloi, whose journal, *Antennae*, has featured contemporary taxidermy art, publishes his own book on the topic, in which he "moves beyond botched taxidermy" to a new model, "speculative taxidermy."[28] His movement "beyond" delimits the earlier model as "a product of its time," that time being an enervating postmodernism, which "bore a passive pessimism at its core—one that eventually tired audiences."[29]

I, as an audience member, am not yet tired of "botched taxidermy," but I am finding it can be hard to distinguish from "rogue taxidermy," also previously featured in *Antennae* and defined by Robert Marbury as "pop-surrealist art characterized by mixed-media sculptures containing traditional taxidermy materials used in an unconventional manner."[30] I am not as worried about "crap taxidermy," a fuzzy fan category—"every bug-eyed, misshapen, awkward, or just-plain-wrong piece of taxidermy that I was able to find online"[31]—but the line between "rogue" and "botched" seems thin. "Botched taxidermy"—disavowed by own maker, relegated to an earlier time, difficult to define—seems to have mutated toward its own obsolescence.

Still, I decide to retain the concept: it is Baker's prerogative to renounce "botched taxidermy" and Aloi's to move "beyond" it, but it is also mine to retain it. I do not mind being late, and I like to go back to classics, including recent ones. I sort through Baker's original examples: Singer's taxidermy does not seem at all "playful," but this adjective does apply to German artist Thomas Grünfeld, whose series *Misfit* combines taxidermy body parts from different species. Reading Baker, I realize I have seen one of Grünfeld's *Misfits*, in an exhibition on *Unnatural Science* at Mass MoCA, the Massachusetts Museum of Contemporary Art, which is north by northwest from me; I somehow missed its exhibition on animal-centered art, but I have seen many others there.[32] The Grünfeld work I saw was *Misfit (St. Bernhard)* (1994), a taxidermy sculpture with the body of a St. Bernard dog and the head of a sheep. It was a large figure, installed at the entrance to the exhibition, reclining on a platform and looking alertly from its sheep eyes atop its dog's body. This figure might have seemed an ominous avatar of forced hybridity: sheep-slash-dog, emphasis on the violence of the slash. I found it rather delightful.

When I looked at *Misfit*, I was thinking about *Frankenstein*, not taxidermy, although now I can see how closely related they are. Victor Frankenstein is like a taxidermist manipulating different corpses; Shelley takes this manipulation further, into reanimation, while Grünfeld hyperbolizes the hybridity involved

FIG. 11.

Thomas Grünfeld, *Misfit (St. Bernhard)*, 1994. Courtesy of the artist and Galerie Jousse Entreprise, Paris.

FIG. 12.

Nina Katchadourian, *Chloe*, installation proposed for San Diego Museum of Natural History (never realized), 1994. Courtesy of the artist.

in his project. In *Misfit (St. Bernhard)*, he also hyperbolizes the idea of breed mixture, turning mixed-breed dog into multispecies animal.

He is not the only artist to work with dogs: Emily Mayer taxidermies them herself, sometimes posing dogs apparently dozing—"sleeping animals are much more comforting and believable"—and sometimes making them comic, as in *The Dog's Bollocks*, in which a taxidermied rat holds a jar containing a dog's testicles.[33] That last title requires American translation—the "dog's bollocks," a British idiom, means the best—but no translation is required for *I'm Dead* (2012), a work by English artist David Shrigley, in which a taxidermied dog stands on its hind legs, holding a sign that says, "I'm dead." In *I'm Dead*, the dog's human posture and sign-holding make taxidermy comically artificial, while the words of the sign—in another version of first-dog voice—suggest that "the dog objects to being dead or made to look alive, or likely both."[34]

If the taxidermied dogs of Shrigley and Mayer open the door to comedy, then that door is slammed by Jordan Baseman's *The Cat and the Dog* (1995), in which the artist mounted on a wall a cat and a dog with their bodies skinned but their taxidermied full heads attached. This work brutally violates the distinction between domestic pet and hunted animal. The line between pet and natural history specimen is blurred more gently by Nina Katchadourian's *Chloe* (1994), in which the artist placed a taxidermied pet dog, a Pomeranian, in a vitrine for an exhibition of contemporary art in the San Diego Museum of Natural History, only to find that the museum "refused to exhibit the piece, stating that it was offensive, and that people would find the situation confusing and that children might get upset. [Katchadourian] pointed out that Chloe was genetically very much like the Coyote who lived in a nearby diorama . . . but to no avail."[35] The museum would only display the empty vitrine; Katchadourian exhibited the dog in an art gallery instead.

The boundary-blurring dogs of Katchadourian and Basemen seem to me not dissimilar to the dogs of Tring; all move uneasily among pets, trophies, and specimens. Also, the postcard of the Tring dogs reminds me of a genre of contemporary art photographs analyzed by Stephanie Turner as "remediating" natural history taxidermy—changing its context from science display to art gallery.[36] Diane Fox's photographs, for example, highlight the glass of the natural history taxidermy case; she includes "reflection" on the lists of materials for her artworks.[37]

Here, I will do the remediation, imagining the Tring postcard exhibited in an art gallery. There—I envision—its green background might seem a parody of a verdant natural setting, and its odd grouping of dogs, mismatched gazes and postures, might appear as deliberate artifice. There, the Tring postcard could have a touch of the taxidermy comedy of Mayer's *The Dog's Bollocks* or Shrigley's *I'm Dead.*

And the Tring gallery as a whole seems to have a bit of "botched taxidermy" in it. It is not that the bodies of the dogs are made of mismatched parts, as in Grünfeld's *Misfits*—quite the contrary: they are "purebred" wholes—but that they do not go with the other species in a natural history exhibition; the "botch" is at the level of the museum as a whole. Assessing the Tring dogs, Poliquin suggests, "Perhaps the human-dog bond is too intimate for such post-mortem bodily invasions."[38] Perhaps; there seem to be multiple invasions here. In its intimacy, the human-dog bond already crosses a species boundary, so the taxidermy dog in the museum crosses a boundary itself about boundary crossing. When Katchadourian attempted to exhibit *Chloe* at the San Diego Museum of Natural History, she was staging a similar botch, juxtaposing beloved domestic canine and natural history coyote. Works like Chloe extend rather than invent the weirdness of the Victorian museum.

Tring (opened 1892) and *Beautiful Joe* (published 1894) are contemporaries, and there are points of connection between the museum of taxidermied dogs and the novel in first-dog voice. Taxidermy is one such connection: it makes brief but striking appearances in *Beautiful Joe.* In this chapter, I analyze taxidermy in Saunders's work and in a range of other late nineteenth-century English and North American literature. Moving from the theme of voice to that of skin, and from dogs to birds, I analyze conjunctions between taxidermy and literature—what I will call "literary taxidermy"—emphasizing form as well as politics. I show how literature illuminates and challenges the terms of taxidermy, while taxidermy provides metaphors of form, as well as content, for literary texts. Politically, literary taxidermy often exaggerates the violent hierarchies inherent in actual taxidermy, although it can also allow for political reversals. Aesthetically, literary taxidermy reveals a complex relation between interiors and exteriors. Literary taxidermy, I argue, in its focus on the surface of skin, seems the inverse to a novel in first-dog voice like *Beautiful Joe*, but it is also its complement, for both forms explore animal interiors as well as exteriors.

I first interpret the representation of taxidermy in fiction by H. G. Wells and nonfiction by William T. Hornaday, suggesting that their works depict taxidermy politically as a series of violent hierarchies—particularly those of race and gender—and formally as an invented set of paper-like surfaces and embodied interiors. I emphasize their depictions of taxidermied birds, which were linked in this era with aesthetic production and with female consumption.

Returning to Marshall Saunders, I argue that she offers a very different representation of avian taxidermy in *Beautiful Joe* and her later memoir *My Pets*. These discussions of mounted birds, which highlight their connections to dogs and women, will also involve a short detour to representations of avian taxidermy in the films of Alfred Hitchcock. In cinematic and literary ways, the birds and the dogs of taxidermy repeatedly attempt to revivify animals—not by offering first-animal voices but by getting under their skins.

2.

The late nineteenth century was a major moment in the aesthetic development as well as public display of Anglo-American taxidermy. Featured in natural history museums, animals were preserved with more advanced methods, positioned in more lifelike poses, and grouped together in dioramas with environmental habitats, a practice that would reach its apotheosis in Carl Akeley's dioramas at the American Museum of Natural History. Meanwhile, a growing industry of commercial taxidermists served private customers, whether hunters seeking trophies or families preserving pets. Victorians welcomed taxidermy into their everyday lives.[39]

With some notable exceptions, new practices and displays of taxidermy centered on an aesthetics of ever greater realism.[40] This is a paradoxical concept: Jane Desmond—like Poliquin, an indispensable scholar of taxidermy—puts "realism" in quotation marks, and defines taxidermy's realism as built on a set of structural ironies. The main one: "Death is the absolute and always indispensable prerequisite to the process of creating lifelikeness. For the fiction of realism to work, though, this fact . . . must be so masked that it does not interrupt the viewing pleasure." Another: "To be presented as 'lifelike' and 'whole,' the animal body must first be totally disarticulated." Death and disarticulation must be hidden, while something else must be displayed: "The actual skin, with its covering of fur, hair, or feathers, is the absolute prerequisite for taxidermy."[41] In taxidermy, then as now, these were the prereqs for Realism 101: death denied, dismemberment healed, skin displayed.

In its Victorian moment, taxidermic realism drew heavily from multiple media. Desmond links taxidermy to theater: "The relationship between viewer and object is fundamentally theatrical . . . the depicted moment is like an excerpt from a play."[42] Haraway locates Akeley's dioramas at the conjunction of sculpture and photography, with photography "represent[ing] the future and sculpture the past."[43] Other scholars emphasize connections between taxidermy and photography, both "technologies of preservation [that] deal in the frozen moment."[44] Still others focus on film, emerging at this late nineteenth-century moment. Akeley himself invented a movie camera with a moving head, which was able to pan, tilt, and otherwise capture wild animals with greater ease.[45] The film connection is also thematic: early ethnographic cinema offered a kind of ethnic taxidermy, treating human subjects as exotic specimens frozen in time but vivified by the moving image.[46]

Theater, sculpture, photography, cinema: I will bring literature into the mix. Words are not a historical influence on taxidermy in the same way that sculpture and photography are. But there are important connections between taxidermy and literature, starting with the material forms in which literature has appeared. Parchment, the precursor to paper, was customarily made with animal skins; indeed, "the whole of medieval book production operate[d] using what were once living things. The act of writing comprise[d] the touch of human skin on animal skin, goose feather pen in hand, oak gall ink in a horn inkwell close by."[47] The animal trace can be something of a purloined letter, hidden in plain sight: a medievalist confesses, "The origin of parchment in animal skin is easily overlooked. I am guilty of this oversight myself."[48]

Paper has now replaced parchment, although the link between animal skins and book bindings remains. Steven Connor—who wrote a book about skin after the one on ventriloquism; I seem to be echoing his interests, in a different voice—puts the case this way: "The implication of the skin in the idea of the book is more than a metaphor. For centuries of manuscript and book production, books were primarily things of skin."[49] Animal skin, primarily, although occasionally parchment was made of human skin; there were also a small number of books bound in human skin, particularly that of executed criminals or medical subjects.[50] That books made of human skin seem shocking only confirms the degree to which books made of animals do not. Nonhuman animal-made books are so common as to be entirely naturalized—easy to overlook because they are everywhere to see.

What happens when books and taxidermy collide, and books are made of animals in less material but more metaphoric ways? In fiction of the late nineteenth century—the moment of both Tring and *Beautiful Joe*—taxidermy appears both directly and indirectly. Indirectly, in the tableaux vivants scene of the famous novel by Edith Wharton, *The House of Mirth* (1905), wherein "a dozen fashionable women . . . exhibit themselves in a series of pictures"; a scholar has connected the tableaux vivants to taxidermy dioramas of the era.[51] Directly, in an obscure short story by George Washington Cable, a Louisiana novelist known for his interest in Creole life. Cable's "The Taxidermist" (1893) is about a New Orleans taxidermist seen as an artist: "There is a way of making everything—anything—an art instead of a craft or a commerce, and such was the way of this shop's big, dark, hairy-faced, shaggy-headed master."[52]

Both of these examples link taxidermy to art and aesthetics; both also suggest a connection to racial themes. In Wharton's novel, the tableaux vivants practiced by white Northern elites express a desire to freeze white identity, "to secure an American identity impervious to hybridization and change."[53] In Cable's story, the Creole taxidermist occupies a position of cultural difference, if not also racial ambiguity; "Creole" was a category in flux, increasingly accreting the implications of blackness and racial mixture.[54] In Cable's story, the "dark, hairy-faced" taxidermist is dismissed by another character as an "old ourang-outang," closer to the racist imagery of slave than of "master."[55] But Cable—who was known for his support of black equality—condemns this racially marked slur and refutes it; his artist-taxidermist is a hero in the story's climactic fire. A preliminary proposition, then, drawing on Wharton and Cable: literary depictions of taxidermy are inseparable from questions of racial politics as well as aesthetic form.

I am moving past examples too quickly: I slow down and focus on an English story, "Triumphs of a Taxidermist" (1894) by H. G. Wells; I have already cited Wells's images of vivisection in *The Island of Doctor Moreau*. "Triumphs of a Taxidermist," one of his first published stories, has received little scholarly attention. It offers, I argue, a hyperbolic account of the political hierarchies enacted by taxidermy—particularly those of race and gender—while also linking taxidermy to counterfeit, fakery, and the making of fiction itself.

"'Triumphs' is narrated by a man named Bellows who describes an evening spent with an unnamed male taxidermist. The story's opening situates the two men in the taxidermist's small living quarters, with a description of 'the noisome den where he plied his trade': the taxidermist, who is 'in a mood of elation . . . in the time between the first glass of whiskey and the fourth,' is dressed in 'horrible yellow plaid' trousers and a coat 'chiefly of grease upon a basis of velveteen.'" After this brief scene-setting description, the rest of the story consists of a long, boasting monologue by the taxidermist: "There never was a man who could stuff like me, Bellows, never. I have stuffed elephants and I have stuffed moths, and the things have looked all the livelier and better for it" (22).[56]

This is a conversation between men about male power—which is to say, a conversation that enacts the gender norms of Victorian taxidermy. Taxidermy was assumed to be a male pursuit, both in the mounting of hunting trophies and in the creation of animal tableaux in natural history museums; American museum staff advocating new modes of display were known—whatever their

FIG. 13.

Eugene S. M. Haines, *The Taxidermists' After-Dinner Dream*, stereograph, ca. 1870. Photo: Library of Congress, Washington, D.C.

gender—as "museum men."[57] Fantasies of masculine control accompanied the imagery of taxidermy, as in an 1870 photograph by Eugene S. M. Haines.[58] The image depicts a male taxidermist dozing in his study, surrounded by an array of animals he has mounted, including monkey, owl, swan, seal, and boar; it is captioned "The taxidermists' after-dinner dream: 'We thought all nature subservient to our will." Haraway notes of the hunter that "the eye is infinitely more potent than the gun. Both put a woman to shame—reproductively."[59] The caption's plural "we" conveys a community of potent male eyes as well as a relay among their looks. A male hunter has shot the animals, a male taxidermist has mounted them, and a male photographer has represented them: reproduction—of the animal, of the dream, of the image itself—is a collective male fantasy of birth.

Wells's story is continuous with such masculine fantasies. The between-men intimacy of his opening tableau does not seem particularly erotic—the "horrible yellow plaid trousers" repel rather than attract—but it is hyperbolically homosocial. The taxidermist's claim "There never was a man who could stuff like me" offers another scenario of male reproductive power.

Wells immediately introduces a different form of hierarchy to this scenario, for this same opening paragraph continues, "And I have stuffed human beings—chiefly amateur ornithologists. But I stuffed a nigger once" (22). Wells stops here—the first paragraph of the story ends here—as will I: this is a shocking passage. The first sentence crosses the defining boundary of taxidermy—using human bodies—with a comic focus on "amateur ornithologists," who presumably stuff birds. The second sentence, however, changes tone and crosses a different boundary, into overt racism. Human taxidermy and racist violence were related: there was a reported case of human taxidermy in which the body of an African man was sent to London by a zoologist and stuffed and exhibited by a taxidermist there; this event was reported by the London *Times*, and it is possible Wells knew of it.[60] The term "nigger" was well established as a racist slur by this time, though it remained widespread in British fiction; this was the decade of Joseph Conrad's novel *The Nigger of the Narcissus* (1897).[61] In Wells's story, the line "I stuffed a nigger" seems calculated, by the taxidermist and by Wells, to shock. Its racism is reinforced in the taxidermist's next sentences, which begin a new paragraph: "No, there is no law against it. I made him with all his fingers out and used him as a hat-rack" (22). Racism is enacted in the transformation of the black body into skinned specimen, taxidermy mount, and "hat-rack."

What are the politics of this moment? As in *The Island of Doctor Moreau*, which he was writing at the same time, Wells collapses boundaries between human and nonhuman. *The Island of Doctor Moreau* can be seen as a critique of racism, insofar as the disgust that its white narrator feels toward characters like the "black-faced man" gives way to his sense that they are all atavistic animals; the novel ends with him back in ostensibly civilized London but fearing that "[he] too was not a reasonable creature, but only an animal tormented with some strange disorder in its brain."[62] It is less clear whether "Triumphs of a Taxidermist" is criticizing the taxidermist's racism or the racism of a culture that already imagines black bodies as commodified servants. The taxidermist is described as a seedy and unctuous figure—literally, wearing a coat "of grease"—but his racist slur is not protested by the narrator within the story. In the silent gap between "I stuffed a nigger" and "No, there is no law against it" is only the implication that Bellows has asked about the legality of the project, which the taxidermist has confidently asserted ("No, there is no law"). But the space for outrage is blank.

The rest of the story continues this structure: it is a monologue punctuated only by gaps where the narrator presumably responds with comments or questions for the taxidermist. The next revelation is that the taxidermist has faked specimens: "You know I have made some dodos and a great auk. No! Evidently you are an amateur at taxidermy. My dear fellow, half the great auks in the world are about as genuine as the handkerchiefs of Saint Veronica. . . . We make 'em of grebes' feathers and the like" (23). Dodos and auks were well-known extinct species; Wells pairs them with religious relics and exposes both as objects for fakery and payoff. For his character, taxidermy is a highly profitable scam: "Even if they suspect an egg they do not like to examine it too closely. It's such brittle capital at best." Taxidermic specimens are like counterfeit money; the fake eggs are "brittle capital" for hatching a fortune.

The taxidermist goes even further: "'All this is merely imitating Nature. I have done more than that in my time. I have—beaten her. . . . I have *created* birds,' he said in a low voice. '*New* birds. Improvements. Like no birds that was ever seen before.' He resumed his attitude during an impressive silence" (23–24). The next paragraph begins: "Enrich the universe; *rath*-er" (24). Presumably, Bellows has asked if the taxidermist's motive is financial enrichment—more "brittle capital"—but the response, "enrich the universe," suggests his aims are higher. First making his own eggs, now making his own bird, the male taxidermist is playing both P. T. Barnum and Victor Frankenstein, "beat[ing]" God and Mother Nature.

Note the focus, in a tale of taxidermy, on birds. Avian taxidermy has its own long history; popular and portable, it was technically feasible before large-animal taxidermy. In the nineteenth century, its significance changed in relation to aesthetics, science, and politics. Aesthetics: A new standard of art was set by John James Audubon in the watercolor portraits of *The Birds of America* (1827–38). Audubon trained as a taxidermist, and his practice was to hunt, mount, and then paint birds; some of his birds "appear as if they have just escaped from the taxidermist's workshop."[63] Science: Ornithology became professionalized after midcentury (British Ornithological Union, founded 1858; American Ornithologists' Union, 1883). Live birds were studied with greater precision, and dead birds were understood anew; this was the era of the "discovery" of species extinction, with species like the auk becoming icons of mass death.[64] Politics: In addition to the politics of extinction, avian taxidermy relied on the politics of collection. Audubon aimed to catalog every North American bird, while colonial officers serving the British empire generated an "avian imperial archive."[65] Huge bird taxidermy collections—Lord Rothschild, at Tring, amassed more than three hundred thousand bird skins—enshrined this archive for museum viewing. Private households also exhibited taxidermied birds under glass domes in the parlor.[66]

Wells's story punctures the aesthetic and scientific value with which avian taxidermy was invested in this period; for his taxidermist, birds are a commodity to invent and sell. The taxidermist so scorns "amateur ornithologists" that he has them stuffed. Conversely, he praises himself as an ornithologist extraordinaire, inventing as well as identifying species; his best is "a masterpiece. . . . I made it out of the skeletons of a stork and a toucan and a job lot of feathers. Taxidermy of that kind is just pure joy, Bellows, to a real artist in the art" (24). The commercial impulse to create "brittle capital" repeats in the image of the "job lot of feathers," birds sold cheaply in bulk. The "real artist" is the con artist, profiting from taxidermy that crosses boundaries between fake and real animals and between mounting animals and stuffing humans.

The taxidermist offers the narrator one more account of taxidermy encroaching on the human: "He proceeded to tell me of how he concocted a most attractive mermaid, and how an itinerant preacher, who could not get an audience because of it, smashed it because it was idolatry. . . . But as the conversation of all the parties to this transaction . . . was uniformly unfit for publication, this cheerful incident must still remain unprinted" (24). The mermaid suggests the well-known story of P. T. Barnum's "Feejee Mermaid," a fraudulent specimen made of fish and monkey parts; the taxidermist's version of the mermaid sexualizes this hybrid—"a most attractive mermaid"—and mixes it with religion.[67] Bellows, the narrator, increases the titillation of the story by refusing to narrate it in full. Insisting the story remain "unprinted," he assumes the Barnumesque role of carnival barker, using the mermaid to lure the reader and to cement the story's bonds between men.

As the story concludes, Bellows resumes his narration in a more sober vein: "The reader unacquainted with the dark ways of the collector may perhaps be inclined to doubt my taxidermist, but so far as great auks' eggs, and the bogus stuffed birds are concerned, I find that he has the confirmation of distinguished ornithological writers. And the note about the New Zealand bird certainly appeared in a morning paper of unblemished reputation, for the

Taxidermist keeps a copy and has shown it to me" (24–25). After criticizing amateur ornithologists, the taxidermist now mocks "distinguished" professionals; their "confirmation" deepens his con. The final lines turn toward the circulation of stories to readers of the "morning paper"—and, in turn, to the readers of this story itself, which was first published in the *Pall Mall Gazette*. The movement is thematically and literally toward paper, its "unblemished reputation" suggesting a virginal female body kept, if not made, by, the taxidermist. "Triumphs of a Taxidermist" ends with paper on which words describe animal skins: taxidermy about taxidermy, or parchment on parchment.

The political attitudes of the story remain ambiguous. Wells reinforces the racist violence of "I skinned a nigger" by withholding any punishment for the taxidermist and, more important for the reader, any condemnation by a narrator. But the story also presents the taxidermist as greedy, obnoxious, and monomaniacal, with the form of the dramatic monologue enhancing the hyperbole of his voice. The story criticizes this taxidermist, and perhaps all taxidermy; at minimum, Wells pulls back the curtain on both the ostensible benevolence of the taxidermist and the realist illusions of taxidermist form. Haraway notes that the power of taxidermy in its realist natural history heyday lay "in its magical effects: what is so painfully constructed appears effortlessly, spontaneously found, discovered, simply there if one will only look."[68] This story takes away the magic, shows the staging of the spontaneity and the calculated misdirection of the look. In Wells's "Triumphs of a Taxidermist," turn-of-the-century taxidermy is politically a world of bigotry and formally a world of fakery.

And a world of fiction, not only because it is a short story but also because it focuses on the creation of counterfeits and forgeries: in this story, "the 'art' of the fiction writer is like that of the taxidermist. Each creates an illusion of a new reality."[69] Taxidermy leads to fiction-writing and is also founded on it: "Triumphs of a Taxidermist" depends for its effects on Wells's imagery, his characterizations, and his scripting of the taxidermist's near-monologue—that is, on literary techniques. This is literary taxidermy in several senses: taxidermy described as and through the techniques of fiction with an emphasis on the intertwining of animal skins and paper surfaces. More succinctly, if speculatively, this is fiction as taxidermy.

3.

A different version of literary taxidermy emerges in a genre that might seem less interested in the tools of fiction: the handbook. First, the author:

Before Carl Akeley, the most famous taxidermist in America was William T. Hornaday (1854–1937). He was the founding president of the Society of American Taxidermists, the longtime director of the Bronx Zoo, another Teddy Roosevelt associate, and also a zoologist, naturalist, hunter, and conservationist. These last two may seem like opposites—killing versus saving animals—but Hornaday, like Roosevelt, considered both hunting and taxidermy to be acts of conservation. Literally, taxidermy preserved vulnerable animal species; symbolically, it helped conserve a different species perceived to be under threat: white Anglo-Saxon manhood. Hornaday was uncomfortable with the flux of modern life and hostile to the influx of immigrants to America. His long career included an unusually direct expression of the political links between taxidermy and racism: in 1906, as director of the Bronx Zoo, he approved the exhibition of a living man named Ota Benga, an African "pygmy," in the Monkey House alongside an orangutan. Ota Benga killed himself in 1916.[70]

Hornaday was also a prolific author, and I focus here on his *Taxidermy and Zoological Collection: A Complete Handbook for the Amateur Taxidermist, Collector, Osteologist, Museum-Builder, Sportsman, and Traveller*. The *Handbook* was one of the best-known and best-selling taxidermy manuals (a robust genre in this period in England and America); first published in 1891, it was reprinted numerous times. It is a large volume, a how-to with altruistic goals: "This work is offered as my contribution to the science of zoology and the work of the museum-builder. . . . My only desire [is] that it may be the means of materially increasing the world's store of well-selected and well-preserved examples of the beautiful and interesting animal forms that now inhabit the earth and its waters" (vii).[71] These prefatory claims stand in stark contrast to Wells's portrait of the taxidermist as a corrupt huckster; Hornaday's taxidermist is sincere and selfless.

As in Wells's story, though, Hornaday presents the taxidermist as an all-powerful male creator and his taxidermy as a kind of inventive fiction. The *Handbook* features extensive discussion of what Hornaday considered his major innovation as a taxidermist: the use of interior structures on which animal skins were shaped and mounted, which he claimed to have invented and called "manikins."[72] Several chapters explain how to build manikins, which Hornaday presents as elaborate sculptural creations, made in multiple phases with wire, iron, wood, and twine and then the whole covered in clay: "When the manikin has been fully covered with clay from end of nose to tip of tail . . . you then have a complete clay statue of the animal" (149). The manikin precedes the taxidermic mount: "You can actually model the skin down upon the body, and it will not only take the exact form of the manikin—every depression and every elevation—but it will also *keep* it" (149). As his illustrations attest, manikins constitute distinct new forms in their own right.

Hornaday's manikins expose, even as they purport to perfect, the manufacture behind taxidermic realism. Here is his definition: "The term *manikin* is applied to the made-up figure of an animal over which a skin is to be adjusted, and made to counterfeit the actual form and size of a living animal" (140). The terms of the "counterfeit" and the "made-up" are not far from those of Wells's huckster; at minimum, this language suggests taxidermy as the artistic invention rather than the realist re-creation of animal forms.

The manikin also complicates the relation between surface and depth in taxidermy. Taxidermy draws attention to the animal's surface skin and fur. In so doing, it confirms how humans often see animals—negatively, as surfaces only, "lacking the substantiality found in the 'depth' of human interiority."[73] There are numerous ways to refute this lack: Ron Broglio, whom I just quoted, argues for revaluing the animal surface as "a site of productive engagement with the world of animals."[74] Hornaday's writing suggests another avenue, which is to recognize, in the case of taxidermy, how the reproduction of the surface often involved the production of depth. As his *Handbook* describes, Hornaday manufactures a new form of animal depth on which "every depression and every elevation" of the surface is then molded. At the same time, that new depth itself generates a new surface—a second skin, on the manikin itself, of clay. Hornaday's manikins celebrate, above all, the power of the taxidermist, showing "the absolute control the operator is able to exercise over the form of his subject from first to last" (141).

The literal control the taxidermist exercises over these materials is matched by the control of his literary persona: "There is supreme pleasure in crowning a well-made manikin with a handsome skin, and seeing a specimen take on perfect form and permanent beauty as if by magic. It is then that you begin to be proud of your work; and finally you revel in it. You say to yourself, '*This* is art!'—and so it is,—but let your work speak for itself" (149).[75] The taxidermist is a magician-ruler, taking "crowning" joy in crowning the manikin; he seems a still-reveling Prospero—or perhaps a happier Victor Frankenstein. The animal that results can "speak for itself," but it is equally Hornaday's literary voice that the *Handbook* constructs.

Throughout the *Handbook*, the taxidermist's art relies on paper. Manikins are "equally successful in the treatment of a thick-hided elephant and a small dog with a skin as thin as writing-paper" (141). Here skin is "as thin

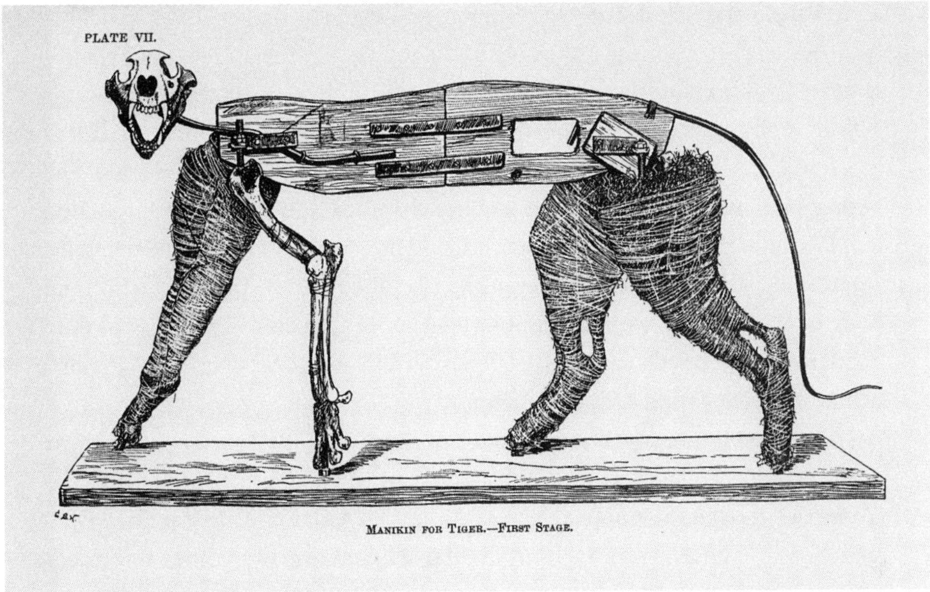

FIG. 14.

William T. Hornaday, "Manikin for Tiger—First Stage" and "Manikin for Tiger—Completed," from *Taxidermy and Zoological Collecting: A Complete Handbook for the Amateur Taxidermist, Collector, Osteologist, Museum-Builder, Sportsman, and Traveller*, 1893. Photo: James Gehrt.

as writing-paper," but elsewhere the simile drops out; skin is inextricable from actual paper, for the final layer of the manikin is the application of papier-mâché: "This material is absolutely indispensable in taxidermic work. . . . It is used in filling up holes, seams, and cracks, in modeling the mouth parts of specimens that have been mounted with the mouth open," and more (151). The best papier-mâché is made with paper pulp from "the Bureau of Engraving and Printing in Washington, from mutilated paper currency" (152). Paper with a particular kind of writing—the marks of money—is used for perfecting the body of a taxidermy mount. Complementing Wells's transformation of fake taxidermy into "brittle capital," the "counterfeit" of taxidermy comes, in part, from the recirculation of paper currency.

The most important link between taxidermy and "writing-paper" inheres in the parallel Hornaday establishes between the taxidermy mount and the *Handbook* itself. Other books on taxidermy, Hornaday declares, are bad constructions: "The average book on taxidermy contains four times too much 'padding,' and not one quarter enough practical information" (viii). Hornaday overtly eschews such "padding." For example, in a section on what food and clothing the naturalist should take into the field, he demurs: "These subjects I propose to leave entirely alone. They make excellent 'padding' for a work of this kind when there is a lack of really useful information with which to fill up; but every man feeds and clothes himself according to the dictates of his temperament, his purse, or his own sweet will" (4). The bad "padding" of other taxidermy books is supplanted by the useful interiors of Hornaday's own mounts and, now, of his own book. Hornaday's *Handbook* offers manual as manikin: literature as taxidermy.

I have been stressing the aesthetic dimensions of Hornaday's model of literary taxidermy, but as in Wells's story, these aesthetics embed relations of power. There is no equivalent here to the slur of Wells's fictional taxidermist—"I stuffed a nigger"—but Hornaday's real-life exhibition of Ota Benga is continuous with the racist hierarchies in the Wells story. A complementary alignment between animals and native peoples informs his first book, *Two Years in the Jungle: The Experiences of a Hunter and Naturalist in India, Ceylon, the Malay Peninsula and Borneo* (1886). Hornaday introduces this project as "a ceaseless warfare for specimens": "I had no other assistance than such as could be rendered by ignorant and maladroit native servants."[76] The "maladroit native servants" are both backdrop and complement to Hornaday's "warfare for specimens." The American naturalist reprises the British colonial project in India; here as elsewhere, we see "natural history as an aspect of imperial violence."[77]

Complementary relations of power also suffuse Hornaday's depictions of the practice of taxidermy, even without reference to other humans. Here is a characteristic passage: "Make a long, perpendicular slit in the skin behind each foreleg and in each flank. . . . Through these openings you can introduce your metal filling tools . . . and give the interior a complete overhauling. . . . Through these holes you command the entire body of the animal at every point, and now you must work out your own salvation" (133). Here, the "entire body" under the taxidermist's "command" seems not only that of the animal but also that of the body politic: the taxidermist "overhauling" the animal "interior" is metonymic with the Westerner penetrating a geographic interior of a non-Western country. So too does this language suggest the "overhauling" of a U.S. interior made uncertain by immigrants. The goal, in each case, is to "work out your own salvation," a phrase echoing St. Paul and thus sanctifying the taxidermist, though suggesting that salvation has not yet been accomplished. The project of "overhaul" is an incipient rather than a completed performance of power.

Male power—note the phrase "his temperament, his purse, or his own sweet will." As in Wells's story, the *Handbook* offers masculinity as the foundation of a taxidermic authority. The man who commandingly introduces his tools through the "slit[s]," "openings" and "holes" of the animal's body exercises a penetrative power that at once feminizes the animal, excludes human women, and usurps female reproductive power. Masculinity reigns, although that phrase "his own sweet will" also seems defensive, as if his wife keeps trying to tell him what to take in the field. Masculinity also seems a somewhat belated foundation for the naturalist's reproductive authority. For example, "The duty of a naturalist to his specimen begins when he levels his gun at it in the field. Do not shoot a specimen to pieces, or mutilate it beyond recognition by its own mother" (13). The gaze of the naturalist human is preceded by that of the animal mother; she constitutes an uneasy standard of "recognition" against which the human measures his destructive "duty."

Another female presence, this one human, shapes the *Handbook* more obliquely. As in Wells's "Triumphs of a Taxidermist," Hornaday features birds as a medium for the taxidermist's godlike skill. At the outset, he names birds as the inspiration for the ideal taxidermist—"He must be a man of tireless energy, incapable of going to bed so long as there are birds to be skinned" (3)—and he devotes four chapters to avian taxidermy. Mounting birds requires virtuous commitment: "Do not be discouraged if your first bird is a dead failure. . . . If you have a love for taxidermy, and the patience and perseverance to back it up, you are bound to succeed" (190).

However, Hornaday knows that there is a dystopian version of avian taxidermy, the dark shadow to his vision of "patience and perseverance." In the preface, he laments the "gulls, terns, herons, egrets, ibises, and spoonbills [that] are being slaughtered wholesale for the equally bloodthirsty goddess of Fashion" (vii). In his book *Our Vanishing Wild Life* (1913), he devotes a chapter to this outrage: "It is high time for the whole civilized world to know that many of the most beautiful and remarkable birds of the world are now being *exterminated* to furnish millinery ornaments for women's wear."[78] His target is women's hats made with dead birds, a fashion craze in this era, incorporating either bird feathers or taxidermied bird bodies. Widespread protest arose against the decimation of bird populations for these hats, which were termed "murderous millinery." The protests culminated in protectionist legislation at the turn of the century in America and in 1920 in England.[79]

Like other elements of the conservation movement, the critique of murderous millinery was often organized along lines of race and class. This is from the foreword to *Our Vanishing Wild Life*, by Henry Fairfield Osborn, then the president of the New York Zoological Society: "The people of all the New England States are poorer when the ignorant whites, foreigners, or negroes of our southern states destroy the robins and other song birds of the North."[80] The book itself includes a chapter entitled "Destruction of Song Birds by Southern Negroes and Poor Whites." The millinery trade was also associated with Jewish business owners, and its consumers were seen as vulgar strivers "attempt[ing] to cross class lines by aping the fashions of the debauched rich."[81] The preservation of avian species relied on, and further ratified, elite Northern white manhood.

Attacks on women were central to the campaign against murderous millinery. While women "wore taxidermied rodents, moles, foxes, insects, reptiles, monkeys and even cats," bird hats were the most visible of these, and popular culture vilified hat-wearing women.[82] So great was public interest in women wearing bird hats that "the new bird lovers often talked much more about women than birds."[83] The *New York Times* collapsed the distinction in an 1898 editorial attacking the trend: "'Feather-headed women', as indeed they are in more ways than one, is a term which might be used more frequently. . . . Surely they invite . . . such public stigma by exhibiting themselves as they do in the relics of murdered innocence."[84]

A full-page illustration by John Hyde from *Frank Leslie's Illustrated Weekly* (1883) traces the gender dynamics of such critiques. In the upper-left-hand corner, a male hunter shoots; in the upper right, a male taxidermist mounts the bird; in the lower left, a woman shopper, presumably with a husband who controls the purse strings, views taxidermied hats on display; and in the lower right, she poses with hat on head and fur-trimmed cloak. Tracing the political economy of the bird-hat trade, the illustration might potentially condemn the men who manufacture and profit from it, but as the last image suggests, it instead blames the female consumer. The title of the illustration, meanwhile, underscores other affinities between women and birds: "The Cruelties of Fashion—Fine Feathers Make Fine Birds" plays on the slang of women as sexually attractive "birds," an American as well as English idiom. "Birds of America" could be as much sexual catalog as Audubon taxonomy; in the campaign against murderous millinery, women were seen as symbolically feather-headed, sexually "fine birds."

In Hornaday's *Handbook*, the attack on women is implicit: birds killed for the female "bloodthirsty goddess of fashion" are murdered for women consumers. Hornaday himself supported woman's suffrage and was, in the assessment of a recent biographer, "a feminist by the standards of the day."[85] In Hornaday's *Handbook*, however, a different kind of gender politics is at work: a world in which women's relation to taxidermy is either absent or murderous, while the male taxidermist is the salvation of animal life, regenerating himself as well as animals through his art.

In both Wells and Hornaday, then, expressions of male violence against animals and persons converge with elaborate accounts of fictive creation. In their works, the literary and the taxidermic are not so much form (literature) taking on content (taxidermy) but intersecting modes of representation. Hornaday's emphasis on manikins provides another kind of bridge between taxidermy and literature. Like a novelist who creates characters with interiority, the taxidermist who builds "interior mechanisms" for animals manufactures depth. In turn, a novelist who creates interiors for his animal characters extends the process whereby the taxidermist builds his manikins. His, or hers: it is time to return to Marshall Saunders.

4.

Here is a moment in *Beautiful Joe* that I have not yet mentioned. It is a reminiscence told by an old dog named Jim to Beautiful Joe: "I often stop in the street and look up at fine ladies' bonnets, and wonder how they can wear little dead birds in such dreadful positions. Some of them have their heads twisted under their wings and over their shoulders, and looking toward their tails, and their eyes are so horrible that I wish I could take those ladies into the woods

FIG. 15.

John N. Hyde, *The Cruelties of Fashion*, from *Frank Leslie's Illustrated Newspaper*, 1883. Photo: Library of Congress, Washington, D.C.

and have them see how easy and pretty a live bird is, and how unlike the stuffed creatures they wear" (92). This is another critique of taxidermied bird hats, but it offers a different view of the issue from that provided by Hornaday or the *New York Times*.

In the campaign against "murderous millinery," women were political activists rather than just targets: for example, they founded Audubon Society chapters and inaugurated a campaign for bird-free hats called "audubonettes."[86] Their activism could take literary routes: another animal autobiography of the era, Virginia Sharpe Patterson's *Dickey Downy: The Autobiography of a Bird* (1899), includes a sustained critique of murderous millinery. The bird-protagonist of this novel recounts at length the following episode: "I saw six ladies' hats trimmed with dead birds. . . . How my heart sickened as I gazed at these pleasant, refined, soft-voiced women flaunting the trophies of their cruelty in the beautiful light. . . . Had they no compassion for the feathered mother who had been robbed of her young for the sake of a hat?"[87] As Annie Dwyer notes, Patterson's novel influenced legislation prohibiting illegal game; the introduction to *Dickey Downy* was written by the legislation's senate sponsor.[88]

Saunders was not active in such legislative campaigns, so far as I know; she did not join the Audubon Society until 1908.[89] But her novels constitute another form of avian activism, as Jim's anecdote in *Beautiful Joe* suggests. Her critique in *Beautiful Joe*, like Patterson's in *Dickey Downy*, is less about condemning "feathered-headed women" than about seeking to educate them: "I wish I could take those ladies into the woods and have them see how easy and pretty a live bird is, and how unlike the stuffed creatures they wear." The problem with women is not that they are permanently feather-headed but that they are temporarily ignorant.

She also introduces an intermediary—the animal narrator, in this case a double example of first-dog voice, since the speaker is Jim, who is speaking to Joe, who is speaking to us. The anecdote is part of Jim's story, a cautionary tale detailed in a chapter called "A Ruined Dog," which begins, "'I was a sporting dog,' he said, bitterly" (89). For his first three years, he was happy: "[My owner] used to hire me out to shooting parties. I was a favorite with all the gentlemen. I was crazy with delight when I saw the guns brought out" (89). But one day, drunken hunters shot at him: "I was never the same dog again. I was quite deaf in my right ear, and though I strove against it, I was so terribly afraid of even the sight of a gun that I would run and hide myself whenever one was shown to me" (91). Jim is still psychologically scarred: "I have a happy home here, and I love the Morris boys; but I often wish that I could keep from putting my tail between my legs and running home every time I hear the sound of a gun" (92). It is not only that Saunders redirects her critique of murderous millinery; it is also that she embeds it, through the voice of Jim, in a critique of murderous masculinity.

Jim's specific canine identity is important: he is a "bird dog," trained not "to bite the birds when he was bringing them back to any person who was shooting with him" (88). Nineteenth-century bird dogs could be several breeds—traditionally, retrievers, pointers, or spaniels—but they all functioned as extensions of the hunter's gun, trained to see birds only as corpses. Jim's testimony—"how easy and pretty a live bird is"—marks the possibility of a bird dog's conversion from retrieving dead birds to appreciating live ones, from avian predation to admiration; this conversion is notably feminized, as Jim becomes "a great pet with Mrs. Morris" (92). The chapter ends with an anecdote about Jim carrying a box of seeds home for the family's pet canary. Trained to carry the corpses of birds, his mouth now holds their food, redefining the "bird dog" as an ally between canine and avian species.

Saunders repeats her critique of avian taxidermy a few chapters later in a different character's voice. An adult human, Mrs. Wood, gives a long speech to the children at the Band of Mercy meeting about murderous millinery:

> All over America [birds] are hunted and killed. Five million birds must be caught every year for American women to wear in their hats and bonnets. Just think of it, girls. Isn't it dreadful? Five million innocent, hard-working, beautiful birds killed, that thoughtless girls and women may ornament themselves with their little dead bodies. . . .
>
> In Florida cruel men shoot the mother birds on their nests while they are rearing their young, because their plumage is prettiest at that time. The little ones cry pitifully, and starve to death. . . .
>
> I am sorry to tell you such painful things, but I think you ought to know them. You will soon be men and women. Do what you can to stop this horrid trade. . . . My last words to you are, "Protect the birds." (164–65)

Here a female human rather than a male dog is making the case: her target is initially "thoughtless girls and woman" who wear murderous millinery, then it shifts to "cruel men [who] shoot mother birds." This progression echoes but alters the circuitry of the "The Cruelties of Fashion" illustration; the final exhortation here is to both boys and girls—"soon . . . men and women"—to stop this trade. The attack on millinery gathers force from the preceding critique of avian taxidermy offered by Jim. "To bird-dog" as a verb has another meaning: to pursue something persistently. We might think of Saunders as bird-dogging the topic of avian taxidermy and, in so doing, challenging the pejorative equation between women and birds.

There is a longer tradition of women writers doggedly—bird-doggedly—challenging this equation. Here is a woman scientist who works with parrots: "You might think that an MIT- and Harvard-trained scientist working at various universities would be given a certain amount of deference, but as a woman working with a bird, I found it was sometimes the opposite."[90] Woman scientist with a bird: birdbrained. The scientist, recognizing this equation, perseveres. Here is another example, a theorist whose laughing-Medusa essay remains a hallmark of "French feminism": "Birds, writing and many women are considered abominable, threatening, and are *rejected*, because others, the rejectors, feel something is taken away from them."[91] The theorist rejects this rejection, as do others. The pejorative equation between female and bird brains is so irrelevant that it does not even arise in a memoir by a woman training a very tough bird; in this account, "H" stands for hawk, but "hawk" does not so much stand in for the writer's brain as perch metonymically on her writing hand.[92]

Another strain of avian imagery protests the caging of birds, in a critique of racial as well as gender norms. Maya Angelou, entitling her 1969 memoir *I Know Why the Caged Bird Sings*, was quoting Paul Laurence Dunbar, whose poem "Sympathy" (1898) ends with this same line.[93] And here is another example from the same year as Dunbar: "A green and yellow parrot, which hung in a cage outside the door, kept repeating over and over: 'Allez-vous-en! Allez-vous-en!'" This is the opening of Kate Chopin's novel *The Awakening* (1898), now a feminist classic, then a scandalous account of a married woman having affairs and ultimately drowning herself. The opening image signals that she is a caged bird; the parrot's words—*allez-vous-en*, "go away"—suggest the woman's own imminent refusal of her world. This uncaging and refusing does not end well, as a bird image in the seaside suicide scene confirms: "A bird with a broken wing was beating the air above, reeling, fluttering, circling disabled down, down to the water."[94] This is the "feather-headed woman" remounted—the bird-woman as a foundation for a fictional treatment of feminism.

Beautiful Joe is not *The Awakening*, but it too offers a resistant perspective on the alignment of women with birds. More specifically, it rejects an alignment between women and taxidermied birds and instead promotes, via reformed bird dogs, a vision of women as political reformers. The taxidermist himself is not directly assailed, as he will be, for example, in Willa Cather's *A Lost Lady* (1923), where a bullying young man, equipped with sharp tools obtained from "a taxidermy outfit from the *Youth's Companion*," captures a live woodpecker and deliberately slices its eyes; he names the bird "Miss Female."[95] Saunders deplored taxidermy, but *Beautiful Joe* does something different with the role of the taxidermist. The novel as a whole implicitly takes on the power of this role for Saunders herself.

It is time—past time—to discuss the woman taxidermist. She appears often in the contemporary taxidermy art world: I have already named the artists Diane Fox, Nina Katchadourian, Emily Mayer, Polly Morgan, Angela Singer, and Bryndís Snæbjörnsdóttir. Half the taxidermists included in a contemporary anthology are women; in some taxidermy classes, instructors and almost all students are women.[96] It is unclear "why everyone and their mother seems to be into mounting animal carcasses lately." This is a query from an article called "Meet the Lady Taxidermy Artists of Brooklyn"—a title that sounds like a carnival barker's invitation, with the lady taxidermist presented as a new form of freak.[97]

But if "it seems ironic that it has been young, female artists who have so wholeheartedly embraced the current turn toward taxidermy," the irony is not, historically, complete.[98] The history of taxidermy does include some women. In nineteenth-century Britain and America, domestic manuals encouraged middle-class women to take up taxidermy, especially of birds and insects, as a decorative art and domestic craft.[99] And some women were taxidermists in the outdoorsy vein. A taxidermist named Martha Maxwell hunted her own specimens; worked with large mammals; opened her own Rocky Mountain Museum of taxidermy in Boulder, Colorado; and exhibited her specimens at the 1876 Centennial Exhibition in Philadelphia. Her biography intertwines with that of feminist reform movements—she was educated at coed institutions, wore bloomers, and supported suffrage—as well as with American women writers; Julia Ward Howe wrote, "I consider this lady collector a marvel."[100] Maxwell's taxidermy career suggests the particular flexibility the American West afforded some white women in this era for conventionally masculine activities. A photograph of Maxwell shows her sitting next to a table of animals she has mounted, brush in one hand and gun propped up along the table's side; the caption "in the work room" positions her outside of domesticity, as a hunter and taxidermist. Maxwell has now been recovered as "the patron saint of the Rogue Taxidermy movement."[101]

Unlike Martha Maxwell, Marshall Saunders was not a producer of taxidermy, nor did she consume it. She embraced live animals: a profile of her

FIG. 16. *Martha Maxwell, In the Workroom*, ca. 1876. Photo: Library of Congress, Washington, D.C.

in the *Toronto Star* was entitled "Pigeon on Her Head When Author Talked; Miss Marshall Saunders, Friend of Birds, Etc., Celebrates 70th Birthday."[102] I have found only one instance in which she did not respond to taxidermy with repulsion: in a diary entry about an acquaintance who "[has] a fine collection of stuffed birds—nearly two hundred," she states, "Usually I hate to look at stuffed birds but these are so life like—he has so cleverly preserved natural attitudes that there is nothing unpleasant abt. seeing them."[103] Here, "life like" and "natural attitudes" trump her habitual "hate," the exception proving her antitaxidermy rule.

Rather, Saunders's interest was in the literary register of taxidermy. I have emphasized her differences from Wells and Hornaday, but in the construction of the taxidermist as artist, she has affinities with them. "Taxidermy," says Wells's narrator, "is just pure joy . . . to a real artist in the art." Or Hornaday:

"You say to yourself, '*This* is art!'—and so it is,—but let your work speak for itself." Like Wells and Hornaday, Saunders moves into the realm of artistic making, constructing as well as reproducing animal forms. The novel rejects the violence against animals endemic to taxidermy but adopts its posture of art-making and its enlivening of animal forms.

In this context, the signature formal trait of *Beautiful Joe*—its impossible animal narrator—suggests a version of literary taxidermy taken to its logical conclusion. Rather than just offering a taxidermy specimen that "speak[s] for itself," Saunders provides an entire novelistic world of animals speaking. Taxidermy seems the complement of first-dog voice, both its inversion and its extension. Inversion: The animal novel written in first-person voice animates the animal from the inside out, while taxidermy revivifies the animal from the outside in. The novel in first-dog voice invents the animal interior, while the taxidermy dog remounts the animal exterior. Extension: As Hornaday's *Handbook* shows, taxidermy concerns itself with invented interiors too, particularly in the form of the manikin. The verbal interiors of first-dog voice emulate and expand the invented interiors of taxidermy.

It is not just that taxidermy appears in passing in *Beautiful Joe* as a plot point and object of political critique; it is that the novel as a whole, with its animals speaking in first-dog voice, is a sustained act of literary taxidermy. The animal is the object—both surface skin and interior manikin—on, through, and with which the novel is written.

5.

Thinking about taxidermy, I have moved from dogs to birds, with bird dogs providing a hinge between them. H. G. Wells and William Hornaday, both chroniclers of avian taxidermy, are already strange enough company for Marshall Saunders, but someone even stranger has been on my mind: Alfred Hitchcock. The most famous cinematic images of avian taxidermy are in *Psycho* (1960), where Norman Bates's comment to Marion Crane, "You eat like a bird," echoes the stuffed birds on the walls of his overstuffed parlor, who loom over and next to him, cast shadows, and fill the frame. They become food for conversation in his dinner with Marion, when Norman says to her, "My hobby is stuffing things. You know—taxidermy. I guess I'd just rather stuff birds because I hate the look of beasts when they're stuffed. . . . Some people even stuff dogs and cats, but I can't do that. I think only birds look well stuffed because they're kind of passive to begin with." Norman favors birds because

FIG. 17.
Parlor taxidermy in *Psycho*, dir. Alfred Hitchcock, 1960.

of their passivity—or rather, the passivity he imposes on them: birds are not "passive to begin with."[104]

Nor are the women for whom they stand. The violence that Norman effects on birds is what he has already imposed on his mother—whom he calls "as harmless as one of those stuffed birds"—and will soon impose on Marion, stabbing her until her body has the stillness of a taxidermy specimen. His avian taxidermy is a preemptive solution to the prospect that human women might harm him; throughout the film, "the equation between women and 'stuffed birds' is clear."[105] The stuffed birds of the film provide a vocabulary for its murdered female bodies and also an idiom for its titular insanity: Norman goes cuckoo and parrots his mother.

And there is another possible metaphoric equation here: the taxidermist as movie director. Asked by François Truffaut about the "stuffed birds," Hitchcock responded, "I was quite intrigued with them: they were like symbols. . . . [Norman] knows the birds and he knows that they're watching him all the time. He can see his own guilt reflected in their knowing eyes."[106] The taxidermied birds, "like symbols," are omnipotent watchers within the film, but its most powerful voyeur, with the most "knowing eyes," is Hitchcock. This connection twins the male voyeur—character and director—with the feminized body, complementing the argument of Tania Modleski, in what remains my favorite book about Hitchcock, that his films betray "men's fascination and identification with the feminine."[107] In *Psycho*, birds are at once antonym and manikin to masculinity, and taxidermy is both a parlor trick of the mise-en-scène and a metaphor for the skin of the film itself.

There are other avenues for exploring taxidermy in Hitchcock: for example, the scene set in a London taxidermist's shop in the 1956 remake of *The*

Man Who Knew Too Much; Hitchcock was very keen on this setting, specifying that "obscene eviscerations are in progress" there.[108] The setting is a digression caused by an error: Jimmy Stewart, searching for his kidnapped son, visits the shop because he mistakenly thinks that the words "Ambrose Chapel" signify a person and not a place, the actual chapel where his son is being held. But the choice of taxidermy for this digression matters: the trickery of taxidermy, wherein dead animals seem alive, provides a visual analogue for the misleading homophone that sets the scene in motion. And the error guides the film as a whole: we could see the taxidermy shop as a microcosm—a profane chapel—for Hitchcock's own "obscene eviscerations" of the psyche throughout.

But I will leash the taxidermy birds of *Psycho* to the avian world of *The Birds* (1963). This film does not seem, at the outset, to take up dead animals; actually, it begins with two live dogs. In San Francisco, Hitchcock appears, escorting his own white terriers out of a pet shop; this is the shop into which Melanie Daniels (Tippi Hedren) will enter and where she and Mitch Brenner (Rod Taylor) will engage in a prolonged flirtation over "lovebirds" in cages, one of whom is metaphorically Melanie, an unhappy rich girl ("Back in your gilded cage, Melanie Daniels," says Mitch). The director is shown removing his dogs from the world of birds in cages, "as if he has liberated the two terriers."[109] These are only two of many dogs saturating the Hitchcock canon: "There is an opening for a scholarly paper on the subject of Hitchcock and dogs."[110] Eventually, someone else slips through the opening, arguing that "dogs offered [Hitchcock] strategic dramaturgical possibilities for establishing action and relationships that could not be shown otherwise."[111] I will stay here with *The Birds* and note only that the film opens by leashing birds to dogs, women, and Hitchcock himself.

Once they appear, the birds of *The Birds* both evoke and alter taxidermy. To generate the attack sequences, Hitchcock famously combined live birds with animatronic ones, such technologies inheriting the realist mantle for which taxidermy was once the state of the art. The birds of *The Birds* are like taxidermy specimens moved from stillness to frenzy, gone wild—rewilded. Like the stuffed owl in *Psycho*, they watch and know; they have the "bird's-eye" view, the omniscient overhead shot of cinema. Think of the famous sequence in which Tippi Hedren sits obliviously on a bench outside a school as birds mass behind her on the jungle gym; for a moment, the birds perch on the metal grid like taxidermied specimens imprisoned in a natural history display. Then they take flight, attacking the schoolchildren and their schoolteacher; they make a prison break and wreak murderous havoc. The viciousness of this film's birds is infamously irrational: in a scene of nonexplanation, a British

FIG. 18.
Birds in playground in *The Birds*, dir. Alfred Hitchcock, 1963.

woman ornithologist explains that birds of different species will neither flock together nor attack without motivation. If we interpret them as the extension of the taxidermy birds of *Psycho*, though, their actions are not unmotivated: their attacks reverse the taxidermist's violence against them.

These attacks are linked, as in *Psycho*, to women. The birds have been interpreted as the embodiment of maternal rage, "extensions of Lydia's hysterical fear of losing her son"; they have been seen as versions of Melanie, herself a kind of "avian female."[112] Certainly, the birds threaten women on-screen, as they horribly did on set. In Tippi Hedren's memoir, she recounts how she was attacked by live birds during the filming of the bird scenes. For the attic scene, "I heard Hitchcock yell 'Action!' and right on cue, the handlers began hurling those live birds at me. It was brutal and ugly and relentless. . . . I just kept saying to myself over and over again, 'I won't let him break me. I won't let him break me.'"[113] Throughout the production, Hitchcock harassed Hedren. Here the live birds metaphorically embody the "action"—"brutal and ugly and relentless"—of male sexual assault, which Hedren, unbroken, resisted.

If we see these birds as emblems of avian taxidermy, then they also avenge the violations of the male taxidermist—and, perhaps, of the female consumer of dead animals. Remember the opulent mink coat Melanie wears when she first visits Bodega Bay, the coat she is wearing when gulls first swoop down to attack her in a boat. In any case, the threat posed by the birds—as symbolic women, perhaps to actual women—does not resolve: at the end, thousands of birds fill the frame while Tippi Hedren makes an escape that seems only temporary. The birds are quite still in this moment—the frozen pose again evokes taxidermy—but they seem massed for large-scale battle. Angry birds: avian taxidermy, seeking apocalyptic revenge.

I realize that Hitchcock seems to have erupted into this discussion out of nowhere, but he was here already. In the film *White Dog*, the actress-protagonist has a Hitchcock poster on the wall of her Los Angeles home, and as if that allusion were not direct enough, when she visits her dog-injured friend in the hospital, she brings the book-length interview with the director, indispensable for any cinephile—I have already quoted from it—known as *Hitchcock/Truffaut*. The white German shepherd of Samuel Fuller's movie seems a different animal from Hitchcock's own beloved terriers, but not really; Fuller was a big Hitchcock fan.

It is harder to hitch Hitchcock to Saunders, but I will give it a try. I have suggested that Hitchcock pursues avian taxidermy as an ambiguous mark of male violence and as the source of angry-bird revenge. This dual use of avian taxidermy can also be found, I suggest, in another of Saunders's books: *My Pets: Real Happenings in My Aviary* (1908), from which I have already quoted the anecdote of Billy, the fox terrier who loved to be photographed. *My Pets* is an animal biography about Saunders's large home aviary; such aviaries were not uncommon then.[114] It contains chapters on her owls, robins, mockingbirds, pigeons, hawks, canaries, cardinals, sparrows, swallows, hummingbirds, and finches.

Avian biography has its own lineage, anchored in Audubon's essays on the histories and habits of the birds he painted. The essays of his *Ornithological Biography* create "a framework in which birds, like humans, [are] granted the special form of subjectivity that relies on a communicable interiority."[115] The words of an Audubon essay provide avian "interiority"; Audubon's history as a taxidermist provides another framework for thinking about the connections between avian insides and outsides. Although Audubon's taxidermy predated the interior manikins of Hornaday, his mounts also provided a form of interior for the bird. To put it another way, Audubon's avian essays, giving body to the flat surfaces of his watercolors, offer another variant of literary taxidermy.

Sometimes Audubon's avian biographies explored the animal interior by invoking specific humans, as in his comparison of the bald eagle to George Washington: "[Washington] was brave, so is the eagle; like it, too, he was the terror of his foes; and his fame . . . resembles the majestic soarings of the mightiest of the feathered tribe."[116] This is as much Manifest Destiny as manifest interiority—not that the two are mutually exclusive. Like Audubon's *Ornithological Biography*, *My Pets* mixes interior and exterior, human and avian: "Whenever a new bird enters an aviary, he has to find his place—he is just like a new-comer in a community of human beings" (35).[117] *My Pets* also offers, inter alia, the reverse: human memoir bird-ized, female autobiography via avian biography.

All of this is anchored—I am anchoring it—with the imagery of avian taxidermy. Like *Beautiful Joe*, *My Pets* has an overtly negative relation to avian taxidermy. The book includes the same critique of murderous millinery given twice in *Beautiful Joe*, this time in a nonfiction context. Early in the memoir, Saunders describes a beloved owl of her childhood named Betsy, who died after eating a fish head. "When her soft, gray body became cold, I held her in my hand close to the fire and, with tears in my eyes, wished for a miracle to restore her to health" (28). Saunders's own mother steps in to comfort her daughter: "It was impossible for me to conceal my emotion, and my mother . . . generously took the little feathered creature to a taxidermist" (28). But the result horrifies Saunders:

> Betsy was the first and last bird I shall ever have stuffed. I daresay that man did the work as well as it could be done, but I gazed in dismay at my Betsy when she came home. That stiff little creature sitting on a stick, with glazed eyes and motionless body, could not be the pretty little bird whose every motion was grace. Ever since the day of Betsy's death, I can feel no admiration for a dead bird. Indeed, I turn sometimes with a shudder from the agonized postures, the horrible eyes of birds in my sister women's hats—and yet I used to wear them myself. My present conviction shows what education will do. If you like and study live birds, you won't want to wear dead ones. (28–29)

This is a more explicit critique than in *Beautiful Joe*: Saunders represents taxidermy more overtly as a violation, making birds "glazed," "agonized," and "horrible"; she offers a more directly gendered scenario in which male taxidermist violates female birds; and she condemns more clearly—but also with more explicit sympathy—the "sister women" who wear taxidermy birds as fashion.

Also notable: The taxidermy critique is here part of a memory of mothers and daughters. Saunders's mother honors her daughter's grief by taking the bird to the taxidermist for revivification. The Betsy project fails, but in a literary sense, it succeeds, for *My Pets* constitutes another project of literary taxidermy. As a biographer, Saunders can revive birds in writing as she, her mother, and the taxidermist could not in life.

She can also remount the story of herself: this narrative about revivified birds is also, indirectly, one of female independence. The memoir begins in

1899, when Saunders is "studying boy life"—presumably, teaching—"in the charming Belmont School, twenty-five miles from San Francisco" (11), a place within the orbit of the Bodega Bay of Hitchcock's *The Birds* but far more benign, bird-wise. This is where she acquires four owls, "motherless balls of down" (12); she moves into a cottage in Berkeley with her sister Rida; she has a carpenter build them an aviary. She also acquires, temporarily, "One Sierra collie dog, Teddy Roosevelt by name, in whose upbringing I was assisting, [who] used to tremble as he stared at [the birds], partly from jealousy, partly because he recognized lawful prey in them" (13). This is all in the opening chapter, which depicts California as a zone of freedom, in which women attend university, teach, and raise dogs and birds. The aviary is a domain over which Saunders has symbolic power, while the household of sisters is one in which she is master of a dog president. Teddy bear patriarchy becomes matriarchy, women ruling topsy-turvy over Teddy Roosevelt.

After she returns to Halifax to live with her family, however, this zone constricts. There Saunders has a "basement aviary . . . just under my study and my father's" (43). When a visiting child says, "'You must feel as if you were in heaven, Miss Saunders, when you get into this basement with all your animals.' In some embarrassment I replied that I did not consider the basement of my father's house an ideal place. Some day I hoped to have a better home for my birds" (88). This sounds potentially gothic—the daughter underground, immured in "the basement of my father's house." The underground space seems "not ideal" for either Saunders or her birds. Elsewhere in *My Pets*, Saunders concedes, "I probably project a little too much of my own personality onto bird bodies, but by dint of drinking and eating, sleeping, playing, and passing day after day with bird companions, I feel myself enabled to interpret some of their bodily and facial expressions, and I can surely and safely say that the uncaged bird is a happy bird" (215). In her father's basement, Saunders seems herself to be at risk of becoming a caged bird.

But there is an escape. Saunders has an elaborate extension built to the aviary in her family's Halifax house in 1903, with an internal route through which birds can fly from basement to roof: "At present I have no birds in cages. All are free. In the basement aviary they have fifteen feet by thirty-two of space. From it they enter the elevator that is twenty feet high and ascend to the roof-veranda and sunroom" (199). Saunders offers the aviary as an architectural way out for birds to ascend to a roof-veranda: a sunny state, perhaps a version of California. The aviary is the antithesis to taxidermy, an escape from confinement for birds—and perhaps for Saunders herself. The memoir ends with her praising "our little brothers and sisters of the air, that have a right to exist and to lead their own lives" (283), a right that applies, implicitly, to Saunders herself. By the end of the memoir, both birds and women are uncaged and happy, flying free.

I have offered a liberatory trajectory for this narrative of literary taxidermy, but I am overstating the case. An aviary is not necessarily freedom; an aviary is a bigger cage. In a diary entry, Saunders wrote, "My birds are not socialists. . . . There is always a boss."[118] The birds are still, as she says, "my pets"; she is their boss and owner. Saunders's aviary allows its inhabitants to fly more freely, but they still cannot fly away. Her suggested titles for the volume, before the publisher settled on *My Pets* included *Captive Birds*, *Birds and Their Friends in Captivity*, and *Jail-Birds!*[119]

Also, I am leaving something out from *My Pets*. Remember my preliminary proposition that literary taxidermy is connected to questions of race; I have tracked this proposition through Wells and Hornaday. *My Pets*, like other bird biographies, is ostensibly apolitical, but references to racial and national difference suffuse Saunders's narrative. Some are images of people of color: "I was in the habit of renewing the trees in my aviary every few months by burning old ones and getting some of the colored people about Halifax to bring in fresh ones from the country" (216–17). The "colored people about Halifax," like the trees, are represented here as a renewable natural resource for the aviary, and themselves a source of birds: "I one day expressed a wish to have some bluejays in the presence of a bird-fancier, and shortly afterward he arrived with a pair that he had bought from a woman near Halifax, in one of the colored settlements composed of descendants of Southern Negroes" (253). Remember Saunders's account of Ellen, who was "like a Southern mammy"; here the "descendants of Southern Negroes" supply birds and trees.

And there is another kind to racialized language in *My Pets*. The sunroom passage continues, "Better than cages, better than aviaries is the broad blue sky, and the boundless fields; but of course, one cannot release delicate foreigners in our Northern climate" (199). The language is ostensibly apolitical, "foreigners" not intentionally implying immigration or race. Similar references saturate the book: of her Japanese robin, for example, Saunders remarks, "I was intensely interested in this foreigner that never for an instant lost his foreign look, his foreign ways, and yet who seemed more at home than any native bird in my aviary" (276–77). It is hard not to see political connotations in this account of the "foreign look." This is Saunders's assessment of sparrows: "Poor little brown immigrants, how many enemies and how few friends they have . . . they always remind me of true Anglo-Saxon stock. They protect the family, they fight all strangers, and 'Colonize, colonize,' is their motto" (239). The language comes close to naming "little brown immigrants," then swerves contrarily to its opposite, the colonizing "true Anglo-Saxon stock." The actual history of African Americans who migrated north to Canada—"colored settlements composed of descendants of Southern Negroes"—abuts the ornithological metaphors of "captives" and "brown immigrants." The bird metaphors do not merge with these human histories, but they do not remain entirely separate from them. The language of immigration and foreignness seems to be hiding in plain sight; that plain sight—that is, the apparent distance of bird biography from human politics—may be what enables the hiding.

And sometimes the literal and metaphoric become ensnared. Here is Saunders's account of finches "brought to America from Africa, Asia, and Australia":

> Many of these finches are bred in captivity, but in most cases they are wild, and are caught by natives with more or less cruelty. . . . They drop into blankets spread by the cunning Negroes and are given to captains of vessels in exchange for mock jewelry or rum.
>
> . . . The voyage is long, and overcrowding and disease do their work. The wonder is that any survive. Fancy the contrast between the splendors of the African forest and the horrors of this crowded ship!
>
> Upon arriving in America the bird-dealers take the tiny captives in hand, open their filthy cages, put them in clean ones, and exhibit them in their windows.
>
> . . . Of course, the birds in most cases die, but the Negro goes on getting his rum, the captain gets his money, and the dealer makes a living. (268–69)

This is an account of a slave trade that literally describes birds, but metaphorically describes people, particularly in its language of the Middle Passage ("The voyage is long, and overcrowding and disease do their work. The wonder is that any survive"). The metaphors replace humans with birds, who are the sympathetic sufferers of the journey. The focus on the exhibition of "captives" in America also displaces the racist display of the human other—akin to that of Ota Benga, whose presence in the Bronx Zoo was approved by Hornaday.

Meanwhile, the overt references to black people in this passage are pejorative: slavetraders are "cunning Negroes," and the cycle continues because "the

Negro gets his rum." The passage not only displaces human onto avian enslavement but also makes "Negroes" into villains. The memoir's overtly declared human projections onto birds combine with covert projections about humans. Saunders's avian biographies create a metaphoric skin—as thin and as thick as paper—through which are made visible human relations of power as well as literary questions of form.

6.

"The ideal viewer completes the imaginary act of resurrection that taxidermy invites": I am not anyone's "ideal viewer," but I too respond to taxidermy's invitation to resurrection.[120] Tring, in particular, leaves its mark; I remain on the lookout for taxidermy. Visiting England again, I persuade friends to accompany me to the Booth Museum of Natural History in Brighton. Like Tring but on a smaller scale, the Booth Museum is another taxidermy project built by a Victorian obsessive, in this case the naturalist Edwin Booth, "a fanatical ornithologist, determined to source a specimen of every British bird."[121] Opened in 1874, it features over three hundred display cases filled with taxidermy birds posed in small habitat dioramas within rectangular cases built all along the walls and layered on top of each other. These displays remain unchanged, as Booth stipulated when he left the collection to the city; newer, supplementary exhibitions include a re-created Victorian parlor with taxidermied birds under glass domes and a glass vitrine holding Booth's boots and guns. This is the natural history, sportsman-conservator model of taxidermy, an English-eccentric version; it is the world of men, birds, and bird dogs. These dogs are not in evidence here, though apparently they are in Booth's diaries, where he recorded the names of his dogs but not his wife.[122]

Learning this last detail makes me think of Jim, the reformed bird dog of *Beautiful Joe*, lamenting his participation in the hunting process that leads to taxidermy hats. It also makes me think of my own dog, Frankie. The golden retriever as a breed was invented in England in the late nineteenth century by one Lord Tweedmouth; it was bred as another bird dog to retrieve the master's hunted game.[123] Frankie has never hunted, though he enjoys coming upon dead animals, and happily picks them up, holds them in his strong jaws, and runs to me with their heads and tails dangling from his mouth. He cannot help this, his own version of bird-dogging; he—his ancestors—was bred for this purpose.

I, on the other hand, can help it: liking taxidermy, that is—even though it is a world of weaponized dogs and hunters' guns as well as dead animals

FIG. 19.

Candida Lacey, *Booth Museum of Natural History, Brighton.* Used by permission of Candida Lacey.

on display. I cannot redeem this world, nor do places like the Booth Museum invite me to try. In its rectangular grid of cells, each frozen in Victorian time as the taxidermy froze the birds stuffed within them, the museum resembles nothing so much as a large bird prison. It is hard even to see into some of the displays, so dominated are they by the structure of the grids and the glare of the glass in them. The glass, the grids, the guns: all seem evidence for the political horrors of the birds incarcerated within and of the medium itself.

And yet still I look, bird-doggedly, at the mounted animals, and still I smile—neither feather-headed nor birdbrained—at taxidermy's insurmountable wonders.

CHAPTER 4

Mounting and Mourning

1.

In the years when Frankie is being treated for cancer, he and I disappear into the world of the Tufts animal hospital at least once every three months for all-day checkups, complete with ultrasounds and X-rays. Many of the people in the waiting room have driven long distances to get there, and they exude goodwill and camaraderie; the place is far friendlier than any human hospital I know. The canine oncologists are expert, but it is their kindness that undoes me, as does that of Frankie's wonderful local veterinarian, who discusses each option carefully with me and cheers him along every step of the way. At my vet's office and at Tufts, the staff are mostly women; noncoincidentally, Tufts is the only hospital I know where the staff say "I love you" to the patients. After each of Frankie's visits, I receive a detailed written report, which ends with something wildly at odds with the clinical tone of the medical narrative: for example, that Frankie "is a wonderful dog and always a pleasure to work with."[1] Even if they write this about every dog, even if it is meant to sweeten the pill of the bill, it still pulls me in.

As does the institution, the animal hospital built on the grounds of an insane asylum—Grafton State Hospital, the "farm colony" for the nearby Worcester Lunatic Hospital. Tufts has three freestanding hospitals, one each for small animals, large animals, and "exotics"; the small-animal hospital alone serves more than twenty-six thousand animals each year.[2] It is an animal wonderland, into which I easily tumble. For example, the sign at the entrance road has four listings, each with a directional arrow: "Client Parking / Dogs & Cats / Staff Parking / Horses." Although the sign is intended for humans, it looks to me as though it is meant for members of all four groups to read—the

"Dogs & Cats" nosing their vehicles to one lot, the horses self-propelling their horsepower to the other.

Still, the mood is serious, it is tiring to go there, and I see terrible things. One day, a couple rushes into the ER cradling a small, still dog, and shortly thereafter they are sitting outside, crying, with a vet; I overhear the word "cremation." The bleakness of such moments reminds me of one of my favorite works of contemporary fiction, a short story about a mother grappling with her baby's cancer: "'I've never heard of a baby having chemo,' the Mother says. *Baby* and *Chemo*, she thinks: they should never even appear in the same sentence together, let alone the same life."[3] I admire this story's mix of pathos and humor, as well as its self-reflexive shrewdness about turning suffering into art: "'A little light chemo. Don't you like that one?' says the Mother. '*Eine kleine* dactinomycin. I'd like to see Mozart write that one up for a big wad o' cash.'"[4] "The Mother" is the creation of the author, Lorrie Moore; she got a big wad o' well-deserved acclaim, maybe even some cash, for this short story, which appeared in the *New Yorker* and then in her collection *Birds of America*—this title presumably riffing on Audubon, another reworking of the bird-woman analogy. I have read this story so many times that I occasionally hear the narrator's wry voice in my head—for example, when "Frankie" and "chemo" seem like two words that should never even appear in the same sentence together.

But I hesitate to say more about Moore, because my reference to her story implicitly positions Frankie as a baby, an analogy about which I mean to be vigilant. Ethnographies of human-dog interactions confirm that "the owner's communicative behavior displays distinct characteristics much like those used in interactions with a child."[5] These characteristics seem distinctly embarrassing, particularly when the owners are women. An animal surgeon at Angell Animal Medical Center in Boston voices the risk: "These days the majority of my clients implore me to understand that their pet *is* their child. One woman even spawned a disturbing image that I consider both her Labradors as physically coming from her womb!"[6] The male surgeon is appalled by the female client whose disturbed mind, womb-like, has "spawned" monster-dogs; to him, she is herself a kind of monster—a female grotesque. I do not share this woman's thinking, but I also do not feel as strong a need to condemn it; I have spent a lot of time with monster stories. More troubling to me is how Frankie's treatment participates in the gigantic industry of dog goods and services. I often enjoy this industry, particularly its cultural wing—for example, I happily subscribe to *Bark*, the "dog culture magazine"—but I am acutely aware of its inequities and excesses, which are data for the field of "critical pet studies."[7] These excesses are now exemplified, for me, in the fantastic expenses of Frankie's medical care. I am, though, so grateful for this care. It has—people have—saved Frankie's life.

I am trying to live with Frankie's cancer—with the relief of sending it into remission and then with the fear following its return. I see a related labor at work in *Topsy: The Story of a Golden-Haired Chow* (1940) by Marie Bonaparte—French writer, Poe scholar, princess, psychoanalyst, analysand, and ally of Sigmund Freud; she helped him flee Nazi Vienna for London. She wrote a memoir about her dog after she—the dog, Topsy—had been treated for oral cancer. *Topsy* is a series of vignettes divided into two sections, "Topsy Is Ill" and "Topsy Is Healed." You would think that the vignettes of "Topsy Is Healed" would be joyful, and they do open with a happy scene, in which Bonaparte takes the dog to the Mediterranean coast to run "by the sea, inhaling the wind and the storm," saying, "Topsy . . . I am prouder to have almost magically prolonged your little life, than if I had written the *Iliad*" (123).[8] But this Homeric kvelling gives way to grimmer thoughts: "Topsy is probably cured, and will never know, in her new-born joy of living, that she touched, last spring, the frontiers of death. For Topsy does not know that there is a country where she and I will go one day, whence no one returns, and that is darker than the darkest of nights" (135). The dog's successful treatment leads to the dark "frontiers of death."

This is an odd way to describe recovery, but I understand why Bonaparte, having started to mourn, finds it difficult to stop: she is now in a forward-looking mode, anticipating future losses. These are both human and canine: "Topsy, should I die before you, my image, an uncertain phantom, will haunt you when you sleep . . . if I were dead, sometimes in a dream you would think you saw me again" (155). This passage finds a dead Bonaparte coming back to life in the dreams of her dog, a gothic image that reminds me of Mary Shelley's introduction to *Frankenstein*, in which Shelley claimed to have envisioned the monster initially in a dream: "I saw the hideous phantasm of a man stretched out, and then, on the working of some powerful engine, show signs of life, and stir with an uneasy, half vital motion."[9] The reminder also marks a contrast: Shelley dreams of a nonhuman, while Bonaparte imagines a nonhuman dreaming of her.

Still, Bonaparte and Shelley converge not only through the nonhuman but also through mourning. *Frankenstein* is, as a feminist critic first showed, a personal meditation on mourning; several of Mary Shelley's children were stillborn or died in infancy, and she wrote in her journal, "Dream that my little baby came to life again, that it had only been cold, and that we rubbed it before the fire, and it lived. Awake and find no baby."[10] In the novel, the dream repeats—"I thought," says Victor Frankenstein, "that if I could bestow animation upon lifeless matter, I might in process of time . . . renew life where death had apparently devoted the body to corruption"—and then that dream comes true; of course, it does not end well.[11] As for *Topsy*, it ends with Bonaparte's role in revivifying Topsy—"It is I who . . . took you to the rays which made it possible for you, Topsy, to see the spring this year" (163)—but also with Topsy's role in keeping Bonaparte from death: "She guards me, and by her presence alone must bar the entrance of my room to a worse ill, and even to Death" (164). "Death" gets the last word in *Topsy*, but the book itself, with its anticipatory postmortems, keeps both dog and author alive.

To put it another way, *Topsy* seems a preemptive form of literary taxidermy, Bonaparte mounting the dog in narrative form while Topsy is still alive. In its Victorian heyday, taxidermy was sometimes preemptive. In addition to acknowledging species that were already extinct—like the auk in Wells's story "Triumphs of a Taxidermist"—taxidermists also looked to preserve species that would soon disappear. Here is Hornaday again, in *Taxidermy and Zoological Collecting: A Complete Handbook for the Amateur Taxidermist, Collector, Osteologist, Museum-Builder, Sportsman, and Traveller*: "It is already too late to collect wild specimens of the American bison. . . . Very soon it will also be too late to collect walrus, manatee, fur seal, prong-horn antelope, elk, moose, mountain sheep, and mountain goat." The task of the taxidermist is to stave off future loss: "If the naturalist would gather representatives of all these forms for perpetual preservation, and future study, he must set about it at once."[12] Hornaday's logic followed the "preservation paradox" anatomized by Nigel Rothfels, wherein "killing, photographing, and pickling animals" were seen as "preserving them [and] saving them."[13] As a prophylactic against future species death, taxidermy preempted mourning with mounting.

Sometimes species extinction involved both preemptive and retrospective mourning. The passenger pigeon, for example, was infamously hunted to extinction, reduced from billions to one; in 1914, the last pigeon—"Martha," as she was named—"was sent to the Smithsonian for taxidermic preservation and display, and mourned as the avatar of extinction." Mourning for Martha had actually begun earlier: "For two decades before Martha died, a collection of writings accumulated that now read as a kind of preliminary postmortem: pet theories, purported sightings, rewards announcements (all futile), the reminiscences, eulogies and protests that eulogies were premature."[14] Postmortem writing lost its preliminary after Martha died; premature eulogies became elegiac laments.

Taxidermied passenger pigeons embodied this transfer from anticipatory to retrospective mourning, as individual specimens mounted before 1914 later became emblems of an entire lost species. A century later, artists have amplified these connections between mounting and mourning anew. Rosamond Wolff Purcell's *Passenger Pigeon* (2013), for example, is one of many photographs Purcell took of natural history specimens in the Western Foundation of Vertebrate Zoology in California; I am lucky to be able to look at the actual photograph, at the Mount Holyoke College Art Museum.[15] It shows two passenger pigeon "study skins," a minimalist form of taxidermy in which the bodies of birds were removed and replaced with cotton, and the specimens laid flat for further study. The study skin was intended neither for public display, as in the natural history museum, nor for private remembrance, like a taxidermied pet. It was meant to serve as stored scientific data—unbeautified, unindividuated, and unmourned.

By contrast, Purcell's photograph shows passenger pigeon study skins as corpses to be mourned. The top bird almost seems to be resting, but the bottom one definitely is not. It is unnaturally torqued in what looks like postmortem rigidity, beak straining upward, head lifted off the ground. Two specimen labels are visible, one camouflaged amid the white feathers of the top bird and the other nestled under the brown tail feathers on the bottom. But the words on these labels are not legible; Purcell does not redeem the specimens into scientific utility.

Instead, she positions them—embalmed and monumental—so that they seem to be lying in state. They await a commemorative burial that presents itself here not once but twice: in the casket-like green space where the birds rest within the image and in the respectful funeral provided by the photograph itself.

This is a funeral for species extinction as well as specimen death. Purcell writes, "The extinct Passenger Pigeon, with its sunset colors and history of massacre, is a relic that evokes great melancholy. . . . The two birds before me—thanks to the light and despite tell-tale identification tags—levitate above the stage."[16] Purcell responds to extinction's "melancholy"—I will return to this word—by making the birds "levitate." This verb suggests a magician's act, a theatrical illusion of movement that will never come again, for species as for specimen. The passenger pigeon cannot reverse its "sunset," but through the magic of photography—twinned here with taxidermy—the "relic" can at least find a visual reliquary through which it can be mourned.

FIG. 20.

Rosamond Wolff Purcell, *Passenger Pigeon*, 2008 capture; 2013 print. Digital color print photograph. Purchase with the Henry Rox Memorial Fund for the Acquisition of Work by Contemporary Women Artists. Mount Holyoke College Art Museum, South Hadley, Massachusetts. Photo: Laura Shea, 2013.28. Used by permission of Mount Holyoke College Art Museum and Rosamond Wolff Purcell.

Mourning for the dog, whether Bonaparte's Topsy or a taxidermied pet, does not carry this species elegy. In the Victorian era, while species of birds disappeared, dogs proliferated—one species, many breeds—and were mourned in increasingly elaborate ways. Analyzing Victorian Britain, Teresa Mangum shows the profusion of elegies, eulogies, stories, novels, memoirs, portraiture, photographs, sculpture, and other monuments used to commemorate beloved dogs. Some of these were new forms of memorialization: for example, dog cemeteries were founded in London, Paris, and New York. Some were connected to individuals: Sir Walter Scott famously enshrined his dogs in statuary, epitaphs, poetry, and fiction. Scott's commemorations were anticipatory as well as retrospective: he had a statue of his dog Maida made in advance of the dog's death, "in anticipation of the need to mourn and memorialize the loss to come."[17]

Commemoration could also proceed in reverse, with representations of dogs seeming to grieve their owners. Real animals do grieve in various ways: they "may refuse to eat, lose weight, become ill, act out, grow listless, or exhibit body language that conveys sadness or depression."[18] In the Victorian era, representations of animal grief over human death abounded. I have already named Greyfriars Bobby, the terrier famous for keeping vigil over his master's grave; he was an icon of canine mourning as well as fidelity—of mourning as the ultimate version of fidelity. Canine mourning could improve upon human mourning: in Sir Edwin Landseer's painting *The Old Shepherd's Chief Mourner* (1837), a dog plaintively perches his head on an empty bed, presumably still awaiting his master's touch. Or his master's voice? I am back to the painting by Francis Barraud, in which the dog sits on a coffin mourning his master, the painter's brother; again the dog seems chief mourner—mourner in chief. The depiction of the mourning dog says most about the master: here as elsewhere, the canine reveals most about the human. Mangum suggests that images of mourning dogs reflect a wish for the human "to *be* monumentalized by an animal's grief."[19]

Beautiful Joe shows up—an honorary Brit—in Mangum's discussion of another prominent feature of Victorian animal memorialization: the representation of aged dogs. The elderly Joe, like other older dogs, represents human anxieties about aging, "in the face of our older human companions, of our aging selves, and of death itself."[20] In all human-made commemorations of the dog, mourned and mourning, the animal reflects the human; so too in my discussion of Frankie, not yet aged but potentially near death. My mourning comments are an anticipatory commemoration of him and presumably also a song of myself.

I cannot decode this song, but I can analyze the dog novels of Marshall Saunders. In this chapter, I analyze animal mourning—both mourning by animals and mourning for animals—in *Beautiful Joe* and its sequel, *Beautiful Joe's Paradise* (1902), which offers an explicit plot of animal afterlife and an implicit fantasia of taxidermic revivification. I analyze mourning in psychoanalytic terms, on a loose leash to Freud, to suggest the expansive psychic power—generative as well as shattering—involved in representations of animal mourning.

I will introduce these arguments through an investigation of the foundational case study of psychoanalysis, wherein dogs anchor an explicit account of human mourning and an implicit story—this is Freud, after all—of repressed sexual desires. Turning to Marshall Saunders, I will argue for the organizing role of animal mourning, melancholic and masochistic, in *Beautiful Joe* and then, more redemptively, in *Beautiful Joe's Paradise*. Finally, I find a sequel to this sequel—less redemptive, more radical—in a recent representation of women, dogs, and loss: Kelly Reichardt's film *Wendy and Lucy* (2008).

2.

What the world of the Tufts animal hospital most reminds me of is an element of my own childhood. As a girl, I was—you will not be surprised to learn—dog-oriented; I lived intensely inside the *umwelt* of our English springer spaniel. She gave birth to seven puppies when I was seven, in the bedroom one of my sisters and I shared; we put a piece of string exactly halfway across the floor to delineate our sides, and the puppies were born on her side of the string, but they roamed the house for the next two months and became my childhood pack. A mixed-breed dog duo, canine father and daughter, also enlivened my youth; we won the father as a raffle prize at a Purim carnival, and the daughter was an accidental result of the father's wandering. When I was about ten, I imagined being a veterinarian—for dogs only—and created a mock-animal hospital. It had an examining table made of cardboard, an X-ray machine of tinfoil wrapping around paper-towel tubing, and an elaborate pharmacy of medications I thought suitable for dog ailments. Decades later, I came across the hospital while helping my parents pack up the house in Illinois in which they had lived for decades. The house was crammed with stuff; my father, a historian by profession, had saved everything. He and I found the hospital, mostly intact, in the basement; the "equipment" could not be saved, but the "pharmacy" was pristine. I packed it up and mailed it to myself in Massachusetts, and now it sits in front of me.

It is a strange child's toy, medical and morbid. My childhood pharmacy includes bottles labeled "Vitamin E," still filled with what look like kidney beans; "Aspirin—5 grain" (multicolored plastic discs, from a board game); "Bicarbonate of Soda" (sand); "Fleantis—Flea Powder" (salt), and "Diarrhea Stopper" (coffee beans). Some of the bottles are spice jars, some are Tic Tac holders, and at least one is a miniature alcohol bottle from an airplane, but most are empty prescription pill bottles from my parents. The oddest entry is a spice jar labeled "Epsom Salts," filled with hundreds of tiny balls of laboriously wadded-up tinfoil. I admire artworks with apothecary themes—especially Joseph Cornell's pharmacies—but my jar seems to be evidence of psychological compulsion rather than artistic creativity. I had some obsessive traits as a child, and the tiny tinfoil versions of "Epsom Salts" look to me like diagnostic criterion numero uno for a case of childhood obsessive-compulsive disorder. OCD itself seems linked to dogs, a species known for agonizingly repetitive behaviors, like worrying a bone or scratching an itch. These are general idioms, but there are breed-specific versions of canine OCD—the fox terrier, for example, is known for chasing patches of light, while the German shepherd snaps at flies.[21] The whole hospital seems to enshrine doglike obsessiveness as well as obsession for dogs; it looks like a diorama of my childhood psyche.

Now I have gone back to the dogs of my childhood, the self-revelations of the autobiographical animal. The artifact of the dog hospital suggests a modest interest in dog illness, but a greater one in dog cure; I seem to have had fantasies of Frankensteinian power, of reviving animals with pills and play. These fantasies are a bit worrying. For example, the choice of a diarrhea-stopper or the way I turned my parents' pill bottles into toys: I seem to be presenting myself as a set of symptoms ripe for analysis. You know who the analyst would be: I have already talked about one "SF," the filmmaker Samuel Fuller—two if you count his daughter, Samantha Fuller, who played the granddaughter in *White Dog*—and another is demanding to be heard.

I prefer, though, to talk back to Sigmund Freud, master's voice of psychoanalysis, veterinarian to the Viennese psyche, massive dog-lover. There are other impulses to do so: the centennial of Freud's 1909 lectures at Clark University, down the road from the Tufts animal hospital, prompts new reflections on his only American visit.[22] I have been rereading Freud's own *Five Lectures on Psycho-analysis*, the book adapting his lectures at Clark; in an early greatest-hits way, these lectures outline hysteria, repression, dreams, transference, sublimation, and other topics, all overtly framed as Freud's self-introduction to Americans: "Ladies and Gentlemen,–It is with novel and bewildering feelings that I find myself in the New World, lecturing before an audience of expectant enquirers."[23] In scientific quarters, there is no longer such an expectant audience, nor so many admirers. Freud's model of the "talking cure" has been displaced by findings about brain biochemistry, along with the chemicals to treat those findings; the pharmacy—the big-pharma kind, not my childhood toy—is now the main source of treatment. The American Psychoanalytic Association has concluded that while Freudian psychoanalysis is alive in humanities departments, in psychology departments it is "dessicated and dead."[24] This phrase seems overdetermined—to use a Freudian term—if not downright gothic, like the "dessicated and dead" mother of Norman Bates. *Psycho* intertwines taxidermy with psychoanalysis, and neither comes out looking good.

Still, Freud is already in this chapter, and not only because of the adjacencies of geography or the accident of anniversary. He is in my account of women who treat dogs as their children, and my reflections on my childhood attachment to dogs: these are topics that come into view through his analytical methods. And if Freud is already in this dog story, so too are dogs in stories about Freud—his own beloved dogs, for example, were present during his analytic sessions and are disproportionately featured in the family home movies at the Freud Museums in London and Vienna.[25]

There are many stories involving Freud and dogs: for example, Bonaparte's *Topsy*. I do not know if there is an *Uncle Tom's Cabin* allusion in this dog's name, but there is definitely a Freud connection in *Topsy* the book. Literally, Sigmund and Anna Freud translated *Topsy* into German; symbolically, Bonaparte was writing about the oral cancer that would kill Freud.[26] I would say there is a triangle formed by Freud, Bonaparte, and Topsy except that there is also one formed by Bonaparte, her own father—also dead of cancer—and Topsy, and there is another one formed by Topsy, Sigmund Freud, and Anna Freud. Freud, dogs, and women writers converge in too many biographical triangles to count. Now I have offered the beginnings of another one: Freud, Frankie, and me.

And dogs are also in stories—psychoanalytic case studies, but I think of them as literary stories—written by Freud. Animals in general: "In nearly every essay he wrote, Freud mentions animals: animal examples, animal anecdotes, animal metaphors, animal idioms, and . . . animal phobias."[27] Dogs in particular: for example, they play an important role in the story of Anna O., the opening case study in Freud and Josef Breuer's *Studies on Hysteria* (1895). Anna O. was the twenty-one-year-old "hysteric" with many symptoms, including a cough, the inability to eat, disturbances of speech and vision, partial paralysis, and trancelike "absences." After her treatment—she was actually Josef Breuer's patient, Breuer later talking to Freud about her, Freud then pronouncing freely on her—Freud concluded that "when they were brought to verbal utterance the symptoms disappeared." Anna O. herself came up with the phrase "talking cure."[28]

One prominent symptom of Anna's hysteria was initially inexplicable: "She would take up the glass of water that she longed for, but as soon as it touched her lips she would push it away like someone suffering from hydrophobia." It turned out that a dog was the key: "One day during hypnosis she grumbled about her English 'lady-companion,' whom she did not care for, and went on to describe, with every sign of disgust, how she had once gone into this lady's room and how her little dog—horrid creature!—had drunk out of a glass there. . . . After giving further energetic expression to the anger she had held back, she asked for something to drink, drank a large quantity of water without any difficulty, and awoke . . . thereupon the disturbance vanished, never to return." This was the turning point in the treatment: "Never before had anyone removed a hysterical symptom by such a method or had thus gained so deep an insight into its causation." Freud's insight was that Anna's symptoms were "a display of mourning." Specifically, "in the episode of her lady-companion's dog, she suppressed any manifestation of her very intense disgust, out of consideration for the woman's feelings; while she watched at her father's bedside she was constantly on the alert to prevent the sick man from observing her anxiety and her painful depression."[29] The anecdote of the "horrid" dog reveals "painful depression" about the father; the dog is a symbol of what is repressed—disgust and anger, anxiety and depression—in the hysteric, which is then expressed and talking-cured.

I could stop there, with the "little dog" as a foundation of psychoanalysis. Freud even uses my favorite punctuation mark here, the semicolon, to make the formative connection between dogs and mourning; at least, he does so in this translation. But I would be remiss not to note that there is another dog in the Anna O. story: "She drew much benefit from a Newfoundland dog which had been given to her and of which she was passionately fond. On one occasion, though, her pet made an attack on the cat, and it was splendid to see the way in which the frail girl seized a whip in her left hand and beat off the huge beast with it to rescue his victim."[30] This story—recounted in the *Studies in Hysteria* version of the Anna O. case, omitted from the *Five Lectures* one—seems, at first, the opposite of the other: in contrast to her dislike of the "little dog," Anna O. is "passionately fond" of the large Newfoundland. But she recoils from this animal too, even more dramatically: she attacks it—the dog's gender is not specified, at least not in translation—to defend a cat. There is a probable connection between Anna's "sign of disgust" at the little dog's lips on the drinking glass and her rejection of the big dog's violence. There is a possible connection of both dogs to foreignness. The little dog is associated with the Englishwoman, and the big one is named for a Canadian province; I will come back to this topic. Both are foreign to the Austrian Anna. And there is a definite link between Anna's behavior in the two anecdotes: her act of "giving energetic expression to the anger she had held back" becomes her action of going decisively forth with the whip.

How does one interpret, in the Newfoundland story, the description of "beat[ing] off the huge beast"? Freud gives his all-purpose interpretive guide in the *Five Lectures*: "Psychoanalytic research traces back the symptoms of patients' illnesses . . . to impressions from their *erotic life*" (his emphasis, of course).[31] There is a famous erotic backstory to Anna O: "When the treatment had apparently reached a successful end, the patient suddenly made manifest to Breuer the presence of a strong unanalysed positive transference of an unmistakably sexual nature."[32] This is Freud's early translator, James Strachey, in a footnote; a more detailed version was later provided by Freud, who claimed that Breuer stopped treatment because he found Anna "confused and writhing in abdominal cramps. Asked what was wrong with her, she cried, 'Now comes Dr. B's child!'"[33] This account of an imagined childbirth has been contested as fact and reinterpreted as myth: critics have argued that this story is less about Anna's desire for Breuer than about "the sexual responses of male doctors to their patients"; that it signals the centrality of the mother to Freud, "the specter that drives him forth"; and that the key to the case is the Freud-Breuer relation, a between-men story of "men's financial, intellectual, and erotic exchanges."[34]

I am focusing on the dogs, not the men, but even so, the image of Anna "beat[ing] off the huge beast" seems erotically charged. Even leaving aside the masturbatory dimensions, in English, of the phrase "beating off," the dog in this image seems a metaphor for sexual aggression, which the woman must subdue into submission; that aggression might come from another human, or it might be Anna's own sexual desire. More Freud, from *The Interpretation of Dreams*: "Wild beasts are as a rule employed by the dream-work to represent passionate impulses of which the dreamer is afraid . . . wild beasts are used to represent the libido, a force dreaded by the ego and combated by means of repression."[35] The story with the "horrid dog" also suggests "passionate impulses" of both attraction and aversion. The lady companion and the dog drink from the same glass: is this sharing of lips on glass a symbolic kiss between Anna and the companion? Is Anna's hydrophobia homophobia?

I started off talking about death, but now I seem to be talking about sex. This combination is already embedded, in an off-color way, in the taxidermic idea of "mounting" an animal. One commentator puts it this way: "I've never personally wanted to go about mounting an animal. (And here we first arrive at the unfortunate middle-school pun that lies at the heart of taxidermy: 'mounting,' *har har*. It's a goofball double-entendre this book will by needs be lousy with.)"[36] Sexual connotation is here relegated to parentheses, downgraded to "middle-school pun" and "goofball double-entendre." Freud removes the parentheses; the goofball double entendre is his point d'appui, and the connections between sex and death drive him. I will leave the sexual connotations of taxidermic "mounting" aside, but I still want to understand sexual possibility in the Anna O. story.

Perhaps I am moving too quickly past the dogs, using them only as conduits for interpreting sexual desires between people. Perhaps the more important imagined kiss is between the lady and her little dog and the "passionate attachment" in these stories is that of humans for dogs. Freud does not have much to say on this topic: in *Three Essays on the Theory of Sexuality*, a very short section on "Sexually Immature Persons and Animals as Sexual Objects" lumps pedophilia and bestiality together. This seems brief, compared to Freud's usual detail in discussing sexual practices and desires.[37]

I look elsewhere: separate from Freud, there is a robust history of dogs represented as erotically linked to humans. For example, of "dog love and same-sex love" narrated together and, in a more theoretical frame, of queer studies and animal studies intertwined: "While it would be false to equate the two, relations between the two epistemological regions of *queer* and *animal* abound."[38] That is putting it abstractly; there are more specific examples. A famous American reference point: Alfred Kinsey found in his sexual surveys that "three quarters of the women who confessed that they had occasionally committed bestiality had made love with a dog."[39] A specific example: "The dog is most commonly used for cunnilingus. Dogs have an ideal tongue for the purpose. . . . Every dog is a potential lapdog."[40] The lapdog pleasuring the lady appears frequently in fiction. For example, in *The History of Pompey the Little*, the English eighteenth-century novel, the lapdog has an intimate relation to his human mistress: "When she awoke in a morning, she would

FIG. 21.
Woman and dog in *White Dog*, dir. Samuel Fuller, 1982.

embrace him with an ardour, which the happiest lover might have envied."[41] Although lapdogs may have "enjoy[ed] a better reputation in the nineteenth century . . . associated with proper domesticity rather than with sexual satisfaction," they did not entirely lose—nor have they lost now—their connotations as objects and agents of sexual desire, especially for women.[42]

In such representations of human-canine contact, sometimes one species seems to stand in for another—for example, in Fuller's film *White Dog*. The overt romance in the film is human, heterosexual, and intraracial: the white actress Julie has a boyfriend, a white man named "Roland Gray," the name an apparent homage to the novel's author, Romain Gary. But Roland is a lackluster presence, and he disappears in the second half of the film. By contrast, there are highly charged moments between Julie and an African American woman friend, and between Julie and a white woman animal trainer. Kristy McNichol, who plays Julie, had a strong lesbian following; Fuller's original choice for the role, Jodie Foster, had an even stronger one. But these details are outside the film—extradiegetic—and the glances between women are just that: glancing. There is also a developing friendship between Julie and Keys, the African American male trainer, which noticeably stops short of romance; they have a getting-to-know-you dinner in which the other trainer is present, and a policeman stops by. Perhaps, if not so heavily policed, their relationship would cross the boundary of interracial sexuality: the opposite of but also the complement to the interracial hatred that the film so hyperbolically presents.

But I am burying the lead: the most sustained relationship Julie has in the film is with the dog, and it is developed in ways that seem more suitable to a Hollywood romantic couple. In one scene, he picks up her lingerie from the floor and they play tug-of-war with it; in another, after he comes home injured in a fight, she washes him in the bathtub, stroking him tenderly through a steamy mist. It's not just me imagining this: studio memos asked for a "moving and emotional love story between a human and an animal."[43] In this "love story," the dog is a love-object in himself, but he also gestures toward a queerer world of relationships between women, as well as across race.

Now I seem to have drifted far from Freud, although not really; it is more as though I am on one of those long retractable leashes, the kind allowing the illusion of independent movement, which is then dispelled at the push of a button. Freud has me on such a leash, pushing my buttons: he is the foundational model of a critic who uncovers concealed psychosexual terrain. In the case of *White Dog*, the terrain is not well hidden; even the Hollywood studio executives suggested it. In the case of Anna O., the terrain is obscured. My speculation about the erotic possibilities of her dog stories relies on others' versions of Anna—men's versions, relayed between Breuer and Freud. It would be good to know what Anna herself would say. She was, in real life, a woman named Bertha Pappenheim, who became a journalist, activist, and feminist—she translated Mary Wollstonecraft's *A Vindication of the Rights of Woman* into German—and altogether an accomplished figure.[44] Not that Pappenheim, who refused to discuss her treatment, would necessarily offer, or be able to offer, the sexual "truth" of her story. Even so—and as usual with Freud—one wants to hear the woman's story along with the master's voice.

So I will hazard only a limited set of claims here about Freud: that the founding case of psychoanalysis is based, in part, on a woman talking about a dog as a way to talk about mourning; that one of her dog stories leads to another, its opposite but also its complement; and that the dog stories together may lead not only to mourning for humans but also to "passionate attachments" of ambiguously erotic kinds. Uncovering these attachments is only a start: from the *Five Lectures*, "The hypothesis of repression leaves us not at the end but at the beginning of a psychological theory."[45] I will give Freud the last word, for the moment, and make my way back to Marshall Saunders.

3.

Mourning by and for animals saturates *Beautiful Joe*. Joe's mother, who dies after her master murders her puppies, is not the only animal mother in the novel who is shattered by grief. I have already mentioned the story a boy tells about his English uncle: "One day when he was hunting in the Punjab, he saw a mother monkey carrying a little dead baby monkey. Six months after [he saw the] same monkey still carrying dead baby monkey, all shriveled up. Mother monkey loved her baby monkey, and wouldn't give it up" (159). Profound maternal grief recurs when Laura rescues a stable of neglected animals, among them a cow whose calf has died: "The cow, poor unhappy creature [never] lost a strange, melancholy look from her eyes. . . . It always seemed to me that [she] was thinking of her poor dead calf, starved to death by her cruel master. . . . Even the farm hands called her 'Old Melancholy,' and so she got to be known by that name, or Mel, for short" (214).

"Old Melancholy": a proper name, also a condition about which psychoanalysis has something to say; I said I would come back to the idea of "melancholy," and I knew I could not leave Freud out for long. In "Mourning and Melancholia" (1917), Freud contrasts these terms: mourning is "normal" grief, through which the lost object is let go; melancholia is unresolved, ceaseless, and "pathological" grief, in which the lost object itself has been lost.[46] "Mourning and Melancholia" has become a focal point of cultural theory. Scholars interpret melancholia in relation to political as well as personal loss: postcolonial melancholia, racial melancholia, Left melancholia.[47] Melancholia is no longer mourning's whipping boy; it is seen as productive rather than destructive, "a persistent condition, a state, indeed, a structure of desire."[48] And mourning is still going strong as a scholarly tool—for example, as an organizing framework for studies of nineteenth-century American literature.[49]

In *Beautiful Joe*, the dog, monkey, and cow who mourn their losses seem embodiments of melancholia, stricken with unresolved grief, carrying corpses rather than letting them go. These animal mothers sound like symbolic humans, melancholic over lost children. In an era of high infant mortality, representations of dead human children saturated popular culture: "Dying is what children do most and do best in the literary and cultural imagination of nineteenth-century America."[50] The animal mothers in this novel seem, in particular, like enslaved mothers, whose children were seized, sold, and tortured at every turn. Here again is Mel: "It always seemed to me that [Mel] was thinking of her poor dead calf, starved to death by her cruel master." "Master" here again echoes the slave master; one legacy of slavery seems that of maternal melancholia—"Mel, for short."

But I have gone intraspecies again, replacing an all-animal cast of grieving mothers and children with an all-human one. The purpose of the novel is an interspecies one, to persuade human readers to support animal welfare; one mechanism for ensuring this support is for readers to mourn the mourning animals within the novel. This mechanism again recalls *Uncle Tom's Cabin*, which appeals specifically to "mothers of America" to "pity those mothers that are constantly made childless by the American slave-trade!"[51] *Beautiful Joe* is addressed to children, but it too asks the human reader to "pity those mothers made childless."

Inside the novel too is a human mother figure mourning animals in an anticipatory mode: Joe will die one day, leaving Miss Laura with loss. Late in the novel, she and Harry have a discussion about whether dogs go to heaven. Harry notes that "Dr. Johnson believed in a future life for animals, as also did Wordsworth, Shelley, Coleridge, Jeremy Taylor, Agassiz, Lamartine, and many Christian scholars" (237). Laura simply wishes it would be so: "I think I would be happier in heaven if dear old Joe were there. . . . I think I should be lonely without him" (238). She is the novel's chief human mourner, more metaphoric mother than "Christian scholar."

But human mourning over animals need not be routed through mothers; I said I would be wary about maternal metaphors. Another route: In *Melancholia's Dog*, Alice Kuzniar theorizes literary representations of dog death, emphasizing melancholia, in the Freudian sense. She suggests that the human-dog relationship already tends toward the melancholic when the dog is alive, because "the very fact that animals are mute and that we desire to be close to them renders us melancholic" and also because the lack of official acknowledgment when a dog dies "exacerbates the melancholic."[52] The works she analyzes—twentieth-century nonfiction by women writers about dogs, including *Topsy*—labor to turn "stuck" melancholia about dog death into "unstuck" mourning.

These works reveal the dog's death only at the end, balancing between two temporal modes, which she terms the "not yet" and the "no longer." "No longer" corresponds, in a Freudian sense, to mourning, and acknowledges the dog's departure; "not yet" corresponds to melancholia and attempts to bring the dog back. Lingering in the "not yet," these works show a "keen desire to resurrect the dog, willingly to suspend disbelief in order to imagine it still alive."[53] At the same time, the act of writing is redemptive: these authors "work through the process of mourning by giving voice to the loss. They countervail depressive muteness."[54] Representations of dog loss are organized by pairs: mourning and melancholia, "not yet" and "no longer," muteness and voice.

Beautiful Joe seems to pivot on these pairings. The novel features both stuck melancholia—the monkey "still carrying [her dead baby monkey], all shriveled up"—and unstuck mourning. Look at Joe's own response to his mother's death: "There she lay, a little, gaunt, scarred creature, starved and worried to death by him. Her mouth was half open, her eyes were staring. She would never again look kindly at me at night to keep me warm. Oh, how I hated her murderer!" Joe's mother is stuck, but Joe is not. He attacks Jenkins—"I gave him a savage bite on the ankle" (60)—and later, when he reencounters Jenkins as a burglar, he captures him; Jenkins is sent to prison for ten years, and Joe, triumphant, is praised for his valor. But the bigger return on his mourning is the story itself, as it translates his mutilation into first-dog voice. We could see his voice—unusually "wicked" and full of "pleasure" at this moment—as a way of overcoming his grief at his mother's death, of turning mute melancholy into vocal mourning.

Beautiful Joe is linked to melancholia, mutilation, muteness, and something else: masochism. Here is Joe on his mother's relation to Jenkins: "I have seen him use his heavy whip to punish her until her body was covered with blood. When I got older I asked her why she did not run away. She said she did not wish to, but I soon found that the reason she did not run away was because she loved Jenkins. Cruel and savage as he was, she yet loved him, and I believe she would have laid down her life for him" (54–55). "Cruel and savage as he was, she yet loved him": the account of the master's whipping leads to the mother's apparent masochism. I have already noted the prominence of whipping in *Black Beauty* and *Uncle Tom's Cabin*, discussing it in relation to racial slavery, from which it cannot be disentangled. Neither can whipping be entirely separated from erotic frames of reference. The whipping in *Black Beauty*, for one critic, is "unquestionably erotic," not only because it echoes plots of human flagellation common elsewhere in British Victorian culture, but also because the literature of flagellation had "an originary association with inter-species violence and sexuality. It is no coincidence that a Victorian slang term for flagellation was 'horsing.'"[55] Another critic specifies the sexual allure of whipping in Stowe, arguing that masochistic desires are a surprisingly strong current in nineteenth-century U.S. women's writing. Her study also highlights the well-documented history of *Uncle Tom's Cabin* as a sexual stimulant: Freud noted that many of his patients with masochistic fantasies masturbated to Stowe's novel.[56]

Can we similarly interpret the novel known as "the *Uncle Tom's Cabin* of the dog" as a novel of masochism? In the same moment when *Beautiful Joe* was being written, the term was being defined by Richard von Krafft-Ebing: "By masochism I understand a peculiar perversion of the psychical sexual life in which the individual affected . . . is controlled by the idea of being completely and unconditionally subject to the will of a person of the opposite sex;

of being treated by this person as by a master,—humiliated and abused."[57] This definition sounds rather narrow—why, specifically, a person "of the opposite sex"? Why "a person"? "A master" seems more general, less species-specific. Freud's definition is broader: in masochism, "satisfaction is conditional upon suffering physical or mental pain at the hands of the sexual object."[58] Here, again, is Joe on his mother: "I used to ask her why she followed such a brute of a man, and she would hang her head, and say that sometimes she got a bone from the different houses they stopped at. But that was not the whole reason. She liked Jenkins so much, that she wanted to be with him" (58–59). The female who masochistically "follow[s] such a brute of a man" cannot control her desires, for which she gets "a bone" as reward.

There is sadism in the novel too: when Joe reencounters Jenkins as a burglar, for example, "I felt as if I could tear him to pieces. I have never felt so wicked since. I was hunting him, as he had hunted me and my mother, and the thought gave me pleasure" (125). The critic explicating flagellation in *Black Beauty* extends the argument to *Beautiful Joe*: "Taking pleasure in violence . . . is something that nearly all of the characters in the novel, animal and human, share."[59] These pleasurable effects seem to vary by gender: sadism is linked to the novel's male characters and masochism to its female characters. Masochism is also followed by mourning, as in the case of Joe's mother, who loses her children after "follow[ing] a brute." This link extends across species too: Miss Laura's love for Joe is so great that his loss makes the prospect of heaven painful to her.

Or perhaps all human dog-love is a kind of masochism. The comparison between dog and child is here a contrast: some children may die before their parents—especially in the era of *Beautiful Joe*—but almost all dogs, then and now, will die before their owners. Kuzniar notes that dog-owning tends toward the melancholic because dogs cannot speak; perhaps the melancholic tendency also springs from the imminent loss of dogs. To get a dog, with its short life-span, is—sooner or later—to lose a dog: the mourning, if not the melancholia, is built in. To know this and yet still to proceed seems close to masochistic, although I do not mean this in the sexual sense. It is more that dog-loving has the same emotional valence Freud ascribes to masochism, in which "satisfaction is conditional upon suffering physical or mental pain." When the dog becomes ill, then the master who witnesses his pain risks even more masochism.

Now I am at risk of speaking about Frankie and my years of caring for him—of suffering from his suffering. Reading Kuzniar, I have had a shock of recognition, a sense of my own dog story falling within her terms. Anticipating Frankie's death, I am between the "not yet" and the "no longer" of dog death, though by the time you read this, I will almost certainly have tipped to the latter, with anticipatory mourning moving into retrospection. I am mourning his death in advance—too early, though probably not by much.

Of course, Frankie himself does not have that sense of anticipation; he does not tell time in the way that humans do. Reading a clock, like reading a book, is something that I can do but he cannot. Presumably, this asymmetry affects how he experiences illness. The pediatric analogy again beckons: "The Baby won't suffer as much as you,' says the Surgeon . . . [Babies] are like a different race, a different species: they seem not to experience pain the way *we* do."[60] This is Lorrie Moore's narrator, again, in her short story. Like "a different species"—here and elsewhere in the story, the child seems not unlike a pet: "A few afternoons last month, at snacktime, she placed a bowl of Cheerios on the floor for him to eat, like a dog."[61] Moore's mother-narrator offers the baby-dog analogy ruefully, but—this time, at least—I will embrace it: Frankie the dog sometimes seems like a baby in a pediatric oncology ward. I do not share Moore's critique, in her story, of the world of pediatric oncology, but like her narrator, I too hate the patient's suffering.[62] The suffering is from the care as well as the cancer. It can feel sadistic to inflict medicine on Frankie, as well as masochistic to await his death.

I would rather not dwell on this; I will go back to Marshall Saunders. I do not see her as a masochist, sexually or otherwise. But I need to mention something about her biography, which I probably should have brought up earlier. Just outside the fictional world of *Beautiful Joe*, a death lurks. Not a dog death—the canine model for Beautiful Joe lived until 1899—but a human death, that of Saunders's beloved younger sister Laura, who had died, at age seventeen, a few years before she began writing *Beautiful Joe*.[63] I have argued that within the novel, the character of Miss Laura celebrates female authority, heading its world of animal reform. The fictional Laura also mourns the dead sister—though the "also" is putting it backward; the mourning undergirds the celebration.

The novel's mourning mothers and sons seem, in this context, yet another set of psychic displacements: they substitute for sororal mourning. When Miss Laura speculates on whether Joe will ascend to heaven, she herself occupies the heavenly afterlife of fiction, wherein the real Laura Saunders can live again. Read biographically, *Beautiful Joe* seems a narrative in which melancholia—unstuck into fiction as anticipatory mourning—brings a sister back to life.

4.

I have not forgotten ventriloquism, the production of voice from a nonliving being. Ventriloquism can also be a form of mourning, as in a documentary entitled *Her Master's Voice* (2012), directed by Nina Conti, an English actress who learned ventriloquism from a now-dead ex-lover, Ken Campbell. The film intertwines her pilgrimage to an American museum of ventriloquism with a meditation on her late mentor; she memorializes him by speaking through her dummies and in so doing, gives voice to her own mourning.[63] On the other hand (though this seems an odd phrase when discussing ventriloquism), the museum itself—"Vent Haven" in Fort Mitchell, Kentucky—seems stuck in some form of melancholia. It features a room packed with hundreds of dummies from the medium's history, carefully posed, sometimes arrayed in rows, their "lives" and the names of their ventriloquists memorialized in captions.[64] Vent Haven is dummy heaven, but a heaven awaiting revivification—new lifelines yet to be thrown to thrown voices, new opportunities awaiting for dummies to be on other hands.

In the sequel to *Beautiful Joe*, *Beautiful Joe's Paradise*, Marshall Saunders provides a literary version of such revivification, adapting the "not yet" of dog death into a full-fledged narrative of animal afterlife. There is symbolic ventriloquism as well as literary taxidermy at work here. *Beautiful Joe's Paradise* offers another depiction of animals remounted in narrative, a project taken to its logical extreme: not only a revivification through the form of first-dog fiction but a fictional plot centered on bringing dead animals back to life. The sequel offers a redemptive narrative that transmutes melancholia into redemptively uncanny mourning.

That is the claim; here is the plot: *Beautiful Joe's Paradise; or, The Island of Brotherly Love* is a novel told in the first-person voice of a human boy, Sam Emerson, who lives in San Francisco and whose beloved dog, Ragtime, is killed by a cruel neighbor boy as the novel opens. Distraught, Sam falls into a sleep from which he awakens into the company of talking monkeys, who transport him, by hot-air balloon, to a place in the Pacific called the "Island of Brotherly Love." In this setting, amid tigers, kangaroos, elephants, swans, and other animals—all reanimated from the dead—Sam is reunited with the revivified Ragtime and then with Beautiful Joe, who serves as president of the island. In the book's twenty-nine chapters, Sam goes on numerous adventures and learns about the island's highly organized systems of governance and discipline. At the end, Beautiful Joe leaves the island to reunite in heaven with Miss Laura, who has just died, and Sam returns to San Francisco, reuniting with his mother. He plans to write the story of *Beautiful Joe's Paradise* and become active in the animal welfare movement: "It is going to be my business in life to talk about animals" (362).[65]

The novel's prefatory texts establish Saunders as the novel's chief mourner. First, the dedication: "To the memory of Nita, Best loved of my dogs, this book is affectionately dedicated by her sorrowing Mistress." In the preface, she explains,

> For a long time I have had in mind a story bearing on the immortality of animals. Some four years ago, while walking with my father, I sketched the outline of this paradise for animals that I so earnestly wished to write about. He was much interested, and said at once, "You should make your old favourite Joe the hero of this paradise." Almost shocked at the idea of trading, as it were, on the popularity of the dear old animal, I said, firmly, "I can not do that. I shall never bring Joe into another story."
>
> However, last autumn, when in great grief over the death of a beloved dog, my mind turned strongly to my animal story, old Joe was ever before me. He, and only he, was suited to preside over the happy republic where the animals found themselves after death.
>
> Struggle against it as I would, Joe constantly confronted me, and as his death has occurred since the publication of the story of his life, I at first reluctantly, then gladly, introduced my former friend into a second story.
>
> This is my apology for a sequel—an after-part—which in many cases is of doubtful discretion. (n.p. [5–6])

This preface interweaves three pairings: human-canine, father-daughter, and author-book. The dogs here are also tripled: the real-life "beloved dog" Nita; the real-life dog who inspired *Beautiful Joe*; and the fictional character of Joe, who urges her to write. In agreeing to his wishes, Saunders herself becomes another version of Fido—faithful, deferential, apologetic. The sequel, in turn, becomes a response to mourning, a revivification—"a second story, an after-part"—of previous dog and previous novel.

The father's presence here seems double-edged, generative but also coercive. Earlier, I noted Saunders's handwritten inscription, "My father's hand," atop the photograph of Billy in *Beautiful Joe*, and I suggested that Billy might be a version of the daughter herself. Similarly, Waterston, reading the full

Saunders oeuvre, notes a consistent "rejection of older-generation males in Saunders's fiction" and suggests a source in her "beloved but daunting father."[66]

The "but" is brought into focus in Saunders's 1927 mini-memoir, "The Story of My Life": "The first library I remember was my dear father's. Like Prospero, he prized his books above a dukedom" (43).[67] This is an affectionate tribute from a daughter-Miranda, but then comes a less positive memory: "I was allowed very few novels," only those by Charles Dickens and Sir Walter Scott; in particular, "'Jane Eyre' was not permitted. . . . Books of reference, classics, *et alii*, I did not need to get from the library. My father had them all. It was the fiction my soul craved." The difficulty of fathers prohibiting daughters from reading fiction goes back a generation: "My sympathetic mother comforted me by saying that when she was a girl she had to secrete 'Uncle Tom's Cabin,' or her father would have banished it from the house" (43). At the end of the essay comes another story of paternal prohibition: "As a child, I remember being stood in a row with my brothers and sisters. 'Children,' he would say, 'Bring me all your gift books. . . . I am going to an outlying part of the province where the boys and girls have little reading matter.' How we used to protest! But the books went—and he being dead yet speaketh" (44). The last phrase is meant as a tribute, but it suggests an ambiguity to the father's role. The father who encourages Saunders to write a new book carries traces of the father who bans her old ones. He too speaks, Prospero-like, in the master's voice, which Saunders at first protests but then obeys, "reluctantly, then gladly." The preface to *Beautiful Joe's Paradise*, then, provides an origin story in which dog loss generates writing and a daughter's plan to stay mute is overcome by a father's insistence on her resumption of voice.

With its combination of fathers, daughters, dogs, and mourning, the preface offers an echo of the Anna O. story, but I am drawn to another Freudian dimension of it: its uncanniness. "The Uncanny" remains, after many readings, my favorite essay by Freud. Its model of the uncanny as a return of repressed material—material traversing the lines between animate and inanimate, dead and living—seems endlessly applicable. Freud's main examples are dolls, waxworks, and automata; although he does not discuss them, the ventriloquist's dummy would fit perfectly in this list, as would the taxidermied animal.[68] The uncanny is "that species of the frightening that goes back to what was once well known and had long been familiar"; that "species of the frightening" could—perhaps should—include some animals.[69]

Beautiful Joe's Paradise seems uncanny in several ways. The origin story of the preface presents the form of the sequel as a kind of uncanny rebirth.

Its multispecies plot repeatedly relies on uncanny return. That return is not frightening; rather, it transmutes the melancholic into joyful fantasy. It also brings a daughter's power to Saunders, who establishes her own fantasy island where dead animals live and her characters rule.

The first chapter of the novel sets up this fantasy of empowered uncanny revivification. It is entitled, simply, "Dead." When Sam finds his dead dog, "I picked him up . . . he was as limp as a doll. I held him in my arms. I didn't know there was such a difference between a dead dog and a live one. . . . Where was Ragtime? A few minutes ago he had been screaming, jumping, yelping—now he was only a warm heap of bones and flesh" (13). Here is a dog held in a human's arms, an embrace that seems less erotic than parental and a tableau of the "no longer" of death.

The name of the dog should be noted. Ragtime, as a musical form, was then reaching its peak of popularity, seen as "the music not just of black Americans, but of all Americans."[70] Saunders's choice of "Ragtime" seems meant to showcase her knowledge of U.S. culture. Perhaps "Ragtime" also has racial connotations here, with Saunders bringing together a black musical form marked by syncopated liveliness with a dog who was "screaming, jumping, [and] yelping" while alive. Racially marked on not, "Ragtime" the dog connotes liveliness, the better to emphasize his shocking deadness.

The dog's death leaves the human inconsolable, with Sam literally unable to let go of the animal: "'He's slept with me every night for ten years. Let me have him once more.' Then I broke down. You would have thought I was a girl" (17). This is grief so profound that Sam refuses to cede the corpse; he sounds like the monkey carrying around the shriveled corpse in *Beautiful Joe*. In Freud's terms, he has moved into "the crushed state of melancholia," wherein the mourner "reproaches himself, vilifies himself"—in this case, condemns himself as being like "a girl."[71] Sam voices self-hatred taken to self-annihilation: "Why, you might as well die yourself at once, and be done with it. Life wasn't worth living. I wished I could lie down beside Ragtime" (18).

The Island of Brotherly Love transforms this melancholic state into an uncanny zone that is idyllic rather than frightening. In "The Uncanny," Freud notes, "Children are not afraid of their dolls coming to life—they may even want them to. Here, then, the sense of the uncanny would derive not from an infantile fear, but from an infantile wish."[72] In *Beautiful Joe's Paradise*, Sam falls asleep sobbing, the canine corpse "limp as a doll" in his arms, and the monkey persuades him to give up the corpse on the promise of the Island of Brotherly Love: "'Will he come to life? . . . And be just as he was here?' 'Exactly'" (22). And it is so: "I saw those compact feet kick out, that long flat head raise itself. I saw, saw—for I snatched the cloth of gold [covering the animal] aside. . . . Then I had my dog in my arms, and I thought I should die of joy" (37). The desolate posthumous human-canine embrace has become a joyful living one.

Think, again, of the biographical backstory for *Frankenstein*: Mary Shelley dreaming of her dead baby coming back to life. Or think of taxidermy: the "heap of bones and flesh" is given a new interior mount. The moment fulfills what Jane Desmond calls the "as-if-ness" of taxidermy—"the invitation to imagine as alive that which patently is not."[73] From suicide to "joy": the as-if fantasy of the uncanny double erases mourning and melancholia.

The Island of Brotherly Love is like an anti–island of Doctor Moreau or an uncanny Oz. The latter seems a deliberate allusion: L. Frank Baum's *The Wizard of Oz* (1900) had appeared to great success two years before.[74] Like Baum's wizard, a ventriloquist, Saunders makes Rag speak:

> "Rag! Rag! Rag!" I said, "you've been dead, but now you're alive. I'll never be mad at anything again, never in my life. I'm jam full of thanks."
>
> "So am I, master," he said.
>
> I nearly fell over the edge of the car into the sea.
>
> *So am I, master!* Why, Rag was speaking too . . . that Rag had found a voice, was the biggest surprise in my life.
>
> "Why, Rag," I gasped, when I recovered my centre of gravity, "can you talk? Do you know what I say?"
>
> "I've always partly understood you," he said, coolly, "now I know every word," and his dear old eyes shone like black stars. (38–39)

For any reader of *Beautiful Joe*, the speech of Rag is an uncanny return of the earlier novel's first-dog voice, here made literal in the dog who can talk. When the character of Joe appears, he further intensifies the uncanny. Sam first sees him from afar and learns only that he is "the President": "A sturdy, medium-sized dog sat under the trees" (60). Then he is revealed as Joe: "There he sat, well-preserved, firm-looking, a wise old dog, with his missing bits of ears and tail grown on again" (62). Joe's transformation into president is no less shocking than the regeneration of his ears and tail—an uncanny undoing of his lost limbs that accompanies the reversal of his death.

This moment of revivification has already appeared in the novel, in its frontispiece illustration. Captioned "A sturdy, medium-sized dog sat under the trees," the image shows the dog that we will know in five chapters to be

FIG. 22.
Charles Livingston Bull, *Beautiful Joe's Paradise*, frontispiece, 1902. Photo: James Gehrt.

Joe atop a hill, body intact, surrounded by a horse, two other dogs, and birds in the sky. The frontispiece revivifies the dog—live, lively, intact, on top—from the outset, anticipating the revivification to come.

The artist is Charles Livingston Bull, a prolific illustrator, a specialist in images of animals—and also, before he turned to illustration, a professional taxidermist; he succeeded William Hornaday as chief taxidermist at the National Museum in Washington, and his taxidermy mounts were admired by Teddy Roosevelt.[75] I am no longer surprised to learn of this prior career; taxidermists appear so often in nineteenth-century culture, Audubon onward. What seems notable is how Bull's taxidermy training dovetails with the novel itself. *Beautiful Joe's Paradise* provides another instance of literary taxidermy, wherein readers are transported to a zone of uncanny animal revivification.

FIG. 23.
Charles Livingston Bull, *Beautiful Joe's Paradise*, illustration of journey to the Island of Brotherly Love with the caption "We were going up and up," 1902. Photo: James Gehrt.

Bull's illustration of transportation within the novel—Sam's journey by hot-air balloon to the island—highlights the uncanniness of this zone. An image depicts the hot-air balloon along with one of the two swans that guide it, one of the three monkeys within the balloon, the luminous moon behind them; the caption is "We were going up and up." Sam is not in the image, which foregrounds the delicate lines of the swan: "Bull's forte was design: an ordered spacing of unbalanced forms."[76] The imbalance of scale—giant swan, tiny monkey—implicitly positions the viewer in midair as well, vertiginously near the swan's wing in the impossible journey from San Francisco to the island.

The emphasis on the hot-air balloon, within both image and text, seems another deliberate reference to Baum's *The Wizard of Oz*, wherein a balloon brought the Wizard to Oz before the start of the story and helps him depart Oz near its end; Bull also illustrated Baum. But Baum's balloon is tethered to the mundane world of the Wizard: when he decides to leave Oz, it is because "[he was] tired of being such a humbug."[77] While the Wizard supervises the construction of the balloon—Dorothy sews the silk—he comes to the limits of his knowledge when it lifts off without her. The balloon in Oz is only a tool of the bumbling humbug.

In *Beautiful Joe's Paradise*, by contrast, the balloon retains its magic: "We were going up and up, and I expected to gasp and have a catching in my throat as if I were in a swing. But there was nothing of the sort. It just seemed as if there was a sweet little breeze blowing by the balcony, that took us in its arms, and bore us right over the Bay. In going with it we felt nothing, no rocking motion, nor rushing motion, nor any kind of motion, but just the sweeping away of things beneath us" (28–29). The balloon's workings are enigmatic, its movements "just the sweeping away of things beneath us"; this description names only the mode of transport, while the image pairs the balloon with avian flight. In both versions, the balloon operates as a metaphor for the magical mechanics of the novel. In another version of literary taxidermy, the balloon transports readers to the uncanny zone of the island.

Within that zone, Saunders revivifies the bodies of texts as well as animals. Sam and his monkey guide discuss who Beautiful Joe is by referring to the previous novel:

> "Joe, old Joe," I gasped. "Of course I've read of him, but he's a story-book dog. I thought this paradise was only for real animals."
>
> "Can't an animal be a real animal and a story-book animal too?"
>
> "The book said he was real, still I didn't believe it."
>
> "Well, he truly was a real dog—people used to read his story, then go to see his living self. He died a year or two ago, and we brought him here in an air-ship. His false body is buried near his home, and if you choose, you can see it when you go back to America." (61–62)

The term "false body" is arresting enough on its own, and it has an additional connotation. It was sometimes used in taxidermy to describe the internal mount: "Sometimes the false body forms only a simple mass in which to embed the supporting wires."[78] In a novel about dead animals returning to life, taxidermy here may supply a vocabulary for dramatizing literary revivification.

This passage sets up several doubles—apart from the "false body" of the dead Joe and the real one on the island, there are "real animals" and "story-book animals," the dead Joe and the "living self." These are less doppelgängers than multiples, which is how Freud imagined the uncanny double: "The constant recurrence of the same thing . . . the same characters, the same destinies, the same misdeeds, even the same names, through successive generations."[79] The double counters death, providing "a defence against annihilation."[80] On the Island of Brotherly Love, such "defences" abound. Doubled "false bodies" are everywhere: A fish tells Sam, "I dare say you've eaten the false bodies of some of my family" (145), while a sparrow says that Sam's mother, back in San Francisco, is "not too anxious, because the doctor tells her that your false body will soon come out of its trance" (134). When Sam returns home, his mother asks him if he wants to see Rag's embalmed body, and he replies, "Oh, yes, but I left Rag alive and well. This is only his false body" (363). "False bodies" are everywhere, available to be consumed or awakened into uncanny life.

A different kind of uncanniness is embodied by Bella the parrot, who resurfaces in *Beautiful Joe's Paradise*. "You're a gay old resurrectionist," Sam tells her, to which she responds, "I'm the belle of the Island, the belle of the Island. . . . Pretty Bella, lovely Bella, sweet Bella" (75). While "gay" did not then have its modern sexual meaning, it did connote immorality; Bella speaks for the pleasures of rebellion, including self-love—presumably she is parroting others' praise of her as "pretty," "lovely," and "sweet." As a parrot, she already renders other speech uncanny; as a dead parrot resurrected, she has become her own uncanny double.

Bella's speech is, in turn, parroted by Sam, who is both the book's narrator and also the author, by conceit, of the novel we are reading: "I have just been looking at the pile of paper I laid out to write this story on. . . . I used to wonder how folks did it, but I see now you just take your paper, make up your mind what to leave out, and start in" (322). By novel's end, he is done: "[Though I] haven't got on so very well, what with my trying to keep slang out, and fit nice-sounding words in . . . I've got down what I wanted to say" (365). End of story, although also the start of another one: when Sam tells his mother where he has been, she calls in a doctor—"I told him he had been fooled by a false body" (363)—and then "an editor friend of hers published a very good story in his paper, called 'The Strange Hallucination of a Boy'" (363–64). Sam has become a journalistic subject, although the story's title also sounds like a

Freudian case study. Immortalized in "The Strange Hallucination of a Boy," Sam has become an uncanny analysand—the case of Sam E., the Sam-Man.

The "story in the paper" forms one model of representation named within the novel; the photograph is another. Sam says to Joe, "I'm surprised not to find you larger. You used to look larger in your pictures," Joe replies, "Oh, I was afraid of the photographer's camera. . . . I used to sit in front of one to please Miss Laura, but it frightened me terribly" (111–12). While Joe may be frightened by photography, his character in this novel is a kind of postmortem photograph, like photographs that depicted dead children—and, less commonly, pets—posed as if sleeping.[81] The novel, like the photograph, makes him "look larger"—undead, uninjured, and presidential.

Photography makes a brief appearance here, but fiction remains Saunders's preferred medium for animal revivification, as it was Freud's own choice for the uncanny: "Fiction affords possibilities for a sense of the uncanny that would not be available in real life."[82] One more example: "Nita: The Story of an Irish Setter" (1904), published two years after *Beautiful Joe's Paradise*.[83] "Nita" is a short story about the separation of Mary, a girl sent from California to the East Coast for her ill health, from her beloved dog, Nita. Nita, sold away by the child's mother, is sent to a cruel man who "gave her a cut with a whip" (6) and then rescued by a kind vet; learning that "the child is dying of grief over the parting from the dog" (19), the vet arranges for Nita to be sent East, and finally, "there was a reunion such as one is seldom privileged to witness" (22). "They shall never be separated again," declares the chastened mother at story's end, "'Where Mary goes her dog goes.' . . . And she kept her word. Mary and the dog are at present viewing together the wonders of Switzerland" (22).

In this story, dog loss is temporary, "dying of grief" is reversible, and revivification lasts. Mary reunites with her chastened mother as well as her lost dog; the recovery is that of girl "dying of grief" as well as of a dog. "Where Mary goes her dog goes" sounds like a line from "Mary Had a Little Lamb" ("everywhere that Mary went, / the lamb was sure to go"), with a travelogue ending. Still, although the story ends happily, the dog will not live forever; dog death is the ultimate destination within the story, as well as its real-life foundation in the loss of Saunders's own Nita. The "wonders of Switzerland" are a paradise, but only a temporary one, allowing the reader to imagine a fantasy zone wherein mourning and melancholy are both banished and—if only this were true—nobody dies at all.

5.

There are now so many ways to mourn dogs. Jane Desmond interprets pet cemeteries and pet obituaries, both on the rise, as new forms of mourning that grant pets the value of being grieved.[84] These forms of mourning seem, historically speaking, familiar; even the new media—like online pet memorials—seem like extensions of the pet-memorialization, pet-taxidermy moment of the Victorians. In an anthology on animal mourning practices, Margo DeMello expands the contemporary moment to include one essay on "freeze-drying Fido" through taxidermy and another on dog owners who freeze their male animals' semen.[85] The documentary *Furever* (2014), directed by Amy Finkel, respectfully surveys even more media with which people commemorate their animals—for example, jewelry, pottery, vinyl records, and bullets. Taxidermy, which is evoked in the film in modes from freeze-drying back to mummification, was the filmmaker's inspiration: *Furever* began when Finkel befriended a taxidermist with a business in pet dogs.[86] The next wave, already breaking for the rich, is dog cloning.[87] Even this option, though, seems less an avatar of a sci-fi future than an evocation of earlier moments, especially the pet-mourning, taxidermy-obsessed Victorian past.

The whole idea of mourning dogs with taxidermy seems creepy to me; my interest in taxidermy has its limits, after all. In the late nineteenth century, as Saunders's story of her revulsion against her taxidermied bird in *My Pets* attests, there was already a recoil against pet taxidermy, and this recoil continues now in different ways. Domestic pets are prohibited in taxidermy competitions, and Emily Mayer, the British artist, describes her resistance to working with pets as follows: "I try and talk potential clients out of it as most of them don't really want a piece of taxidermy, they want their animal back, and that's not something I can give them."[88] That's not something anyone can give them—"them" meaning the people I see at Tufts, "them" meaning, at some point not far in the future, me.

I am not sure what to expect from myself when Frankie dies. Sociologists studying pet loss use language that does not draw me in: "The pet owner's level of attachment to a deceased pet, the perceived degree of understanding received from others about the loss, and the level of other stressful events . . . combine to have a significant predictive value in grief outcome."[89] I find another kind of remembrance more compelling: the Dog Chapel in the northern Vermont town of St. Johnsbury, built by the artist Stephen Huneck, known for his brightly colored woodcut prints of retrievers.[90] The Dog Chapel has pews with dogs carved at their base, stained-glass windows featuring dogs, and a "remembrance wall" for people to record memories of dogs; by the time I visit, in summer 2011, the entire interior has become a remembrance wall, with notes about beloved dogs crammed and layered, floor to ceiling, on every inch of every wall. I have come here after a day spent at another venue in St. Johnsbury, the Fairbanks Museum; like Tring and the Booth in England, this is a natural history museum opened in the 1890s by a wealthy collector and filled with taxidermy.

Seeing the Fairbanks Museum and the Dog Chapel back to back, I realize that the chapel also offers a kind of literary taxidermy. It too puts dead animals on display, mounting their images and written notes about them. The effect is, to me, moving—bathos alchemized to pathos, whimsy leavened with grief. Grief for lost people as well as dogs: When I visit, the walls include tributes to the artist, Stephen Huneck, who killed himself early in 2011, apparently "despondent over having had to lay off most of the employees of his art business."[91] I see condolence notes about him alternating with commemorations of dogs. Stories of human and canine mourning are so often intermixed, here combined in the writing on the wall.

One more example, a film overtly interleaving dogs, people, and loss: This is *Wendy and Lucy* (dir. Kelly Reichardt, 2008), about a woman and her dog—the film's eponymous protagonists—on the road in Oregon, en route to Alaska, where Wendy (played by Michelle Williams) is hoping to earn good money working in fisheries. Poor, getting poorer, Wendy suffers a series of reversals, getting arrested for shoplifting, having her car break down, sleeping in a scary park, and above all, losing Lucy; she finds her but then cedes her to a new owner who can provide her with house, yard, and food; the film ends with Wendy back on the road, now solo, traveling by train. Directed by Kelly Reichardt, a woman filmmaker—a filmmaker—*Wendy and Lucy* is based on a short story, "Train Choir" by Jon Raymond. It is an art film, exquisitely austere, praised as "one of the most stripped-down existential quests since Vittorio De Sica sent his unemployed worker wandering through the streets of Rome searching for his purloined bicycle."[92] The comparison to *Bicycle Thieves* is apt, except that Lucy is no bicycle but a sentient being—part companion, part child, part alter ego, all dog; she is less stolen than lost, in several senses. *Wendy and Lucy*, I suggest, links dogs and loss in several distinctive ways—with unusual formal intimacy, within a framework of political as much as psychological loss, and with a melancholic outcome that resists the taxidermic lure of uncanny revivification.

FIG. 24.
"I'm Lost" poster in *Wendy and Lucy*, dir. Kelly Reichardt, 2008.

Before Lucy is lost, she is loved, in a way that mixes genres: the scenes of woman and dog evoke both the wide-open spaces of the male buddy road movie and the intimate domestic interior of the "woman's film." The opening of the film is a long shot of trains moving in a railroad yard, a quintessential setting for a male on-the-road story. Similarly, the second shot is of Lucy in the woods with Wendy, who is a slight androgynous figure, dressed in shorts and a plaid shirt: it seems to be the tableau of a boy and his dog—except that it is not. The difference gender makes is suggested in a scene shortly after, in which Wendy and Lucy awaken, together, having slept in the front seat of the car; this scene makes the vehicle a domestic interior in which Wendy's first movement, mother-like, is to stroke Lucy. The intimacy between woman and dog extends to every register of the film, from the close-ups of Lucy's head, which reinforce the presence of her gaze, to the minimalist soundtrack, which features Wendy's humming and Lucy's panting. This is not the typical master's voice, but an interior dialogue of voices, human and canine serving as each other's vocal partner and acoustic mirror.[93] Wendy and Lucy constitute a cross-species love affair, a mother-daughter tableau, and two parts—mirrored, echoed—of a split self. Lucy is played by the director's own pet, also named Lucy, which means that the intimate human-animal relationship here is also that of director and dog.[94]

The loss of Lucy is represented in ways that emphasize these forms of intimacy. "The word 'loss' itself has a double meaning when it comes to the dogs in our lives": sometimes it means dead, sometimes missing.[95] *Wendy and Lucy* works with both meanings. After Wendy returns from the police station to find Lucy is gone, she makes posters to try to locate her. The lost pet poster is its own genre, potentially "a heartbreaking story about love, loss, and friendship."[96] In Raymond's "Train Choir," the poster is described as follows: "[She] filled out the Lost Dog poster to the best of her ability. . . . Her writing was not pretty, but the important data was all there: name, breed, and even a picture of Lucy sleeping on the grass that Verna [Wendy] kept in her pocket at all times."[97] The film transforms this brief passage into an almost silent two-minute sequence that dramatizes the convergence, visual and aural, of person and dog.

The sequence begins with Wendy in a diner, completing the poster, which includes a photograph of Lucy and the words "I'm Lost / Floppy Ears / Sharp Eyes / Yellowish-Brown / Friendly / Face / Please help." The shot of this poster, over Wendy's shoulder, links the dog's body with that of Wendy; we see her hand producing the "I," in another version of first-dog voice. Wendy is then shown photocopying and posting the copies, mutely, herself a kind of tracking animal. Finally, she calls out, "Lucy," finding her own voice through naming the dog. Throughout, the human voice still presides: it is Wendy who speaks, and Kelly Reichardt who makes the film. But Lucy is necessary to this sequence, as she was to the making of the film: "One big reason she was cast was because she tends to destroy Kelly's apartment when left alone, so she had to be on set anyway."[98] Lucy the dog seems to have her own voice of demand, or at least destruction, in the film's production.

The master here—Wendy, and behind the camera, Kelly Reichardt—could be any human, though her "I" seems specifically female. I am reminded of a subgenre of the "woman's film" known as the "maternal melodrama," anatomized by scholars in the first wave of feminist film theory. These are films centered on mother-child rupture: "Maternal melodramas are scenarios of separation, of separation and return, or of threatened separation—dramas which play out all the permutations of the mother/child relation."[99] A foundation of the genre is *Stella Dallas* (dir. King Vidor, 1937), in which a mother loves her daughter above all others; their bond is ruptured repeatedly—and ultimately, self-sacrificingly, by the mother herself. *Wendy and Lucy* may seem an unusual candidate for the maternal melodrama: melodrama is commonly understood as all about excess, "characterised by an extravagantly dramatic register and frequently by an overtly emotional form of address."[100] Extravagance and emotion customarily come out in the genre's mise-en-scène; for example, Stella Dallas's excess explodes in her ruffly, gewgawed, girly costumes. In *Wendy and Lucy*, by contrast, Wendy is boyish, stripped down in her clothes and behavior, and the film is spare rather than extravagant; this film is a minimalist melodrama. But it is a maternal melodrama nonetheless. It features women, it dramatizes an intimate bond between mother-like and childlike figures, and it turns on the loss of a beloved.

A loss inseparable from gender—and also from class. In *Stella Dallas*, poverty sets the story in motion; Stella's desire to escape the grinding life of a factory town in Massachusetts pushes her to land a rich husband; she gets money but remains unrefined; she eventually pushes Laurel away to give her a better chance at a classy life, without her embarrassingly vulgar mother. In *Wendy and Lucy*, we know little of the backstory, but it is poverty that results in Wendy's first loss of Lucy: no money, hence shoplifting, hence arrest, hence not being there for Lucy, who is taken away in her absence. And no money means no respect: the smug grocery clerk who turns her in says, "If a person can't afford dog food, they shouldn't have a dog." As in *Bicycle Thieves*, the problems of money permeate, take up time and space, and colonize all else. An analysis of *Wendy and Loss* focuses on its moments of weariness, stillness, and waiting, emphasizing Wendy's "suspension in this dead time of economic evanescence."[101] The "suspension" is of Lucy as well as Wendy, the evanescence of economy producing the pet who is lost—missing, maybe dying.

There is no happy ending to this story, even after—especially after—the lost dog is found. Remember Saunders's "Nita," in which the lost dog and the girl, reunited, live happily ever after: "Where Mary goes her dog goes. . . . Mary and the dog are at present viewing together the wonders of Switzerland." In *Wendy and Lucy*, by contrast, there is no Switzerland, no wonder, no money. In Raymond's "Train Choir," Verna—the Wendy character—reflects on her options:

> Verna crouched and let Lucy lick her face through the holes of the fence. . . .
>
> A dog could love anyone, she thought. A dog could be happy almost anywhere . . .
>
> And by the same token, a dog could forget anyone, too. They were loyal, but only to whoever was around. . . .
>
> The tears began gently, but then, quickly, came with more power. Soon Verna's whole body was quaking. She felt like rusty nails were being pried from her chest. She crouched there and let the sun hit her. The sun was still free, she thought, though probably not for too much longer.
>
> "I lost the car, Lu," Verna said, sobbing. "I'm sorry . . . " And already the decision was made.[102]

FIG. 25.
Woman and dog in *Wendy and Lucy*, dir. Kelly Reichardt, 2008.

The ruptures represented here are multiple: the fence that divides woman from dog, the dog's potential memory loss, the class-loss of the car, and finally the woman's decision to renounce the dog. As in the maternal melodrama, the effect is heartbreaking—here, pursued into metaphor, "rusty nails . . . pried from her chest"—and tears are the result, within the story and in its effect on the reader. Verna moves from internal thoughts to spoken words, but the most salient sound in the passage is her sobbing, a feminized and wordless version of the "master's voice" that seems close to a dog's own howl.

In the film, the pathos of rupture is enhanced by visual doubling. The renunciation sequence begins when Wendy, having arrived at Lucy's new home, sees Lucy, who is shown from behind; it ends when Wendy, having left Lucy, is shown from the same angle. Between these paired shots are moments of merger—Wendy leaning down to talk to Lucy, Lucy kissing her through a chain-link fence—that are constrained by the barrier of the chain-link fence. Wendy apologizes to Lucy with the same dialogue from the story ("I'm sorry, Lu . . . I lost the car . . . I'll make some money, I'll come back . . . Be good."), but again her words are secondary not only to the sound of her sobbing but also to the image of the fence. As with the cage in *White Dog*, a metal boundary separates human and dog, but it operates differently here. In *White Dog*, human and dog are antagonistic, and the fence keeps the human alive; in *Wendy and Lucy*, theirs is a relationship of intimacy, and the fence imposes an unwilling separation. Both fences forge forms of incarceration, human as well as animal—for Wendy, incarceration in mourning, incarceration of class.

This ending is wrenching: minimalist melodrama, maximal effect. It reminds me of the ending of *Stella Dallas,* when Stella, having renounced Laurel, watches Laurel's wedding, sobbing, in the rain, her face framed by the jail-like bars of a metal fence—like Wendy, loving and losing Lucy, sobbing through the chain-link, fenced in by class. Patricia White makes this connection too: "*Wendy and Lucy* ends on a note of deserved *Stella Dallas*-scaled pathos—all Wendy can call her own is her point of view."[103] Although Stella strides off diagonally into the future, a smile on her face: the final shot is ambiguous, but there is at least a chance that renunciation has brought her some joy.[104] Not so here: the final two shots of the film reprise the first two but in a melancholic way. Wendy is walking in the woods, but without Lucy; the tableau of girl and dog is now just girl. And then a shot of the train, with Wendy on it—the vehicle of mobility now signals pain. Wendy is lost even though—especially because—Lucy is found. There are no rejuvenations here, upgrades to the uncanny: Lucy's death is "not yet," but Lucy as Wendy's companion is "no longer." On the road, Wendy is solo, inconsolable.

On the road—that most American activity—to where? *Wendy and Lucy* is set in the Pacific Northwest; Ketchikan, Alaska, is Wendy's destination, where she hopes to find well-paying work in a fishery—a mirage of the American dream, ever receding on the horizon. But there is another country through which, presumably, she must pass to get to Alaska: by land or ferry, she must traverse the Pacific coast of Canada.

Canada—the other side, its Atlantic coast—is whence Marshall Saunders came. I seem to have been everywhere but Canada in these chapters—from New England to the South to California and from the United States westward to the Pacific location of the "Island of Brotherly Love" and eastward to the United Kingdom. I have traversed the Anglo-American divide with particular frequency, conjoining Stowe and Alcott with Sewell and Woolf, Hornaday with Wells; some continental Europeans—Freud, Bonaparte, Krafft-Ebing, Rothschild—have slipped in as well. But I have sidestepped Canada at almost every turn. It is time to go back on the road.

CHAPTER 5

CanLit

1.

In summer 2010, I travel to Canada to learn more about Marshall Saunders. I have corresponded with archivists about her papers there, and I have reread the published accounts of her life, the most detailed of which is by Elizabeth Waterston.[1] I am focusing, finally, on the role of Canada in her writing, so I return to her biography via geography: Saunders was born in 1861 in rural Nova Scotia, then moved to Halifax, where her father was a well-known minister; at fifteen, she went to Edinburgh for one year of schooling and to Orléans for another; she returned to Halifax and began writing fiction; visiting her brother in rural Ontario, she met the dog who became "Beautiful Joe." After the novel's success, Saunders spent two years in Boston, then traveled more, zigzagging across North America on both the Canadian and U.S. sides; she lived for a time in San Francisco—where *Beautiful Joe's Paradise* is anchored and *My Pets* begins—with her sister Rida, then came home to Halifax; in 1909, she apparently had a mental breakdown and went to Maine; she recovered and moved to Toronto, living there for thirty years, often with another sister, Grace. She wrote many more novels; she was active in Canadian civic life; she cofounded a branch of the Canadian Women's Press club with her friend Lucy Maud Montgomery, author of *Anne of Green Gables* (1908); she was awarded a CBE from the Queen in 1934; she died in Toronto in 1947 at eighty-five. She is commemorated in "Beautiful Joe Park" in Meaford, Ontario, on the Georgian Bay, and her papers are at Acadia University, in Wolfville, Nova Scotia, on the Bay of Fundy.

I need to shift my frame of reference for this geo-biography. For example, I associate 1861, the year of Saunders's birth, with the Civil War and the Confederacy, but in Canada, this was the decade of Confederation: in 1867, four provinces—Ontario, Quebec, New Brunswick, and Nova Scotia—united to become a Dominion, other provinces joining later, the whole autonomous but not sovereign, still linked to mother-country England. Canadian Confederation will have a sesquicentennial celebration in 2017, but this 150th anniversary has not yet shown up on my radar, although I am anticipating the Civil War sesquicentennial, 2011–16, with interest. I understand that my association for this historical moment—Confederacy rather than Confederation—reflects my ignorance of Canada as well as my training as a scholar of Civil War literature. My perspective is provincially U.S. American—I mean "provincial" not in the denotative sense (Saunders's home province was Nova Scotia) but in the connotative one, wherein it is synonymous with small and small-minded.

Provincialism in the pejorative sense has been a defining antagonism for Canadian writers at least since Confederation, after which they "were able to assume that an emergent national literature was in the wings."[2] In the wings, perhaps, but that national literature did not take center stage until a century later, when "CanLit" emerged. This term is both the general shorthand for "Canadian Literature" and a more specific historical designation for the mid-twentieth-century production, promotion, and celebration of Canadian literature. Now a half century past its emergence, CanLit has been self-scrutinized at every turn, that self-scrutiny itself becoming part of Canadian popular culture, the world of "Mondo Canuck"—though that is an insiders' title; I would not use it, nor be able to declare as its authors do that reflecting on CanLit is part of a tradition of "obsessive Canadian self-examination."[3] There are still enthusiastic celebrations of the moment when CanLit had its "arrival," breaking its bounds of provincialism, turning Canada "from a country without a literature to a literature without a country."[4] But many others offer critiques of CanLit. For example, a writer distances himself: "CanLit is the literary equivalent of representational landscape painting, with small forays into waterfowl depiction and still lifes. . . . Am I CanLit? No. I'm Canadian and write books."[5] Scholars criticize the biases of the category and the resulting exclusions of its canon. Some aim to broaden CanLit into "Trans.Can.Lit," aiming to adapt its legacy for different ends—less nationalist, more multicultural.[6]

Although this term too has a different valence in Canada: "multiculturalism" has been official government policy since the Canadian Multiculturalism Act of 1988, and as such is now often criticized from the left as well as right, seen as self-congratulatory, neoliberal, watered-down; for some scholars, it "sidetracks race and class for a celebration of cultural difference."[7] Contemporary Canadian cultural studies criticizes the celebration, bringing into view the "unsettled remains" left by Indigenous, Francophone, Acadian, Asian Canadian, and African Canadian writers marginalized in Canadian culture.[8] Each of these unsettlings is itself unsettled, starting with their terms: Rinaldo Walcott, for example, prefers "black Canadian" to "African-Canadian," because scholars need to "recogniz[e] that something important does happen here."[9] Customarily that recognition does not happen, "here"—Canada—or anywhere: as Katherine McKittrick puts it, in a Canada assumed to be all-white, black people are "unexpected, shocking, concealed in a landscape of systemic blacklessness."[10] Not only is black Canadian writing yet to be acknowledged fully in Canadian literary studies; it is also neglected within contemporary frameworks of the black Atlantic.[11]

Contemporary issues of Canadian multiculturalism and blackness may seem distant from the nineteenth century of Marshall Saunders, but they are not: an earlier literature only comes into view via the lenses of scholars, writers, and publishers. I start to situate Saunders in a literary genealogy of Canadian women writers. I have already named one who was her friend: L. M. Montgomery, also from the Maritimes, also associated with popular books for children; unlike Saunders, Montgomery is still famous, her *Anne of Green Gables* series still read, her home on Prince Edward Island a thriving tourist site.[12] Waterston identifies Saunders as one of a "silenced sextet" of nineteenth-century Canadian women writers. I do not recognize the names of the other five, though I am guessing that they are also unknown to most Canadians; they were women who "subsequently disappeared from view."[13] Only one other nineteenth-century Canadian woman writer has stayed in view: Susannah Moodie, whose memoir *Roughing It in the Bush* (1852) registered her unhappy migration from England to Canada. Moodie, in turn, was the subject of an early book of poems by Margaret Atwood, the most famous figure of CanLit. I wonder if there is a line of affiliation from Saunders back to Moodie or forward to Atwood.

But now I am reproducing the whiteness of the CanLit canon; I want to decenter it from the start. I start again. Born in 1861, the same year as Marshall Saunders, was poet and performer E. Pauline Johnson, Mohawk name Tekahionwake, daughter of a Mohawk father and a British mother; her biography "blurs the borders of what it means to be Native, a woman, and Canadian."[14] Border-blurring seems built into women's writing of this period: another Saunders contemporary, Sui Sin Far, was born Edith Maud Eaton in England to a British father and a Chinese mother, and lived in Seattle, San Francisco, Boston, and Montreal; scholars now situate her fiction and journalism in an even broader transnational circuit that includes Jamaica.[15] Mary Ann Shadd, black editor and abolitionist, born and raised in the United States, wrote *A Plea for Emigration* (1852) in the same year as *Roughing It in the Bush*—emigration here meaning black people moving north to Canada rather than white people coming west from Britain.[16] Situated in transnational frameworks, Moodie herself looks different: she transcribed the Caribbean slave narrative of Mary Prince, and a pioneering scholar of black Canadian literature sees *Roughing It* as itself a "displaced 'slave narrative.'"[17] Johnson, Far, Shadd, Moodie: contemporary scholarship helps me understand any genealogy of nineteenth-century Canadian women writers as transnational and multiracial from the start.

For me, this understanding involves reorientation: I have read Sui Sin Far before, but under the rubric of Asian American—that is, Asian U.S.—literature, and I studied Mary Ann Shadd, who lived in Canada for only a decade, as an African American writer. Reconstructing black Canadian literature means admitting short-term residents and acknowledging chronological gaps. George Elliott Clarke—the pioneering scholar I just quoted; also a poet and playwright by genre and a Nova Scotian by origin—locates Nova Scotia as the genesis of black Canadian writing and anthologizes its literary history, but his examples from 1860 to 1960 are sparse.[18] This absence, as another scholar summarizes, is national rather than provincial: "After the outpouring in the nineteenth century, a resurgence of black Canadian writing occurred only after the increase in Caribbean immigration from the mid-1950s on."[19]

This gap contrasts with the abundance of African American literature at the turn of the century: for example, Anna Julia Cooper, Frances Harper, Pauline Hopkins, and Ida B. Wells—to start with the women, as I like to do—as well as W. E. B. Du Bois, Booker T. Washington, Charles Chesnutt, and Paul Laurence Dunbar. I was hoping to find black Canadian fiction contemporary with *Beautiful Joe*; earlier, situating it in conversation with African American literature, I deferred discussion of its Canadian context. Not that America needs to be the basis of comparison: Walcott, for example, asserts that "the comparison is not Black Canada/African America; the comparison is Black Canada/Black Britain."[20] Still, I do not want to analyze Saunders's depictions of race in Canada without showing black Canadian alternatives.

That is putting it too tentatively: I wish to understand Canadian literary history with themes of race and multiculturalism at the center and with black writers as active participants in the story. I will analyze these themes elsewhere in Saunders's oeuvre, and I will find relevant black Canadian intertexts for her work. I know, for example, that she wrote a novel on Acadians in Nova Scotia and another featuring black Canadian characters in Halifax: *Rose of Acadia* (1898) and *Jimmy Gold-Coast* (1923), respectively. To analyze Saunders as a Canadian writer, I need to understand how her novels represent boundaries of race and culture as well as species.

The species issue is already prominent in CanLit criticism; as a Canadian literature scholar summarizes, "Animals are so fundamental to our writing that it might indeed be said that our literature is founded on the bodies of animals—alive or dead; anthropomorphized or 'realistic'; indigenous or exotic; sentimental, tragic, magical, and mythical."[21] This scholar is herself riffing on a line from Margaret Atwood's *Surfacing*: "Do you realize . . . that this country is founded on the bodies of dead animals?"[22] I have read this novel, a feminist classic, but I was then thinking about feminism, not Canada, nor animals; I will have to return to it, reflecting on the origin of species in Canadian literature. Already, it seems as though these species are usually wild ones. Wild animals are the currency of Canada—literally: "Look at Canadian money and stamps—you'll see beavers and moose and caribou and loons."[23]

I am not sure how the dog fits into the nation. There are dog breeds with Canadian names, like the Labrador retriever, but presumably they are not embodiments of Canada; being canine is not like being Canadian—that is, having a nationality. Dogs are the property of nationally specified human citizens; they are not passport-holding citizens themselves. There is the "canine good citizen," an obedience program trademarked by the American Kennel Club; a book called *Citizen Canine* argues that developments in animal law, increased uses in military service animals, and other social changes are rapidly advancing American dogs—U.S. American dogs—to the status of "fellow citizens."[24] But the idea of a dog as an "American citizen" sounds odd, as does a hyphenated identity like "canine-American," let alone something more specifically provincial within the worlds of dogs and nations. I do not think of Frankie, for example, as a "golden retriever–New Englander."

Still, there is a strange relationship, at once incidental and intimate, between dog breeds and geographic regions. The Bernese mountain dog, the Havanese, and the Chihuahua do not represent Bern, Havana, or Chihuahua—or, expanding from the part to the whole, Switzerland, Cuba, or Mexico—but at the same time, dog breeds are not separable from the regions in their names. I have already mentioned the English bulldog, avatar of nationhood, and the German shepherd, whose militarization in Germany set the terms for its later use by U.S. police in the civil rights era. These breed-nation affiliations could be volatile: after World War I, the German shepherd became so associated, pejoratively, with all things German that it was briefly renamed "Alsatian" in England, while the dachshund was called the "liberty hound" in the United States.[25] I do not know the histories of Canadian breeds, which seem to cluster on Marshall Saunders's Atlantic coast: Labrador, Newfoundland, Nova Scotia duck tolling retriever. I would like to know if Saunders—herself a Nova Scotia retriever of animal stories—forged new connections between dogs and provinces and, on a bigger scale, among animals and nations.

It is time to summarize what lies ahead: in this chapter, I analyze what roles animals play in the representation of nations; to put it more personally, I say what I did on my summer vacation. That last phrase does not sound scholarly enough. I am pulling at the leash of disciplinary imperatives again—in this case, the need for me, as a scholar trained in the literature and culture of the United States, also a U.S. American by biography, to be responsible to a Canadian author. I respect this responsibility, and I try to be faithful to its scholarly imperatives; I attend carefully to the work of Canadian literature scholars and hope that they—you—will find evidence of this attention in the endnotes. It is just the tautness of the leash—the demand for seriousness of style—that I resist. Let me try again.

In this chapter, I explore, through a series of zigzags in time and space, the Canadian dimensions of Saunders's writing. I first foreground the cultural and species flux in her fiction, analyzing depictions of ethnicity, race, and animals in her novels *Rose of Acadia* and *Jimmy Gold-Coast*. To suggest alternative ways of understanding this flux, I analyze a more recent Canadian novel, Lawrence Hill's *The Book of Negroes*.

Turning to *Beautiful Joe*, I situate its apparent evacuation of Canada in the context of the preoccupation with animals in Canadian literature. I situate Saunders in resistant response to the "nature fakers" animal-writing controversy of her moment and in uncertain filiation with the most iconically Canadian of women writers, Margaret Atwood.

Finally, I analyze the Saunders archives in Nova Scotia—the "summer vacation" part—where I find materials that highlight themes of female voice and animal skin. The archives do not fix the geographic locations that arise in this inquiry. They suggest, rather, shifting spaces in which women, animals, and nations overlap and in which CanLit—both canine and Canadian—is at once an oxymoronic identity and a cross-species fiction.

2.

Early Canadian writers, Carole Gerson argues, "operated in a trans-national framework: triangulated with Britain and the US in the case of anglophone writers."[26] Marshall Saunders fits this framework, Trans.Can.Lit in an old-school way: she traveled to Scotland and France in her youth, and she lived frequently in the United States. Her interest was professional as well as personal: for Canadian authors in the late nineteenth century, the United States was increasingly where the publishing industry and markets lay. America became the new capital of capital, while Britain remained the imperial home of culture; Saunders's favorite authors—Scott and Dickens—were Scottish and English.

What Canada meant, for a writer, was still uncertain. From a writer in 1886: "We are still an eminently unliterary people."[27] This was Sara Jeanette Duncan, another contemporary of Saunders, well known in her day; I find this quotation in an anthology of Canadian literature published in 1975 that itself begins, "Yes, there is a Canadian literature. It does exist."[28] Saunders is not in this anthology, nor in a more recent, less defensive survey of Canadian literature in her era.[29] It is hard to find her voice among the shifting tones of CanLit criticism.

I cut out the CanLit middleman and find an example of Saunders's place as a Canadian in *Types of Canadian Women and of Women Who Are or Have Been Connected with Canada* (1903), an early volume of boosterism, boosting Canadian women and, through them, Canada itself.[30] This book is heavy and glossy, with one woman per page, a block of text under her photograph and her Canadian address listed on the bottom; it seems like a kind of field guide to Canadian women, a human *Birds of Canada*.

Although there was an actual *Birds of Canada* (1872), by Alexander Milton Ross, as well as a *Birds of Ontario* (1894), by Thomas McIlwraith. I find an essay championing McIlwraith, and am startled to see its mention of *Beautiful Joe*: "I'm not about to argue that Margaret Marshall Saunders's Beautiful Joe . . . is in any way comparable to Melville's white whale or that McIlwraith's whining loon is a direct relative of the demonic bird [in] Thoreau's *Walden*."[31] I was not aware that anyone was in danger of likening *Beautiful Joe* to *Moby Dick*, although it turns out that this is not the first time it has happened: "I lack the courage to take students from 'Call me Ishmael' to 'My name is Beautiful Joe.'"[32] I do not see why male critics repeatedly compare Saunders to Melville to demote her. It seems odd to make this a matter of men's "courage" and thereby to insult both woman and dog.

Marshall Saunders.

MISS MARSHALL SAUNDERS.

From a photograph by Gauvin & Gentzel, Halifax.

Miss Margaret Marshall Saunders, who has become one of the foremost writers of animal stories in the world, is the daughter of a Baptist clergyman, the Rev. E. M. Saunders, D.D., and his wife, Maria Kisborough Freeman, and was born in Milton, Queen's County, Nova Scotia, April 13th, 1861. She claims descent from John Alden, the first pilgrim from the *Mayflower* to set foot on Plymouth rock, the same who, with his wife, Priscilla, is immortalized in Longfellow's "The Courtship of Miles Standish." On her mother's side she counts descent from another *Mayflower* pilgrim. Born amid romantic surroundings, Miss Saunders early became a student and a writer. After completing her education in France, she returned to Canada, and did her first work for newspapers and magazines. Her first story, "My Spanish Sailor," appeared in 1887. This was followed by "Beautiful Joe,"* the autobiography of a dog, which won the $200 prize offered by the American Humane Education Society for the best story illustrative of the kind or cruel treatment of domestic animals and birds in the Northern States, and other animal stories which have been extensively read. She has also written love stories, which, in the opinion of Katharine Hale, have "an irresistible charm." The best known of her works, in addition to those we have mentioned, are "Daisy," "Charles and his Lamb," "The House of Armour," "Rose à Charlitte," "The King of the Park," "For the Other Boy's Sake," "Deficient Saints," "For his Country," "Her Sailor" ("My Spanish Sailor" rewritten), "'Tilda Jane," and "Beautiful Joe's Paradise." Miss Saunders has seen much of the world, and is described as one who possesses genius, heart and insight. Residence : *28 Carlton Street, Halifax, N.S.*

* The subject of this story died at Meaford, Ont., September 13th, 1899, in the eighteenth year of his age.

305

FIG. 26.

Henry James Morgan, Marshall Saunders entry, *Types of Canadian Women and of Women Who Are or Have Been Connected to Canada*, 1903. Photo: James Gehrt.

Types of Canadian Women praises both. I start with the text: Under her photograph is her signature, "Marshall Saunders"; under this, the photograph's caption, "Miss Marshall Saunders"; and at the start of the text, "Miss Margaret Marshall Saunders"—a progression that firmly feminizes her. The entry also nationalizes her, presenting her Canadian—or, to be more precise, Haligonian: "Residence: 28 Carlton Street, Halifax, N.S." However, her origins are U.S. American: "She claims descent from John Alden, the first pilgrim from the *Mayflower* to set foot on Plymouth rock. . . . On her mother's side she counts descent from another *Mayflower* pilgrim."[33] Saunders is represented here as a double-Mayflower American—a blue blood or, in dog terms, a purebred.

The dogs on the page, though, push the pilgrimage back to Canada. The photograph shows Saunders with the fox terrier Billy, a similar image to the frontispiece of *Beautiful Joe*, though this dog looks right at the reader; presumably, he too lives in Halifax. A note at the bottom of the page reasserts the Canadianness of the original *Beautiful Joe* dog: "The subject of this story died at Meaford, Ont." The "subject of this story" was also, presumably, a subject of the Queen, or at least his owner was. It would not be right to say that Canadians were the lapdogs of the British, but neither were they self-ruling masters. The first entry in *Types of Canadian Women* confirms British sovereignty: it is for "Her Royal Highness the Princess Louise," daughter of Queen Victoria; Louise "recently gave expression to the pride she felt in having once lived among the Canadian people."[34] Saunders is triangulated on a map in which America is the rock, Britain the rule, and "the Canadian people" a source of pride to the patronizing English—less colonial lapdog than ornithological wonder.

As Saunders knew, the idea of "the Canadian people" as a unified group is a canard. I like using this term here—literally the French noun for duck, figuratively an idiom for an unfounded idea—because Saunders herself pursues literary connections between avian species and Canadian peoples. But I am getting ahead of myself: Saunders's many novels include one about Acadians, *Rose à Charlitte* (1898). It has been recovered by Gwendolyn Davies—whose scholarship on Canadian literature has been indispensable to me—and reprinted as *Rose of Acadia*.[35]

Some context for the novel: Acadians came to Nova Scotia from France and were expelled in the eighteenth century by the British, the expulsion known as *le grand dérangement*; the Acadian diaspora extended into the Caribbean, Africa, and Europe, as well as throughout the Americas; some Acadians later returned to Nova Scotia, built communities, and celebrated cultural identity, fighting ongoing prejudice. Saunders lived in an Acadian community in Nova Scotia in summer 1897, whence she gathered material for the novel. *Rose of Acadia* focuses on two Acadian—here, "Cadien"—heroines, Rose and Bidiane, as encountered by a visiting Bostonian, Vesper Nimmo. Rose eventually marries Vesper after a long, impediment-strewn romance, while Bidiane, more modern, marries an Acadian politician, rides bicycles, and supports suffrage.

To understand this novel, I need to understand more about Nova Scotia from here in Massachusetts. Not that I am the first to do so: the most famous literary account of Acadian expulsion was Longfellow's narrative poem *Evangeline* (1847), which he wrote without having been to Nova Scotia, composing it from Cambridge. He embodied Nova Scotia's Acadian history in the romantic—in both senses—struggle of the titular heroine to reunite with a husband separated by expulsion. His invention was so influential that after *Evangeline*, Nova Scotia experienced a tourist boom, becoming "New England's therapeutic outpost, offering stressed-out American urbanites a chance . . . to recover their vital energies."[36] Its history imagined from afar, Nova Scotia became New England's spa for renewal.

Although this cultural history is new to me, the literary representation of Acadians is not. I have read about different Acadians: "Cajuns"—that is, Acadians who settled in the U.S. South after their expulsion from Nova Scotia—appear prominently in this same historical moment in the fiction of Kate Chopin and other "local color" U.S. writers. I need to move my sense of Cajun to Acadian from the U.S. South up to the Atlantic coast of Canada and to think of the local in "local color" as transnational. This is, generally, a good goal for scholars: "Partitioning the cultures of North America . . . has limited our reading of individual works and genres, and obscured opportunities for innovative cultural analysis."[37]

Rose of Acadia itself seems antipartition, offering instructions for how New Englanders can understand Acadians: its male protagonist, Vesper, journeys from Boston to Nova Scotia, and when he arrives, he is forced to unlearn stereotypes. Given an Acadian newspaper, for example, he sees that it is "in fluent modern French, which greatly surprised him, as he had expected to be confronted by some curious patois concocted by this remnant of a foreign race" (40–41). In an even more pointed refutation of bias, an Acadian character acerbically remembers the visit of a woman journalist, accompanied by her dog, who wrote an article that was "the nonsense, the drivel, the insanity . . . 'Among the Acadiens, Quaintness Unrivalled, Archaic Forms of Speech, A Dance and a Wedding, The Spirit of Evangeline, Humorous Traits, If You

Wish a Good Laugh Go Among Them!'" This writer "had nothing to go on—nothing—nothing" (85–86). This is Saunders mocking her own image as the dog-friendly author of *Beautiful Joe* and criticizing the ethnographic impulse, presumably also her own, to invent "Quaintness Unrivalled" out of "nothing." This passage seems surprisingly self-reflexive and self-critical. Compared to other novels about Acadia—I rely on a scholar of Canadian literature to write this sentence—*Rose of Acadia* is unusual in "its concern to de-mythologize the Expulsion of the Acadians."[38]

Still, other elements of the novel make of Acadians what Vesper first suspected: a "foreign race." The novel seems to use race as synonymous with heritage ("the Acadiens were courageous,—they were a brave race" [347]), with blood ("It was the best blood of France that had settled Acadie" [179]), and with culture ("she acutely appreciated the racial differences about her. There were two worlds in her mind,—French and English" [265]). But the connotation is also of a foreignness linked to racial difference. Robin Bates argues that anxieties about racial intermingling are central to the novel, particularly in the character of Bidiane's aunt, an Acadian woman named Mirabelle Marie Watercrow; she is "fat [and] good natured" (256), comic and vulgar, and speaks in dialect. Mirabelle, Bates argues, "embodies hybridity in an imagined cosmos where purity stands out as the highest ideal."[39] Her hybridity inheres not only in her Acadian identity but also in her Indigenous heritage; Mirabelle's grandmother is described as "a squaw" (373). Though Bidiane is presented in contrast to her aunt ("Very little of the Indian strain had entered her veins, except a few drops were exhibited in a passion for rambling in the woods" [373]), she is her kin, and "a few drops" are presumably enough to mark her as impure. In such themes as the ideal of purity and the fear of hybridity, race is central to the novel—"vitally constitutive," Bates argues, of its meaning.[40]

Though Bates situates *Rose of Acadia* alongside other Maritime Canadian novels, I am struck by the potential affinities between Nova Scotia "Cadiens" in Canadian fiction and Cajuns in U.S. literature. The cultural geography of Kate Chopin's Louisiana is different from that of Saunders's Nova Scotia. In *The Awakening*, for example, the Francophone characters who embody the aristocratic traits Saunders ascribes to "pure" Acadians are Creole, not Cajun; Chopin features a more elite version of Louisiana Creole than the "dark, hairy-faced, shaggy-headed" protagonist of George Washington Cable's "The Taxidermist." But Saunders, like Chopin, represents Cajuns as "both primitive and passionate," reflecting a hierarchy in which they "were considered 'lesser' whites."[41] Nova Scotia "Acadiens" like Saunders's Mirabelle seem linked to Louisiana "Cajuns" transnationally, not so much by the content of their culture as by their authors' depiction of white anxieties about it.

Another connection: I have already noted the prominence of bird imagery in *The Awakening*, and what I most notice about *Rose of Acadia* is its many avian metaphors. Here is an Acadian man likened to a cardinal: "Those resplendent creatures in the male sex are usually clothed in gay red jackets. This male's plumage was also red, but . . . it had a trimming of pearl buttons and white lace." (50). An Acadian woman who has never left Nova Scotia is a "little owl," while her sisters are "overdressed birds of paradise, in their rustling silk blouses, big plumed hats, and self-conscious manners" (167). Most strikingly, Mirabelle Marie Watercrow "plunges about among them like a huge, unwieldy duck" (458–59). The crow-named Mirabelle seems to embody an avian as well as Acadian grotesque.

These negative bird metaphors are not incidental to the novel's emancipated presentation of its Acadian heroines, Rose and Bidiane. Rather, birds function as a fixed nonhuman margin against which the Acadian women's possible migration to whiteness may be measured. Rose and Bidiane, higher in class, will fly into white modernity, but hybrid Mirabelle will remain forever immobile. Saunders may know that stereotypes of Acadia are canards, but her quintessential Acadian is a "huge, unwieldy duck."

The Acadians of *Rose of Acadia* also take shape in relation to another racial presence. At the turn of the century, Nova Scotia had a substantial black population with a multilayered migration history, which included enslaved people brought by the British and French, black Loyalists relocating after the American Revolution, Maroon communities from the Caribbean who were deported to Nova Scotia, and refugee slaves heading north on the Underground Railroad.[42] Saunders interacted with at least a little of this history: I have already noted her mention of Nova Scotia "colored settlements" in *My Pets*, as well as her memories of "the irresponsible though kind-hearted Ellen, the coloured woman who assisted my mother." Other traces of black labor mark her provincial history more indirectly: the family of Saunders's mother, the Freemans, were "West Indies merchants" who used the port of Halifax, and Saunders remembered childhood treats of "tamarinds, raisins, cones of sugar, and other delicacies from the West Indies."[43] Such details mark Halifax's participation in a black Atlantic circuit of commerce; Nova Scotia "delicacies" like West Indian "cones of sugar" were built on the black labor of the slave trade.

In *Rose of Acadia*, the black Atlantic surfaces only fleetingly. In Boston, Vesper's mother chides a visiting Acadian boy for his hostility to her African American servant, reminding him that "you have seen colored people on the Bay [of Fundy]" (244); among Acadians, Vesper sees a "negro" selling "cocoanuts," "probably obtained from some schooner" (257). These images locate black people, like the novel's avians, in contrast to the more mobile and ambiguous group of Acadians. Black people function as an even more fixed margin against which the novel's Acadian heroines may measure, and further purify, their symbolic whiteness.

A quarter century later, Saunders represented black Canadians more directly, in *Jimmy Gold-Coast, or the Story of a Monkey and His Friends* (1924), a novel set in Halifax that overtly brings together racial and animal themes. This novel is narrated in first-animal voice by an African monkey, Jimmy, and ostensibly centered on the fall from grace and redemption of the monkey's white human master, Mr. Napier Gordon MacGregor MacHadra, known as "Nappy." But its main human character is a black woman known as "Nonnie," who works for Nappy's family and on whom Jimmy is focused throughout: "I took a good look at her. She was quite an elderly woman, and very, very fat and black, and as shiny as sealing-wax. . . . My master was beaming all over, for he loved this old woman whom I found out later had brought him up" (19).[44] Nappy remains devoted to Nonnie—"Whom did he love the most? . . . It was Nonnie once, and Nonnie twice, and Nonnie all the time" (171–72)—and Nonnie, in turn, comforts Nappy when he is sick in prison, singing, "Poor little pickaninny, frightened by a bear, run to your mammy" (281).

This vocabulary is painfully familiar. A decade after *Jimmy Gold-Coast*, Margaret Mitchell's *Gone with the Wind* (1936) will cement it in the character of Mammy. Nonnie is a racist stereotype—no more a realistic depiction of black life in Nova Scotia than, say, *Gone with the Wind* shows black life in the U.S. South—and another Africanist persona invented by white norms. The character is complementary with Saunders's nonfiction descriptions of black Nova Scotians. In a 1906 diary entry, for example, she describes a visit to a church in Preston, Nova Scotia. En route to the church, she declares of a woman fixing her husband's necktie, "Pretty to see the old blackie dressing her mate"; upon arrival, she notes, "Coloured people . . . greet each other in a lively rollicking way. Busily slapping on shoulders or backs but no rowdyism."[45] The terms of praise—"pretty," "no rowdyism"—are structured by hierarchy and stereotype. Nonnie in *Jimmy Gold-Coast* is another "lively rollicking" black person, an "old blackie." The novel brings black people into the orbit of white characters as objects of picturesque condescension and as fantasy figures benevolent toward the white people for whom they labor.

That such racist images suffuse the writings of a middle-class white writer of this era is unsurprising. The yield of such images is literary, not biographical. As Morrison writes, the goal of analyzing an Africanist presence is not to determine "a particular author's attitudes toward race" but to investigate "the ways in which a nonwhite, Africanist presence and personae have been constructed . . . and of the literary uses this fabricated presence has served."[46] In the case of *Jimmy Gold-Coast*, the "nonwhite, Africanist presence" of the novel is articulated in a distinctive way as both transnational and cross-species. Transnational in that Nonnie locates herself as initially from the United States ("I am an American citizen. . . . I comes slap out of Florida" [245]), currently Canadian ("I'se a Novy Scoshun now" [246–47]), and ancestrally African ("My great-granfadder was a king in Africa" [122]). Cross-species in that Nonnie expresses an affinity with Jimmy from the start: "'Bless its little heart,' said this nice old black creature, and she fondled me as if I had been a baby" (21). Nonnie's cross-species bond is a maternal compensation: "She said she had never had a baby of her own, and though I must never for a minute compare myself with a human being, I was like a nice little animal infant for her" (257). This is, again, a racist narration of stereotype, reproducing associations of black people with monkeys. The caution that Nonnie offers—"I must never . . . compare myself with a human being"—is disregarded by Nonnie herself; likening Jimmy to "a nice little animal infant," she affiliates black people with monkeys.

The conjunction of an animal narrator and blackness recalls *Beautiful Joe* but to different effect. *Beautiful Joe*, I argued, opens the way to a potential critique of the racist metaphorical equation of black people with animals; it suggests this critique through its imagery of mimicking parrots and trickster monkeys as well as enslaved dogs. *Jimmy Gold-Coast*, by contrast, reinforces that equation, with a racist collapse between "Mammy" and monkey. That Joe aligns, at least potentially, with antiracism and Jimmy with racism is less an inconsistency in Saunders's writing over a quarter century than an illustration of the differing political effects of racial connotations in animal representation. For example, when these connotations remain implicit, as in *Beautiful Joe*, first-animal voice has more potential to disrupt stereotype, but when racial difference is explicitly embodied, with a monkey linked to a black woman—or a duck conjoined with an Acadian woman—racist stereotype takes over. For Saunders herself, the primary interest in each case was the creation of first-animal voice. In *Jimmy Gold-Coast*, for all the novel's imagined migrations among Canada, the United States, and Africa, its crossing of species boundaries is its only committed form of repatriation.

This white-authored fantasy is not, however, the only way to imagine the fictional conjunction of animals, blackness, and Canada. For comparison, I now zig forward to a black Canadian novel from 2007; this also means a zag backward, as this novel is set in the eighteenth century. Lawrence Hill's *The Book of Negroes* (2007), highly celebrated in Canada, is narrated by a black woman, Aminata Diallo, in her old age, beginning with her life as a girl in Africa; she is kidnapped into slavery, endures the Middle Passage and enslavement in South Carolina, escapes to New York City, serves the British during the American Revolution, migrates to Nova Scotia with other black Loyalists promised freedom by the British, journeys to Sierra Leone, and winds up in Britain in abolitionist circles in 1802. The Nova Scotia section, crucial to the novel, emphasizes Canada as a site of racism rather than respite. The author deliberately aimed to criticize a mythology of virtue in which African Americans "migrating from Manhattan to Nova Scotia, hopefully to find themselves in Canaan . . . find that they are sorely disappointed. Their experiences in Nova Scotia fly in the face of the Canadian promise of this being a land of greater kindness."[47] That is Lawrence Hill interviewed about the novel, exposing the history of racism beneath Canada's idealization as slave-refuge Canaan.

And this is Aminata narrating within the novel: "I have long loved the written word, and come to see in it the power of the sleeping lion. . . . In the absence of an audience, I will write down my story so that it waits like a restful beast with lungs breathing and heart beating" (101).[48] This quotation signals my interest in the novel: its representation of animals. The "sleeping lion" and "restful beast" are just two of the many animal images that saturate the novel and that constitute one of its significant themes.

Animal imagery starts in the first paragraph, when Aminata asserts that even now, in her old age, "I can still smell trouble riding on my wind, just as surely as I could tell you whether it is a stew of chicken necks or pigs' feet bubbling in the iron pot on the fire. And my ears still work just as good as a hound's" (1). These sentences turn from actual animals, dismembered into food, to an animal simile, "as good as a hound"; this movement from the literal to the literary highlights the narrator's control over animal imagery. The same movement recurs repeatedly: Aminata initially remembers her mother, a midwife, as so skilled that "she even helped a donkey stalled in labour" (12); then, imagining her birth, she describes herself "sliding from my mother like an otter from a riverbank" (13).

Once Aminata is enslaved, she repeatedly deploys animal metaphors as a survival strategy: in South Carolina, "The best approach was to follow the [white man's] conversation like a well-trained dog" (129). Elsewhere her metaphors directly animalize white people, as when she describes one of the first white men she sees in Africa as "a new breed of man. Spin speckled, like that of a washed pig" (44). She animalizes institutions as well as individuals: "[The slave ship] was an animal in the water. It rocked from side to side like a donkey trying to shake off a bundle, climbing on the waves like a monkey gone mad. The animal had an endless appetite and consumed us all" (57).

As her account of the ship continues, donkey and monkey give way to a sustained animal metaphor: "I imagined the biggest lion of my land . . . living and breathing and hungry. It seemed as if we were being taken straight into its anus" (63). The metaphor of the slave ship as a lion anus privileges Aminata's own imaginative power, and it gives others power too:

> My expression, *anus of a lion*, raced through the stacks of men. . . . [One] gave off a deep booming laugh that echoed inside the hold. . . . One man asked the question, and all the others answered.
>
> "Where are we?" the one said.
>
> "Sister says anus of a lion," two men called back.
>
> "I say where are we?" one called.
>
> "The anus of a lion," more men called back.
>
> One man asked, "Who is the sister who visits us?"
>
> "Aminata . . . "
>
> In the darkness, men repeated my name and called out their own as I passed. They wanted me to know them. Who they were. Their names. That they were alive, and would go on living. (66)

Aminata's lion-anus metaphor is so powerful that it produces laughter, naming, and solidarity.

At stake in Aminata's use of animal imagery is a refutation of a history of representing Africa only through animals. Aminata herself uses animal imagery to describe the African landscape: of the mountains near the slave ship, "One of them rose like an enormous lion" (54), and from her childhood, she remembers, "Sierra Leone—Lion Mountain rose up so sharply . . . that I wanted to reach out and touch it" (375). But she rejects the way non-Africans reduce Africa to its animals: "When people ask about my homeland now, they all seem to be fascinated by dangerous beasts. Everybody wants to know if I had to run from lions or stampeding elephants. But it was the man-stealers I had to worry about most" (42). She particularly objects to Africa's representation in maps, as in one she encounters in a South Carolina library: "I saw a lion and an elephant sketched in the middle of the land called Africa. . . . But the map told me nothing of where I came from" (211). Scrutinizing another such map, she concludes, "This 'Mapp of Africa' was not my homeland. It was a white man's fantasy" (212).

In Nova Scotia, by contrast, she encounters these lines from Jonathan Swift, which also comprise one of the novel's epigraphs: "So geographers, in Afric-maps, / With savage-pictures fill their gaps; / And o'er unhabitable downs / Place elephants for want of towns." Aminata finds, "Swift had expressed the very thing I was feeling now. These weren't maps of Africa" (368). Swift galvanizes her, as does a better map, which lists "Sierra Leone" and town names she recognizes; she decides to leave Canada with an expedition to Sierra Leone. That this expedition is unsuccessful does not undo the importance of maps to her sense of self. On the last page of the novel, she asserts: "I would like to draw a map of the places I have lived. . . . There would be no elephants for want of towns, but rather . . . a woman balancing fruit on her head, another with blue pouches for medicine, a child reading, and the green hills of Sierra Leone" (470). In this map: no animals.

Aminata's idea of eliminating animals from the map of Africa complements her skill as a maker of resistant animal images, from pigskin white man to lion-anus slave ship. In each case, she controls the means of cultural production, whether the literary making of animal metaphors or the cartographic representation of Africans as animals. That control is lacking in Marshall Saunders's *Jimmy Gold-Coast*, not only because it is written by a white writer whose account of black Nova Scotia does not venture outside the terrain of racist stereotype, but also because that novel's black female character is imprisoned within animal metaphors not of her own making. The Canada of Hill's novel, by contrast, centers on a self-narrating African woman who banishes the monkeys and elephants of "white man's fantasy." In so doing, she locates Nova Scotia in the black Atlantic and leaves Canada—anti-Canaan, in Hill's revision of CanLit—far behind.

3.

Exploring Canada in Marshall Saunders's novels, focusing on her depictions of culture and race, I have skipped over *Beautiful Joe*. Also, I have ignored the animals with which Canada is usually associated—not monkeys and elephants but more northern mammals in a colder climate; in *The Book of Negroes*, when Aminata arrives in Nova Scotia, she is told, "We must get some furs for you. Good thing for deer, moose and bear" (317). Deer, moose, and bear are more characteristically Canadian, especially in the rendered form of fur—"rendering" providing a particularly apt verb in the context of animal representations, explicated by Nicole Shukin as both "making a copy" and the "industrial boiling down and recycling of animal remains."[49] Rendered alongside these quintessentially Canadian animals is another one: the beaver, an official emblem of Canada since 1975, and "Canada's fetish insofar as it configures the nation as a life form that is born rather than made."[50]

This passage echoes Simone de Beauvoir ("one is not born a woman, but becomes one"), whose own nickname, "Castor," was French for beaver—but such echoes are scarcely necessary for the woman question to arise. Beaver, fur, fetish: a feminist analysis of Canadian animals seems required. The traffic in beaver updates the traffic in women, circulating metaphoric female genitalia between men. It seems as much a fantasy about masculinity as femininity, portable to other nations: in British boys' fiction about the Canadian fur trade, "trapping and trading in the wilderness represents a raw masculine energy that affirms widespread notions of British Imperial destiny."[51] Although some women, Canadian and otherwise, liked beavers too. A queer interpretation finds erotic possibilities for women, "seductive, but troubling," in the Canadian fetish of fur.[52]

The fetish has other political dimensions. It obscures the violence perpetrated against Indigenous peoples, as well as against animals themselves.[53] Canadian taxidermy—popular in the nineteenth century, often made from wildlife hunted in the Rockies—similarly promoted its white makers and demoted or obscured Indigenous peoples; Canadian culture aligns "taxidermically preserved animals and caricatured mannequins of aboriginal peoples."[54] Animal fur and taxidermic mount: two sides of the same Canadian loonie, converting the animal into an image of national identity from which human violence has been expelled.

Canadian literature accordingly features dead wildlife. To start with the gold standard, or at least the Nobel Laureate: Alice Munro's short story "Vandals" (1993) depicts a male taxidermist in rural Ontario who sexually assaults a girl. The story is told through the memories of the girl, now a woman, who describes the taxidermy in detail—"shelves of stuffed and mounted animals, some quite tiny and bright, and some large and suitable for shooting"—but the sexual assault only briefly. The language of murdered animals comprises the connective tissue between the two: after the assault, "he collapsed heavily, like the pelt of an animal flung loose from its flesh and bones."[55] Munro offers a feminist critique of the taxidermist, making him a mounter of both animals and girls, and himself "an animal flung loose."

But I have started near the end: "Vandals" implicitly critiques a century-long tradition of Canadian fiction focused on animals, whose start was contemporary with the writing of Marshall Saunders. These were the wild animal stories of writers Ernest Thompson Seton, author of *Wild Animals I Have Known* (1898), and Charles G. D. Roberts, author of *The Kindred of the Wild* (1902). Animal-wise, Seton and Roberts are Canadian literature's founding fathers, although their paternity was also questioned at the moment of birth, in the controversy that became known as the "nature fakers." This began in 1903, when a writer named John Burroughs published an attack on Seton, Roberts, and others for anthropomorphizing animals. The condemnation prompted a flurry of defenses and attacks; eventually Teddy Roosevelt weighed in, coining the term "nature fakers."[56]

In scientific terms, the nature faker controversy turned on disputes over animal behavior, fueled by debates over Darwinian evolution; in literary terms, it condemned fiction for masquerading as nonfiction. As Burroughs put it, "The line between fact and fiction is repeatedly crossed and . . . a deliberate attempt is made to induce the reader to cross too and to work such a spell upon him that he shall not know that he . . . is in the land of make believe."[57] This attack suggests anxiety about masculinity as well as fictionality, with the male reader ensorcelled under a "spell" in the make-believe Oz of fiction. The nature faker is a confidence man, a connection Roosevelt made explicit: "The fables [of the nature fakers] bear the same relation to natural history as Barnum's famous artificial mermaid bore to real fish and mammals."[58] Like Barnum conning his customers with the Feejee Mermaid—or H. G. Wells's taxidermist defrauding his customers—the nature faker fools the reader, and the artificial mermaid is his female bait. Wild animals seem to enter the Canadian scene as feminized fictions conning their male readers.

While the nature fakers controversy was a debate waged by men, Marshall Saunders circulated in the same marketplace with these writers; for example, Charles Livingston Bull, who illustrated *Beautiful Joe's Paradise*, also illustrated books by Roberts and Seton.[59] In his preface to *The Kindred of the Wild*, Roberts named "'Beautiful Joe' and 'Black Beauty' [as] deservedly conspicuous examples" of an outmoded style of animal writing: "It is no detraction from the

FIG. 27.

Nina Katchadourian, *My Pets*, from the series *Once Upon a Time in Delaware / In Quest of the Perfect Book*, 2014 ("Sorted Books" project, 1993 and ongoing). Used by permission of Nina Katchadourian.

merits of these books, which have done great service in awakening a sympathetic understanding of the animals . . . to say that their psychology is human. Their animal characters think and feel as human beings would think and feel under like conditions."[60] Ironically, having termed *Beautiful Joe* as anthropomorphic, Roberts would then be accused of the same transgression. Perhaps this is not an irony but an underlying affinity: Saunders was herself engaged in "nature fakery," anthropomorphizing overtly through first-dog voice.

Another connection between Saunders and the nature fakers emerges from an unexpected source: the artist Nina Katchadourian, whose taxidermy dog—*Chloe*, the Pomeranian she tried to exhibit in a natural history museum—I have already mentioned. In an enchanting project entitled *Sorted Books*, Katchadourian juxtaposed physical books and photographed their titles in combination to create a form of visual poetry.[61] Customarily, she used book spines, but in one instance, when a museum invited her to work with their collection of turn-of-the-century illustrated books, she juxtaposed full covers. Her pairings include one of Marshall Saunders's *My Pets* and Ernest Thompson Seton's *Wild Animals at Home*.

The viewer need not know anything about Saunders or Seton for this photograph to have an effect. The two covers share design elements—coloring, typography—and an animal theme; the large paw print on the right seems to enlarge and defamiliarize the small paws of the animals featured on the left. The artist "consider[s] *Sorted Books* a type of portraiture," and here the portrait shows two modes of domesticated animals: the proprietary control over "My Pets" and the less stable experiment of "Wild Animals at Home."[62] The effect of the dual portrait is at once comic and affectionate.

In the context of the artist's interest in mounted animals, we could also see the juxtaposition of book covers as effecting a kind of literary taxidermy. If we consider a book's cover as a kind of skin for the body of the text, this image makes meaning in its recombination of cover-skins; it offers literary taxidermy in an affirmatively botched mode. Moreover, if we read this photograph in relation to the original nature fakers debate, it seems to redress Marshall Saunders's abjected place among male authors of wild animal stories. With the two book covers presented as parallel, Saunders does not seem an outmoded participant to be left behind, as Roberts had claimed, but an equal participant in this literary conversation. The juxtaposition of the titles *My Pets* and *Wild Animals at Home* suggests that the wild/domestic, male/female binaries of animal fiction were less hierarchical absolutes than complementary modes.

That is my speculation, but here is Saunders herself discussing her relation to the nature fakers in a letter to her publisher:

> There is a great outcry now from the President down against writers of my school. I consider that Mr. Long [William Long, another writer targeted as a nature faker] is being persecuted. . . . However there is some truth in the assertion that children should not read too many tales where non-human animals are endowed with human intelligence. For example in proposing "Beautiful Joe" for supplementary reading in a school a severely practical teacher might object to the dog telling the story in the first person. Of course man [many] incidents in the story are true but a conversing dog could never be true to life so these persons say. Therefore out of deference to these new prejudices, and also because it suited me better to do so, I have kept everything in this latest book [*My Pets*] strictly veracious.[63]

Condemning attacks on accused nature fakers as "persecut[ion]," Saunders concedes that *Beautiful Joe* is open to criticism. Her concern, however, is with the pedagogic dangers of the speaking-dog character to children rather than the emasculating effect of anthropomorphized wildlife on men. Her assertion that *My Pets* is "strictly veracious" is on grounds of preference—"because it suited me better to do so"—as well as "deference" to pedagogy and presidents.

I would like to take the terms of Saunders's reclamation further. Minus the pejorative, wrestled back from the accusatory mode, "nature fakery" seems like a positive way to think about Saunders's use of first-animal voice in *Beautiful Joe*. The novel is nature fakery expanded into first-dog voice.

Also, it is Canada fakery: *Beautiful Joe* is Canadian, but not about Canada; it is a book written by a novelist raised in Nova Scotia and based on an experience in Ontario, but set in New England. The change of setting was, as I have noted, a market constraint: Saunders entered her manuscript in a contest sponsored by the American Humane Education Society, which specified that the entries must have U.S. American settings. The constraints for Canadians now work in the other direction: twentieth-century legislation mandated that radio and television broadcasting reflect significant amounts of Canadian content.[64] There is an official phrase for this, "CanCon," and no equivalent term in the United States—"AmCon" being its own unmarked default, a totalizing norm.

But market constraint is the start, not the end, to what is significant about the U.S. American setting of *Beautiful Joe*. The rules of the contest did not specify that she use New England: "[There were] *three* prizes of two hundred dollars each for the best and most useful stories of not less than one hundred 'Black Beauty' pages, on (1) The *kind and cruel treatment of domestic animals and birds in our Southern States and Territories.* (2) *The kind and cruel treatment of domestic animals and birds in our Western States and Territories.* (3) *The kind and cruel treatment of animals and birds in our Northern States.*"[65] This description triangulates the United States into southern, western, and northern regions, asymmetrical categories—South and West are still expanding into "Territories," while the "Northern States" are fixed. Marshall Saunders, clearly reading these instructions carefully, chose to narrow "Northern States" to New England.

Which was its own imaginative zone, in flux at this moment. Historically, "New England" comprises six states—Maine, New Hampshire, Vermont, Connecticut, Rhode Island, Massachusetts—and it is a real place; I live there. But it is also, and always has been, an imagined region, and in the late nineteenth century, "New England" was undergoing vigorous reinvention. This was the moment, for example, of the Colonial Revival, new buildings that looked back architecturally. Historians have shown how such inventions often responded defensively to the present—for example, attempting to ward off waves of immigrants then transforming New England.[66] These immigrants included nearly half a million Maritime Canadians in search of work in New England factories.[67]

Saunders deplored this migration—she called Boston "a huge pulp mill into which Nova Scotia throws many of her sons and daughters"—but she too offered a cultural reinvention of New England, using its grist for her own mill.[68] It is not just that *Beautiful Joe* is set in New England but that it is so precisely mapped onto it. Joe is born on "the outskirts of a small town in Maine called Fairport" (54); "The summer after I came to [the Morrises], Jack and Carl went to an uncle in Vermont, Miss Laura went to another in New Hampshire, and Ned and Willie went to visit their holidays with a maiden aunt who lived in the White Mountains" (131). Boston recurs repeatedly, from a simple shout-out to the "American Humane Education Society in Boston" (150)—the organization sponsoring the competition that *Beautiful Joe* won—to an account of an old woman pained by animal cruelty ever since she was "a little girl walking the streets of Boston" (138).

This specificity is a bluff, a nation faker. Gwendolyn Davies has shown that "Fairport, Maine," in *Beautiful Joe*, its main city, is Halifax in disguise. Saunders's papers include a map of Halifax annotating it as the "Fairport" of the novel, with a marginal note, "B. Joe written abt. Halifax but was moved to Maine to comply with conditions for taking prize. Fairport Maine is Halifax Nova Scotia."[69] Keridiana Chez gives one kind of metaphor for this transformation: "*Beautiful Joe* is, in effect, a quilt of Canadian facts woven with American details."[70] I think of it as another version of literary taxidermy: the novel seems a mounted animal, with American fur on a Canadian manikin. *Beautiful Joe* covertly vivifies Canada by remounting it under the skin of the United States.

What happens to Canada in this transformation? There are just a few references to it in the novel, and they all concern animals. One comes in a series of anecdotes about Newfoundland dogs. In the first, Joe sees boys throwing sticks for two Newfoundlands, who then start fighting: "It was terrible . . . to see the way in which they tore at each other's throats" (100); in the second, a friend's dog is treated poorly: "The Drurys' Newfoundland watch-dog Pluto had arrived from New York, and he told Jim and me that he had had a miserable journey" (132); and in the third, Joe describes "a brave Newfoundland dog, that saved eight lives by swimming out to a wrecked sailing vessel, and getting a rope by which the men came ashore" (167). The Newfoundland moves from a posture of aggression to victimization to heroism.

Newfoundland was a popular dog breed; exported in the late eighteenth century from Canada to the United Kingdom, it became known for its strength, bravery, and loyalty.[71] Several examples of the breed have already come up in these pages: the unnamed Newfoundland who frightened Freud's Anna O. and—much more typical of the breed's positive image—Lord Byron's beloved pet Boatswain, Emily Dickinson's companion Carlo, and Eliza's loyal Bruno in *Uncle Tom's Cabin*. Newfoundland was also Britain's earliest Canadian colony, though it did not formally become a province until 1949; its people have historically been denigrated within Canada, and "Newfie" jokes are a category of ethnic slur.[72] So the Newfoundland as a dog became a valued early export of Canada, while the "Newfie" as a person later became a ridiculed citizen within it. That "Newfoundland" recurs in *Beautiful Joe* seems, to me, to evoke the region as well as the dog. Saunders's heroic Newfoundland suggests a shout-out to CanCon, emphasis on the "con"; like a trick of the confidence man, her dogs stand in affirmatively for its absent Canadian people.

This interpretation may be a stretch, but look at the other reference to Canada in the novel. It comes when Joe is visiting the farm with Mr. Wood, who speaks of pigs, "by no means the stupid animals that some people considered them. He had had pigs that were as clever as dogs." The smartest are Canadian:

> He said the most knowing pigs he ever saw were Canadian pigs. One time he was having a trip on a sailing vessel, and it anchored in a long, narrow harbor in Canada, where the tide came in with a front four or five feet high called the "bore." . . . Every day at low tide, a number of pigs came down to look for shell-fish. Sometimes they went out for half a mile over the mud flats, but always a few minutes before the tide came rushing in, they turned and hurried to the shore. Their instincts warned them that if they stayed any longer they would be drowned. (213–14)

The long, narrow harbor must be Nova Scotia's Bay of Fundy, which has a famously high tidal range; its dramatic differences between low and high tides cause a wave called a tidal bore. Pigs may be "as clever as dogs," but here they are "knowing" in their own terms. Pigs are often emblems of disorder, poverty, and dirt, as well as a figure for insult—for example, "Men are pigs." In the nineteenth century, there was also a counterimage of pigs as learned animals; at the turn of the century, Barnum & Bailey Circus advertised exhibitions of pigs playing cards.[73] Saunders's learned pigs know something more practical: how to save themselves from drowning.

In *Beautiful Joe*, then, Canada is represented by pigs, certainly, and dogs, possibly, along with water, mud, and shellfish—but no humans. There is another way to look at the almost total absence of Canada within the novel, its reduction to the condition of low tide. It is an enactment of a classic theme in CanLit: the erasure of Canada itself. "I wasn't aware that I lived in a country with any distinct existence of its own. At school we were being taught to sing 'Rule Brittania' and to draw the Union Jack; after hours we read stacks of Captain Marvel, Plastic Man and Batman comic books"[74]: these are early sentences in Margaret Atwood's *Survival*, her famous 1972 study of Canadian literature; they implicitly update Sara Jeanette Duncan's nineteenth-century lament of Canada as a "barren literary horizon," here a space blotted out by "Rule Brittania" and Batman. *Survival* catapulted Atwood into celebrity, catalyzing self-examination in the new era of CanLit, and prompted ferocious criticism, in part because of Atwood's feminism, her reputation in this era being that of "a medusa with a razorblade in her mouth."[75] Medusa-made or not, *Survival* seems to have lost its place in the CanLit canon; a recent anthology on Canadian cultural studies, for example, barely mentions it.[76] I can tell that the field has moved past *Survival*, but I don't want to do so. As you have seen, I like going backward to early works when studying new fields; it is a necessary, often revelatory, part of the scholarly zigzag.

I read *Survival* now, and it seems to overlap with Marshall Saunders. By overlap, I mean that the missing Canada of the aggressively New Englandized *Beautiful Joe* seems an enactment of the literary space of Canada as Atwood describes it—not only erased but animalized. Fiction about "animals caged, trapped and tormented" is Atwood's first example of Canadian literature, and she devotes a whole chapter to animals: "Those looking for something 'distinctively Canadian' in literature might well start right here."[77] Her focus is on Seton's *Wild Animals I Have Known*, not for its potential nature fakery but for its portrayal of animals as victimized, suffering, and dying; Seton, Atwood argues, offers stories "about animals *being* killed, as felt emotionally from inside the fur and feathers."[78] A key quotation from Seton: "The life of a wild animal *always has a tragic end*."[79] A key quotation from Atwood: "If animals in literature are always symbols, and if Canadian animal stories present animals as victims, what trait in our national psyche do these animal victims symbolize?"[80] Her answer to this riddle: the Canadian is a "threatened victim."[81] The equation is that Canadianness equals victimization.

You could interpret *Beautiful Joe* as an early version of this equation. The Canadian pigs fleeing their tidal drowning are threatened victims, as is the Newfoundland who had "a miserable journey" on the train—and as is Beautiful Joe. With his docked ears and tail, Joe enters the novel in a condition of supreme victimization. He is a Canadian dog docked of his Canadianness—but to be docked of Canadianness is also, in this equation, to be an exemplar of Canada.

For Atwood, the solution is to reject victimization: "This above all, to refuse to be a victim. Unless I can do that I can do nothing. I have to recant, give up the old belief that I am powerless and because of it nothing I can do will ever hurt anyone" (222).[82] Actually, these words are from the end of her novel *Surfacing*; Atwood finished it just before starting *Survival*. I go back to *Surfacing* now and notice how they share themes, including Canada and animals.[83]

Taxidermy—the enshrinement of the victimized animal—appears frequently in *Surfacing*, exemplifying for Atwood the domination of humans over animals and of U.S. Americans over Canadians. At a gas station are "three stuffed moose . . . dressed in human clothes and wired standing up on their hind legs, a father moose with a trench coat and a pipe in his mouth, a mother moose in a print dress and flowered hat and a little boy moose in short pants, a striped jersey and a baseball cap, waving an American flag" (16). Flag-waving is a prelude to American violence toward animals, as in a grisly scene with a dead heron: "Why had they strung it up like a lynch victim? . . . The only relation they could have to a thing like that was to destroy it. . . . It must have been the Americans" (138). The simile equates American lynching with taxidermy, although Canadians are not blameless in the making of a country "founded on the bodies of dead animals." It is important for nations as for individuals to take responsibility: "This above all, to refuse to be a victim . . . I have to recant, to give up the old belief that I am powerless and because of it nothing I can do will ever hurt anyone" (222).

The "I" here is, not coincidentally, a woman. The Canada of Atwood's *Survival* seems feminized, in the negative sense: lurking behind the equation Canadianness = victimization, especially for those made anxious by the razorblade-wielding Medusa, is another one: victimization = feminization. In *Surfacing*, Atwood solves the equation: the Canadian protagonist is affirmatively female, and she rejects any connection to victimization. "This above all, to refuse to be a victim" is the exhortation of Atwood's unnamed protagonist after she has journeyed solo through the northern Ontario wilderness and into the wild of her own psyche, which is rebellious and sad and, by the end, semi-mad, albeit in a complex, yellow-wallpapery way. In the novel, women are connected to Canada and animals in many ways, including a discussion of Canada as a "split beaver," puns intended (141). This novel was published in 1972, a foundational year in the women's liberation movement—for example, *Ms.* magazine began then—and feminism is an active presence in the novel. A character says of his wife, "I'm all for the equality of women; she just doesn't happen to be equal and that's not my fault, is it?" (163).

I like the ironic comedy of that comment, as well as the dark humor in Atwood's tableau of the U.S. American family as a taxidermy trio of Canadian moose. It seems a way of taking earnest critique—for example, the idea that Americans are animals—and twisting it with wit. I take pleasure in bringing to the surface Atwood's humor more than her nameless narrator's own final "surfacing," which is represented in terms of animals. The narrator at novel's end: "I laugh, and a noise comes out like something being killed: a mouse, a bird?" (222). The woman's voice emerges as that of a resistant victimized animal, a bird of Ontario making noise, but no longer human speech.

This brings me back to *Beautiful Joe*, which begins where this passage ends: with images of animal mutilation providing the foundation of the voice of a nonhuman "I." This is only a loose connection to Atwood. Saunders is not mentioned in *Survival*, even in the chapter on animals. By contrast, *Beautiful Joe* is name-checked in the work of Carol Shields, another eminent Canadian woman writer. In Shields's novel *The Stone Diaries* (1993), a list of the lifetime reading of the Canadian female protagonist begins, "*Black Beauty, Anne of Green Gables, Freckles, Twice Told Tales, Beautiful Joe*."[84] Shields is constructing a fictional protagonist and Atwood a nonfiction critique, but still, in the early 1970s, when her feminist voice was emerging, Atwood was paying homage to Susannah Moodie, not Marshall Saunders.

Then I find a tight connection between Atwood and Saunders, hidden in plain sight. At the start of *Surfacing*, as the narrator introduces the major characters, here is her boyfriend, Joe: "From the side he's like the buffalo on the U.S. nickel, shaggy and blunt-snouted, with small clenched eyes and the defiant but insane look of a species once dominant, now threatened with extinction. That's how he thinks of himself, too: deposed, unjustly. Secretly he would like them to set up a kind of park for him, like a bird sanctuary. Beautiful Joe" (10). I get a chill when I read this last sentence; it feels uncanny. Surely someone has discussed this allusion to Saunders: I check Atwood criticism, but there are only brief mentions of it as parodic.[85] That may be, but what is the point of the parody? Another perplexity is the allusion's placement, at the end of a paragraph in which animal images run amok, buffalo followed by bird. The paragraph seems Atwood's way of introducing animals as symbolically overdetermined beings, always serving as the tail end of the human simile ("like the buffalo . . . like a bird sanctuary"). "Beautiful Joe" has his own sentence, a two-word animal sanctuary, but the sentence also extends the other animal metaphors of the paragraph. Human Joe is like Beautiful Joe, who is himself a novel-length symbol. The allusion is also funny, offering a heads-up to readers who can recognize it, a sly flipping of the coin. Heads on the U.S. nickel is the buffalo, and tails is the Canadian writer's canine creation—the dog with the missing ears and tail.

Throughout Atwood's novel, Joe is hyperbolically equated with animals by a narrator self-conscious about such equations: "[In some stories,] the animals are human inside and they take their fur skins off as easily as getting undressed" is followed by "I remember the hair on Joe's back, vestigial, like appendices and little toes. . . . Everything I value about him seems to be physical" (65–66). And later: "'[Joe]seems out of sorts' David said, 'maybe he has worms; when you get back to the city you should take him to the vet'" (119–20). Joe's animalistic characterization throughout seems a gender reversal: "Atwood's novel—in backgrounding and silencing Joe, in reducing him to a mere physical presence, and in associating him with nature—[does] to him what traditionally has been done to female characters in literary texts."[86]

In animalizing Joe, Atwood is revivifying Saunders, albeit aslant: the original beautiful Joe is human inside, while Atwood's Joe is animal inside—"take[n] to the vet," cut down to size. If the human character seems a parody of the canine one, the reference overall offers a witty update, in which Atwood adapts a more genteel woman writer for an overtly feminist critique. Atwood's use of Saunders seems canny, and the collision between them seems, to me, uncanny.

Doubly so when, eventually, I meet her—Margaret Atwood, not Marshall Saunders—and ask her if she intended the Saunders allusion in the novel; she says no, and she cannot, at that moment, recall ever having read *Beautiful Joe*.[87] I am disappointed by this, but my argument does not require authorial intention—at least, not Atwood's; it requires my own. So I will be dogged about my claim: Atwood's novel, intentionally or not, revises *Beautiful Joe*. The "Can" in "CanLit," in the case of Atwood, is ambiguously canine but ever canny.[88]

4.

Another zigzag: I have gone backward into the twentieth century in advance of my 2010 trip, finding Saunders in Atwood's foundational feminism. And I have also gone forward, past this moment, to more recent scholarship on Canadian literature; you can tell this if you read the endnotes to the preceding pages. It is time to narrate that trip, wherein I travel in August 2010 to Wolfville, Nova Scotia, where Saunders's papers are housed in Acadia University, and then to Halifax, where she grew up and spent her early adulthood.

Wolfville is a university town set in a beautiful watercolor landscape: the farms of the Annapolis Valley, a lush quilted patchwork, meeting up with the long layers of the Bay of Fundy, which keep changing with the tides, their wavy harbors morphing into sprawling mudflats. As usual, though, I am drawn to the weirder elements of the picturesque. For example, in tiny Wolfville Harbour, a plaque explains the movements of the bay as follows: "Why are the tides so high? . . . Much like a father pushing his daughter on a swing, the gentle Atlantic tidal pulse pushes the waters of the system causing a large to-and-fro oscillation." This seems an oddly gendered metaphor, even more so in the French version alongside it.[89] Some things seem odd to me by virtue of being familiar, uncanny repetitions of home: for example, the nearby town of Amherst, whose name is that of the town next to me in Northampton. And Halifax seems wonderful: water everywhere, surrounding a city filled with bookstores and cafes, with a friendly, art-school vibe.

That is, I know, a paragraph written by a tourist; I am continuing in a long history of New Englanders traveling to Nova Scotia to idealize its landscape. I am following, for example, in the footsteps of Hezekiah Butterworth, whom I have already introduced as the introducer of *Beautiful Joe*. He was famous in his day for a series of travel books for young people with the title Zig-zag Journeys, unabashedly cast as exoticizing picaresques: for example, one was called *Zig-zag Journeys in India; or, The Antipodes of the Far East*. The series included *Zig-zag Journeys in Acadia and New France* (1885), in which he declares, "The tourist on his way to Halifax will, of course, stop over for a day or two at Wolfville or Grand Pré, and visit the Land of Evangeline."[90] Like Butterworth, I am journeying in "the land of Evangeline," and I make a visit to Grand Pré, which is ground zero for the reinvention of Nova Scotia following Longfellow's poem; the site was developed in the early twentieth century by a railroad company aiming for more business. I am on my own zigzag journey, and I too risk railroading Nova Scotia.

Still, as you know, I like the zigzag, and I do not reject tourism. I find Grand Pré moving, and I spend several hours absorbing its account of Acadian expulsion and exile. I have a similar response to St. George's Island, now a pastoral dot in Halifax harbor, but once a carceral space where Acadians were quarantined during *le grand dérangement*. A Canadian colleague has alerted me to visit the monument to Africville, a once thriving black Canadian community of Halifax; it was catastrophically razed in the 1960s for "urban renewal." The only sign of Africville now is a plaque in a park on the edge of town, beneath the looming span of a bridge. This is the violent zigzag of history as made by the razor's edge of racism—another Canadian anti-Canaan, another landscape marked by *dérangement*.[91]

The area formerly known as Africville is also now a leash-free dog park; I encounter many dogs there and around Halifax and Wolfville, including literary ones. In Wolfville, for example, an independent bookstore features a book by a Canadian woman writer, just published by a local press, which opens with a prose poem about famous women writers and their dogs.[92] I see many dogs and dog stories here, but little trace of the once-famous dog-story writer Marshall Saunders.[93] In Halifax, there are many plaques for notable figures, but I see none for her. I spend time looking for her family's houses in the Halifax neighborhood of Spring Garden; with the help of a librarian, I find that two of the houses still exist.[94] They are nicely maintained clapboards, but I see no evident commemoration of Saunders herself.

Except in her papers in the archives at Acadia University: seven large boxes of correspondence, journals, manuscripts, and miscellany. Between my first inquiry to the archivist and my visit to Acadia, the papers have been cataloged and summarized in a lengthy finding aid; this is a form of order I greatly respect as an erstwhile archivist myself, not to mention the daughter of a historian.[95] I have my own scholar-father, who is a meticulous historian of ordinary life, a master of the archives and the making of biography from elusive scraps.[96] I am not nearly as careful as he would be, though I do read through every folder.

These are, first and foremost, the papers of a professional writer, dominated by correspondence about publishing, editions, and rights. The questions I have been considering in a literary vein—say, the "translation" of a dog's voice into words—appear here in more pragmatic terms. For example, the Swedish publisher of *Beautiful Joe* writes to Saunders, "We have no such name in Swedish as 'Joe', and we could not possibly use 'Joseph' for the book, because in Swedish you know that is a 'holy' name and altogether 'too good' for a dog. The name 'Tasso' is a familiar name among the Swedes, and as a rule when the aristocratic people have a very fine dog they call it 'Tasso.' It was the best name we could adopt."[97] "Aristocratic people": something about Joe's humble origins seems to have gotten elevated in translation to the Swedish. Although elevation in translation is what occurs in the novel's first paragraph, wherein "only a cur" becomes "Beautiful Joe." And remember Saunders's description of her success: "I have had the honour of leading the old Ontario dog around the world on a chain of translations." The transformation of "Tasso" seems part of the migration, across nations and species, built into the novel from the start.

The role of Canada in the "chain of translations" is recounted here. In a 1921 speech, Saunders remembered, "When I started writing I met with so little encouragement in Canada that I went to American earth—but without the slightest resentment. My publishers knew that I was a Canadian, they knew I loved my own country best, but it never made any difference to them."[98] "American earth" presumably refers to her choice of U.S. publishers, though it also suggests the U.S. geography into which she translated the source material of *Beautiful Joe*. This phrase is also an embedded animal metaphor, "going to earth" describing what a hunted animal does. Saunders crosses species as she describes traversing geography, making herself an animal in charge of the hunt for literary success.

To see the Canadian earth next to the American, I look for the map of Halifax that became translated into "Fairport," a map first analyzed by Gwendolyn Davies. Here it is, in a folder with materials for *Jimmy Gold-Coast*. At the top, as promised: "B. Joe written abt. Halifax but was moved to Maine, to comply with conditions for taking prize. Fairport Maine is Halifax Nova Scotia." She continues, "In this neighborhood is the house beautiful Joe was written about. Same house figures in Jimmy Gold-Coast." Saunders has also added other terms, such as "penitentiary": this setting features in *Jimmy Gold-Coast*, when Nappy is imprisoned there. Also on this map is an annotation of a real event, "narrows where explosion took place"—this was in 1917, when a cargo ship blew up in the harbor, killing three thousand people.[99] The map is a shifting atlas of Saunders's geographic imagination, translating narrow Fairport to the narrows of Halifax, making *Beautiful Joe* contiguous with *Jimmy Gold-Coast*, updating 1894 to 1924, and blending fact with fiction.

Bringing the Fairport of *Beautiful Joe* forward into twentieth-century Canada, the archives also move the novel outward, to the transnational circuitry of the black Atlantic. In a bound journal from 1891, for example, Saunders noted attending a "Colored people prayer meeting," and she saved a newspaper clipping on "The Maroons of Jamaica."[100] The most prominent U.S. representation of African Americans is mentioned in the same journal: "Great prejudice against novels when Father & Mother were young. Were allowed to read U. Tom's Cabin however. That was exempt from general rule. Father tells of old deacon who when his daughter was reading it aloud to him exclaimed, Oh I hope it isn't a novel!"[101] *Uncle Tom's Cabin* appears here in the context not of slavery but of novel-reading. The entry recalls but contradicts Saunders's memory elsewhere of her mother as a girl, when "she had to secrete 'Uncle Tom's Cabin,' or her father would have banished it from the house"; in the journal anecdote of the deacon, the mother is exempt from the prohibition on Stowe. Still, in both accounts, *Uncle Tom's Cabin* forms part of a story of rebellious daughters reading fiction.

And writing it: an undated speech, "How I Began to Write," offers a revealing origin story for the emergence of her writerly voice. Saunders starts by recounting her mother, who "owned a tiny dog that she called little Al. She had a night-dress for him and put him to bed as if he had been a baby."[102] This story evokes the fictional cross-species mother-child duos of Nonnie and Jimmy in *Jimmy Gold-Coast* and of Laura and Joe in *Beautiful Joe*. Unlike in the animal novels, though, the memoir's figure of authority is the father: "While extolling my mother . . . I must not forget my late revered father," and father's "dearest friend, the late Dr. Rand, Chancellor of MacMaster University" encouraged her to write.

As Saunders recalls, she talked with her sister Rida about what to write:

> "What shall I do?" I said in a solemn voice, "Dr. Rand wishes me to describe our exquisite winter scenery . . . "
>
> "Don't you do it," said Rida, "write something with blood and murder in it—lots of blood. People like that." . . .
>
> For three weeks Sister Rida did the housekeeping, and I scribbled. Finally the story was written. . . . Rida pronounced it excellent. Something which we did not discuss prevented our showing this effusion to my father or our hero Dr. Rand. I think we felt that gentlemen whose favorite reading was Hebrew and Greek, and whose pastime was Shakespeare would not appreciate this gem I had produced.
>
> "Where shall we send it?" asked Rida, surveying in dismay the religious and literary journals on my father's study table.
>
> "I don't know," I said. "Let's go down town." . . .
>
> Rida sat down on a bench and put her hand on what was then the 'Frank Leslie Magazine,' now the 'American.' "Send it there."
>
> I sent it, and to our mingled delight and amazement a cheque for forty dollars came flying from New York.

In this account, the sisters overturn the world of the fathers so thoroughly that the results cannot be discussed with them. "Something with blood and murder" comes to life in New York; America, idealized, is the place of publishing freedom. The story itself, Saunders notes in this essay, was intriguingly entitled "A Gag of Blessed Memory"; its text proves curiously elusive.[103]

Its origin story, though, is evocative: it reminds me of another American writer, Louisa May Alcott, who similarly began her literary career in the shadow of an august father and his even more august friend, Ralph Waldo Emerson. I think of high tide in the Bay of Fundy: "Much like a father pushing his daughter on a swing, the gentle Atlantic tidal pulse pushes the waters of the system causing a large to-and-fro oscillation." In this oscillation, both daughters—Alcott and Saunders—swung high and also in some unexpected directions. Like Saunders, Alcott wrote pseudonymous "blood-and-thunder" stories and sent them to a precursor New York publication, *Frank Leslie's*

Illustrated Weekly. Alcott dramatized this part of her career in *Little Women*, where Jo delights in publishing "blood-and-thunder" tales until her eventual husband, Prof. Bhaer, persuades her to stop. Saunders mentions reading *Little Women* in her Edinburgh journal at age fifteen.[104] This scene in "How I Began to Write" sounds like an homage to Alcott, with male prohibition as the start rather than the end to the writing of sensation stories.

This account is also, like *Little Women*, a story of sisters. The death of Saunders's sister Laura inspired the character of Miss Laura in *Beautiful Joe*; another sister, Grace, would be Saunders's assistant during her Toronto years. Here the featured sister is Rida, with whom Saunders lived in San Francisco, in the household with Teddy Roosevelt the collie and her first birds. Rida helps Marshall take flight, cleaning so that her sister may write.

The memoir continues with a lull—"I had come to the end of matrimonial plots. I had no real interest in love affairs, and for some time I wrote and sold nothing"—and then she finds her subject: "My attention had at last fallen on the animals about my feet." Animals fuel the daughter's rise: she writes *Beautiful Joe* and travels with Rida "gaily to Boston and California and New York. . . . I wrote more stories and Rida criticised and typewrote them. Everywhere literary circles were interested in the dear old Canadian dog who was born and lived in Ontario and was transported to Maine only to comply with the conditions of the American prize competition." Here, again, is the geographic translation from Canada to New England, named as a market imperative but also implying a gender transformation: the woman leaving the father's nest, with the sister serving the helpmeet role.

The memoir ends with an account in which animals seem to substitute for married life: "My waggish sister decided that perhaps after all it was better to go to the dogs than to worry about the problems of married life that are never-ending and which lead unmarried folk into the dismal swamp of Literary Land." Animals seem a solution to "the dismal swamp of Literary Land," and also, perhaps, to "the problems of married life" themselves. With the help of sisters—and in contrast to the demands of husbands—the voice of the writer has emerged.

I appreciate the dog puns in the final sentence: the successful author "gone to the dogs" according to the "waggish sister." I have finally brought dogs into view; it is odd to have left them out of this account of the Acadia archive for so long. They are everywhere in Marshall Saunders's papers, professionally and personally. One folder in the collection consists, in its entirety, of a "Toronto Bitch License" for the fox terrier she called "Billie Sunday"—the name of a famous U.S. evangelist, Saunders having adopted the dog in New York after hearing Sunday preach.[105] Folders entitled "Family Pictures" are filled with photographs of dogs, horses, and birds; there are more images of animals than of people. On the backs of photos, annotations describe the dogs as fully as the people.

A more sustained example: In the materials for a novel called *Wandering Dog*, a typed list of "Principal Characters. Human Beings" is followed by one for "Principal Characters. Dogs."[106] In these folders is the exhaustive research Saunders conducted for how to illustrate these dog characters, among them newspaper clippings and cards advertising championship dogs; this is the era when dog breeds and shows came to the fore. One card is labeled "Study for collie dog, Sir Walter Scott"—there's the dog-loving Scott of her childhood novel-reading, here the name for a dog character—and another, a picture of a champion terrier, is annotated, "This dog's face idealized would do for the hero of story—Boy, the fox-terrier. Should have a little different face-marking—more tan on head, less black—tan under eyes is effective—Boy must be a bright, intelligent, alert, active kind of a dog."[107] Not only do such meticulous notes confirm the importance that Saunders attached to her fictional dogs; they also suggest that the publication of her dog fiction was less an invention from scratch than a revivification of dogs already alive as "Principal Characters" in her mind. This project seems to me another version of literary taxidermy—a reanimation rather than a creation and a making of animal interiors as well as exteriors.

I should develop these connections more fully—for example, see if there is any mention of actual taxidermy in the Acadia archives; I only think to do this after I have left. A bigger project: figuring out how to conjoin the archives with my analyses of race and culture in Saunders's novels. I developed these analyses after I went to Wolfville, but I put them first in this chapter because I wanted race and culture in Saunders's Canada to be central from the start. I need to do more work to see how the parts are connected—not only the parts of this chapter but also the parts of literary history, of the CanLit canon and its many counterhistories. As usual, I have only gotten as far as showing the seams.

This to-do list is daunting, but I will take it as a sign of promise, not error. Archival work may answer some questions, but it should raise others; one's relation to the archives is not that of one-way discovery but of back-and-forth, even tidal, movements: "Much like a father pushing his daughter on a swing, the gentle Atlantic tidal pulse pushes the waters of the system causing a large to-and-fro oscillation." I should go back. Someday, I will.

5.

But all of this will have to wait; a lot has happened since my first trip to Nova Scotia. For example—but it is more than an example—my father, the historian, has died. Remember that dog stories mourn human as well as canine loss.

6.

Also, I am distracted from this, my pet project, by my actual pet, because Frankie is sick again. His illness has returned and metastasized, and there will be no more surgery or chemotherapy. I do not want to leave him again for long. A different CanLit: Canada, canine, cancer.

7.

Instead, I will leave you with three objects from the Acadia archive. I cannot make them speak, but I will describe their surfaces. One: The original manuscript of *Beautiful Joe*.[108] It is handwritten, crumbly, messy, a motley combination of big and small pieces of paper in different stages of decomposition. Thc handwriting is replete with strikeouts, blank spaces, and meta-annotations: on the contents page, for example, is the note, "6 months writing it"—this doesn't seem long at all, to me. But what most interests me is on the reverse side of the paper. Saunders used various kinds of scratch paper—for example, some from the "Canadian Bank of Commerce"—but the majority of her pages are written on the back of a typed fund-raising letter from her father about his church. There are dozens of copies of this letter, which begins with "the resurrection of the dead" and then asks for contributions—"Give the Board the unspeakable privilege of acknowledging the receipt of a good collection from each church"—turning neatly from spiritual resurrection to financial growth. The father's words are the foundation for the daughter's manuscript—empowering, "a father pushing his daughter on a swing." But also, perhaps, disempowering—or at least distracting: the daughter turns the father's text over, makes his words face the ground, so that she may write.

Two: The Braille edition of *Beautiful Joe*. This is shelved with many translations in the Acadia rare book stacks: for example, *Beautiful Joe* in Spanish (*Jose el Hermoso*) and, farther afield, Esperanto (*Bela Joe Autobiografio e Hundo*). The Braille edition comprises two large volumes; its many pages are clean, crisp, and textured with Braille dots. Inside volume 1 is a 1934 letter to Saunders from the National Institute of the Blind in London, presenting the volume to her; inside volume 2 is a label, "Beautiful Joe was put into Braille in London England by request of Dr. S. C. Swift of Toronto."[109] These are the only parts of these volumes that I can read. I feel like Beautiful Joe, trying to read a book: I am as blind to Braille as he is to words.

I am uneasy about this analogy. Disability studies scholars are scathing on the glib use of blindness as a metaphor: for example, "I hope we can . . . abandon the cliches that use the word 'blindness' as a synonym for inattention, ignorance, or prejudice."[110] Still, I think that there is something complementary about starting these pages with a book that a dog cannot write and ending with a book that I cannot read. Both impossibilities catapult me, in turn, to other senses: touch, the fingertip reading the raised marks on a Braille page; smell, the nose of the dog encountering his *umwelt*. Other senses, other stories.

Three: The slides that Saunders used to illustrate her public lectures in the 1920s and 1930s, when she was hard up for money. The slides are in two leather-covered cases, shoebox-sized, sealed with leather straps, each filled with about fifty glass slides.[111] There is no written guide to these. I unfurl the straps, open the boxes, and raise the slides gingerly to the light. There are many, many slides of animals. Instead of images of people who might ordinarily populate a life, there are photographs of animals, some with the writer, many solo. Ten, at least, of Saunders and her dog Billy; photos of goats, birds, chickens, rabbits, monkeys, frogs; here is a frog with a dog. One Saunders scholar, describing the writer's Toronto years with her sister Grace, puts it disparagingly: "The focus of the presentations, indeed, of their lives, became increasingly obsessive about birds and animals."[112] "Obsessive" seems unnecessarily harsh. As you know, I favor the obsessive. I prefer to think of these slides as another version of autobiography via animals, with the animals not so much substituting for people as occupying their own space in between animal biography and human autobiography.

The combinations of animal images into a slideshow seems like Saunders's own taxidermy, botched in the best sense. There is, indeed, a trace of taxidermy in the leather-covered boxes for the slides. It is the long, thin leather straps especially that invoke the skins of animals, furling and unfurling around the box, remounting the slides within. I am as interested in the straps as in the slides, though I recognize that I might be looking at the wrong thing, like the child who plays with the wrapping paper instead of the toy within. I have always liked the wrapping paper—too much so, you might say; you might say that this book is a whole lot of wrapping paper scraps botched together rather than the box. But surely that is what any piece of writing is: words wrapped like skin around somebody's guts—yours, mine, Frankie's?

Coda

Eventually, in March 2014, Frankie dies, six years after his initial illness and just short of his fourteenth birthday. He lives so long, even after the second recurrence of cancer, that his death seems to be from old age. His final collapse comes when I am away at a conference on nineteenth-century literature, preparing to give a paper on literary taxidermy—material that you read, in a different form, three chapters ago. I fly home to Massachusetts; the strangeness of missing a lecture on dead animals to tend to an actual dying animal is not lost on me. Shortly thereafter, Frankie is euthanized at home. It is very quick: before, he is still and quiet, breathing; after, the breathing stops. Everybody—including his wonderful veterinarian and caretaker, along with the same friend who drove me to Tufts in the gothic darkness six long years before and, of course, me—cries.

Now the prospect of mourning flips, as you and I knew it would, from anticipatory to retrospective. It is no less difficult for all the advance notice I have had, nor because I have been studying and writing about dog loss in academic terms—at least, in the mostly academic terms of the chapters you have just read. An animal studies scholar, Jessica Pierce, confronts this relationship between dog-death and dog-scholarship directly in a book that assesses both end-of-life bioethics and the last year of the life of her own pet, Ody: "At the same time as I began writing my daily journal about Ody, I was finishing a large college-level textbook on bioethics. . . . Soon enough, the bioethics book was done, and before me sat, clear as day, my next project: to write about caring for our aging and dying animals."[1] Before her sat the "next project": a book waiting like a faithful dog—or perhaps the bioethicist was the obedient one, obeying the command of the dog's body. She was acting as a dogsbody to Ody, as well as to the writing imperatives of academia.

I like the word "dogsbody," a noun meaning drudge, servant, or lackey—origin: British naval slang; also a verb, "to dogsbody." I do not use it ordinarily, but now it has gained multiple meanings in my life. Taking care of Frankie near the end—repeatedly rising at night to calm him, stooping to clean his excretions, slowing to walk and hoist him—is a kind of drudgery; I feel like a dogsbody to his decline, the labor made heavier by knowledge of what comes next.

Now, after his death, I feel like a dogsbody to the demands of mourning. These demands are double: Frankie's death comes not long after my father's, and sometimes I am startled by the way one loss evokes another—both, for example, have become compact boxes of ashes—and mourning ricochets between them. Apparently, this ricochet is common: "After any major loss, including the death of an animal companion, many people find previous losses coming to mind. . . . Please try to keep a positive perspective if you find yourself revisiting past losses."[2] "A positive perspective" is not, generally, my forte.

Still, I go once again to Provincetown and scatter Frankie's ashes there. (Reader, do not worry: I do not have him taxidermied. After Frankie dies, it seems even odder to me that people taxidermy their dogs. I do not think taxidermy would bring Frankie back; it would make him seem even deader.) This is a surprisingly buoyant experience—watching traces of the dog's body disappearing into the salty currents of both bay and ocean, where Frankie frolicked. Being at home is harder: for example, not having the dog's body under my own feet, as I sit, now, and try to write. Frankie liked this position, up to a point: when he thought it was time for a walk, he would stand and use his snout to flip my fingers up from the keyboard. I keep waiting for this interruption; its absence makes it hard to write at all.

Anyway, what should I write? I understand that this book, my "pet project," has been made possible by my pet, and now my pet has died. After Ody died, Jessica Pierce finished her book with deliberate unevenness. Her bioethics chapters are polished and measured, but the diary entries on her dog's decline are raw and end abruptly: "I intended to keep writing after he died, as a way to process the grief. But I found that I couldn't. So it all stops abruptly, as his life did."[3] The final entry ends with a fantasy of Ody coming back to life: "In a kind of dream, I push back my chair, step into the doorway where he waits, and take his soft red head into my hands."[4] In this fantasy, the mournful parent-child separation so central to the maternal melodrama—Stella Dallas divided from Laurel, Wendy from Lucy, Jessica from Ody—is undone. The dog who waits, faithful to and beyond the end, is reunited with the master, here the mistress, and she, in turn, is able to enter the threshold space of the doorway and "take his soft red head into [her] hands." Pierce finds solace in a fantasy of revivification, "a kind of dream" in which human and dog again embrace.

Others develop this fantasy of revivification explicitly in fiction. This is the short story "The Dog Hair" by Lydia Davis, in its entirety:

> The dog is gone. We miss him. When the doorbell rings, no one barks. When we come home late, there is no one waiting for us. We still find his white hairs here and there around the house and on our clothes. We pick them up. We should throw them away. But they are all we have left of him. We don't throw them away. We have a wild hope—if only we collect enough of them, we will be able to put the dog back together again.[5]

Davis is known for her extremely short fiction, and here the miniature offers a microcosm of mourning. The story offers an arc of response to dog loss: the beginning registers the completeness of the dog's absence ("No one barks. . . . No one [is] waiting"); the middle marks an oscillation between resignation and denial, or perhaps mourning and melancholia ("We should throw them away. . . . We don't throw them away"); and the end creates an image of revivification ("We will be able to put the dog back together again"). The structure is synecdochic, with the part standing for the whole: the shortness of the story is a compressed version of a longer narrative, while the unidentified "we" represents the whole human domain and "white hairs" stand for the dog's body. The story also reads, to me, as a fantasy of literary taxidermy, with taxidermy transferred from its usual domain, the animal's skin, to his fur. The intensity of this fantasy is suggested in the phrase "wild hope" and, especially, in the dash that follows it; hope soars in that dash. The story suggests a hope dashed, but also inspired, by the hair-thin remaining fragments of the dog's body.

I understand that dashed hope—that hope, dashed—from the six years of preemptive mourning for Frankie that I have already done. Now that the mourning is posthumous, I am not certain how to conclude. These pages now constitute a sort of obituary for Frankie, though I have not rendered his canine biography very fully. Another cultural critic takes on such a project, interweaving a biography of her late pet, the Great Grisby, with more scholarly discussions of historical dogs.[6] Rather than provide an obituary, I defaulted to literary criticism in the paragraph you just read about Lydia Davis's "The Dog Hair." That, after all, is what I am trained to do, as an English professor.

For all my intellectual wanderings, I remain Fido-like to the imperatives of close reading.

I have aimed for fidelity in my own close readings of Marshall Saunders's prose. Images of animal revivification, I have argued, suffuse Saunders's writing, from the fantasia of animal afterlife in *Beautiful Joe's Paradise* to the fantasy of animal speech in *Beautiful Joe.* Her images contrast with but also complement other modes for representing dead animals in this period, particularly those of taxidermy. I have moved through and beyond Saunders's writing, offering "first-dog voice" and "literary taxidermy" as larger frameworks for understanding representations of animals. Within these frames, the energies of mourning animate animal representation; these forms aim to bring animals—their interior and exterior elements, their melancholic and redemptive effects—back to life.

In making these arguments, I like to think that I have gone beyond the confines of the pet project to contribute to literary and cultural history, to feminist criticism, and to scholarship about animals. I have aimed to make these contributions through my methods as well as my conclusions. These methods have involved the usual suspects of scholarship—reading primary literature and secondary criticism, applying theory, following footnotes, visiting archives, and consulting with scholars—but also zigzag journeys to unlikely sites, a personal dog-illness story, and stylistic experiments in an eccentric first-person voice. I have presented these methods as intrinsic, not ancillary, to the scholarly findings; I have shown that the zigzag and the eclectic voice are not detours and flourishes but ends in themselves.

Or at least, I hope to have shown these things. You, of course, may dash that hope as you like, though it is only human—I recognize the strangeness of this phrase in this context—that I wish for it to remain undashed.

In the meantime, I decide to make one more trip, prompted by a dog's body—not that of Frankie, though of course he is lurking in here somewhere, but that of the nineteenth-century dog who was the original for *Beautiful Joe.* I know this will be a project with limited findings. I quoted Erica Fudge's framing of the problem at the outset of this book: "Animals are 'inarticulate'; they do not leave documents."[7] The original Beautiful Joe wrote no memoirs or novels, as Saunders did. But I do not want to leave the real dog behind: just because Joe did not represent himself does not mean I should leave him out of the story.

Here is the known biography of the historical Joe, as it comes into view in discussions of Saunders. He was born around 1882 in rural Ontario and

FIG. 28.
Beautiful Joe postcard from the Osborne Collection of Early Children's Literature. Courtesy of Toronto Public Library.

lived for years with a cruel owner who cut off his ears and tail. In 1890, he was rescued and adopted by a man named William Moore, who owned a grist mill in Meaford, and he subsequently lived with the Moore family, who apparently named him Beautiful Joe. Marshall Saunders enters the story after William Moore's daughter, Louise, became engaged to Jack Saunders, Marshall's brother; Marshall Saunders met Joe while on an extended visit to Jack and Louise in Meaford in 1892. She later remembered, "I became greatly attached to [him]. . . . I used to go for walks with this dear old dog whose ears and tail had been cut off."[8] After Saunders returned to Halifax and wrote *Beautiful Joe*, Joe remained with the Moores for the rest of his long life. He accompanied Mr. Moore around town, though he apparently remained "a skittish dog, wary of strangers."[9] He died in 1899, the exact date noted in the entry on Saunders in *Types of Canadian Women*: "The subject of this story died at Meaford, Ont., September 13th, 1899, in the eighteenth year of his age."[10] Joe was buried in Meaford. In 1963, his gravesite was marked with a plaque and a park was named for him, and in 1994, an organization named the Beautiful Joe Heritage Society was founded and now remains.

I decide to visit Meaford. It is summer 2014—a few months after Frankie's death, exactly four years after I went to Nova Scotia. On this trip, I notice how frequently the subject of dead animals comes up in Canada: in the online Air Canada check-in, for example, I am asked if my checked baggage includes "hunting bounty—horns/antlers." This reminds me of Atwood's *Surfacing*—"Do you realize . . . that this country is founded on the bodies of dead animals?"—and also makes me think about my own scholarly process. I too am going hunting in Canada for bounty, in the form of information about Beautiful Joe. I do not want to reduce Canada to antlers, even though I know that whatever I find will become—to switch to the metaphor provided by Joe's human family—grist for my writerly mill.

In Meaford—a small town on the Georgian Bay, two hours' drive from Toronto—members of the Beautiful Joe Heritage Society meet me at the Meaford Museum, which has an exhibit on Saunders, and take me through Beautiful Joe Park. The park contains many monuments, developed over several decades. In addition to a memorial cairn and historical plaque at Beautiful Joe's gravesite, there is a sculpture of the original dog, a plaque commemorating Marshall Saunders, and a kiosk entitled "Paradise Island" featuring rows of small engraved plaques that people buy to honor their dead pets; the name comes from *Beautiful Joe's Paradise*. There are also monuments to service dogs, to canine police units, and to Sirius, the only dog who died in service in the September 11 attacks. Most of these monuments are sited along a wooded path at the front of the eight-acre park; there are also some nonmonumental features: a small branch of a river running through it, a pavilion for people to picnic under, and a long path on which people walk their living dogs.[11]

During and after my park tour, I talk with three members of the Beautiful Joe Heritage Society. I learn about their painstaking efforts to realize each feature of the park I have just seen and of their hopes for further development, including building a bridge across the stream to where a parking lot would be able to host tourist buses. They are dedicated and impassioned, albeit with different passions—some for Saunders, some for *Beautiful Joe*, and some for the novel's animal welfare legacy. Some are active in animal rescue

FIG. 29.
Gunter Neumann, Margaret Marshall Saunders monument, Beautiful Joe Park, Meaford, Ontario. Photo: author.

efforts, while others speak more generally about compassion for animals; the motto of the organization is "Working toward a more humane world." About Meaford, they are united: they want to promote it through increasing the visibility of *Beautiful Joe*. Our conversation is instructive, energizing, and also a little unnerving for me; this project has been so much my pet project that I am not used to sharing my enthusiasm with others. I understand, though, that their wish is for *Beautiful Joe* to cease being anyone's "pet project," with its implications of narrowness; they wish for Meaford and *Beautiful Joe* to be known in the broadest ways, and I hope they achieve these wishes.

As they show me, the most recent addition to the park is the plaque to Marshall Saunders, erected only in 2013; it is an angled slab with an image of the author etched from a photograph taken in the 1920s. Saunders on the slab looks very different from the 1890s photographs with which I am more familiar; here she looks very modern, wearing a chic cloche hat. I realize how far into the twentieth century she got: past suffrage, mostly past the exigencies of the male pseudonym—her plaque here deliberately honors "Margaret." Seeing her image in Meaford, I also realize anew how much she transformed the Beautiful Joe story, provincially speaking. I have stressed her Americanization of Canada, but first she had to transform Ontario into Nova Scotia. The marked-up map in the Acadia archives, wherein Nova Scotia became New England, itself wiped out a prior Ontario geography; she reprovincialized the dog before she renationalized him. This seems another kind of CanCon, emphasis on the "con": one province was converted by a writer to another, by a writer who was also deprovincializing herself, gender-wise, from Margaret into Marshall. In the Meaford park, the CanCon is restored: the province returns to Ontario, the writer's name to Margaret.

In the park, though, Saunders is only a sideline: the main theme is dead dogs. This is another version of the Dog Chapel in Vermont, but with a wider range of commemorative modes, from the plaques on Paradise Island, which record personal grief (a strikingly named example: "Beautiful Josephine, 1966–1982, The Best Friend Ever"), to the 9/11 dog monument, which marks the most public of calamities. The monument consists of two tall, asymmetrical stones; mounted on one is a small cross fashioned from metal beams of the actual World Trade Center. An inscription honors Sirius, "K-9 Partner of Officer David Lim, World Trade Center, Lost September 11, 2001." Several elements of this story merit analysis—for example, the role of dogs in 9/11 and the story of Officer Lim, who has been termed "a Chinese-American hero of 9/11."[12] My interest is in how this site alters the *Beautiful Joe* legacy. Like the plaques of Paradise Island, the Sirius monument moves the Saunders novel forward to contemporary dog loss. But the monument also plunges the novel into global geopolitics, changes its context from children to adults, shifts its focus from the feminized world of the domestic pet to communities of men—police, politicians—and alters its tone. Sirius makes *Beautiful Joe* more serious.

Beautiful Joe himself is commemorated in both a gravesite cairn and a statue. There are many cairns in Canada; I have just seen a memorable one in the town where I am staying, Owen Sound, which served in the nineteenth century as a northern terminus of the Underground Railroad. The Black History Cairn, built in 2004, commemorates this history: shaped like an open room, it has a floor of stones that re-create the patterns of quilts made by slaves; the design is by Bonita Johnson de Matteis, herself a descendant of slaves who escaped to Owen Sound.[13] I am in Owen Sound during its annual Emancipation Festival and visit the cairn after hearing the festival's keynote address by George Elliott Clarke. I have read Rinaldo Walcott's critique of Clarke as privileging "an authentic older and rural black Canada"—of which Owen Sound might be considered part—"set against an inauthentic newer and urban black Canada"; I recall Lawrence Hill's critique of the mythology of Canada as a slave-refuge Canaan.[14] I know that black Canada is neither a monolith nor set in stone. Still, the talk offers another resounding refutation of the presumed "blacklessness" of Canada, while the Black History Cairn

FIG. 30.
Beautiful Joe dog cairn, Beautiful Joe Park, Meaford, Ontario. Photo: author.

suggests the importance of the commemorative site as the bedrock—or at least one crucial stratum—of self-representation.

As the Beautiful Joe cairn, of course, does not: animals do not design or build structures to represent themselves. The Beautiful Joe cairn is a simple cylinder of stones surrounded by a fence, with a wordy memorial plaque on top; it was erected in 1963.[15] Made by and for humans, this is not a dog's cairn, though that phrase sounds odd, because a "cairn" is also a breed of dog, the Scottish cairn terrier; Toto, in the film version of *The Wizard of Oz,* is a cairn terrier. The Scottish connection seems fitting for Saunders, who first left Canada for Edinburgh and who named a dog character for the dog-loving Sir Walter Scott. Even the Toto link seems apt, as the echoes of *The Wizard of Oz* in *Beautiful Joe's Paradise* are so strong. The cairn seems strangely, albeit abstractly, suitable for Joe. It is almost a statuary version of a pun: a cairn cairn.

The statue of Beautiful Joe, though, recognizably depicts the actual dog. It, like the Saunders memorial, was designed by Gunter Neumann, a local businessman, and unveiled in 2005; a locally published edition of *Beautiful Joe* reproduces the image of the sculpture on the cover, where it looks bigger and

FIG. 31.
Gunter Neumann, Beautiful Joe monument, Beautiful Joe Park, Meaford, Ontario. Photo: author.

more monumental.[16] In person, the sculpture is small, life-size; it is slightly elevated to waist level for an adult or eye level for a child. It is modest, inviting, and—this seems the opposite of the monument to Sirius—cute.

In its scale and sweetness, the figure seems different from other public statues of real-life dogs. For example, there is a statue in New York's Central Park of Balto, a husky who transported lifesaving medicine in Alaska in 1925; it is large and elevated, more in the mode of monumental heroism.[17] The Beautiful Joe sculpture is much cuter than Balto—and more disturbing. For the tail of the sculpture is clearly cut off halfway down, its end sliced off horizontally, and the ears are missing, the jagged edges ridged in metal. I have argued that the missing body parts in *Beautiful Joe* are the basis for the novel's first-dog voice, with its mutilation first signaling muteness, then prompting voice. In the sculpture, the mutilation is, in some ways, less visible—you could look at the sculpture from some angles and not see it—but in other ways, more important. Once you see them, the edges registering the missing body parts are permanently there, frozen in time and space; they are unnervingly tactile and three-dimensional. This is a monument to canine mutilation, evoking pain, suffering, and scarring.

Such evocations are common in memorials of humans: think of war memorials registering the martyrdom of soldiers. There are some public monuments to animals in war: one in London, for example, honors "all the animals that served, suffered and died alongside the British, Commonwealth and Allied forces in the wars and conflicts of the 20th century."[18] In the Beautiful Joe Park, the monument to Sirius extends this tradition, albeit without depicting the dog's body; his sacrifice is implicitly sanctified as martyrdom through the symbol of the cross. By contrast, the Beautiful Joe

FIG. 32.
Gunter Neumann, Beautiful Joe monument, Beautiful Joe Park, side view. Photo: author

monument freezes the dog's body in the aftermath of mutilation, without the redemptive context—redemptive for humans anyway—of national service. I think afresh about chronology: the real dog spent eight years with the cruel owner before being rescued, an excruciating span; this duration is obscured in *Beautiful Joe*, where Joe is still young when he is rescued. I think of the description of the real Beautiful Joe as "a skittish dog, wary of strangers." For "skittish," I now read "traumatized."

This is usually an adjective for humans, describing an event and its aftermath: in one influential formulation, trauma consists "in the *structure of its experience* or reception: the event is not assimilated fully at the time, but only belatedly, in its repeated *possession* of the one who experiences it"[19] In trauma studies, "the one who experiences it" is assumed to be human, but it is increasingly recognized that animals can experience trauma, too: a book on *Animal Madness* is eloquent on this theme.[20] In the United States, recognition of PTSD in dogs has focused on those who served with the military in Iraq and Afghanistan; their trauma as veterans brings them closer to the category of "citizen canines."[21]

Of course, the distinction between trauma sustained in military service and other trauma may be lost on the dogs themselves. Another inscription on the London monument to animals in war is this: "They had no choice." Service animals have no choice about their service, and to a dog, presumably, pain is pain—like the pain of Beautiful Joe, feeling his tail and ears mutilated and becoming "skittish."

Or the pain of my dog, Frankie, when his cancerous tumor grew and hemorrhaged. I am back to where I began: the moment of Frankie's collapse. This was a moment of physical trauma; I remember him whimpering. So too did the effects of his surgeries seem traumatic for him, and he could not understand that they were to end his suffering rather than to prolong it. He "had no choice" about these treatments; the choice—like the dog himself—was mine. I am lucky that the trauma did not seem to scar him, psychologically, as far as I could tell: for example, he ran willingly into the Tufts animal hospital on subsequent visits and guided me eagerly on evening walks to the local veterinarian's office, where he stood outside the door wagging his tail and waiting to be let in. I know I risk projection in stating this, but still: to the end, he remained an extremely happy dog—goofy, joyful, unskittish.

I cannot quite say the same for me. You knew this: seeing Frankie collapse, rushing him to the hospital, witnessing his suffering, waiting for the cancer's return, I was traumatized too. I hasten to qualify this statement: this was a very moderate human trauma, in the scheme of things. My turn to *Beautiful Joe* represents, in its nonscholarly vein, an attempt to write about this trauma; these chapters dramatize a "repeated possession of the one of who experiences" trauma—the one being, in this case, me.

The "possession," turned into a writing project, has been uncanny but not unpleasurable; its satisfactions have emerged, for me, in the crafting of style, especially the dogged pursuit of punning and the deliberate mapping of a literary zigzag. And they have emerged in the actual zigzag journeys that have brought me along bayswaters, from Cape Cod Bay to the Bay of Fundy and the Georgian Bay.

Which is where I am now, in Meaford: I look at the dog's sculpture again, and am disturbed anew by its mutilated tail. It resonates with an awful story I have just read in the local newspaper: "A dead dog found in the Welland Canal with a brick tied to its legs may have been alive when it was thrown into the water."[22] It is horrible to think of the suffering of this real dog and of the real Beautiful Joe, when his tail and ears were cut off. This moment is enshrined in the shape of the sculpture. And yet the sculpture is also cute; its metal seems pettable. Any adaptation of *Beautiful Joe* must wrestle with this oxymoronic combination of the cute and the mutilated.

I return to the Beautiful Joe Park the next day on my own, for a second look, and the sculpture looks different: someone has put a hat and a skirt on it. I think that people in the Beautiful Joe Heritage Society would not like this. They have told me of other episodes of vandalism at the park: the cross on the Sirius monument was damaged in 2007, and some memorial plaques on the Paradise Island kiosk were ruined earlier this year.[23] The damage to the cross was iconoclastic, breaking a religious icon, while the destruction of the plaques seems a more personal blasphemy; I would not like it, myself, if a plaque for Frankie were defaced. In this context, the female clothing on the sculpture of Beautiful Joe could be seen—as feminization so often is in popular culture—as humiliation.

But—speaking only for myself—I like it. The clothing does not seem, to me, like humiliation; it seems like affectionate transformation. I also like how the cross-dressing—across gender, across species—implicitly brings the figures of the dog and the woman closer together; I have argued for their affiliation throughout this book. The clothing on the sculpture does not skirt the dog-woman affinity but embraces it. She was woman; he was dog.

In Toronto, a few days later, I see the Saunders-Joe couple again in an entirely unexpected place. Late at night, I am awakened by my phone; the television is still on and it catches my attention. I hear the words "Beautiful Joe" and see a white man speaking energetically on the screen. He seems to be talking about dogs, Marshall Saunders, and Meaford—the screen briefly becomes a montage of different covers of *Beautiful Joe*—and he concludes, "That's something you might not know about Canada!" The whole of this is so unlikely that I assume I am dreaming.

Back at home, though, when I look this up, it turns out to have been real. What I saw was a one-minute entry in a recurring segment, "Something You Might Not Know About Canada," on a talk show on the CBC. Each segment features a different celebrity talking about an achievement of a Canadian in an ironic, mock-nationalist tone—though I am not sure about the tone; maybe it is the irony that is itself being mocked, in a mix of self-deprecation and self-appreciation. The deprecation-appreciation mix is evident in the breezy choice of topics for other entries in this series: not, say, the award-winning fiction of Margaret Atwood or Alice Munro, but such lower-brow Canadian achievements as poutine. My eye for CanCon keeps sliding toward popular culture, particularly in its most ironic modes. My hipster hotel in Toronto, for example, sells a product line called "Canadiana," which includes toiletries named for important years in Canadian history; I am now able to identify the hand cream called "1867" as honoring the year of Canadian Confederation.[24] I like the idea of a nation turned into a lotion: ideas about national identity are often used as cultural emollients, to soften the skins of ideology. Now ideas about *Beautiful Joe* are showing up as mock-ironic emollient of "Canada" on late-night television.

The *Beautiful Joe* segment of "Something You Might Not Know About Canada" is presented by a Canadian-born actor known for tough-guy roles. This is most of what he said:

> So Joe was a real-life mutt who'd been through a lot. How he dealt with such vicious abuse and had such a big heart . . . became the stuff of legend up here in Canada. Halifax author Margaret Marshall Saunders was so inspired by Joe and the tribulations he had gone through and the size of his heart that she decided to write a novel about him. The story of Beautiful Joe was such a smash hit it became Canada's first million-seller as a novel. Look, I don't know who let the dogs out, but I do know one thing—I know the name of the dog that brought world-wide attention to animal cruelty. And that's Beautiful Joe from Meaford, Ontario. . . . And that is something you might not know about Canada.[25]

This segment originally aired a while ago, and it just so happens that this episode was rerun at the moment I awakened. The odds against this seem so formidable that I feel the uncanny has hailed me directly. The television segment even honors the dog, as I have been trying to do in these pages, rather than moving directly to the human—attention is being paid to "the dog that brought world-wide attention to animal cruelty. And that's Beautiful Joe from Meaford, Ontario."

Of course, this segment is also in the realm of ironic self-mockery, with absurdity generated in the contrast between male actor and cute topic. The woman writer is probably the butt of some joke here. Still, my "pet project" has really gone public—or rather, it was never mine alone. It has long belonged, at minimum, to the dedicated people I met in Meaford, the Canadian literary critics who have written about Saunders, and the animal studies scholars interested in dogs. Now it has been broadcast—at least briefly, in reruns—on the CBC, temporarily my Canine Broadcasting Channel.

Back in New England, it is time to change the channel on my psyche and go back to school. At home, I am ever aware of Frankie's absence, but at work, I find frequent reminders of avian presence. The Mount Holyoke campus includes a surprising amount of bird taxidermy, including one item now housed in the art museum called *Birds of Mary Lyon's Time* parlor dome (1845). It is a glass dome filled with taxidermied birds, from the period when such items were becoming favored decorations for the Victorian parlor. This is a good example of its genre, with eighteen brightly colored birds arrayed on artificial branches atop false grass, the whole encased under a dome.

The bird-woman connections evoked by this object are multiple. Such domes were linked to the feminized domestic space of the parlor; sometimes

FIG. 33.
Lucius Hyde (American, 1799–1872), *Birds of Mary Lyon's Time* parlor dome, 1845. Glass, wood, feather, cloth, and wire. Joseph Allen Skinner Museum, Mount Holyoke College Art Museum, South Hadley, Massachusetts. Photo: Jim Gipe, SK 2006.2166.INV. Used by permission of Mount Holyoke College Art Museum.

they were even made by women; small-animal taxidermy was seen as a domestic art. In this case, the taxidermist was a local man, Lucius Hyde, but the object was given to one woman, "Mrs. John Dwight"—a.k.a. Nancy Shaw Everett, who attended Mount Holyoke in its opening year, 1837—and it is named for another, Mary Lyon, who founded the college. The birds are all local species of "Mary Lyon's Time" and of her space. After a half century with Mrs. and Mr. John Dwight, the dome made its way back to Mount Holyoke, and in a book about the college at its 1937 centennial, I find this description: "The 'Birds of South Hadley' are in their glass-domed cage. Miss Lyon's Bible is in the corner cupboard, and her thimble . . . and the green velvet bag in which she collected money for the first endowment."[26] In this account of presidential personal effects, the taxidermied birds share space with Bible, thimble, and money-bag—praying and sewing being obligatory duties for the nineteenth-century woman and fund-raising the requirement, then as now, of a college president. With this provenance in mind, I see the object as reworking the woman-bird

FIG. 34.
James Gehrt, *Canada Warbler*, 2013. Courtesy of the artist.

connection, so often pejorative, in an empowering way: the bird-woman as a powerful female president.

But the object also seems ominous to me. The glass is too evident a metaphor for constriction, for the carceral space of a dome. If I think about this object in relation to Marshall Saunders, she seems closer to the birds under glass than to the woman writer outside it. As do Mount Holyoke students, massed in groups—one was the original recipient of this dome, but others are potentially bird-women encased within it. I feel a little implicated in this dome's carceral space too; it might hold faculty as well. Maybe any woman—president, student, teacher, scholar—is potentially immobilized, imprisoned, and displayed as a bird under glass.

Fortunately, I find more air to breathe in another Mount Holyoke taxidermy specimen, as remediated by a contemporary American photographer, James Gehrt. This image depicts one of many avian specimens originally used for science instruction; no longer useful as pedagogy but not deemed art, these are arrayed in limbo-land in glass vitrines on the lower floors of a science building. This photograph, in black and white, is titled *Canada Warbler*, and it shows the natural history side of taxidermy—birds posed on sticks, labeled as specimens—without any illusions of revivification.

The emphasis in the photograph is on the transfiguring eye of the photographer, who makes the tones black and white, the shading into shadows, and the bird's shape into a softened blur on the left-hand side of the frame. The bird in the foreground is in focus in its deadness: stuck on its wedge, adjacent to its sole nature-faking leaf. I find this photograph more invigorating than *Birds of Mary Lyon's Time*: less colorful but also less confined by glass. Or rather, the main glass here is the photographer's lens—the refiguring lens of art-making.[27]

I also like the label within the photograph. It is partly missing, so that "Canada" looks like "nada": Spanish for nothing. This makes me think of Marshall Saunders, the "Canada Warbler" of these pages. She fell into the "nada" of historical obscurity, as well as the "nada" against which succeeding generations of CanLit defined itself. My project, restoring the "Ca" of the bird label—its CanCon—has also been to make Saunders sing.

I recognize that she is singing through my voice box. Saunders crafted Joe's first-dog voice, and I have used her writing, prosthetically, to craft my own first-person voice. This is my own form of literary taxidermy, revivifying Saunders in an archive of texts that moves from the nineteenth century to now. Repurposing the idea of botched taxidermy, I have also cited some contemporary artists working in this mode. This archive is shaped along a manikin of my own story—or, at least, the partial and stylized version of that story I have offered in these pages.

Here is one more art citation, metaphorically stretched on a manikin of me: in Toronto, on the same Joe-research trip, I see a small exhibition at the Royal Ontario Museum on the passenger pigeon—remember, this was 2014, the centennial nonhappy birthday of the extinction of the species. For this exhibition—a fine-art room in a natural history museum—Canadian artist Sara Angelucci photographed taxidermy specimens at the museum and combined them, through Photoshop, with nineteenth-century cartes de visite. In *Aviary (Female Passenger Pigeon/extinct)* (2013), the bird's head covers the woman's, its beak extending her nose, its wings resting on her ears, while the woman's eyes and hair remain, and her collar is visible. This version of botched taxidermy (in my view; I do not know if the artist embraces this term) seemed both poignant and funny, to me. It seemed to comment, sympathetically, on the way women have been castigated as feather-headed birdbrains, and it seemed, more specifically, to adapt the taxidermied bird hat: the bird has been

FIG. 35.

Sara Angelucci, *Aviary (Female Passenger Pigeon/extinct)*, 2013. Courtesy of the artist.

moved from atop a woman's head to her face. Angelucci has noted the connection of this work to bird hats, as well as her interest in Victorian women as "keepers of the family album" and as taxidermists.[28] She describes the *Aviary* portraits as "chimera suspended in a state of empathy."[29]

The literary critic in me always stops to examine the words, and I like this phrase. A chimera is a fantastic hybrid creature; the "state of empathy" is Angelucci's attitude, her interest in honoring the histories of birds and women. Like all the human subjects in the *Aviary* series, the woman in this photograph has no proper name. But I give her several: I think of her as Martha, the last passenger pigeon, as Margaret, and as Marshall. I see a version of Saunders in this Canadian bird-woman. I too have tried to present Saunders as a chimera suspended in a state of empathy—her empathy for animals, with all the political flaws of her era; my own empathy for her, presumably with my era speaking through me as well. This last is harder for me to assess. Metacriticism is notoriously difficult to undertake in a mirror.

Of course, I am probably the only viewer who would have the impulse to connect Marshall Saunders with Angelucci's *Aviary (Female passenger pigeon/extinct)*, let alone to link her to the "nada" of Gehrt's *Canada Warbler*. This is the monomania of the pet project, in which I see and hear Saunders everywhere. Unlike my experience seeing Beautiful Joe on television, there is no CBC broadcast to ratify these viewings. I should stop. So I will.

Although—one more peep—I do not think, in the end, that it is necessary to disavow the idea of a pet project. All scholarly projects are, in the end, someone's pet project; otherwise, they would never get written. At the beginning of any tale, scholarly or personal, is something hounding the writer; in my case, the hound was Frankie. I was able to leash him to more academic goals, which I will repeat here once more, speaking a scholarly master's voice. The goals of that academic project are recovering a woman writer, rethinking the politics and aesthetics of animal representation, and providing a self-reflexive model of interdisciplinary exploration. That sentence is true, but putting it that way takes the "pet" out of the project; it does not tell the whole tale.

At the nose of the story, at the end of the tail, are two dogs' bodies: Beautiful Joe (ca. 1882–1899) and Frankie Young (2000–2014).

Acknowledgments

While acknowledgments customarily reveal the personal story behind the scholarly one, I have already eroded this distinction. Nonetheless, I want here to name many people—and two dogs—who made this book possible. Colleen Boggs and Susan McHugh intervened at an early stage with remarkably generous and detailed feedback on the manuscript; Rebecca Tishler, student turned colleague, enabled its final stages with meticulous assistance. Simone Davis was a key interlocutor throughout, and she and Peter Armstrong provided incomparable hospitality in Ontario. For support in Canada, I am grateful to scholars Mary Chapman and Carole Gerson and to Gwendolyn Davies, who generously shared her Saunders expertise by email; to librarians and archivists at Acadia University, Toronto Public Library, Halifax Public Library, Meaford Museum, and Mount Allison University; and to Beautiful Joe Heritage Society members Evelyn Dean, Viv Baker, and Michael Biggins. In England, Candida Lacey and Eve Burman-Lacey offered two generations of friendship and professed avid enthusiasm for taxidermy.

Mount Holyoke College generously supported publication costs, for which I thank dean of faculty, now president, Sonya Stephens. At Mount Holyoke, I am grateful for suggestions and support from colleagues in English, film studies, and elsewhere, including Chris Benfey, Bettina Bergmann, Robin Blaetz, Leah Glasser, Christian Gundermann, Bob and Fi Herbert, Gail Hornstein, Anthony Lee, Amy Martin, Jenny Pyke, William Quillian, Karen Remmler, Erika Rundle, Robert Shilkret, Kate Singer, Ajay Sinha, Paul Staiti, Thomas Wartenberg, and Don Weber. Special thanks to Valerie Martin for inviting me to dinner with Margaret Atwood and to Iyko Day for providing Canadian, especially Haligonian, guidance. My students, especially in "The Nonhuman" and "Hitchcock and After," energized and sharpened my thinking about animals. The wonderful Mount Holyoke College Art Museum, especially Ellen Alvord and Wendy Watson, encouraged my writing and teaching on the nonhuman. I was assisted throughout by administrative and library staff, including Cynthia Meehan and Rozelynn Douglas, who called *Beautiful Joe* "adorable." I am greatly indebted to James Gehrt, who has tirelessly created beautiful images for me, including his own photographs, for years; I could not have completed this project without him.

Support and suggestions have come from colleagues near and far, including Anna Botta, Darcy Buerkle, Paul Erickson, Teresa Goddu, Jim Hicks,

Barbara Kellum, Dana Leibsohn, Rebecca May, Kirsten Twelbeck, Laura Wexler, Ara Wilson, and Sandy Zagarell. I am very grateful to Faith Barrett for inviting me to discuss the introduction with her students and to Mary Louise Kete for joining me on a research day in Vermont. I thank Brigitte Fielder and Lesley Ginsberg for a conference talk that didn't end up happening and Susanne Opfermann and Birgit Spengler for another one that did. Related projects helped this one, and I thank Istvan Csicsery-Ronay for inviting me to review new books about dogs and the Civil War Caucus for welcoming my speculations about Lincoln's dog. I appreciate the artists who encouraged my use of their work here, particularly Sara Angelucci, James Gehrt, Nina Katchadourian, and Rosamond Wolff Purcell. Nigel Rothfels enthusiastically welcomed me to the Animalibus series at Penn State Press. I thank Kendra Boileau, Alex Vose, Regina Starace, Sam Martin, and others at the press.

For their care for Frankie, I am grateful to Dr. Leanne Ksiasek and the remarkable staff at Northampton Veterinary Clinic and to Dr. Lisa Barber, Dr. Kristine Burgess, Dr. Suzanne Rau, and others at the Tufts University Cummings School of Veterinary Medicine. Bridget Ryan warmly welcomed Frankie into her pack, and dog-whisperer Hanni Beyer Lee provided amazing palliative support for him. Neighbors Sharon Goldstein and Jim Rader and Silas and Linda Kopf buoyed Frankie and me. Janice Dumond offered vital cross-species support.

Elissa Forman drove Frankie to the Tufts animal hospital, and her friendship has sustained me in numerous ways, as has that of Judith Frank and Elizabeth Garland, Nina Gerassi-Navarro, Lisa Beskin, and the Systors, especially Lisa Hunter. William Cohen doggedly supported this book throughout. Without hounding me, Laura Green indefatigably and indispensably edited it into being. Marilyn Young, Emily Young, Sarah Young, Jeff Goll, Thomas Witz, Davia, Isabel, Noah, and Ruby fortified me with human family, and Emily provided expert counsel. Tippi Young reintroduced dog joy. I remember always Alfred F. Young, whose historian's spirit vivifies these pages, and Frankie Young, whose canine one does too. As I finish this book, I grieve the loss of my mother, Marilyn Young.

An earlier version of a small section of chapter 4 was published as "Passenger Pigeon" in the Mount Holyoke College Art Museum online series "Objects of Our Affection," 2016, https://artmuseum.mtholyoke.edu/blog/passenger-pigeon. Used by permission.

Notes

INTRODUCTION

1. Anna Schuleit, "Grafton State Hospital," *1856.org*, http://www.1856.org/grafton/grafton.html. For more information on this artist, now known as Anna Schuleit Haber, see https://anna-haber.com/.

2. On the Northampton State Hospital, see J. Michael Moore, *The Life and Death of Northampton State Hospital: The Experience of Work in an Institution for the Mentally Ill* (Northampton, MA: Historic Northampton, 1994); and Moore and Anna Schuleit Haber, *Northampton State Hospital: Images of America* (Charleston, SC: Arcadia, 2014).

3. See Helen Lefkowitz Horowitz, *Alma Mater: Design and Experience in the Women's Colleges from Their Nineteenth-Century Beginnings to the 1930s* (New York: Knopf, 1984), 14.

4. Anna Schuleit [Haber], "The State Hospital: In Memoriam," *1856.org*, http://www.1856.org/documentation.htm.

5. On Freud and William James, see Saul Rosenzweig, *Freud, Jung, and Hall the King-Maker: The Historic Expedition to America (1909)* (Seattle: Hogrefe & Huber, 1992), 171–74; on Freud and Emma Goldman, see 132–34.

6. Sigmund Freud, "An Autobiographical Study" (1925), in *The Freud Reader*, ed. Peter Gay (New York: W. W. Norton, 1989), 32–33.

7. Nick Trout, *Tell Me Where It Hurts: A Day of Humor, Healing, and Hope in My Life as an Animal Surgeon* (New York: Broadway, 2008); Dr. Nancy Kay, *Speaking for Spot: Be the Advocate Your Dog Needs to Live a Happy, Healthy, Longer Life* (North Pomfret, VT: Trafalgar Books, 2008).

8. George T. Angell, *Autobiographical Sketches and Personal Recollections* (Boston, 1892), 59, 60.

9. On Angell's abolitionism, see Janet M. Davis, *The Gospel of Kindness: Animal Welfare and the Making of Modern America* (New York: Oxford University Press, 2016), 42–44.

10. Peter Singer, *Animal Liberation* (1975; repr., New York: Ecco, 2002), xx.

11. Gary L. Francione, "Animals—Property or Persons?," in *Animal Rights: Current Debates and New Directions*, ed. Cass R. Sunstein and Martha C. Nussbaum (New York: Oxford University Press, 2004), 132.

12. Katherine C. Grier, *Pets in America: A History* (Orlando: Harcourt, 2006), 173.

13. This was Angell's complete endorsement of *Black Beauty*:

THE "UNCLE TOM'S CABIN" OF THE HORSE. For more than twenty years *this thought* has been upon my mind. *Somebody* must write a book which shall be as widely read as *"Uncle Tom's Cabin," and shall have as widespread and powerful influence in abolishing cruelty to horses as "Uncle Tom's Cabin" had on the abolition of human slavery.* Many times, by letter and word of mouth, I have called the attention of American writers to this matter and asked them to undertake it. At last the book has come to me—not from America, but from England, where already over *ninety thousand copies have been sold.* (*Autobiographical Sketches and Personal Recollections*, 94)

Many works of social reform were hailed as "the *Uncle Tom's Cabin* of a cause"; see Carolyn Karcher, "Stowe and the Literature of Social Change," in *The Cambridge Companion to Harriet Beecher Stowe*, ed. Cindy Weinstein (Cambridge: Cambridge University Press, 2004), 211.

14. Elizabeth Young, *Disarming the Nation: Women's Writing and the American Civil War* (Chicago: University of Chicago Press, 1999), 24–68.

15. Hezekiah Butterworth, introduction to *Beautiful Joe: An Autobiography*, by [Margaret] Marshall Saunders (Philadelphia: Charles H. Banes, 1893 [1894]), 7. The publication date for the novel is sometimes listed as 1893, when Saunders won the prize from the American Humane Education Society and, having retained copyright, secured a publisher in the American Baptist Publication Society. The majority of scholars use the date 1894, when the novel was actually published. I use 1894.

16. Elizabeth Waterston, "Margaret Marshall Saunders: A Voice for the Silent," in *Silenced Sextet: Six Nineteenth-Century Canadian Women Novelists*, ed. Carrie MacMillan, Lorraine McMullen, and Elizabeth Waterston (Montreal: McGill-Queen's University Press, 1992), 137.

17. Mark Doty, *Dog Years: A Memoir* (New York: HarperCollins, 2007), 64.

18. See, for example, Susan Baker, *Provincetown Dogs* (Hanover: University Press of New England, 2000); and Barbara E. Cohen, *Dog in the Dunes, Revisited* (North Truro, MA: Fields Press, 2005).

19. [Margaret] Marshall Saunders, *Beautiful Joe: An Autobiography*, Phoenix Edition (Philadelphia: Charles H. Banes, 1903).

20. Margaret Marshall Saunders, *Beautiful Joe*, Beautiful Joe Heritage Society Special Edition (Meaford, Ontario: Beautiful Joe Heritage Society, 2004); Saunders, *Beautiful Joe*, introd. Gwendolyn Davies (Halifax, Nova Scotia: Formac, 2001); and Saunders, *Beautiful Joe*, ed. and introd. Keridiana Chez (Peterborough, Ontario: Broadview, 2015). Two other Canadian reprints are Saunders, *Beautiful Joe* (Toronto: Puffin Canada, 2009); and Saunders, *Beautiful Joe*, 100th anniversary edition (Owen Sound, Ontario: Ginger Press, 1994).

21. Jeremy Bentham, *Principles of Morals and Legislation*, in *The Animals Reader: The Essential Classic and Contemporary Writings*, ed. Linda Kalof and Amy Fitzgerald (Oxford: Berg, 2007), 9; Singer, *Animal Liberation*, 7–9.

22. Elizabeth Young, *Black Frankenstein: The Making of an American Metaphor* (New York: New York University Press, 2008).

23. Steve Baker, *The Postmodern Animal* (London: Reaktion, 2000), 56, 75.

24. Steve Baker, "Beyond Botched Taxidermy," in *Dead Animals; or, the Curious Occurrence of Taxidermy in Contemporary Art*, ed. Jo-Ann Conklin (Providence: Brown University / David Winton Bell Gallery, 2016), 43–58.

25. I have written in this voice before: see Elizabeth Young, "Mourning Pictures and Magic Glasses," *Massachusetts Review* 54:3 (Fall 2013): 539–55 and 54:4 (Winter 2013): 629–52.

26. Robert Rosenblum, *The Dog in Art from Rococo to Post-Modernism* (New York: Harry N. Abrams, 1988), 11.

27. See Marjorie Garber, *Dog Love* (New York: Touchstone, 1997).

28. Two relevant inquiries: Lori Merish, "Cuteness and Commodity Aesthetics: Tom Thumb and Shirley Temple," in *Freakery: Cultural Spectacles of the Extraordinary Body*, ed. Rosemarie Garland Thomson (New York: New York University Press, 1996), 185–203; and Sianne Ngai, "The Cuteness of the Avant-Garde," *Critical Inquiry* 31:4 (Summer 2005): 811–47. By the time I complete this book, the latter article has become Sianne Ngai, *Our Aesthetic Categories: Zany, Cute, Interesting* (Cambridge: Harvard University Press, 2012), 53–109.

29. Gilles Deleuze and Felix Guattari, *A Thousand Plateaus: Capitalism and Schizophrenia*, in *Animals Reader*, 43.

30. Alice A. Kuzniar, *Melancholia's Dog: Reflections on Our Animal Kinship* (Chicago: University of Chicago Press, 2006), 6.

31. Angell, "Sentiment, Sentimental," in *Autobiographical Sketches and Personal Recollections*, appendix, 34.

32. Donna J. Haraway, *When Species Meet* (Minneapolis: University of Minnesota Press, 2008).

33. Donna J. Haraway," Companions in Conversation" with Cary Wolfe, *Manifestly Haraway* (Minneapolis: University of Minnesota Press, 2016), 254.

CHAPTER 1

1. Garth Stein, *The Art of Racing in the Rain* (New York: Harper, 2008); Andrew O'Hagan, *The Life and Opinions of Maf the Dog, and of His Friend Marilyn Monroe* (Boston: Houghton Mifflin, 2010).

2. John Berger, *King: A Street Story* (New York: Pantheon, 1999); Paul Auster, *Timbuktu: A Novel* (New York: Henry Holt, 1999), 56. On *King*, see Andy Merrifield, *John Berger* (London: Reaktion, 2012), 121–23; on *Timbuktu*, see Laura Brown, *Homeless Dogs and Melancholy Apes: Humans and Other Animals in the Modern Literary Imagination* (Ithaca: Cornell University Press, 2010), 113–16, 139–43.

3. Amy Hempel and Jim Shepard, eds., *Unleashed: Poems by Writers' Dogs* (New York: Three Rivers Press, 1995).

4. [Barbara Bush], *Millie's Book: as Dictated to Barbara Bush* (New York: Harper Perennial, 1992); Charles Siebert, *Angus: A Memoir* (New York: Crown, 2000). On *Millie's Book*, see Colleen Glenney Boggs, *Animalia Americana: Animal Representations and Biopolitical Subjectivity* (New York: Columbia University Press, 2013), 157–73; on *Angus*, see Karla Armbruster, "What Do We Want from Talking Animals? Reflections on Literary Representations of Animal Voices and Minds," in *Speaking for Animals: Animal Autobiographical Writing*, ed. Margo DeMello (New York: Routledge, 2013), 26–31.

5. Cynthia Huff and Joel Haefner, "His Master's Voice: Animalographies, Life Writing, and the Posthuman," *Biography* 35:1 (Winter 2012): 153–69.

6. See Tess Cosslett, *Talking Animals in British Children's Fiction, 1786–1914* (Burlington, VT: Ashgate, 2006), 63–92. On U.S. animal autobiographies following *Beautiful Joe*, see Annie Dwyer, "Animal Autobiography and the Domestication of Human Freedom," *Arizona Quarterly* 71:2 (Summer 2015): 1–30. On the structure of animal autobiographies, see also Lars Bernaerts, Marco Caracciolo, Luc Herman, and Bart Vervaeck, "The Storied Lives of Non-human Narrators," *Narrative* 22:1 (January 2014): 68–93; and David Herman, "Animal Autobiography; Or, Narration Beyond the Human," *Humanities* 5:4 (2016): 82.

7. Frances Power Cobbe, *The Confessions of a Lost Dog* (London, 1867). On this novel, see Monica Flegel, "Mistresses as Masters: Voicing Female Power Through the Subject Animal in Two Nineteenth-Century Animal Autobiographies," in *Speaking for Animals*, 89–101.

8. Francis Coventry, *The History of Pompey the Little; or, The Life and Adventures of a Lap-Dog*, ed. Robert Adams Day (London: Oxford University Press, 1974). On "it" narratives, see Mark Blackwell, ed., *The Secret Life of Things: Animals, Objects, and It-Narratives in Eighteenth-Century England* (Lewisburg: Bucknell University Press, 2007).

9. Theodore Ziolkowski, "Talking Dogs: The Caninization of Literature," in *Varieties of Literary Thematics* (Princeton: Princeton University Press, 1983), 97. Analyses of Kafka's story in an animal studies context include Marianne DeKoven, "Kafka's Animal Stories: Modernist Form and Interspecies Narrative," in *Creatural Fictions: Human-Animal Relationships in Twentieth- and Twenty-First-Century Literature*, ed. David Herman (New York: Palgrave Macmillan, 2016), 19–40; and Neema Harel, "Investigations of a Dog, by a Dog: Between Anthropocentrism and Canine-Centrism," in *Speaking for Animals*, 49–59.

10. On these developments in the United States, see Diane L. Beers, *For the Prevention of Cruelty: The History and Legacy of Animal Rights Activism in the United States* (Athens: Swallow Press / Ohio University Press, 2006); Janet M. Davis, *The Gospel of Kindness: Animal Welfare and the Making of Modern America* (New York: Oxford University Press, 2016); and Katherine C. Grier, *Pets in America: A History* (Orlando:

Harcourt, 2006). On European contexts, see Harriet Ritvo, *The Animal Estate: The English and Other Creatures in the Victorian Age* (Cambridge: Harvard University Press, 1987); and Kathleen Kete, *The Beast in the Boudoir: Petkeeping in Nineteenth-Century Paris* (Berkeley: University of California Press, 1994).

11. See Mark Seltzer, *Bodies and Machines* (New York: Routledge, 1992), 166–72.

12. Jennifer Howard, "Presses, Journals, and Meetings Buzz with Animal Studies," *Chronicle of Higher Education* 56:9 (October 23, 2009): B9.

13. Susan McHugh, *Dog* (London: Reaktion, 2004).

14. Jennifer Mason, *Civilized Creatures: Urban Animals, Sentimental Culture, and American Literature, 1850–1900* (Baltimore: Johns Hopkins University Press, 2005).

15. "Theories and Methodologies: Animal Studies," *PMLA* 124:2 (March 2009): 472–575.

16. Jacques Derrida, "The Animal That Therefore I Am (More to Follow)," originally published in English in *Critical Inquiry* 28:2 (2002): 369–418, reprinted in *The Animal That Therefore I Am*, ed. Marie-Louise Mallet, trans. David Wills (New York: Fordham University Press, 2008), 1–51.

17. Marshall Saunders, *Beautiful Joe*, ed. and introd. Keridiana Chez (Peterborough, Ontario: Broadview, 2015); all quotations are taken from this edition unless otherwise noted.

18. See "H-Animal Syllabus Exchange," https://networks.h-net.org/node/16560/pages/27594/h-animal-syllabus-exchange.

19. On the nineteenth-century Band of Mercy, see Beers, *For the Prevention of Cruelty*, 88–89, 97–98, and Davis, *Gospel of Kindness*, 61–64; on the newer Band of Mercy, see Noel Molland, "Thirty Years of Direct Action," in *Terrorists or Freedom Fighters? Reflections on the Liberation of Animals*, ed. Steven Best and Anthony J. Nocella (Herndon, VA: Lantern Books, 2004), 67–74.

20. For reflections on this distance, see Marianne DeKoven and Michael Lundblad, eds., *Species Matters: Humane Advocacy and Cultural Theory* (New York: Columbia University Press, 2013).

21. See Michael Brandow, *A Matter of Breeding: A Biting History of Pedigree Dogs and How the Quest for Status Has Harmed Man's Best Friend* (Boston: Beacon Press, 2015).

22. Gwendolyn Davies, introduction to *Beautiful Joe* by Marshall Saunders (Halifax, Nova Scotia: Formac, 2001), v–xx; Davies, "Marshall Saunders and the Urbanization of the Animal," in *Other Selves: Animals in the Canadian Literary Imagination*, ed. Janice Fiamengo (Ottawa: University of Ottawa Press, 2007), 170–83; Davies, "Margaret Marshall Saunders: Making Regionalism International," in *Literature of Region and Nation: Proceedings of the 6th International Literature of Region and Nation Conference*, ed. Winnifred M. Bogaards (Saint John, NB: SSRC, 1998), 143–56; Davies, *Margaret Marshall Saunders and Beautiful Joe: Education Through Fiction* (Truro, Nova Scotia: Nova Scotia Teachers College, 1995); Carole Gerson, "Margaret Marshall Saunders," in *Canadian Writers, 1890–1920*, ed. W. H. New, *Dictionary of Literary Biography* 92 (Detroit: Gale, 1990), 327–30; Elizabeth Waterston, "Margaret Marshall Saunders: A Voice for the Silent," in *Silenced Sextet: Six Nineteenth-Century Canadian Women Novelists*, ed. Carrie MacMillan, Lorraine McMullen, and Elizabeth Waterston (Montreal: McGill-Queen's University Press, 1992), 137–68; and Waterston, *Children's Literature in Canada* (New York: Twayne, 1992), 95–97.

23. Cosslett, *Talking Animals*, 64–67; Davis, *Gospel of Kindness*, 64–67; Dwyer, "Animal Autobiography," 2, 6–7, 12–14; Erica Fudge, *Pets* (Stocksfield, United Kingdom: Acumen, 2008), 50–52; Marjorie Garber, *Dog Love* (New York: Touchstone, 1997), 67–70, 94–95; Roxanne Harde, "'Better Friends': Marshall Saunders Writing Humane Education and Envisioning Animal Rights," *Jeunesse: Young People, Texts,*

Cultures 1:2 (2009): 85–108; McHugh, *Dog*, 139–42; Teresa Mangum, "Dog Years, Human Fears," in *Representing Animals*, ed. Nigel Rothfels (Bloomington: Indiana University Press, 2002), 35–47; Justin Prystash, "Vectors of a Flea: The Convergence of Species in Victorian Animal Autobiographies," *Mosaic* 49:1 (March 2016): 47–50; Keridiana Chez, *Victorian Dogs, Victorian Men: Affect and Animals in Nineteenth-Century Literature and Culture* (Columbus: Ohio State University Press, 2017), 76–102; and Keridiana Chez, introduction to *Beautiful Joe*, by Marshall Saunders (Peterborough, Ontario: Broadview, 2015), 11–35.

24. See Monica Flegel, *Pets and Domesticity in Victorian Literature and Culture: Animality, Queer Relations, and the Victorian Family* (New York: Routledge, 2015), 56–92.

25. For example, this term is used by Gerson ("Margaret Marshall Saunders," 330) and by Phyllis R. Blakeley ("Margaret Marshall Saunders, the Author of *Beautiful Joe*," *Nova Scotia Historical Quarterly* 1:3 [September 1971]: 237).

26. Flegel, "Mistresses as Masters," 92. On Cobbe's biography, see Sharon Marcus, *Between Women: Friendship, Desire, and Marriage in Victorian England* (Princeton: Princeton University Press, 2007), 53–55.

27. Mary E. Wilkins Freeman, "A New England Nun," in *Selected Stories of Mary E. Wilkins Freeman*, ed. Marjorie Pryse (New York: W. W. Norton, 1983), 120.

28. Leah Blatt Glasser, *In a Closet Hidden: The Life and Work of Mary E. Wilkins Freeman* (Amherst: University of Massachusetts Press, 1996), 36. On Freeman's representation of animals, see Susan M. Griffin, "Understudies: Miming the Human," *PMLA* 124:2 (March 2009): 511–19.

29. For overviews of this recovery, see Thomas L. Erskine and Connie L. Richards, eds., *The Yellow Wallpaper* (New Brunswick: Rutgers University Press, 1993); and Denise D. Knight and Cynthia J. Davis, eds., *Approaches to Teaching Gilman's "The Yellow Wallpaper" and Herland* (New York: MLA, 2003).

30. See, for example, Gail Bederman, *Manliness and Civilization: A Cultural History of Gender and Race in the United States, 1880–1917* (Chicago: University of Chicago Press, 1995), 121–69. For an interpretation of "The Yellow Wallpaper" that focuses on its racial connotations, see Susan S. Lanser, "Feminist Criticism, 'The Yellow Wallpaper,' and the Politics of Color in America," in *Yellow Wallpaper*, ed. Erskine and Richards, 225–56.

31. Jane Tompkins, *Sensational Designs: The Cultural Work of American Fiction, 1790–1860* (New York: Oxford University Press, 1985), xi.

32. Erica Fudge, "A Left-Handed Blow: Writing the History of Animals," in *Representing Animals*, 5.

33. See, for example, Susan Orlean, *Rin Tin Tin: The Life and the Legend* (New York: Simon & Schuster, 2011) and Samuel J. M. M. Alberti, ed., *The Afterlives of Animals: A Museum Menagerie* (Charlottesville: University of Virginia Press, 2011).

34. On Saunders's changes to the novel, see Chez, introduction to *Beautiful Joe*, 30–35; and Davies, introduction to *Beautiful Joe*, xvii–xviii.

35. Frances Power Cobbe, *Life of Frances Power Cobbe* (1894), excerpted in H. G. Wells, *The Island of Doctor Moreau*, ed. Mason Harris (Peterborough, Ontario: Broadview, 2009), 263. On American vivisection debates, see Beers, *For the Prevention of Cruelty*, 119–46. For antivivisection writings relevant to *Beautiful Joe*, see Chez, "Appendix A," in *Beautiful Joe*, 277–81.

36. Wells, *Island of Doctor Moreau*, 94, 124.

37. Elizabeth Stuart Phelps, *Trixy* (Boston: Houghton Mifflin, 1904), 56. On *Trixy*, see Lori Duin Kelly, "Elizabeth Stuart Phelps, *Trixy*, and the Vivisection Question," *Legacy* 27:1 (January 2010): 61–82; and Alyssa Chen Walker, "Bringing the Laboratory Dog Home: Elizabeth Stuart Phelps and the Antivivisection Narrative," *Humanimalia: A Journal of Human/Animal Interface Studies* 4:2 (Spring 2013): 101–29.

38. Mark Twain, "A Dog's Tale" (1903), in *Mark Twain's Book of Animals*, ed. Shelley Fisher Fishkin (Berkeley: University of California Press, 2010), 165, 173. On this story, see also Matthew Guzman, "Vivisecting the 'Animal' in Mark Twain's 'A Dog's Tale,'" *Mark Twain Annual* 13 (2015): 29–42.

39. Quoted in Beers, *For the Prevention of Cruelty*, 125.

40. Alfred Elwes, *The Adventures of a Dog, and a Good Dog Too* (London, 1857), iii; this passage is discussed in Cosslett, *Talking Animals*, 69.

41. See Emma Townshend, *Darwin's Dogs: How Darwin's Pets Helped Form a World-Changing Theory of Evolution* (London: Frances Lincoln, 2009). For discussion of Darwin's animal imagery, see Eileen Crist, *Images of Animals: Anthropomorphism and Animal Mind* (Philadelphia: Temple University Press, 1999), 11–50.

42. Charles Darwin, *The Expression of the Emotions in Man and Animals*, introd. Joe Cain (1890; repr., London: Penguin, 2009), 57–58.

43. Cosslett, *Talking Animals*, 66.

44. Margaret Marshall Saunders, "The Story of My Life," *Ontario Library Review* 12:2 (November 1927): 43.

45. See M. Lynn Rose, "Deaf and Dumb in Ancient Greece," in *The Disability Studies Reader*, ed. Lennard J. Davis, 2nd ed. (New York: Routledge, 2006), 17–31; and R. A. R. Edwards, *Words Made Flesh: Nineteenth-Century Deaf Education and the Growth of Deaf Culture* (New York: New York University Press, 2012).

46. Douglas Baynton, "'A Silent Exile on This Earth': The Metaphorical Construction of Deafness in the Nineteenth Century," in *Disability Studies Reader*, 42.

47. Quoted in Baynton, "Silent Exile on This Earth," 37, 43.

48. On Deaf culture, see, for example, Carol Padden and Tom Humphries, *Inside Deaf Culture* (Cambridge: Harvard University Press, 2006). On the capitalization of Deaf, see Brenda Jo Brueggeman, *Deaf Subjects: Between Identities and Places* (New York: New York University Press, 2009), 9–15.

49. Susan McHugh, *Animal Stories: Narrating Across Species Lines* (Minneapolis: University of Minnesota Press, 2011), 27–64.

50. See Susan Burch and Alison Kafer, eds., *Deaf and Disability Studies: Interdisciplinary Perspectives* (Washington: Gallaudet University Press, 2010).

51. Sunaura Taylor, *Beasts of Burden: Animal and Disability Liberation* (New York: New Press, 2017), 63.

52. Taylor, *Beasts of Burden*, 12. On the evolution of this term, see Victoria Ann Lewis, "Crip," in *Keywords for Disability Studies*, ed. Rachel Adams, Benjamin Reiss, and David Serlin (New York: New York University Press, 2015), 46–48; for an influential theorization, see Robert McRuer, *Crip Theory: Cultural Signs of Queerness and Disability* (New York: New York University Press, 2006).

53. Taylor, *Beasts of Burden*, 43.

54. Julia L. Mickenberg and Lynne Vallone, introduction to *The Oxford Handbook of Children's Literature*, ed. Mickenberg and Vallone (New York: Oxford University Press, 2011), 7.

55. See Beverly Lyon Clark, *Kiddie Lit: The Cultural Construction of Children's Literature in America* (Baltimore: Johns Hopkins University Press, 2003), 77–101.

56. On *Beautiful Joe* as a pedagogic text, see Harde, "Better Friends."

57. Susan J. Pearson, *The Rights of the Defenseless: Protecting Animals and Children in Gilded Age America* (Chicago: University of Chicago Press, 2011), 56.

58. Flegel, *Pets and Domesticity*, 149.

59. Harriet Beecher Stowe, "Rights of Dumb Animals," *Our Dumb Animals* 1:9 (1869): 69. This essay first appeared in slightly different form in *Hearth and Home* 1:2 (1869): 24.

60. On Greyfriars Bobby, see Jan Bondeson, *Amazing Dogs: A Cabinet of Canine Curiosities* (Ithaca: Cornell University Press, 2011), 130–48; and Hilda Kean, "The Moment of Greyfriars Bobby: The Changing Cultural Position of Animals, 1800–1920," in

A Cultural History of Animals in the Age of Empire, ed. Kathleen Kete (New York: Berg, 2007), 25–46.

61. Kete, *Beast in the Boudoir*, 25.

62. Sarah Knowles Bolton, *Our Devoted Friend the Dog* (Boston: L. C. Page, 1902), n.p. [7].

63. See Matthew Algeo, *Abe and Fido: Lincoln's Love of Animals and the Touching Story of His Favorite Canine Companion* (Chicago: Chicago Review Press, 2015).

64. Keith Thomas, *Man and the Natural World: A History of the Modern Sensibility* (New York: Pantheon, 1983), 112–17.

65. Grier, *Pets in America*, 9.

66. Yi-Fu Tuan, "Animal Pets: Cruelty and Affection," in *The Animals Reader: The Essential Classic and Contemporary Writings*, ed. Linda Kalof and Amy Fitzgerald (New York: Berg, 2007), 143.

67. Darwin, *Expression of Emotions*, 114.

68. Quoted in Chez, *Victorian Dogs, Victorian Men*, 18.

69. Chez, *Victorian Dogs, Victorian Men*, 20. For another conceptualization of dogs as prostheses in Victorian literature, see Ivan Kreilkamp, "Anthroprosthesis, or Prosthetic Dogs," *Victorian Review* 35:2 (Fall 2009): 36–41.

70. David Mitchell and Sharon Snyder, "Narrative Prosthesis and the Materiality of Metaphor," in *Disability Studies Reader*, 206; and see Mitchell and Snyder, *Narrative Prosthesis: Disability and the Dependencies of Discourse* (Ann Arbor: University of Michigan Press, 2000). On the multiple meanings of "prosthesis" in disability studies, see Katherine Ott, "Prosthetics," in *Keywords for Disability Studies*, 140–43.

71. Phelps, *Trixy*, 214, 274.

72. Coral Lansbury, *The Old Brown Dog: Women, Workers, and Vivisection in Edwardian England* (Madison: University of Wisconsin Press, 1985), 95.

73. Carol J. Adams, *The Sexual Politics of Meat: A Feminist-Vegetarian Critical Theory* (New York: Continuum, 1990). "Sexism/Speciesism" is a section title in *Animals and Women: Feminist Theoretical Explorations*, ed. Carol J. Adams and Josephine Donovan (Durham: Duke University Press, 1995), 9.

74. Catharine A. MacKinnon, "Feminism, Marxism, Method and the State: An Agenda for Theory," in *The "Signs" Reader: Women, Gender and Scholarship*, ed. Elizabeth Abel and Emily K. Abel (Chicago: University of Chicago Press, 1983), 253; MacKinnon, "Of Mice and Men: A Feminist Fragment on Animal Rights," in *Animal Rights: Current Debates and New Directions*, ed. Cass R. Sunstein and Martha C. Nussbaum (New York: Oxford University Press, 2004), 264.

75. Donna Haraway, *The Companion Species Manifesto: Dogs, People, and Significant Otherness* (Chicago: Prickly Paradigm Press, 2003), 3, 9–10.

76. See Maureen Adams, *Shaggy Muses: The Dogs Who Inspired Virginia Woolf, Emily Dickinson, Elizabeth Barrett Browning, Edith Wharton, and Emily Brontë* (New York: Ballantine, 2007).

77. See, for example, Boggs, *Animalia Americana*, 177–78; Fudge, *Pets*, 70–72; Alice A. Kuzniar, *Melancholia's Dog: Reflections on Our Animal Kinship* (Chicago: University of Chicago Press, 2006), 120–23; McHugh, *Dog*, 99–101; and Kari Weil, *Thinking Animals: Why Animal Studies Now* (New York: Columbia University Press, 2012), 81–96.

78. Virginia Woolf, *Flush: A Biography* (San Diego: Harcourt, 1983), 22–23.

79. Waterston, *Children's Literature in Canada*, 96.

80. McHugh, *Dog*, 142.

81. Chez, *Victorian Dogs, Victorian Men*, 95, and see 89–98.

82. For a different comparison of Alcott and Saunders, see Waterston: "Joe—gruff, self-deprecating, loyal, impetuous—has many of the characteristics of another 'Jo,' the troubled protagonist of *Little Women*" ("Margaret Marshall Saunders," 147).

83. Mangum, "Dog Years, Human Fears," 43.

84. Sarah Amato, *Beastly Possessions: Animals in Victorian Consumer Culture* (Toronto: University of Toronto Press, 2015), 73. See also Keridiana Chez, "Man's Best and Worst Friends: The Politics of Pet Preference

at the Turn of the Twentieth Century," in *American Beasts: Perspectives on Animals, Animality and U.S. Culture, 1776–1920*, ed. Dominik Ohrem (Berlin: Neofelis Verlag, 2017), 175–200.

85. See Elizabeth Ammons, "Heroines in *Uncle Tom's Cabin*," in *Critical Essays on Harriet Beecher Stowe*, ed. Ammons (Boston: G. K. Hall, 1980), 152–65.

86. On Saunders's adoption of the pseudonym, see Waterston, "Margaret Marshall Saunders," 143.

87. John Berger, "Why Look at Animals?," in *About Looking* (New York: Pantheon, 1980), 26. On the rise of animal photography, see Akira Mizuta Lippit, *Electric Animal: Toward a Rhetoric of Wildlife* (Minneapolis: University of Minnesota Press, 2000), 162–97; on the rise of the zoo, see Nigel Rothfels, *Savages and Beasts: The Birth of the Modern Zoo* (Baltimore: Johns Hopkins University Press, 2002).

88. Ann-Janine Morey, *Picturing Dogs, Seeing Ourselves: Vintage American Photographs* (University Park: Pennsylvania State University Press, 2014), 25.

89. See Ruth Silverman, introduction to *The Dog Observed: Photographs, 1844–1988* (San Francisco: Chronicle Books, 1988), xi.

90. Morey, *Picturing Dogs, Seeing Ourselves*, 35.

91. Margo DeMello, "Introduction," *Speaking for Animals*, 1.

92. Steven Connor, *Dumbstruck: A Cultural History of Ventriloquism* (New York: Oxford University Press, 2000), 307.

93. Connor, *Dumbstruck*, 328.

94. Charles Brockden Brown, *Wieland*, ed. Bryan Waterman (New York: W. W. Norton, 2011), 148.

95. On "distant voice" ventriloquism, see Valentine Vox, *I Can See Your Lips Moving: The History and Art of Ventriloquism* (Kingswood, Surrey: Kaye & Ward, 1981), 76, 194–97; on ventriloquism in *Wieland*, see Leigh Eric Schmidt, *Hearing Things: Religion, Illusion, and the American Enlightenment*, excerpted in *Wieland*, 457–70.

96. L. Frank Baum, *The Wizard of Oz* (1900; repr., London: Puffin Books, 2008), 136.

97. Katharine M. Rogers, *L. Frank Baum: Creator of Oz* (New York: St. Martin's Press, 2002), 83.

98. Baum, *Wizard of Oz*, 136–37. On Toto's role, see William Farina, *Man Writes Dog: Canine Themes in Literature, Law and Folklore* (Jefferson, NC: McFarland, 2014), 113–21.

99. On Lewis, see Vox, *I Can See*, 170–72. On Conti, see Sarah Kessler, "Puppet Love: Documenting Ventriloquism in Nina Conti's *Her Master's Voice*," *Camera Obscura* 92 (2016): 61–91. For a theorization of ventriloquism and animal voices, see Norie Neumark, *Voicetracks: Attuning to Voice in Media and the Arts* (Cambridge: MIT Press, 2017), 43–44.

100. Quoted in Connor, *Dumbstruck*, 330.

101. Vox, *I Can See*, 139.

102. Candice Bergen, *Knock Wood* (New York: Simon & Schuster, 1984), esp. 15–133.

103. Helen Davies, *Gender and Ventriloquism in Victorian and Neo-Victorian Fiction: Passionate Puppets* (New York: Palgrave Macmillan, 2012), 13.

104. Deborah Denenholz Morse and Martin A. Danahay make a similar leap: "While Derrida would object to Sewell turning Black Beauty into a puppet for human words, his 'animal autobiography' project is in the same lineage as Sewell's *Black Beauty*" (introduction to *Victorian Animal Dreams: Representations of Animals in Victorian Literature and Culture*, ed. Morse and Danahay [Burlington, VT: Ashgate, 2007], 4).

105. Derrida, "Animal That Therefore I Am," 3–4.

106. Derrida, "Animal That Therefore I Am," 4, 11.

107. Derrida, "Animal That Therefore I Am," 29.

108. For a discussion of this illustration, see Cosslett, *Talking Animals*, 65.

109. [Margaret] Marshall Saunders, *My Pets: Real Happenings in My Aviary* (Philadelphia: Griffith & Rowland, 1908), 251.

110. [Margaret] Marshall Saunders, *Beautiful Joe* (Toronto: McClelland, Goodchild and Stewart, 1918), 73. The annotated copy is in the Osborne Collection of Early Children's Books, Toronto Public Library.

111. Donna Haraway, *When Species Meet* (Minneapolis: University of Minnesota Press, 2008), 20.

112. Susan Fraiman, "Pussy Panic Versus Liking Animals: Tracking Gender in Animal Studies," *Critical Inquiry* 39:1 (Autumn 2012): 89–115.

113. *Lily Does Derrida: A Dog's Video Essay* (dir. Kathy High, 2010–12); for discussion, see Steve Baker, *Artist / Animal* (Minneapolis: University of Minnesota Press, 2013), 201–2, 207–9.

114. Derrida, "Animal That Therefore I Am," 49.

115. Susan McHugh, "Bitch, Bitch, Bitch: Personal Criticism, Feminist Theory, and Dog-Writing," *Hypatia* 27:3 (Summer 2012): 616–35.

116. Heather Steffan, "Introduction to 'The Feral Issue,'" *Minnesota Review* 73–74 (Fall 2009–Spring 2010): 63.

CHAPTER 2

1. Alexandra Horowitz, *Inside of a Dog: What Dogs See, Smell, and Know* (New York: Scribner, 2009), 13–32.

2. See, for example, *Thinking with Animals: New Perspectives on Anthropomorphism*, ed. Lorraine Daston and Gregg Mitman (New York: Columbia University Press, 2005).

3. Horowitz, *Inside of a Dog*, 119.

4. See Alec MacLeod, "The Canine in Conversation: Dogs in Metaphor and Idiom Illustrated," *Dogmatic Technologies*, updated April 20, 2014, http://www.metaphordogs.org.

5. Horowitz, *Inside of a Dog*, 258.

6. Laurel Braitman, *Animal Madness: How Anxious Dogs, Compulsive Parrots, and Elephants in Recovery Help Us Understand Ourselves* (New York: Simon & Schuster, 2014), 36.

7. Erica Fudge, *Animal* (London: Reaktion, 2002), 8.

8. Robert Rosenblum, *The Dog in Art from Rococo to Post-Modernism* (New York: Harry N. Abrams, 1988), 67. On the history of the painting, see Leonard Petts, *The Story of "Nipper" and the "His Master's Voice" Picture Painted by Francis Barraud* (Bournemouth, United Kingdom: Talking Machine Review, 1973). Analyses of the image include Steven Connor, *Dumbstruck: A Cultural History of Ventriloquism* (New York: Oxford University Press, 2000), 386–87; Mladen Dolar, *A Voice and Nothing More* (Cambridge: MIT Press, 2006), 74–77; Fudge, *Animal*, 67–70; Cynthia Huff and Joel Haefner, "His Master's Voice: Animalographies, Life Writing, and the Posthuman," *Biography* 35:1 (Winter 2012): 153–54; Susan McHugh, *Dog* (London: Reaktion, 2004), 97–98; Michael Taussig, *Mimesis and Alterity: A Particular History of the Senses* (New York: Routledge, 1993), 212–25; and Cary Wolfe, *Animal Rites: American Culture, the Discourse of Species, and Posthumanist Theory* (Chicago: University of Chicago Press, 2003), 183–84.

9. Dolar, *Voice and Nothing More*, 77.

10. Advertisement reprinted in Petts, *Story of "Nipper,"* n.p.

11. Barraud, quoted in Petts, *Story of "Nipper,"* n.p.

12. Connor, *Dumbstruck*, 393.

13. *OED Online*, s.v. "master, n.1 and adj.," March 2019, accessed May 28, 2019, http://www.oed.com/view/Entry/114751.

14. Harriet Beecher Stowe, *Uncle Tom's Cabin*, ed. Elizabeth Ammons (New York: W. W. Norton, 1994); all quotations are taken from this edition.

15. Marjorie Spiegel, *The Dreaded Comparison: Human and Animal Slavery*, foreword by Alice Walker, rev. ed. (1988; repr., New York: Mirror Books, 1996).

16. Peter Singer, *Animal Liberation* (1975; repr., New York: Ecco, 2002), 221.

17. Joseph Holt Ingraham, quoted in Lesley Ginsberg, "Slavery and the Gothic Horror of Poe's 'The Black Cat,'" in *American Gothic: New Interventions in a National*

Narrative, ed. Robert K. Martin and Eric Savoy (Iowa City: University of Iowa Press, 1998), 105.

18. Kathleen Kete, "Animals and Ideology: The Politics of Animal Protection in Europe," in *Representing Animals*, ed. Nigel Rothfels (Bloomington: Indiana University Press, 2002), 21.

19. See Boria Sax, *Animals in the Third Reich: Pets, Scapegoats and the Holocaust* (New York: Continuum, 2000), 110–23.

20. Thomas Dixon, *The Clansman: An Historical Romance of the Ku Klux Klan* (New York: Grosset and Dunlap, 1905), 323.

21. Quoted in Michael Lundblad, *The Birth of a Jungle: Animality in Progressive-Era U.S. Literature and Culture* (New York: Oxford University Press, 2013), 132.

22. Lundblad, *Birth of a Jungle*, 132.

23. Thomas Nelson Page, "Marse Chan," in *The Literature of the American South*, ed. William L. Andrews et al (New York: W. W. Norton, 1998), 314, 311.

24. Leon F. Litwack, "Hellhounds," in *Without Sanctuary: Lynching Photography in America* by James Allen et al (Seattle: Twin Palms, 2000), 23.

25. "Cujo," a name now linked with the Stephen King novel about a violent dog, is also associated, in different spellings, with figures of the African diaspora, including Cudjoe, a hero among black Maroons in Jamaica. For an exploration of Cujo, animals, and the Jamaican Cudjoe, see Paul Youngquist, "The Cujo Effect," in *Gorgeous Beasts: Animal Bodies in Historical Perspective*, ed. Joan B. Landes, Paula Young Lee, and Paul Youngquist (University Park: Pennsylvania State University Press, 2012), 57–72.

26. Paul Laurence Dunbar, "The Lynching of Jube Benson," in *The Heart of Happy Hollow*, introd. Eleanor Alexander (1904; repr., New York: Harlem Moon / Broadway, 2005), 112, 113, 117.

27. Paul Laurence Dunbar, *The Sport of the Gods*, introd. William L. Andrews (New York: Signet, 1999), 18, 115, 121–22.

28. Elizabeth Young, *Black Frankenstein: The Making of an American Metaphor* (New York: New York University Press, 2008), 140–52.

29. Philip Armstrong, *What Animals Mean in the Fiction of Modernity* (London: Routledge, 2008), 61–77.

30. Colin Dayan, *The Law Is a White Dog: How Legal Rituals Make and Unmake Persons* (Princeton: Princeton University Press, 2011), 240, 241.

31. Mia Bay, *The White Image in the Black Mind: African American Ideas About White People, 1830–1925* (New York: Oxford University Press, 2000), 119.

32. Quoted in Lundblad, *Birth of a Jungle*, 122.

33. Lundblad, *Birth of a Jungle*, 122.

34. On these projects of rejuvenation, see Gail Bederman, *Manliness and Civilization: A Cultural History of Gender and Race in the United States, 1880–1917* (Chicago: University of Chicago Press, 1995), esp. 170–215.

35. Mark Twain, *Pudd'nhead Wilson and Those Extraordinary Twins*, ed. Sidney E. Berger, 2nd ed. (New York: W. W. Norton, 2005), 24, 49.

36. Mark Twain, "A Dog's Tale" (1903), reprinted in *Mark Twain's Book of Animals*, ed. and introd. Shelley Fisher Fishkin (Berkeley: University of California Press, 2010), 167.

37. Fishkin, introduction to *Mark Twain's Book of Animals*, 28.

38. Jennifer L. Mason, *Civilized Creatures: Urban Animals, Sentimental Culture, and American Literature, 1850–1900* (Baltimore: Johns Hopkins University Press, 2005), 124–34.

39. Mason, *Civilized Creatures*, 134.

40. Chesnutt used the phrase "dog-like fidelity" in a letter quoted in Mason, *Civilized Creatures*, 134.

41. Harriet Beecher Stowe, "Our Dogs" (1865), in *Writings of Harriet Beecher Stowe*, vol. 16, *Stories and Sketches for the Young* (Boston: Houghton Mifflin, 1896), 68, 69. This story was originally published in *Our Young Folks* (1865).

42. Lesley Ginsberg, "'I Am Your Slave for Love': Race, Sentimentality, and Harriet Beecher Stowe's Fiction for Children," in

Enterprising Youth: Social Values and Acculturation in Nineteenth-Century American Children's Literature ed. Monika Elbert (New York: Routledge, 2008), 104. See also Ginsberg, "Of Babies, Beasts, and Bondage: Slavery and the Question of Citizenship in Antebellum American Children's Literature," in *The American Child: A Cultural Studies Reader*, ed. Caroline F. Levander and Carol J. Singley (New Brunswick: Rutgers University Press, 2003), 85–105; and Ginsberg, "Slavery and Poe's 'Black Cat.'"

43. Brigitte Fielder, "'No Rights That Any Body Is Bound to Respect': Pets, Race, and African American Child Readers," in *Who Writes for Black Children? African American Children's Literature Before 1900*, ed. Katharine Capshaw and Anna Mae Duane (Minneapolis: University of Minnesota Press, 2017), 170–72. On Stowe and animals, see also Mason, *Civilized Creatures*, 95–118.

44. Brigitte Fielder, "Race, Species, and Affective Kinship in Nineteenth-Century Abolitionism," *American Quarterly* 65:3 (September 2013), special issue on "Species/Race/Sex," ed. Claire Jean Kim and Carla Freccero, 487–514.

45. Brigitte Fielder, "Black Dogs, Bloodhounds, and Best Friends: African Americans and Dogs in Nineteenth-Century Abolitionist Literature," in *American Beasts: Perspectives on Animals, Animality and U.S. Culture, 1776–1920*, ed. Dominik Ohrem (Berlin: Neofelis Verlag, 2017), 153–73.

46. Harriet E. Wilson, *Our Nig; or, Sketches from the Life of a Free Black*, ed. P. Gabrielle Foreman and Reginald H. Pitts (New York: Penguin, 2009), 24.

47. Karen Kilcup, "Frado Taught a Naughty Ram: Animal and Human Natures in *Our Nig*," *ELH* 79:2 (Summer 2012): 349–51.

48. See John Campbell, "The Seminoles, the 'Bloodhound War,' and Abolitionism, 1796–1865," *Journal of Southern History* 72:2 (May 2006): 260–302; and Youngquist, "Cujo Effect," 63–70.

49. Marcus Wood, *Blind Memory: Visual Representations of Slavery in England and America, 1780–1865* (New York: Routledge, 2000), 97.

50. Colleen Glenney Boggs, *Animalia Americana: Animal Representations and Biopolitical Subjectivity* (New York: Columbia University Press, 2013), 101.

51. See Amy Louise Wood, *Lynching and Spectacle: Witnessing Racial Violence in America, 1890–1940* (Chapel Hill: University of North Carolina Press, 2009), 94–98.

52. Octavia V. Rogers Albert, *The House of Bondage; or, Charlotte Brooks and Other Slaves*, ed. Frances Smith Foster (1890; repr., New York: Oxford University Press, 1988), 73.

53. Harriet Jacobs, *Incidents in the Life of a Slave Girl Written by Herself*, ed. Jean Fagan Yellin (Cambridge: Harvard University Press, 1987), 74, 55.

54. Frederick Douglass, "Farewell to the British People" (1847), quoted and discussed in Boggs, *Animalia Americana*, 105–6.

55. Claire Jean Kim and Carla Freccero, eds., *American Quarterly* 65:3 (September 2013), special issue on "Species/Race/Sex"; Lindgren Johnson, *Race Matters, Animal Matters: Fugitive Humanism in African America, 1840–1930* (New York: Routledge, 2018).

56. Mel Y. Chen, *Animacies: Biopolitics, Racial Mattering, and Queer Affect* (Durham: Duke University Press, 2012); Che Gossett, "Blackness, Animality, and the Unsovereign," Verso, September 28, 2015, https://www.versobooks.com/blogs/2228-che-gossett-blackness-animality-and-the-unsovereign; Sharon P. Holland, "(Black) (Queer) Love," *Callaloo* 36:3 (2013): 659–68; Zakiyyah Iman Jackson, "Animal: New Directions in the Theorization of Race and Posthumanism," *Feminist Studies* 39:3 (2013): 669–85; and Jackson, "Outer Worlds: The Persistence of Race in Movement 'Beyond the Human,'" *GLQ* 21:2–3 (2015), special issue on "Queer Inhumanisms," ed. Mel Y. Chen and Dana Luciano, 215–18; Claire Jean Kim, *Dangerous Crossings: Race, Species, and Nature in a Multicultural Age* (Cambridge: Cambridge University Press, 2015). See also Maneesha

Deckha, "Toward a Postcolonial, Posthumanist Feminist Theory: Centralizing Race and Culture in Feminist Work on Nonhuman Animals," *Hypatia* 27:3 (Summer 2012): 527–45; Kalpana Rahita Seshadri, *HumAnimal: Race, Law, Language* (Minneapolis: University of Minnesota Press, 2012); and Alexander Weheliye, *Habeas Viscus: Racializing Assemblages, Biopolitics, and Black Feminist Theories of the Human* (Durham: Duke University Press, 2014).

57. Bénédicte Boisseron, *Afro-Dog: Blackness and the Animal Question* (New York: Columbia University Press, 2018), 36. See esp. Boisseron's second chapter, "Blacks and Dogs in the Americas," which discusses three works I analyze in this chapter: Stowe's *Uncle Tom's Cabin*, Charles Moore's photographs of German shepherds during the civil rights movement, and Samuel Fuller's film *White Dog* (37–80).

58. Connor, *Dumbstruck*, 387.

59. Marshall Saunders, "The Story of My Life," *Ontario Library Review* 12:2 (November 1927): 42.

60. Margaret Marshall Saunders, "Autobiographical Sketch of Marshall Saunders," n.d., in "Dalhousie A," file 1943.001-SAU/31, Margaret Marshall Saunders fonds, Esther Clark Wright Archives, Acadia University.

61. Toni Morrison, *Playing in the Dark: Whiteness and the Literary Imagination* (New York: Vintage, 1992), 6.

62. Keridiana Chez offers a helpful paraphrase of this line: "This racist analogy seems to say that just as an ugly slave boy has no business being named after the white, cherubic angel of love and the black slave mother who birthed him could not possibly compare to the white goddess Aphrodite, so Joe appears the antithesis of beautiful" (*Victorian Dogs, Victorian Men: Affect and Animals in Nineteenth-Century Literature and Culture* [Columbus: Ohio University Press, 2017], 84). Marjorie Garber also calls attention to the slave imagery in this passage in *Dog Love* (New York: Touchstone, 1997), 68.

63. See Teresa Mangum, "Dog Years, Human Fears," in *Representing Animals*, 37.

64. On the pit bull as a beloved dog at the turn of the century, see Colin Dayan, *With Dogs at the Edge of Life* (New York: Columbia University Press, 2016), 87–88; and Bronwen Dickey, *Pit Bull: The Battle over an American Icon* (New York: Knopf, 2016), 63–64. On the later racialization of this breed, see note 99 later in this chapter.

65. Dickey, *Pit Bull*, 65.

66. Nipper is characterized as a fox terrier by McHugh (*Dog*, 97), as a bull terrier by Dayan (*With Dogs at the Edge*, 87–88), and as "part bull terrier, part fox terrier" by Fudge (*Animal*, 67).

67. McHugh, *Dog*, 128.

68. Harriet Beecher Stowe, "Dogs and Cats" (1865), reprinted in *Who Writes for Black Children?*, 308.

69. Fielder, "No Rights," 174.

70. Frederick Douglass, *Narrative of the Life of Frederick Douglass, an American Slave*, ed. Houston A. Baker Jr. (Harmondsworth, United Kingdom: Penguin, 1982), 51.

71. See Saidiya V. Hartman, *Scenes of Subjection: Terror, Slavery, and Self-Making in Nineteenth-Century America* (New York: Oxford University Press, 1997).

72. Jacobs, *Incidents*, 84, 16.

73. Jacobs, *Incidents*, 8.

74. Douglass, *Narrative*, 77, 78.

75. Anna Sewell, *Black Beauty*, ed. Kristen Guest (Peterborough, Ontario: Broadview, 2016); all quotations are taken from this edition. For discussion of slavery and *Black Beauty*, see Robert Dingley, "A Horse of a Different Color: *Black Beauty* and the Pressures of Indebtedness," *Victorian Literature and Culture* 25:2 (1997): 241–51; Moira Ferguson, *Animal Advocacy and Englishwomen, 1780–1900: Patriots, Nation, and Empire* (Ann Arbor: University of Michigan Press, 1998), 75–104; and Peter Stoneley, "Sentimental Emasculations: *Uncle Tom's Cabin* and *Black Beauty*," *Nineteenth-Century Literature* 54:1 (June 1999): 53–72.

76. On Ginger's abuse, see Ferguson, *Animal Advocacy*, 83–85.

77. Annie Dwyer, "Animal Autobiography and the Domestication of Human Freedom," *Arizona Quarterly* 71:2 (Summer 2015): 4.

78. Dwyer, "Animal Autobiography," 5, 8.

79. Dwyer, "Animal Autobiography," 23–24.

80. See, for example, Robin Bernstein, *Racial Innocence: Performing American Childhood from Slavery to Civil Rights* (New York: New York University Press, 2011).

81. On *Black Beauty* and *Uncle Tom's Cabin*, see Dingley, "Horse of a Different Color," 242–49; and Stoneley, "Sentimental Emasculations."

82. On the history of the "Uncle Tom," see Thomas F. Gossett, *Uncle Tom's Cabin and American Culture* (Dallas: Southern Methodist University Press, 1985), 388–408.

83. Fielder analyzes Stowe's Carlo and Bruno in "Black Dogs," 167–70.

84. Brontë's Carlo was a likely source for Dickinson's dog name. On Dickinson's Carlo, see Maureen Adams, *Shaggy Muses: The Dogs Who Inspired Virginia Woolf, Emily Dickinson, Elizabeth Barrett Browning, Edith Wharton, and Emily Brontë* (New York: Ballantine, 2007), 109–37; and Boggs, *Animalia Americana*, 143–55.

85. John W. Frick, *"Uncle Tom's Cabin" on the American Stage and Screen* (New York: Palgrave Macmillan, 2012), 124.

86. Fielder, "Black Dogs," 163–64.

87. Boggs, *Animalia Americana*, 101.

88. Stowe, "Dogs and Cats," 308.

89. Harriet Beecher Stowe, "Rights of Dumb Animals," *Our Dumb Animals* 1:9 (1869): 69.

90. See Lawrence W. Levine, *Black Culture and Black Consciousness: Afro-American Folk Thought from Slavery to Freedom* (New York: Oxford University Press, 1977), 81–135.

91. Eric J. Sundquist, *To Wake the Nations: Race in the Making of American Literature* (Cambridge: Harvard University Press, 1993), 341. For an animal studies interpretation of these tales, see Christopher Peterson, *Bestial Traces: Race, Sexuality, Animality* (New York: Fordham University Press, 2013), 50–73.

92. Henry Louis Gates Jr., *The Signifying Monkey: A Theory of African American Literary Criticism* (New York: Oxford University Press, 1988), 52.

93. For a different interpretation of this scene, see Justin Prystash, "Vectors of a Flea: The Convergence of Species in Victorian Animal Autobiographies," *Mosaic* 49:1 (March 2016): 49–50.

94. Werner Sollors, *Neither Black Nor White Yet Both: Thematic Explorations of Interracial Literature* (New York: Oxford University Press, 1997), 21, 24.

95. Bruce Thomas Boehrer, *Parrot Culture: Our 2,500-Year-Long Fascination with the World's Most Talkative Bird* (Philadelphia: University of Pennsylvania Press, 2004), 51.

96. Laura Brown, *Fables of Modernity: Literature and Culture in the English Eighteenth Century* (Ithaca: Cornell University Press, 2001), 249.

97. Brown, *Fables of Modernity*, 262.

98. Colleen Glenney Boggs, email to the author, December 14, 2013.

99. Dayan, *With Dogs at the Edge*, 9. On the racialization of this breed, see also Dickey, *Pit Bull*, 217–20, 269–71; Megan H. Glick, "Animal Instincts: Race, Criminality, and the Reversal of the 'Human,'" *American Quarterly* 65:3 (September 2013): 639–59; Kim, *Dangerous Crossings*, 271–75; Heidi J. Nast, "Pit Bulls, Slavery, and Whiteness in the Mid- to Late-Nineteenth Century U.S.," in *Critical Animal Geographies: Politics, Intersections and Hierarchies in a Multispecies World*, ed. Kathryn Gillespie and Rosemary-Claire Collard (London: Routledge, 2015), 127–45; Meisha Rosenberg, "Golden Retrievers Are White, Pit Bulls Are Black, and Chihuahuas Are Hispanic: Representations of Breeds of Dog and Issues of Race in Popular Culture," in *Making Animal Meaning*, ed. Linda Kalof and Georgina Montgomery (East Lansing: Michigan State University Press, 2011), 113–25; and Harlan Weaver, "'Becoming in Kind': Race, Class, Gender, and Nation in Cultures of Dog Rescue and Dogfighting," *American Quarterly* 65:3 (September 2013): 689–709.

100. Kim, *Dangerous Crossings*, 255, 275.

101. Charles Moore, quoted in Michael S. Durham, *Powerful Days: The Civil Rights Photography of Charles Moore* (Tuscaloosa: University of Alabama Press, 1991), 28. On the twentieth-century use of police dogs, see also J. Robert Lilly and Michael B. Puckett, "Social Control and Dogs: A Sociohistorical Analysis," *Crime and Delinquency* 43:2 (April 1997): 123–47; and Tyler Wall, "'For the Very Existence of Civilization': The Police Dog and Racial Terror," *American Quarterly* 68:4 (December 2016): 861–82.

102. Martin A. Berger, *Seeing Through Race: A Reinterpretation of Civil Rights Photography* (Berkeley: University of California Press, 2011), 47.

103. Kathryn Fuller-Seeley and Jeremy Groskopf, "The Dogs Who Saved Hollywood: Strongheart and Rin Tin Tin," in *Cinematic Canines: Dogs and Their Work in the Fiction Film*, ed. Adrienne L. McLean (New Brunswick: Rutgers University Press, 2014), 65. On German shepherds as police dogs, see Susan McHugh, *Animal Stories: Narrating Across Species Lines* (Minneapolis: University of Minnesota Press, 2011), 37–39; and Susan Orlean, *Rin Tin Tin: The Life and the Legend* (New York: Simon & Schuster, 2011), 263–66.

104. For discussion of Warhol's *Race Riot*, see Berger, *Seeing Through Race*, 26–27; McHugh, *Animal Stories*, 37–38; and Anne Wagner, "Warhol Paints History, or Race in America," *Representations* 55 (Summer 1996): 98–119.

105. Quoted in Lisa Dombrowski, *The Films of Samuel Fuller: If You Die, I'll Kill You!* (Middletown: Wesleyan University Press, 2008), 191.

106. *White Dog*, directed by Samuel Fuller (1982; New York: Criterion Collection, 2008), DVD.

107. For discussion of this film, see Susanne Schwerfeger, "Re-education as Exorcism: How a White Dog Challenges the Strategies for Dealing with Racism," in *Animal Horror Cinema: Genre, History and Criticism*, ed. Katarina Gregersdotter, Johan Höglund, and Nicklas Hållén (New York: Palgrave Macmillan, 2015), 126–45. For discussion of related themes in South African film, see Giuliana Lind, "Bullies and Curs: Overlords and Underdogs in South African Cinema," in *Cinematic Canines*, 158–80. For a different meditation on the symbolic meaning of "white dog," see Dayan, *Law Is a White Dog*; Dayan explicitly contrasts her use of the term with that of Romain Gary on 257. She cites the Fuller film in *With Dogs at the Edge*, 8–9, 122.

108. Jonathan Burt, *Animals in Film* (London: Reaktion, 2002), 39.

109. Romain Gary, *White Dog* (1970; repr., Chicago: University of Chicago Press, 2004); all quotations are taken from this edition.

110. J. Hoberman, "Sam Fuller Unmuzzled," Criterion DVD pamphlet for *White Dog*, 8; this essay is also available at the Criterion Collection website, dated November 8, 2008, at https://www.criterion.com/current/posts/847-white-dog-sam-fuller-unmuzzled.

111. Samuel Fuller with Christa Lang Fuller and Jerome Henry Rudes, *A Third Face: My Tale of Writing, Fighting, and Filmmaking* (New York: Knopf, 2002), 489–90.

112. Romain Gary, *Chien Blanc* (Paris: Gallimard, 1970), 31.

113. [Sam Fuller], "The White Dog Talks—to Sam Fuller," *Framework* 19 (1982), reprinted under the title "The White Dog Speaks—to Sam Fuller," DVD pamphlet, 16–25, and available at the Criterion Collection website, July 6, 2012, https://www.criterion.com/current/posts/2372-the-white-dog-speaks-to-sam-fuller. All quotations are taken from the DVD pamphlet edition.

114. [Fuller], "White Dog Talks," 16.

115. [Fuller], "White Dog Talks," 23–24.

116. Fuller, *Third Face*, 73.

117. Young, *Black Frankenstein*, 172–87.

CHAPTER 3

1. Something similar: "I noticed that the label on her antibiotics said 'Patient: Chicken Orlean,' which even in my funk I found

hilarious" (Susan Orlean, "The It Bird," *New Yorker*, September 28, 2009, 31).

2. Miriam Rothschild, *Walter Rothschild: The Man, the Museum and the Menagerie* (London: Natural History Museum, 2008), 52, 111.

3. I believe this was "Dogs Return to Gallery in Museum at Tring," http://www.nhm.ac.uk/about-us/news/2009/February/dogs-return-to-gallery-in-museum-at-tring27259.html, but this link is no longer active. For a similar story, see Adam Banbury, "Stuffed Dogs Now Best in Show as Gallery Six Reopens at Tring," *Culture24*, February 5, 2009, http://www.culture24.org.uk/science-and-nature/art65394.

4. Rothschild, *Walter Rothschild*, 122.

5. Donna Haraway, "Teddy Bear Patriarchy: Taxidermy in the Garden of Eden, New York City, 1908–1936," in *Cultures of United States Imperialism*, ed. Amy Kaplan and Donald E. Pease (Durham: Duke University Press, 1993), 237–91.

6. [Deirdre Janson-Smith], *Visitor Guide: Natural History Museum at Tring* (London: Natural History Museum, 2008), 5.

7. Kim Dennis-Bryan and Juliet Clutton-Brock, *Dogs of the Last Hundred Years at the British Museum (Natural History)* (London: British Museum, 1988), 16.

8. Harriet Ritvo, *The Animal Estate: The English and Other Creatures in the Victorian Age* (Cambridge: Harvard University Press, 1987), 106.

9. Susan McHugh, *Dog* (London: Reaktion, 2004), 66.

10. Rachel Poliquin, "Balto the Dog," in *The Afterlives of Animals: A Museum Menagerie*, ed. Samuel J. M. M. Alberti (Charlottesville: University of Virginia Press, 2011), 97. On taxidermied dogs in the nineteenth century, see also Marjorie Garber, *Dog Love* (New York: Touchstone, 1997), 269–70; Katherine C. Grier, *Pets in America: A History* (Orlando: Harcourt, 2006), 288–90; Kathleen Kete, *The Beast in the Boudoir: Petkeeping in Nineteenth-Century Paris* (Berkeley: University of California Press, 1994), 288–90; P. A. Morris, *A History of Taxidermy: Art, Science and Bad Taste*, rev. ed. (2010; repr., Ascot, Berkshire: MPM, 2012), 154–55; Alexis Turner, *Taxidermy* (New York: Rizzoli, 2013), 26, 74, 108–9; and John Whitenight, *Under Glass: A Victorian Obsession* (Atglen, PA: Schiffer, 2013), 143–47.

11. Grier, *Pets in America*, 288–90.

12. See Liv Emma Thorsen, "A Dog of Myth and Matter: Barry the Saint Bernard in Bern," in *Animals on Display: The Creaturely in Museums, Zoos, and Natural History*, ed. Liv Emma Thorsen, Karen A. Rader, and Adam Dodd (University Park: Pennsylvania State University Press, 2013), 128–49.

13. For examples of mounted dog heads at Tring, see Dennis-Bryan and Clutton-Brock, *Dogs of Last Hundred Years*, 24, 78, 90. For non-Tring examples, see Turner, *Taxidermy*, 91.

14. On the bulldog as an English symbol, see Steve Baker, *Picturing the Beast: Animals, Identity and Representation* (Manchester: Manchester University Press, 1993), 33–73.

15. Michael Brandow, *A Matter of Breeding: A Biting History of Pedigree Dogs and How the Quest for Status Has Harmed Man's Best Friend* (Boston: Beacon Press, 2015), 23–27.

16. Marc Simpson, "Immaculate Trophies," *Essays on Canadian Writing* 68 (Summer 1999): 98.

17. The trade books are Dave Madden, *The Authentic Animal: Inside the Odd and Obsessive World of Taxidermy* (New York: St. Martin's Press, 2011); and Melissa Milgrom, *Still Life: Adventures in Taxidermy* (Boston: Houghton Mifflin, 2010). The estimate of one hundred thousand taxidermy participants is from Milgrom, 31. New histories, appreciations, and how-tos include Divya Anantharaman and Katie Innamorato, *Stuffed Animals: A Modern Guide to Taxidermy* (New York: Countryman Press, 2016); Jane Eastoe, *The Art of Taxidermy* (London: Pavilion, 2012); Robert Marbury, *Taxidermy Art: A Rogue's Guide to the Work, the Culture, and How to Do It Yourself* (New

York: Artisan, 2014); Morris, *History of Taxidermy*; and Turner, *Taxidermy*. The taxidermy reality television shows are *Immortalized* and *American Stuffers*, discussed in Christina M. Colvin, "Freeze-Drying Fido: The Uncanny Aesthetics of Modern Taxidermy," in *Mourning Animals: Rituals and Practices Surrounding Animal Death*, ed. Margo DeMello (East Lansing: Michigan State University Press, 2016), 65–71. The scholarly books include Jane Desmond, *Displaying Death and Animating Life: Human-Animal Relations in Art, Science, and Everyday Life* (Chicago: University of Chicago Press, 2016); and Rachel Poliquin, *The Breathless Zoo: Taxidermy and the Cultures of Longing* (University Park: Pennsylvania State University Press, 2012). See also notes below.

18. On taxidermy as decor, see Turner, *Taxidermy*, 70–117, 172–207. On the Morbid Anatomy Museum, see Joanna Ebenstein and Colin Dickey, eds., *The Morbid Anatomy Anthology* (New York: Morbid Anatomy Press, 2014); and Joanna Ebenstein, *Morbid Anatomy* (blog), http://morbidanatomy.blogspot.com.

19. Poliquin, *Breathless Zoo*, 50; and see her website, http://www.rachelpoliquin.com/ravishingbeasts/.

20. For introductions to this art, see Giovanni Aloi, *Art and Animals* (London: I. B. Tauris, 2011), 24–48; "Rogue Taxidermy," special issue of *Antennae* 6 (Spring 2008) and "Botched Taxidermy," special issue of *Antennae* 7 (Autumn 2008), both ed. Giovanni Aloi; and Jo-Ann Conklin, ed., *Dead Animals; or, the Curious Occurrence of Taxidermy in Contemporary Art* (Providence: Brown University / David Winton Bell Gallery, 2016).

21. Bryndís Snæbjörnsdóttir and Mark Wilson, *Nanoq: Flat Out and Bluesome: A Cultural History of Polar Bears* (London: Black Dog, 2006).

22. Dion first developed these ethical guidelines in 2000; a revised version appears as Mark Dion and Robert Marbury, "Some Notes Toward a Manifesto for Artists Working with and About Taxidermy Animals," in *Dead Animals*, 68–69. Mayer is quoted in Giovanni Aloi, "Rescuing What Had Become a Dying Art," *Antennae* 7 (Autumn 2008): 48. Morgan, foreword to *Art of Taxidermy*, by Eastoe, 13.

23. Singer, quoted in Steve Baker, "'You Kill Things to Look at Them': Animal Death in Contemporary Art," in *Killing Animals*, ed. the Animal Studies Group (Urbana: University of Illinois Press, 2006), 85–86.

24. Steve Baker, *The Postmodern Animal* (London: Reaktion, 2000), 75, 64.

25. "Rather clumsy catch-all" is in Gregory Williams, "Where the Wild Things Are: An Interview with Steve Baker," *Cabinet Magazine* 4 (Fall 2001), http://www.cabinetmagazine.org/issues/4/SteveBaker.php. "Lost much of its critical purchase" is in Steve Baker, "Beyond Botched Taxidermy," in *Dead Animals*, 43.

26. Baker, "Beyond Botched Taxidermy," 51.

27. The exhibition was "Taxidermy: Art, Science and Immortality," Morbid Anatomy Museum, 2016.

28. Giovanni Aloi, *Speculative Taxidermy: Natural History, Animal Surfaces, and Art in the Anthropocene* (New York: Columbia University Press, 2018), 23.

29. Aloi, *Speculative Taxidermy*, 183.

30. Marbury, *Taxidermy Art*, 12.

31. Kat Su, *Crap Taxidermy* (London: Cassell, 2014), 6.

32. Grünfeld's piece is discussed in the exhibition catalog by Laura Steward Heon with John Ackerman, *Unnatural Science: An Exhibition* (North Adams: Massachusetts Museum of Contemporary Art, 2000), 24–25. The museum's exhibition of animal-centered art was "Becoming Animal"; see Nato Thompson, *Becoming Animal: Contemporary Art in the Animal Kingdom* (North Adams: Massachusetts Museum of Contemporary Art / MIT Press, 2005).

33. Mayer, quoted in Aloi, "Rescuing What Had Become a Dying Art," 47.

34. Cliff Lauson, "David Shrigley: Larger than Life (and Sometimes Death)," in *David Shrigley—Brain Activity*, ed. Lauson et al. (London: Hayward, 2012), 29.

35. Nina Katchadourian, "Chloe," *Confusing Animals*, http://www.ninakatcha dourian.com/confusinganimals/chloe.php.

36. Stephanie S. Turner, "Relocating 'Stuffed' Animals: Photographic Remediation of Natural History Taxidermy," *Humanimalia: A Journal of Human/Animal Interface Studies* 4:2 (Spring 2013): 1–32.

37. Diane Fox, "Reframing Animals," *Antennae* 40 (Summer 2017): 31. For more examples of her work, see Fox, "UnNatural History: Black and White," http://dianefox-photography.com/photography/unnatural-history/.

38. Poliquin, *Breathless Zoo*, 215. For recent encounters with Tring, see also Eastoe, *Art of Taxidermy*, 61–69; Madden, *Authentic Animal*, 18–19; and Milgrom, *Still Life*, 137–39.

39. See Sarah Amato, *Beastly Possessions: Animals in Victorian Consumer Culture* (Toronto: University of Toronto Press, 2015), 196–205.

40. The most notable exception: the taxidermy of Walter Potter. See Amato, *Beastly Possessions*, 217–23; Conor Creaney, "Paralytic Animation: The Anthropomorphic Taxidermy of Walter Potter," *Victorian Studies* 53:1 (Autumn 2010): 7–35; and Pat Morris with Joanna Ebenstein, *Walter Potter's Curious World of Taxidermy* (London: Constable, 2013).

41. Desmond, *Displaying Death and Animating Life*, 33, 34, 34.

42. Desmond, *Displaying Death and Animating Life*, 33.

43. Haraway, "Teddy Bear Patriarchy," 259.

44. Michelle Henning, "Skins of the Real: Taxidermy and Photography," in *Nanoq*, 138. For another perspective on this comparison, see Helen Gregory and Anthony Purdy, "Present Signs, Dead Things: Indexical Authenticity and Taxidermy's Nonabsent Animal," *Configurations* 23 (2015): 61–92.

45. Mark Alvey, "The Cinema as Taxidermy: Carl Akeley and the Preservative Obsession," *Framework* 48: 1 (Spring 2007): 23–45.

46. See Fatimah Tobing Rony, *The Third Eye: Race, Cinema, and Ethnographic Spectacle* (Durham: Duke University Press, 1996), 101–16; and Pauline Wakeham, *Taxidermic Signs: Reconstructing Aboriginality* (Minneapolis: University of Minnesota Press, 2008), 14–15.

47. Sarah Kay, "Legible Skins: Animals and the Ethics of Medieval Reading," *Postmedieval* 2:1 (2011): 13. On animals and medieval parchment, see also Bruce Holsinger, "Of Pigs and Parchment: Medieval Studies and the Coming of the Animal," *PMLA* 124:2 (March 2009): 616–23; and Katie L. Walker, ed., *Reading Skin in Medieval Literature and Culture* (New York: Palgrave, 2013).

48. Kay, "Legible Skins," 14.

49. Steven Connor, *The Book of Skin* (Ithaca: Cornell University Press, 2004), 42.

50. Daniel K. Smith, "Bound in Human Skin: A Survey of Examples of Anthropodermic Bibliopegy," in *Morbid Anatomy Anthology*, 380–93.

51. Edith Wharton, *The House of Mirth*, ed. Elizabeth Ammons (New York: W. W. Norton, 1990), 103. The scholarly connection is made by Jennie A. Kassanoff, *Edith Wharton and the Politics of Race* (Cambridge: Cambridge University Press, 2004), 46–47.

52. George Washington Cable, "The Taxidermist," in *Strong Hearts* (New York: Scribner, 1899), 54.

53. Kassanoff, *Edith Wharton and Politics of Race*, 47.

54. On "Creole" in this context, see Christopher Benfey, *Degas in New Orleans: Encounters with the Creole World of Kate Chopin and George Washington Cable* (New York: Knopf, 1997), 118–19; and James Nagel, *Race and Culture in New Orleans Stories: Kate Chopin, Grace King, Alice Dunbar-Nelson, and George Washington Cable* (Tuscaloosa: University of Alabama Press, 2014), 6.

55. Cable, "Taxidermist," 65.

56. H. G. Wells, "The Triumphs of a Taxidermist," in *The Complete Stories of H. G. Wells*, ed. John Hammond (London:

Phoenix, 1998); all quotations are taken from this edition. The story is also reprinted in John Huntington, ed., *The H. G. Wells Reader: A Complete Anthology from Science Fiction to Social Satire* (Lanham, MD: Taylor, 2003), 6–8. For brief discussions of this story, see Huntington, introduction to *H. G. Wells Reader*, xii–xiii; Morris, *History of Taxidermy*, 89; and P. A. Morris, "Stuffed Humans," in *Morbid Anatomy Anthology*, 161.

57. Karen A. Rader and Victoria E. M. Cain, *Life on Display: Revolutionizing U.S. Museums of Science and Natural History in the Twentieth Century* (Chicago: University of Chicago Press, 2014), 18.

58. This photograph was one of many by Haines depicting taxidermied animals in both realist and nonrealist tableaux, published with *Hurst's Stereoscopic Studies of Natural History* (1871–75). James Hurst, the state taxidermist of New York, mounted the animals, and Haines photographed them.

59. Haraway, "Teddy Bear Patriarchy," 260.

60. Morris, *History of Taxidermy*, 97.

61. On the history of the term, see Randall Kennedy, *Nigger: The Strange Career of a Troublesome Word* (New York: Pantheon, 2002); on Conrad's *The Nigger of the Narcissus*, see D. C. R. A. Goonetilleke, "Racism and *The Nigger of the Narcissus*," *Conradiana* 43:2–3 (2011): 51–66.

62. H. G. Wells, *The Island of Doctor Moreau*, ed. Mason Harris (Peterborough, Ontario: Broadview, 2009), 173. For discussions of race in the novel, see Jennifer DeVere Brody, *Impossible Purities: Blackness, Femininity, and Victorian Culture* (Durham: Duke University Press, 1998), 130–69; and Timothy Christiansen, "The 'Bestial Mark' of Race in *The Island of Dr. Moreau*," *Criticism* 46:4 (Fall 2004): 575–95.

63. Antoine Traisnel, "Huntology: Ontological Pursuits and Still Lives," *Diacritics* 40:2 (2012): 9.

64. See Mark V. Barrow Jr., *A Passion for Birds: American Ornithology After Audubon* (Princeton: Princeton University Press, 1998), 107–11.

65. Kristin Greer, "Untangling the Avian Imperial Archive," *Antennae* 20 (2012): 59–71. On the messiness of this "imperial archive," see Ann C. Colley, *Wild Animal Skins in Victorian Britain: Zoos, Collections, Portraits, and Maps* (Burlington, VT: Ashgate, 2014), 49–62.

66. On nineteenth-century bird taxidermy, see also Morris, *History of Taxidermy*, 36–60, 257–70; Poliquin, *Breathless Zoo*, 67–76; and Whitenight, *Under Glass*, 103–58.

67. On the "Feejee Mermaid," see James W. Cook, *The Arts of Deception: Playing with Fraud in the Age of Barnum* (Cambridge: Harvard University Press, 2001), 73–118.

68. Haraway, "Teddy Bear Patriarchy," 254.

69. Huntington, introduction to *H. G. Wells Reader*, xii.

70. On Ota Benga, see Pamela Newkirk, *Spectacle: The Astonishing Life of Ota Benga* (New York: Amistad, 2015). On Hornaday, see Stefan Bechtel, *Mr. Hornaday's War: How a Peculiar Victorian Zookeeper Waged a Lonely Crusade for Wildlife That Changed the World* (Boston: Beacon Press, 2012); and Gregory J. Dehler, *The Most Defiant Devil: William Temple Hornaday and His Controversial Crusade to Save American Wildlife* (Charlottesville: University of Virginia Press, 2013).

71. William T. Hornaday, *Taxidermy and Zoological Collecting: A Complete Handbook for the Amateur Taxidermist, Collector, Osteologist, Museum-Builder, Sportsman, and Traveller*, 7th ed. (1891; repr., New York: Scribner, 1900), vii.

72. Morris disputes this claim in *History of Taxidermy*, 71.

73. Ron Broglio, *Surface Encounters: Thinking with Animals and Art* (Minneapolis: University of Minnesota Press, 2011), xvi.

74. Broglio, *Surface Encounters*, xvii.

75. Poliquin also quotes this passage, in *Breathless Zoo*, 86.

76. William T. Hornaday, preface to *Two Years in the Jungle: The Experiences of a Hunter and Naturalist in India, Ceylon, the Malay Peninsula and Borneo* (New York, 1886), n.p.

77. John Miller, *Empire and the Animal Body: Violence, Identity and Ecology in Victorian Adventure Fiction* (London: Anthem Press, 2012), 61.

78. William T. Hornaday, *Our Vanishing Wild Life* (New York: Scribner, 1913), 114.

79. On the movement against "murderous millinery," see Janet M. Davis, *The Gospel of Kindness: Animal Welfare and the Making of Modern America* (New York: Oxford University Press, 2016), 104–10; Jennifer Price, *Flight Maps: Adventures with Nature in Modern America* (New York: Basic, 1999), 57–109; and Merle Patchett, "Murderous Millinery," in *Fashioning Feathers: Dead Birds, Millinery Crafts and the Plumage Trade* (Edmonton: FAB Gallery, University of Alberta, 2011), exhibition catalogue, http://fashioningfeathers.info/murderous-millinery.

80. Henry Fairfield Osborn, foreword to *Our Vanishing Wild Life*, vii.

81. Davis, *Gospel of Kindness*, 105.

82. Julia Long, "Portable Pets: Live and Apparently Live Animals in Fashion, 1880–1925," *Costume* 43 (2009): 121.

83. Price, *Flight Maps*, 80.

84. *New York Times* July 31, 1898, also quoted in Patchett, "Murderous Millinery."

85. Dehler, *Most Defiant Devil*, 54.

86. On women's leadership in this movement, see Price, *Flight Maps*, 62–73. On "audubonettes," see Patchett, "Murderous Millinery."

87. Virginia Sharpe Patterson, *Dickey Downey: The Autobiography of a Bird* (Philadelphia, 1899), 34–35.

88. Annie Dwyer, "Animal Autobiography and the Domestication of Human Freedom," *Arizona Quarterly* 71:2 (Summer 2015): 2–3; Dwyer also discusses the novel on 15–16.

89. In a 1908 letter, Saunders wrote, "Thank you very much for the information abt. bird societies. I will join the Audubon." Margaret Marshall Saunders, letter to Charles M. Roe, April 8, 1908, in "Correspondence (1908)," file 1943.001-SAU/6, Margaret Marshall Saunders fonds, Esther Clark Wright Archives, Acadia University; this letter is also available online in *Margaret Marshall Saunders: Transcription of the Documents Dated 1906–1914*, http://www.acadiau.ca/~markham/publish&present/MargaretMarshallSaunders.pdf.

90. Irene Pepperberg, *Alex and Me: How a Scientist and a Parrot Uncovered a Hidden World of Animal Intelligence—and Formed a Deep Bond in the Process* (New York: Harper, 2008), 24.

91. Hélène Cixous, "Birds, Women and Writing," in *Animal Philosophy: Essential Readings in Continental Thought*, ed. Matthew Calarco and Peter Atterton (London: Continuum, 2004), 170.

92. Helen Macdonald, *H Is for Hawk* (New York: Grove, 2014).

93. Maya Angelou, *I Know Why the Caged Bird Sings* (New York: Random House, 1969); Paul Laurence Dunbar, "Sympathy" (1899), in *The Collected Poetry of Paul Laurence Dunbar*, ed. Joanne M. Braxton (Charlottesville: University of Virginia Press, 1993), 102.

94. Kate Chopin, *The Awakening*, ed. Margo Culley (New York: W. W. Norton, 1994), 3, 108. On bird imagery in the novel, see Elizabeth Elz, "*The Awakening* and *A Lost Lady*: Flying with Broken Wings and Raked Feathers," *Southern Literary Journal* 35:2 (Spring 2003): 13–27. On Chopin's parrot in an animal studies context, see Bruce Thomas Boehrer, *Parrot Culture: Our 2,500-Year-Long Fascination with the World's Most Talkative Bird* (Philadelphia: University of Pennsylvania Press, 2004), 110.

95. Willa Cather, *A Lost Lady* (New York: Vintage, 1990), 16.

96. In addition to Morgan, Marbury's *Rogue Taxidermy* profiles Lisa Black, Sarina Brewer, Kate Clark, Tessa Farmer, Kate Innamorato, Jessica Joslin, Elizabeth McGrath, Iris Schlieferstien, Mirmy Winn, and Afka Golsteijn of the duo known as "The

Idiots." On the popularity of taxidermy with women, see Claire Voon, "Meet the Ladies who Turn Animal Corpses into Art," *Vice*, October 14, 2014, http://www.vice.com/read/women-are-dominating-the-rogue-taxidermy-scene-666. The Morbid Anatomy instructors, Divya Anantharaman and Katie Innamorato, are featured in Erica Langston, "When Taxidermy Goes Rogue," *Audubon*, March 30, 2016, http://www.audubon.org/news/when-taxidermy-goes-rogue.

97. Carey Dunne, "Meet the Lady Taxidermy Artists of Brooklyn," *Brooklyn*, August 26, 2015, http://www.bkmag.com/2015/08/26/meet-5-of-brooklyns-best-taxidermy-artists/.

98. Gregory and Purdy, "Present Signs, Dead Things," 74.

99. See Miriam Bailin, "The New Victorians," in *Functions of Victorian Culture at the Present Time*, ed. Christine Krueger (Athens: Ohio University Press, 2002), 39; Talia Schaffer, *Novel Craft: Victorian Domestic Handicraft and Nineteenth-Century Fiction* (New York: Oxford University Press, 2011), 120–21; and esp. Beth Fowkes Tobin, "Women, Decorative Arts, and Taxidermy," in *Women and the Material Culture of Death*, ed. Maureen Daly Goggin and Beth Fowkes Tobin (Burlington, VT: Ashgate, 2013), 311–30.

100. On Maxwell, see Maxine Benson, *Martha Maxwell, Rocky Mountain Naturalist* (Lincoln: University of Nebraska Press, 1986); Howe is quoted on 112. For an important new interpretation of Maxwell's work, see Rebecca May, "Natural History and the Unnatural Woman: Reframing Taxidermy as a New Woman's Art" (paper, Annual Conference of Interdisciplinary Nineteenth-Century Studies, Asheville, NC, 2016).

101. Marbury, *Taxidermy Art*, 21; Maxwell is also praised in Anantharaman and Innamorato, *Stuffed Animals*, 29. Other women taxidermists in the period include Elizabeth Hornby, an Englishwoman who mounted the animals she encountered on her travels in Latin America, and Jane Tost and Ada Rohu, a "mother-daughter dream team of lady taxidermists" in Australia. On Hornby, see Elizabeth Hornby in Colley, *Wild Animal Skins*, 78–85; on Tost and Rohu, see Anantharaman and Innamorato, *Stuffed Animals*, 27.

102. "Pigeon on Her Head When Author Talked; Miss Marshall Saunders, Friend of Birds, Etc., Celebrates 70th Birthday," *Toronto Star*, April 13, 1931, 24.

103. Margaret Marshall Saunders, diary entry for March 12, 1907, quoted in *No Place like Home: Diaries and Letters of Nova Scotia Women, 1771–1938*, ed. Margaret Conrad, Toni Laidlaw and Donna Smyth (Halifax, Nova Scotia: Formac, 1988), 240.

104. On the popular conflation of taxidermists with Norman Bates, see Milgrim, *Still Life*, 15, 258; and Marbury, *Taxidermy Art*, 24. On taxidermy in *Psycho*, see Jeffrey Niesel, "The Horror of Everyday Life: Taxidermy, Aesthetics, and Consumption in Horror Films," *Journal of Criminal Justice and Popular Culture* 2:4 (1994): 61–80; and Erika Rothberg, "Norman Can't Leave the Nest: Freudian Theory and the Uncanny Use of Taxidermied Birds in *Psycho*," in *Critical Insights: Alfred Hitchcock*, ed. Douglas Cunningham (Ipswich, MA: Salem Press, 2017), 141–57.

105. Niesel, "Horror of Everyday Life," 69.

106. François Truffaut with the collaboration of Helen G. Scott, *Hitchcock* (1967; repr., New York: Simon & Schuster, 1984), 282.

107. Tania Modleski, *The Women Who Knew Too Much* (New York: Routledge, 1988), 8.

108. Alfred Hitchcock, quoted in *Hitchcock's Notebooks*, ed. Dan Auiler (New York: HarperCollins, 2001), 196.

109. Michael Walker, "Dogs and Cats," in *Hitchcock's Motifs* (Amsterdam: Amsterdam University Press, 2005), 145.

110. Charles Barr, *English Hitchcock* (Moffat, Scotland: Cameron and Hollis, 1989), 186.

111. Murray Pomerance, "Hitchcock's Canine Uncanny," in *Cinematic Canines: Dogs and Their Work in the Fiction Film*,

ed. Adrienne L. McLean (New Brunswick: Rutgers University Press, 2014), 201.

112. Margaret Horwitz, "*The Birds*: A Mother's Love," in *A Hitchcock Reader*, ed. Marshall Deutelbaum and Leland Poague (Ames: Iowa State University Press, 1986), 279; Richard Allen, "Avian Metaphor in *The Birds*," in *Framing Hitchcock: Selected Essays from "The Hitchcock Annual,"* ed. Sidney Gottlieb and Christopher Brookhouse (Detroit: Wayne State University Press, 2002), 290.

113. Tippi Hedren with Lindsay Harrison, *Tippi* (New York: William Morrow, 2016), 57.

114. See Grier, *Pets in America*, 59–66.

115. Jeff Karnicky, *Scarlet Experiment: Birds and Humans in America* (Lincoln: University of Nebraska Press, 2016), 42.

116. John James Audubon, *Ornithological Biography, Writings and Drawings* (New York: Library of America, 1999), 220.

117. [Margaret] Marshall Saunders, *My Pets: Real Happenings in My Aviary* (Philadelphia: Griffith & Rowland, 1908); all quotations are taken from this edition.

118. Marshall Saunders, diary entry for December 6, 1906, reprinted in *No Place like Home*, 239.

119. Margaret Marshall Saunders, letter to Charles M. Roe, February 6, 1908, in "Correspondence (1908)," file 1943.001-SAU/7, Margaret Marshall Saunders fonds, Esther Clark Wright Archives, Acadia University; this letter is also available online in *Margaret Marshall Saunders: Transcription of the Documents Dated 1906–1914*, http://www.acadiau.ca/~markham/publish&present/MargaretMarshallSaunders.pdf.

120. Desmond, *Displaying Death and Animating Life*, 33.

121. Eastoe, *Art of Taxidermy*, 56.

122. "A Biography of Edward Thomas Booth," https://brightonmuseums.org.uk/booth/about/edward-booth. On the Booth Museum, see Morris, *History of Taxidermy*, 264–66.

123. Elma Stonex, "Development of the Breed in Great Britain and Other Lands," in *The Complete Golden Retriever*, ed. Gertrude Fischer (New York: Howell, 1980), 23–27.

CHAPTER 4

1. Dr. Suzanne E. Rau, Tufts University Foster Hospital for Small Animals, Case Summary #171588, Client #357184, 7/15/2008, 2.

2. Catherine O'Neill Grace, "The Foster Legacy," *Tufts Veterinary Medicine* 10:3 (Spring 2009): 6, news.vet.tufts.edu/magazine/tvm_10-3_spring_2009.pdf.

3. Lorrie Moore, "People like That Are the Only People Here: Canonical Babbling in Peed Onk," in *Birds of America* (New York: Picador, 1998), 216.

4. Moore, "People like That," 227.

5. Clifton R. Sanders and Arnold Arluke, "Speaking for Dogs," in *The Animals Reader: The Essential Classic and Contemporary Writings*, ed. Linda Kalof and Amy Fitzgerald (Oxford: Berg, 2007), 64.

6. Nick Trout, *Tell Me Where It Hurts: A Day of Humor, Healing, and Hope in My Life as an Animal Surgeon* (New York: Broadway, 2008), 247.

7. On the dog industry, see Michael Schaeffer, *One Nation Under Dog: Adventures in the New World of Prozac-Popping Puppies, Dog-Park Politics, and Organic Pet Food* (New York: Holt, 2009). For *Bark*, see https://thebark.com/. On "critical pet studies," see Heidi J. Nast, "Critical Pet Studies?," *Antipode* 38:5 (November 2006): 894–906.

8. Marie Bonaparte, *Topsy: The Story of a Golden-Haired Chow*, introduction by Gary Genosko (New Brunswick, NJ: Transaction, 1994); all quotations are taken from this edition.

9. Mary Shelley, introduction to *Frankenstein*, ed. J. Paul Hunter (New York: W. W. Norton, 1996), 172.

10. Shelley, quoted in Ellen Moers, *Literary Women: The Great Writers* (1976; repr., New York: Oxford University Press, 1985), 96.

11. Shelley, *Frankenstein*, 32.

12. William Hornaday, *Taxidermy and Zoological Collecting* (New York, 1893), vii.

13. Nigel Rothfels, "Preserving History: Collecting and Displaying in Carl Akeley's *In Brightest Africa*," in *Animals on Display: The Creaturely in Museums, Zoos, and Natural History*, ed. Liv Emma Thorsen, Karen A. Rader, and Adam Dodd (University Park: Pennsylvania State University Press, 2013), 59.

14. Jennifer Price, *Flight Maps: Adventures with Nature in Modern America* (New York: Basic Books, 1999), 45. On Martha, see also Joel Greenberg, *A Feathered River Across the Sky: The Passenger Pigeon's Flight to Extinction* (New York: Bloomsbury, 2014). On the representation of bird extinction, see Thom Van Dooren, *Flight Ways: Life and Loss at the Edge of Extinction* (New York: Columbia University Press, 2014).

15. Rosamond Wolff Purcell, Linnea S. Hall, and René Corado, *Egg and Nest* (Cambridge: Harvard University Press, 2008). For an expanded discussion of this photograph, see Elizabeth Young, "Objects of Our Affection: Rosamond Wolff Purcell, *Passenger Pigeon*," blog post, *mhcameo*, Mount Holyoke College Art Museum, February 29, 2016, https://artmuseum.mtholyoke.edu/blog/passenger-pigeon.

16. Rosamond Wolff Purcell, "Unrolling the Egg," in *Egg and Nest*, 188.

17. Teresa Mangum, "Animal Angst: Victorians Memorialize Their Pets," in *Victorian Animal Dreams: Representations of Animals in Victorian Literature and Culture*, ed. Deborah Denenholz-Morse and Martin A. Danahay (Burlington, VT: Ashgate, 2007), 25. On pet cemeteries in this era, see Philip Howell, *At Home and Astray: The Domestic Dog in Victorian Britain* (Charlottesville: University of Virginia Press, 2015), 125–49.

18. Barbara J. King, *How Animals Grieve* (Chicago: University of Chicago Press, 2013), 9.

19. Mangum, "Animal Angst," 19. On representations of dogs mourning their owners in this period, see also Keridiana Chez, *Victorian Dogs, Victorian Men: Affect and Animals in Nineteenth-Century Literature and Culture* (Columbus: Ohio State University Press, 2017), 13–15.

20. Teresa Mangum, "Dog Years, Human Fears," in *Representing Animals*, ed. Nigel Rothfels (Bloomington: Indiana University Press, 2002), 46.

21. Laurel Braitman, *Animal Madness: How Anxious Dogs, Compulsive Parrots, and Elephants in Recovery Help Us Understand Ourselves* (New York: Simon & Schuster, 2014), 110.

22. See, for example, Leon Hoffman, "Freud's Adirondack Vacation," *New York Times*, August 29, 2009, http://www.nytimes.com/2009/08/29/opinion/29hoffman.html.

23. Sigmund Freud, *Five Lectures on Psycho-analysis*, trans. James Strachey (New York: W. W. Norton, 1989), 3.

24. Quoted in Patricia Cohen, "Freud Is Widely Taught at Universities, Except in the Psychology Department," *New York Times* "Week in Review," November 25, 2007, https://www.nytimes.com/2007/11/25/weekinreview/25cohen.html.

25. On dogs in Freud's life, see Marjorie Garber, *Dog Love* (New York: Touchstone, 1997), 135–39; and Gary Genosko, introduction to *Topsy*, 1–13. On dogs at the Freud Museum in London, see Amelie Hastie, "Breathing in the Archives," *Camera Obscura* 64 (2007): 181–85; on dogs at the Freud Museum in Vienna, see Ann Pellegrini, "The Dogs of War and the Dogs at Home: Thresholds of Loss," *American Imago* 66:2 (Summer 2009): 231–51.

26. On Freud and Bonaparte, see Lisa Appignanesi and John Forrester, *Freud's Women: Family, Patients, Followers* (New York: Basic Books, 1992), 329–48; Célia Bertin, *Marie Bonaparte: A Life* (San Diego: Harcourt Brace, 1982), 151–209; and Genosko, introduction to *Topsy*.

27. Kelly Oliver, *Animal Lessons: How They Teach Us to Be Human* (New York: Columbia University Press, 2009), 247.

28. Josef Breuer and Sigmund Freud, *Studies on Hysteria*, trans. James Strachey (1895; repr., New York: Basic Books, 2000), 34, 30.

29. Freud, *Five Lectures on Psycho-analysis*, 8–9, 14.

30. Breuer and Freud, *Studies on Hysteria*, 31.

31. Freud, *Five Lectures on Psycho-analysis*, 42.

32. James Strachey in Breuer and Freud, *Studies on Hysteria*, 40, n1.

33. Peter Gay, *Freud: A Life for Our Time* (New York: W. W. Norton, 1988), 67.

34. See, respectively, Appignanesi and Forrester, *Freud's Women*, 82; Madelon Sprengnether, *The Spectral Mother: Freud, Feminism, and Psychoanalysis* (Ithaca: Cornell University Press, 1990), 40; and Wayne Koestenbaum, *Double Talk: The Erotics of Male Literary Collaboration* (New York: Routledge, 1989), 29. On the case as myth, see Mikkel Borch-Jacobsen, *Remembering Anna O.: A Century of Mystification* (New York: Routledge, 1996).

35. Sigmund Freud, *The Interpretation of Dreams* (New York: Avon, 1965), 445.

36. Dave Madden, *The Authentic Animal: Inside the Odd and Obsessive World of Taxidermy* (New York: St. Martin's Press, 2011), 2.

37. Sigmund Freud, *Three Essays on the Theory of Sexuality* (New York: Basic Books, 1962), 14.

38. Alice A. Kuzniar, "'I Married My Dog': On Queer Canine Literature," in *Queering the Non/Human*, ed. Noreen Giffney and Myra J. Hird (Burlington, VT: Ashgate, 2008), 206; Mel Y. Chen, *Animacies: Biopolitics, Racial Mattering, and Queer Affect* (Durham: Duke University Press, 2012), 102. Other relevant discussions include Monica Flegel, *Pets and Domesticity in Victorian Literature and Culture: Animality, Queer Relations, and the Victorian Family* (New York: Routledge, 2015); Susan McHugh, "Queer (and) Animal Theories," *GLQ* 15:1 (2008): 153–69; and Kathy Rudy, "LGBTQ . . . Z?," *Hypatia* 27:3 (August 2012): 601–15.

39. Quoted in Midas Dekkers, *Dearest Pet: On Bestiality*, trans. Paul Vincent (London: Verso, 1994), 137.

40. Dekkers, *Dearest Pet*, 64.

41. Frances Coventry, *The History of Pompey the Little; or, The Life and Adventures of a Lap-Dog*, ed. Robert Adams Day (London: Oxford University Press, 1974), 132.

42. Flegel, *Pets and Domesticity*, 22. On literary representations of lapdogs, see also Laura Brown, *Homeless Dogs and Melancholy Apes: Humans and Other Animals in the Modern Literary Imagination* (Ithaca: Cornell University Press, 2010), 65–89.

43. Quoted in Lisa Dombrowski, *The Films of Samuel Fuller: If You Die, I'll Kill You!* (Middletown: Wesleyan University Press, 2008), 193.

44. See Appignanesi and Forrester, *Freud's Women*, 72–86.

45. Freud, *Five Lectures on Psycho-analysis*, 24.

46. Sigmund Freud, "Mourning and Melancholia," in *Standard Edition of the Complete Works*, trans. James Strachey (London: Hogarth, 1957), 14:250.

47. See, for example, Paul Gilroy, *Postcolonial Melancholia* (New York: Columbia University Press, 2003); Anne Anlin Cheng, *The Melancholy of Race: Psychoanalysis, Assimilation, and Hidden Grief* (New York: Oxford University Press, 2000); David L. Eng and Shinhee Han, "A Dialogue on Racial Melancholia," in *Loss*, ed. David L. Eng and David Kazanjian (Berkeley: University of California Press, 2003), 343–71; and Charity Scribner, "Left Melancholy," and Wendy Brown, "Resisting Left Melancholia," both in *Loss*, 300–19, 458–65.

48. Brown, "Resisting Left Melancholia," 459.

49. See, for example, Mary Louise Kete, *Sentimental Collaborations: Mourning and Middle-Class Identity in Nineteenth-Century America* (Durham: Duke University Press, 2000); and Dana Luciano, *Arranging Grief: Sacred Time and the Body in Nineteenth-Century America* (New York: New York University Press, 2007).

50. Karen Sánchez-Eppler, *Dependent States: The Child's Part in Nineteenth-Century American Culture* (Chicago: University of Chicago Press, 2005), 101.

51. Harriet Beecher Stowe, *Uncle Tom's Cabin*, ed. Elizabeth Ammons (New York: W. W. Norton, 1994), 384.

52. Alice A. Kuzniar, *Melancholia's Dog: Reflections on Our Animal Kinship* (Chicago: University of Chicago Press, 2006), 138, 139.

53. Kuzniar, *Melancholia's Dog*, 142.

54. Kuzniar, *Melancholia's Dog*, 144.

55. Justin Prystash, "Vectors of a Flea: The Convergence of Species in Victorian Animal Autobiographies," *Mosaic* 49:1 (March 2016): 43–44.

56. Marianne Noble, *The Masochistic Pleasures of Sentimental Literature* (Princeton: Princeton University Press, 2000), 126–27.

57. Richard von Krafft-Ebing, *Psychopathia Sexualis*, trans. Franklin S. Klaf (1892; repr., New York: Arcade, 1965), 195.

58. Freud, *Three Essays*, 24.

59. Prystash, "Vectors of a Flea," 48.

60. Moore, "People like That," 217–18.

61. Moore, "People like That," 217.

62. On the critique of medicine in Moore's story, see Pamela Schaff and Johanna Shapiro, "The Limits of Narrative and Culture: Reflections on Lorrie Moore's 'People like That Are the Only People Here: Canonical Babbling in Peed Onk,'" *Journal of Medical Humanities* 27:1 (Spring 2006): 1–17.

63. *Her Master's Voice* (dir. Nina Conti, 2012). For discussion, see Sarah Kessler, "Puppet Love: Documenting Ventriloquism in Nina Conti's *Her Master's Voice*," *Camera Obscura* 92 (2016): 61–91.

64. On Vent Haven, see its website, https://www.venthaven.org. For a critic's assessment of Vent Haven, see Edward Rothstein, "Bright Lights, Wide Eyes: Nostalgic Collections That Speak Volumes," *New York Times*, June 22, 2009, https://www.nytimes.com/2009/06/22/arts/design/22private.html; for artists' responses, see Matthew Rolston, *Talking Heads: The Vent Haven Portraits* (New York: Pointed Leaf Press, 2012); and Laurie Simmons, *Walking Talking Lying* (New York: Aperture, 2005), 42–71.

65. Marshall Saunders, *Beautiful Joe's Paradise:; or, The Island of Brotherly Love: A Sequel to Beautiful Joe* (Boston: L. C. Page, 1902); all quotations are taken from this edition. For brief discussions of the novel, see Chez, *Victorian Dogs, Victorian Men*, 97–98; Roxanne Harde, "'Better Friends': Marshall Saunders Writing Humane Education and Envisioning Animal Rights," *Jeunesse: Young People, Texts, Cultures* 1:2 (2009): 94; and Waterston, *Silenced Sextet*, 153–55.

66. Waterston, *Silenced Sextet*, 167.

67. Marshall Saunders, "The Story of My Life," *Ontario Library Review* 12:2 (November 1927); all quotations are taken from this edition.

68. Steven Connor notes connections between the uncanny and ventriloquism in *Dumbstruck: A Cultural History of Ventriloquism* (New York: Oxford University Press, 2000), 341.

69. Sigmund Freud, "The Uncanny," in *The Uncanny*, trans. David McLintock (New York: Penguin, 2003), 124. For an introduction to the literature on this essay, see Nicholas Royle, *The Uncanny* (New York: Routledge, 2003).

70. Edward A. Berlin, *King of Ragtime: Scott Joplin and His Era*, 2nd ed. (New York: Oxford University Press, 2016), 108.

71. Freud, "Mourning and Melancholia," 248, 246.

72. Freud, "Uncanny," 141.

73. Jane Desmond, *Displaying Death and Animating Life: Human-Animal Relations in Art, Science, and Everyday Life* (Chicago: University of Chicago Press, 2016), 33.

74. Waterston also suggests a connection between *Beautiful Joe's Paradise* and *The Wizard of Oz*, in *Silenced Sextet*, 154.

75. See Karen A. Choppa, "Charles Livingston Bull," in *Charles Livingston Bull, 1874–1932* (Oradell, NJ: Hiram Blauvelt Art Museum, 1994), 7–8; and Walt Reed and Roger Reed, *The Illustrator in America, 1880–1980: A Century of Illustration* (New York: Society of Illustrators, 1984), 91.

76. Douglas Allen, "Charles Livingston Bull: A Bibliography," in *Charles Livingston Bull, 1874–1932*, 67.

77. L. Frank Baum, *The Wizard of Oz* (1900; repr., London: Puffin Books, 2008), 148–49.

78. P. A. Morris, *A History of Taxidermy: Art, Science and Bad Taste*, rev. ed. (2010; repr., Ascot, Berkshire: MPM, 2012), 47.

79. Freud, "Uncanny," 142.

80. Freud, "Uncanny," 142.

81. On dog postmortem photography, see Katherine C. Grier, *Pets in America: A History* (Orlando: Harcourt, 2006), 138–39; and Jay Ruby, *Secure the Shadow: Death and Photography in America* (Cambridge: MIT Press, 1995), 85–87. On child postmortem photography, see Stanley Burns, *Sleeping Beauty III: Memorial Photography: The Children* (New York: Burns Archive Press, 2011); Stacy C. Hollander, *Securing the Shadow: Posthumous Portraiture in America* (New York: American Folk Art Museum, 2016), 193–221; and Sánchez-Eppler, *Dependent States*, 101–48.

82. Freud, "Uncanny," 157.

83. Marshall Saunders, *Nita: The Story of an Irish Setter, Containing also Uncle Jim's Burglar and Mehitable's Chicken* (Boston: L. C. Page, 1904), 1–22; all quotations are taken from this edition.

84. Desmond, *Displaying Death and Animating Life*, 81–140.

85. Christina M. Colvin, "Freeze-Drying Fido: The Uncanny Aesthetics of Modern Taxidermy," and Chrissie Wanner, "Clutching at Straws: Dogs, Death, and Frozen Semen," both in *Mourning Animals: Rituals and Practices Surrounding Animal Death*, ed. Margo DeMello (East Lansing: Michigan State University Press, 2016), 65–71, 73–79.

86. See the website for *Furever*, http://www.fureverfilm.com/. The taxidermy connection is recounted in Anna Jane Grossman, "Preserving Memories of Pets, and Then Some," *New York Times*, October 11, 2011, https://cityroom.blogs.nytimes.com/2011/10/11/preserving-memories-of-pets-and-then-some/.

87. For an early assessment of dog cloning, see Susan McHugh, "Bitches from Brazil: Cloning and Owning Dogs Through the Missyplicity Project," in *Representing Animals*, 180–98.

88. Emily Mayer, quoted in Giovanni Aloi, "Rescuing What Had Become a Dying Art," *Antennae* 7 (Autumn 2008): 47. On the prohibition of domestic animals in taxidermy competitions, see Desmond, *Displaying Death and Animating Life*, 38–39.

89. Gerald H. Gosse and Michael J. Barnes, "Human Grief Resulting from the Death of a Pet," in *Social Creatures: A Human and Animal Studies Reader*, ed. Clifton P. Flynn (Brooklyn, NY: Lantern Books, 2008), 301.

90. On the Dog Chapel, see "Dog Mountain: Home of Stephen Huneck Gallery," at https://www.dogmt.com/Dog-Chapel.html; and Stephen Huneck, *The Dog Chapel: Welcome All Creeds All Breeds. No Dogmas Allowed* (New York: Abrams, 2002).

91. Margalit Fox, "Stephen Huneck, Artist of Dogs, Dies at 61," *New York Times*, February 1, 2010, http://www.nytimes.com/2010/02/01/arts/design/01huneck.html.

92. J. Hoberman, review of *Wendy and Lucy*, directed by Kelly Reichardt, *Village Voice*, December 10, 2008, https://www.villagevoice.com/2008/12/10/wendy-and-lucy/. *Wendy and Lucy* has also been compared to another De Sica film, *Umberto D* (1952); see Katherine Fusco and Nicole Seymour, *Kelly Reichardt* (Urbana: University of Illinois Press, 2017), 47–48.

93. See Kaja Silverman, *The Acoustic Mirror: The Female Voice in Psychoanalysis and Cinema* (Bloomington: Indiana University Press, 1988).

94. Lucy also appeared in Reichardt's film *Old Joy*; the director comments on her presence in "An Interview with Kelly Reichardt," in Fusco and Seymour, *Kelly Reichardt*, 119–20.

95. Garber, *Dog Love*, 242.

96. Ian Phillips, *Lost: Lost and Found Pet Posters from Around the World* (New York: Princeton Architectural Press, 2002), n.p. [1].

97. Jon Raymond, "Train Choir," in *Livability* (New York: Bloomsbury, 2009), 242.

98. James Warner, interview with Jon Raymond, *Identity Theory* March 12, 2009, http://www.identitytheory.com/jon-raymond/.

99. Mary Ann Doane, *The Desire to Desire: The Woman's Film of the 1940s* (Bloomington: Indiana University Press, 1987), 73.

100. John Mercer and Martin Shingler, *Melodrama: Genre, Style, Sensibility* (New York: Wallflower, 2004), 1.

101. Elena Gorfinkel, "Weariness, Waiting: Enduration and Art Cinema's Tired Bodies," *Discourse* 34:2–3 (Spring/Fall 2012): 335. For a complementary analysis of the film in relation to economic decline, see Fusco and Seymour, *Kelly Reichardt*, 35–49.

102. Raymond, "Train Choir," 258–59.

103. Patricia White, "Watching Women's Films," *Camera Obscura* 72 (2009): 159.

104. For an emphasis on the ambiguity of the ending, see Linda Williams, "'Something Else Besides a Mother': *Stella Dallas* and the Maternal Melodrama," in *Feminism and Film*, ed. E. Ann Kaplan (Oxford: Oxford University Press, 2000), 479–504.

CHAPTER 5

1. Elizabeth Waterston, "Margaret Marshall Saunders: A Voice for the Silent," in *Silenced Sextet: Six Nineteenth-Century Canadian Women Novelists*, ed. Carrie MacMillan, Lorraine McMullen, and Elizabeth Waterston (Montreal: McGill-Queen's University Press, 1992), 137–68. On Saunders's biography, see also Phyllis R. Blakeley, "Margaret Marshall Saunders, the Author of *Beautiful Joe*," *Nova Scotia Historical Quarterly* 1:3 (September 1971): 225–38; Keridiana Chez, introduction to *Beautiful Joe*, by Marshall Saunders (Peterborough, Ontario: Broadview, 2015), 11–16, 37–38; Carole Gerson, "Margaret Marshall Saunders," in *Canadian Writers, 1890–1920*, ed. W. H. New (Detroit: Gale, 1990), 327–30; and Karen Sanders, "Margaret Marshall Saunders: Children's Literature as an Expression of Early Twentieth Century Social Reform" (MA thesis, Dalhousie University, 1978). Selections of Saunders's letters and journals have been published in Margaret Conrad, Toni Laidlaw, and Donna Smyth, *No Place like Home: Diaries and Letters of Nova Scotia Women, 1771–1938* (Halifax, Nova Scotia: Formac, 1988), 227–41; and "Margaret Marshall Saunders: Edinburgh Diary, 1876," *Atlantis: A Women's Studies Journal* 6:1 (Fall 1980): 68–82.

2. Cynthia Sugars, introduction to *The Oxford Handbook of Canadian Literature*, ed. Sugars (New York: Oxford University Press, 2016), 2.

3. Geoff Pevere and Greg Dymond, *Mondo Canuck: A Canadian Pop Culture Odyssey* (Scarborough, Ontario: Prentice-Hall Canada, 1996), ix.

4. Nick Mount, *Arrival: The Story of CanLit* (Toronto: House of Anansi, 2017), 2.

5. Douglas Coupland, "What Is CanLit?," *New York Times*, August 22, 2008, http://coupland.blogs.nytimes.com/2006/08/22/what-is-canlit/.

6. Smaro Kamboureli and Roy Miki, eds., *Trans.Can.Lit: Resituating the Study of Canadian Literature* (Waterloo: Wilfred Laurier University Press, 2007).

7. Iyko Day, *Alien Capital: Asian Racialization and the Logic of Settler Colonial Capitalism* (Durham: Duke University Press, 2016), 168.

8. See Cynthia Sugars and Gerry Turcotte, eds., *Unsettled Remains: Canadian Literature and the Postcolonial Gothic* (Waterloo, Ontario: Wilfred Laurier University Press, 2009).

9. Rinaldo Walcott, *Black like Who? Writing Black Canada*, 2nd rev. ed. (Toronto: Insomniac Press, 2003), 27.

10. Katherine McKittrick, *Demonic Grounds: Black Women and the Cartographies of Struggle* (Minneapolis: University of Minnesota Press, 2006), 93.

11. For this critique, see George Elliott Clarke, "Must All Blackness Be American? Locating Blackness in Borden's 'Tightrope Time'; or, Nationalizing Gilroy's *The Black Atlantic*," in *Odysseys Home: Mapping African-Canadian Literature* (Toronto: University of Toronto Press, 2012), 71–85;

and Winfried Siemerling, *The Black Atlantic Reconsidered: Black Canadian Writing, Cultural History, and the Presence of the Past* (Montreal: McGill-Queen's University Press, 2015).

12. See Elizabeth Waterston, *Magic Island: The Fictions of L. M. Montgomery* (Oxford: Oxford University Press, 2008); and Irene Gammel and Elizabeth Epperly, eds., *L. M. Montgomery and Canadian Culture* (Toronto: University of Toronto Press, 1999).

13. Carrie MacMillan, Lorraine McMullen, and Elizabeth Waterston, preface to *Silenced Sextet*, ix.

14. Veronica Strong-Boag and Carole Gerson, *Paddling Her Own Canoe: The Times and Texts of E. Pauline Johnson (Tekahionwake)* (Toronto: University of Toronto Press, 2000), 3.

15. See Mary Chapman, *Becoming Sui Sin Far: Early Fiction, Journalism, and Travel Writing by Edith Maude Eaton* (Montreal: McGill-Queen's University Press, 2016).

16. Mary Ann Shadd (later Cary), *A Plea for Emigration; or Notes of Canada West*, ed. Phanuel Antwi (Peterborough, Ontario: Broadview, 2016).

17. George Elliott Clarke, "This Is No Hearsay: Reading the Canadian Slave Narrative," in *Directions Home: Approaches to African-Canadian Literature* (Toronto: University of Toronto Press, 2012), 21.

18. George Elliott Clarke, *Fire on the Water: An Anthology of Black Nova Scotian Writing*, vol. 1 (Lawrencetown Beach, Nova Scotia: Pottersfield Press, 1991); and Clarke, "A Primer of African-Canadian Literature," in *Odysseys Home*, 328.

19. Siemerling, *Black Atlantic Reconsidered*, 151.

20. Rinaldo Walcott in Phanuel Antwi and David Chariandy, "The Ethics of Criticism: A Conversation with Rinaldo Walcott," *Transition* 124 (2017), special issue on "Writing Black Canadas," ed. Antwi and Chariandy, 56.

21. Janice Fiamengo, "'The Animals in *This* Country': Animals in the Canadian Literary Imagination," in *Other Selves: Animals in the Canadian Literary Imagination*, ed. Janice Fiamengo (Ottawa: University of Ottawa Press, 2007), 5–6.

22. Atwood, quoted in Fiamengo, "Animals in *This* Country," 5.

23. Douglas Coupland, *Souvenir of Canada* (Vancouver: Douglas & McIntyre, 2002), 126.

24. David Grimm, *Citizen Canine: Our Evolving Relationship with Cats and Dogs* (New York: Public Affairs, 2014), x.

25. Michael Brandow, *A Matter of Breeding: A Biting History of Pedigree Dogs and How the Quest for Status Has Harmed Man's Best Friend* (Boston: Beacon Press, 2015), 221.

26. Carole Gerson, "Writers Without Borders: The Global Framework of Canada's Early Literary History," *Canadian Literature* 201 (Summer 2009): 16.

27. Sara Jeannette Duncan, "Saunterings" (1886), reprinted in *The Search for English-Canadian Literature: An Anthology of Critical Articles from the Nineteenth and Early Twentieth Centuries*, ed. Carl Ballstadt (Toronto: University of Toronto Press, 1975), 31.

28. Douglas Lochhead, preface to *Search for English-Canadian Literature*, n.p.

29. Tracy Ware, "Cosmopolitan Nationalism: Canadian Literature of the Confederation Period, 1867–1914," in *Oxford Handbook of Canadian Literature*, 295–313. Elsewhere in the *Oxford Handbook*, Saunders is briefly mentioned twice (668, 856).

30. Henry James Morgan, *Types of Canadian Women and of Women Who Are or Have Been Connected with Canada*, vol. 1 (Toronto: William Briggs, 1903).

31. Christoph Irmscher, "'So That Nothing May Be Lost': Thomas McIlwraith's *Birds of Ontario*," in *Other Selves*, 164.

32. Nick Mount, "In Praise of Talking Dogs: The Study and Teaching of Early Canada's Canonless Canon," *Essays on Canadian Writing* 63 (Spring 1998): 91.

33. Morgan, *Types of Canadian Women*, 305.

34. Morgan, *Types of Canadian Women*, 1.

35. Margaret Marshall Saunders, *Rose of Acadia*, introd. Gwendolyn Davies (Halifax, Nova Scotia: Formac, 2002); all quotations are taken from this edition.

36. Ian McKay and Robin Bates, *In the Province of History: The Making of the Public Past in Twentieth-Century Nova Scotia* (Montreal: McGill-Queen's University Press, 2010), 72. On the cultural history of *Evangeline*, see Ron McFarland, *The Long Life of Evangeline: A History of the Longfellow Poem in Print, in Adaptation and in Popular Culture* (Jefferson, NC: McFarland, 2009).

37. Rachel Adams, *Continental Divides: Remapping the Cultures of North America* (Chicago: University of Chicago Press, 2009), 7.

38. Janice Kulyk Keefer, "Fortunate Falls and Propitious Expulsions: Anglophone Fictions and the 'Acadian Question,'" *International Journal of Canadian Studies/ Revue internationale d'études canadiennes* 10 (Fall 1994): 40.

39. Robin Bates, "Of the Blood: Race, History, and Memory in Formac Fiction's Treasures Series," *Acadiensis* 41:2 (Summer/ Autumn 2012): 186.

40. Bates, "Of the Blood," 184.

41. Michele Birnbaum, *Race, Work and Desire in American Literature, 1860–1930* (Cambridge: Cambridge University Press, 2003), 87.

42. On the history of black Nova Scotia, see Bridglal Pachai, *The Nova Scotia Black Experience Through the Centuries* (Halifax, Nova Scotia: Nimbus, 2007).

43. Waterston describes the Freemans as "West Indies merchants" in "Margaret Marshall Saunders," 139. "Tamarinds, raisins, cones of sugar" is in Marshall Saunders, "The Story of My Life," *Ontario Library Review* 12:2 (November 1927): 42.

44. Marshall Saunders, *Jimmy Gold-Coast, or the Story of a Monkey and His Friends* (Toronto: Hodder and Stoughton, 1924); all quotations are taken from this edition.

45. Margaret Marshall Saunders, "Margaret Marshall Saunders Diary, 1906–1907," in *No Place like Home*, 233–34.

46. Toni Morrison, *Playing in the Dark: Whiteness and the Literary Imagination* (New York: Vintage, 1992), 90.

47. Hill, quoted in Winfried Siemerling, "A Conversation with Lawrence Hill," *Callaloo* 36:1 (Winter 2013): 23; Siemerling analyzes the novel in *Black Atlantic Reconsidered*, 36–52, 170–85.

48. Lawrence Hill, *The Book of Negroes* (Toronto: HarperCollins, 2007); all quotations are taken from this edition.

49. Nicole Shukin, *Animal Capital: Rendering Life in Biopolitical Times* (Minneapolis: University of Minnesota Press, 2009), 20.

50. Shukin, *Animal Capital*, 3.

51. John Miller, "Illustrating the Fur Trade in Boy's Own Adventure Fiction," *Antennae* 24 (Spring 2013): 56.

52. Chantal Nadeau, *Fur Nation: From the Beaver to Brigitte Bardot* (London: Routledge, 2001), 194.

53. Shukin, *Animal Capital*, 4–5.

54. Pauline Wakeham, *Taxidermic Signs: Reconstructing Aboriginality* (Minneapolis: University of Minnesota Press, 2008), 4.

55. Alice Munro, "Vandals," in *Open Secrets* (New York: Vintage, 1994), 279, 292.

56. The controversy is detailed in Ralph H. Lutts, *The Nature Fakers: Wildlife, Science and Sentiment* (Golden, CO: Fulcrum, 1990). For more recent analyses, see Michael Lundblad, *The Birth of a Jungle: Animality in Progressive-Era U.S. Literature and Culture* (New York: Oxford University Press, 2013), 20–24; and Susan McHugh, *Animal Stories: Narrating Across Species Lines* (Minneapolis: University of Minnesota Press, 2011), 212–14.

57. John Burroughs, "Real and Sham Natural History," *Atlantic Monthly* 91 (March 1903): 300.

58. Theodore Roosevelt, "Nature Fakers," *Everybody's Magazine* 17:3 (September 1907): 430.

59. See Douglas Allen, "Charles Livingston Bull: A Bibliography," in *Charles Livingston Bull, 1874–1932* (Oradell, NJ: Hiram Blauvelt Art Museum, 1994), 67–91.

60. Charles D. G. Roberts, *The Kindred of the Wild: A Book of Animal Life* (Boston: L. C. Page, 1902), 27.

61. Nina Katchadourian, *Sorted Books* (San Francisco: Chronicle Books, 2013).

62. Nina Katchadourian, *Curiouser* (Austin, TX: Blanton Museum of Art, 2017), 78.

63. Margaret Marshall Saunders, letter to Charles M. Roe, June 6, 1907, "Correspondence (1907)," file 1943.001-SAU/6, Margaret Marshall Saunders fonds, Esther Clark Wright Archives, Acadia University (hereafter cited as Saunders fonds); this letter is also available online in *Margaret Marshall Saunders: Transcription of the Documents Dated 1906–1914*, http://www.acadiau.ca/~markham/publish&present/MargaretMarshallSaunders.pdf.

64. See Ryan Edwardson, *Canadian Content: Culture and the Quest for Nationhood* (Toronto: University of Toronto Press, 2008).

65. George T. Angell, "Appendix," *Autobiographical Sketches and Personal Recollections* (Boston, 1892), 36; italics in the original.

66. See Joseph A. Conforti, *Imagining New England: Explorations of Regional Identity from the Pilgrims to the Mid-twentieth Century* (Chapel Hill: University of North Carolina Press, 2001), 203–62.

67. See Betsy Beattie, "The 'Boston States': Region, Gender, and Maritime Out-Migration, 1870–1930," in *New England and the Maritime Provinces: Connections and Comparisons*, ed. Stephen J. Hornsby and John G. Reid (Montreal: McGill-Queen's University Press, 2005), 252–63.

68. Saunders, quoted in Nick Mount, *When Canadian Literature Moved to New York* (Toronto: University of Toronto Press, 2005), 8.

69. Gwendolyn Davies, "Marshall Saunders and the Urbanization of the Animal," in *Other Selves*, 175–76.

70. Chez, introduction to *Beautiful Joe*, 13.

71. On Newfoundland dogs, see Jan Bondeson, *Amazing Dogs: A Cabinet of Canine Curiosities* (Ithaca: Cornell University Press, 2011), 162–88.

72. For analysis of "Newfie jokes," as imposed on Newfoundlanders and used by Newfoundlanders themselves, see Christie Davis, *The Mirth of Nations* (New Brunswick, NJ: Transaction, 2002), 109–50.

73. Brett Mizelle, *Pig* (London: Reaktion, 2011), 100.

74. Margaret Atwood, *Survival: A Thematic Guide to Canadian Literature* (Toronto: House of Anansi, 1972), 29.

75. Laura Moss, "Margaret Atwood: Branding an Icon Abroad," in *Margaret Atwood: The Open Eye*, ed. John Moss and Tobi Kozakewich (Ottawa: University of Ottawa Press, 2006), 23. On the reception of *Survival*, see Jane Schlueter, "Canlit/Victimlit: *Survival* and *Second Words*," in *Margaret Atwood: Vision and Forms*, ed. Kathryn VanSpanckeren and Jan Garden Castro (Carbondale: Southern Illinois University Press, 1988), 1–11.

76. Sourayan Mookerjea, Imre Szeman, and Gail Faurschou, eds., *Canadian Cultural Studies: A Reader* (Durham: Duke University Press, 2009). *Survival* is mentioned on 75–76.

77. Atwood, *Survival*, 73.

78. Atwood, *Survival*, 74.

79. Ernest Thompson Seton, *Wild Animals I Have Known* (1898), quoted in Atwood, *Survival*, 74.

80. Atwood, *Survival*, 75.

81. Atwood, *Survival*, 80.

82. Margaret Atwood, *Surfacing* (New York: Warner, 1983); all quotations are taken from this edition.

83. For analyses of animals in *Surfacing*, see Janice Fiamengo, "'It Looked at Me with Its Mashed Eye': Animal and Human Suffering in *Surfacing*," in *Margaret Atwood: The Open Eye*, 171–84; and Robert McKay, "'Identifying with the Animals': Language, Subjectivity, and the Animal Politics of Margaret Atwood's *Surfacing*," in *Figuring Animals: Essays on Animal Images in Art, Literature, Philosophy, and Popular Culture*, ed. Mary S. Pollock and Catherine

Rainwater (New York: Palgrave Macmillan, 2005), 207–27.

84. Carol Shields, *The Stone Diaries* (New York: Penguin, 1993), 355. And sometimes *Beautiful Joe* surfaces elsewhere in contemporary fiction by non-Canadian writers. A very recent appearance is in Sigrid Nunez's novel *The Friend*, when the New Yorker narrator reflects on dog loss by evoking *Beautiful Joe*: "Something bad happens to the dog: a lesson learned early, from childhood books. . . . The autobiography of Beautiful Joe, based on the life of a real dog and abounding in scenes of cruelty, begins with his brute owner slicing off Joe's ears and tail with an ax" (Sigrid Nunez, *The Friend* [New York: Riverhead Books, 2018], 171).

85. Sandra Djwa names the reference as part of a strategy of parody in *Surfacing*; she suggests that as Saunders's novel shows a maimed dog, *Surfacing*'s Joe, "a potter, maims pots." (Djwa, "'Here I Am': Atwood, Paper Houses, and a Parodic Tradition," *Essays on Canadian Writing* 71 [Fall 2000]: 170). There are also brief mentions of this reference in Fiamengo, "It Looked at Me," 172; Evelyn J. Hinz and John J. Teunissen, "*Surfacing*: Margaret Atwood's 'Nymph Complaining,'" *Contemporary Literature* 20:2 (Spring 1979): 225n6; and Sharon Rose Wilson, *Margaret Atwood's Fairy-Tale Sexual Politics* (Jackson: University Press of Mississippi, 1993), 358n5.

86. J. Brooks Bouson, *Brutal Choreographies: Oppositional Strategies and Narrative Design in the Novels of Margaret Atwood* (Amherst: University of Massachusetts Press, 1993), 46–47.

87. Conversation with Margaret Atwood, South Hadley, MA, October 2015.

88. Another play on these terms: Heather Murray, "'Its Image on the Mirror': Canada, Canonicity, the Uncanny," *Essays on Canadian Writing* 42 (Winter 1990): 102–30.

89. In the French placard, "un mouvement semblable à celui d'un père qui pousse sa fille sur une balançoire."

90. Hezekiah Butterworth, *Zig-zag Journeys in Acadia and New France* (Boston: Estes and Lauriat, 1885), 176. For discussion of this work, see McKay and Bates, *In the Province of History*, 101–3.

91. On the razing of Africville, see Jennifer Nelson, *Razing Africville: A Geography of Racism* (Toronto: University of Toronto Press, 2008); on literary representations of Africville, see Siemerling, *Black Atlantic Reconsidered*, 307–16.

92. Elisabeth Belliveau, "A Spell in Eight Parts," in *Don't Get Lonely Don't Get Lost* (Greenwich, Nova Scotia: Conundrum Press, 2010), 8–22.

93. A rare exception: Saunders is mentioned in Murray R. Barkhouse, *Famous Nova Scotians* (Hansport, Nova Scotia: Lancelot Press, 1994), 105–7.

94. For the locations, see Janet Morris, "Where Did They Live? Marshall Saunders (1861–1947)," *The Griffin: A Publication of Heritage Trust of Nova Scotia* 33:2 (June 2008): 7.

95. "Margaret Marshall Saunders Fonds," compiled by Wendy G. Robicheau and Corey Liu, January 2010, available online at http://openarchive.acadiau.ca/cdm/singleitem/collection/acadiaAnnap/id/2573/rec/177.

96. See Alfred F. Young, "An Outsider and the Progress of a Career in History," *William and Mary Quarterly*, 3d series, 52:3 (July 1995): 499–512.

97. Charles S. Banes, letter to Margaret Marshall Saunders, August 15, 1895, in "Correspondence (1883–1896)," file 1943.001-SAU/3, Saunders fonds.

98. Margaret Marshall Saunders, "Address to the Women Teachers Association of Toronto, Nov 26 1921," in "Miscellaneous Published Pieces by Marshall Saunders part B," file 1943.001-SAU/44, Saunders fonds. This quotation is discussed in Mount, *When Canadian Literature Moved*, 29.

99. Margaret Marshall Saunders, annotations to map of Halifax, in "Manuscript [19–?] Entitled 'How I Began to Write,'" file 1943.001-SAU/23, Saunders fonds.

100. Margaret Marshall Saunders, handwritten bound journal, 76, 118, in "Notebook

III, Personal Anecdotes (1891–92)," file 1943.001-SUA/28, Saunders fonds.

101. Margaret Marshall Saunders, handwritten journal, 150, in "Notebook III, Personal Anecdotes (1891–92)," file 1943.001-SAU/28, Saunders fonds.

102. Margaret Marshall Saunders, "How I Began to Write," 3, in "Manuscript [19–?] Entitled 'How I Began to Write,'" file 1943.001-SAU/23, Saunders fonds.

103. I have been unable to locate this story, "A Gag of Blessed Memory," despite extensive searching in all permutations of the *Frank Leslie* publishing world; I invite others to continue this search.

104. *Little Women* was published in two parts, and Saunders commented on the second part, *Good Wives*, in her diary: "Miss Fraser read 'Good Wives' to us—it is a sequel to 'Little Women,' and a very interesting book" ("Margaret Marshall Saunders: Edinburgh Diary, 1876," 78).

105. "Toronto Bitch License," title of file 1943.001-SAU/14, Saunders fonds.

106. Margaret Marshall Saunders, "Principal Characters. Human Beings" and "Principal Characters. Dogs," in "Wandering Dog" manuscript part A, published in 1916 [19–], file 1943.001-SAU/88, Saunders fonds.

107. Margaret Marshall Saunders, annotations to cards for photograph of "Collies & Airedales" and for "Matford Vic," "Wandering Dog" manuscript part A, published in 1916 [19–], file 1943.001-SAU/88, Saunders fonds.

108. Margaret Marshall Saunders, "Manuscript 'Beautiful Joe,'" file 1932.001-SAU/1, Saunders fonds.

109. Marshall Saunders, *Beautiful Joe* (London: National Institute for the Blind, 1934), 1943.001.SAU/94A and 1943.001.SAU/94B, Acadia University Special Collections.

110. Georgina Kleege, "Blindness and Visual Culture: An Eye Witness Account," in *The Disability Studies Reader*, ed. Lennard J. Davis, 2nd ed. (New York: Routledge, 2006), 397.

111. Margaret Marshall Saunders, "Glass Plate Slides," file 1943.001-SAU/42, Saunders fonds.

112. Sanders, "Margaret Marshall Saunders," 65. Waterston notes Saunders's "obsessive substitution of animal concerns for human ones" ("Margaret Marshall Saunders," 137).

CODA

1. Jessica Pierce, *The Last Walk: Reflections on Our Pets at the End of Their Lives* (Chicago: University of Chicago Press, 2012), 3–4.

2. Ken Dolan-Del Vecchio and Nancy Saxton-Lopez, *The Pet Loss Companion: Healing Advice from Family Therapists Who Lead Pet Loss Groups* (North Charleston, SC: CreateSpace Independent, 2013), 10–11.

3. Pierce, *Last Walk*, 14.

4. Pierce, *Last Walk*, 224.

5. Lydia Davis, "The Dog Hair," in *Can't and Won't: Stories* (New York: Farrar, Straus and Giroux, 2014), 4.

6. Mikita Brottman, *The Great Grisby: Two Thousand Years of Literary, Royal, Philosophical, and Artistic Dog Lovers and Their Exceptional Animals* (New York: HarperCollins, 2014).

7. Erica Fudge, "A Left-Handed Blow: Writing the History of Animals," in *Representing Animals*, ed. Nigel Rothfels (Bloomington: Indiana University Press, 2002), 5.

8. Marshall Saunders, quoted in Gwendolyn Davies, introduction to *Beautiful Joe* (Halifax, Nova Scotia: Formac, 2001), xv.

9. Davies, introduction to *Beautiful Joe*, xiii.

10. Henry James Morgan, *Types of Canadian Women and of Women Who Are or Have Been Connected with Canada* (Toronto: William Briggs, 1903), 1:305.

11. See "Beautiful Joe Park," *Beautiful Joe Heritage Society*, https://beautifuljoe.org/the-parks/beautiful-joe-park. For more information on the park, see Ken Haigh, "A Place for Joe," *Niagara Escarpment Views* 20 (Winter 2013–14): 21–23, 43–45.

12. Michael Kwan and Philip Chin, "Remembering the Chinese American Heroes of 9/11," http://www.chineseamericanheroes.org/history/2011Remembering911v4.pdf. On Sirius, see "A Tribute to PAPD K-9 Officer Sirius," *National September 11 Memorial and Museum*, https://www.911memorial.org/blog/tribute-papd-k-9-officer-sirius; and for brief academic mention, Carolyn Merino Mullin, "Now on Exhibit: Our Affection for, Remembrance of, and Tributes to Nonhuman Animals in Museums," in *Mourning Animals: Rituals and Practices Surrounding Animal Death*, ed. Margo DeMello (East Lansing: Michigan State University Press, 2016), 124. On the dogs of 9/11, see Nona Kilgore Bauer, *Dog Heroes of September 11th: A Tribute to America's Search and Rescue Dogs* (Allenhurst, NJ: Kennel Club Books, 2011); and Charlotte Dumas, *Retrieved* (Los Angeles: Ice Plant, 2011).

13. On the Black History Cairn, see "Arts, Culture, and Heritage," *Visit Owen Sound*, https://owensoundtourism.ca/en/arts-and-culture/Black-History-Cairn.aspx.

14. Rinaldo Walcott, *Black like Who? Writing Black Canada*, 2nd rev. ed. (Toronto: Insomniac Press, 2003), 16.

15. The full text of the plaque:

Born in Milton, Nova Scotia, Margaret Marshall Saunders (1861–1947) taught school briefly before starting her career as a novelist. Her second book, "Beautiful Joe," achieved international recognition. Inspired during a visit to Meaford about 1892, it is based on the story of a dog rescued from a brutal master by a local miller, William Moore. This novel, first published in 1894, appeared in several editions and enjoyed phenomenal success. It was printed in at least ten languages and seven million copies had been sold by 1939. Miss Saunders, who settled in Toronto in 1914, was awarded the C.B.E. in 1934 in recognition of her contribution toward securing humane treatment for animals.

16. Margaret Marshall Saunders, *Beautiful Joe*, Beautiful Joe Heritage Society Special Edition (Meaford, Ontario: Beautiful Joe Heritage Society, 2004).

17. See Rachel Poliquin, "Balto the Dog," in *The Afterlives of Animals: A Museum Menagerie*, ed. Samuel J. M. M. Alberti (Charlottesville: University of Virginia Press, 2011), 92–109.

18. "The Animals in War Memorial," http://www.animalsinwar.org.uk/. On the history of dogs in war, see Michael G. Lemish, *War Dogs: A History of Loyalty and Heroism* (Dulles, VA: Brassey's, 1996); on the memorialization of war dogs, see Hilda Kean, "Britain at War: Remembering and Forgetting the Animal Dead of the Second World War," in *Mourning Animals*, 115–22.

19. Cathy Caruth, introduction to *Trauma: Explorations in Memory*, ed. Cathy Caruth (Baltimore: Johns Hopkins University Press, 1995), 4.

20. Laurel Braitman, *Animal Madness: How Anxious Dogs, Compulsive Parrots, and Elephants in Recovery Help Us Understand Ourselves* (New York: Simon & Schuster, 2014), 43–52.

21. David Grimm, *Citizen Canine: Our Evolving Relationship with Cats and Dogs* (New York: Public Affairs, 2014), 212–13.

22. Dan Dakin, "Dog Dumped in Canal with Brick Tied Around Its Legs," *Owen Sound Sun Times* (Owen Sound, ON), August 1, 2014, A2, http://www.owensoundsuntimes.com/2014/08/01/dog-dumped-in-canal-with-brick-tied-around-its-legs.

23. On the Sirius monument vandalism, see John Goddard, "Meaford's 9/11 Dog Memorial Restored," *Toronto Star*, January 2, 2008, http://www.thestar.com/news/ontario/2008/01/02/meafords_911_dog_memorial_restored.html.

On the Paradise Island vandalism, see "Plaques Repaired at Meaford's Beautiful Joe Park," *Meaford Express*, July 7, 2014, http://www.therecord.com/community-story/4618596-plaques-repaired-at-meaford-s-beautiful-joe-park/.

24. The hand cream was marketed by the Drake General Store connected to the Drake Hotel in Toronto; see "1867 Hand Cream," *Drake General Store*, https://www.drakegen

eralstore.ca/our-brands/drake-general-store/1867-hand-cream#.Wxhu_Ioh1Bc.

25. This is the full text of the segment (my transcription):

Hey Canada, I've worked with a lot of Vikings and a lot of bikers, and one thing I've learned is that scars are cool. And in the animal world, no animal was cooler or more scarred than Beautiful Joe. Long before Air Bud, Marley, Hooch, Old Yeller, Benji, ninety-eight out of the 101 dalmatians, there was Beautiful Joe. So Joe was a real-life mutt who'd been through a lot. How he dealt with such vicious abuse and had such a big heart—it became the stuff of legend up here in Canada. Halifax author Margaret Marshall Saunders was so inspired by Joe and the tribulations he had gone through and the size of his heart that she decided to write a novel about him. The story of Beautiful Joe was such a smash hit it became Canada's first million-seller as a novel. [Sound of song, "Who Let the Dogs Out?"] Look, I don't know who let the dogs out, but I do know one thing—I know the name of the dog that brought world-wide attention to animal cruelty. And that's Beautiful Joe from Meaford, Ontario, motherf***** [bleep], mother-bleep-bleep. And that is something you might not know about Canada. (Donal Logue, "Something You Might Not Know About Canada," *George Stroumboulopoulos Tonight*, season 6, episode 141, originally aired April 14, 2013, available at http://www.cbc.ca/strombo/videos/show-clip/donal-logue-beautiful-joe-something-about-canada)

26. Frances Lester Warner, *On a New England Campus* (Boston: Houghton Mifflin, 1937), 279. Information on the provenance of the object is from an early wall label, probably from the 1930s, retained in the collections of the Mount Holyoke College Art Museum.

27. For the work of James Gehrt, see his website, http://www.jamesgehrtphoto.com, and for discussion, see Anthony W. Lee, "Introduction: Light and Air," in *The Weight of Air*, by James Gehrt (Minneapolis: Hadley House Press, 2015), 10–12.

28. Angelucci affirms the connection to bird hats in an interview with Matthew Brower, "Sara Angelucci's Aviary," *Antennae* 41 (Autumn 2017): 99. She discusses women as "keepers of the family album" and as taxidermists in "*Aviary*: Project Statement," http://www.sara-angelucci.ca/filter/Projects/Aviary2013.

29. Angelucci, "*Aviary*: Project Statement."

Index

Page numbers in *italics* refer to images.